Grade Aid

for

Berk

Exploring Lifespan Development

prepared by

Laura E. Berk
Illinois State University

Trisha Mann
Illinois State University

Sara Harris
Illinois State University

Judy Ashkenaz

Pamela Barter

Boston   New York   San Francisco
Mexico City   Montreal   Toronto   London   Madrid   Munich   Paris
Hong Kong   Singapore   Tokyo   Cape Town   Sydney

Copyright © 2008 Pearson Education, Inc.

All rights reserved. No part of the material protected by this copyright notice may be reproduced or utilized in any form or by any means, electronic or mechanical, including photocopying, recording, or by any information storage or retrieval system, without the written permission from the copyright owner.

To obtain permission(s) to use the material from this work, please submit a written request to Allyn and Bacon, Permissions Department, 75 Arlington Street, Boston, MA 02116 or fax your request to 617-848-7320.

ISBN-13: 978-0-205-54705-0
ISBN-10:   0-205-54705-2

Printed in the United States of America

10 9 8 7 6 5 4 3 2 1   11 10 09 08 07

CONTENTS

PREFACE   *vii*

CHAPTER 1   HISTORY, THEORY, AND RESEARCH STRATEGIES   *1*

Brief Chapter Summary   *1*   • Learning Objectives   *1*   • Study Questions   *2*   • Ask Yourself   *15*   • Suggested Student Readings   *15*   • Puzzle 1.1   *16*   • Puzzle 1.2   *17*   • Puzzle 1.3   *18*   • Practice Test #1   *19*   • Practice Test #2   *21*

CHAPTER 2   BIOLOGICAL AND ENVIRONMENTAL FOUNDATIONS   *25*

Brief Chapter Summary   *25*   • Learning Objectives   *25*   • Study Questions   *26*   • Ask Yourself   *34*   • Suggested Student Readings   *34*   • Puzzle 2.1   *35*   • Puzzle 2.2   *36*   • Practice Test #1   *37*   • Practice Test #2   *39*

CHAPTER 3   PRENATAL DEVELOPMENT, BIRTH, AND THE NEWBORN BABY   *43*

Brief Chapter Summary   *43*   • Learning Objectives   *43*   • Study Questions   *44*   • Ask Yourself   *57*   • Suggested Student Readings   *57*   • Puzzle 3.1   *58*   • Puzzle 3.2   *59*   • Practice Test #1   *60*   • Practice Test #2   *62*

CHAPTER 4   PHYSICAL DEVELOPMENT IN INFANCY AND TODDLERHOOD   *65*

Brief Chapter Summary   *65*   • Learning Objectives   *66*   • Study Questions   *66*   • Ask Yourself   *76*   • Suggested Student Readings   *76*   • Puzzle 4.1   *77*   • Puzzle 4.2   *78*   • Practice Test #1   *79*   • Practice Test #2   *81*

CHAPTER 5   COGNITIVE DEVELOPMENT IN INFANCY AND TODDLERHOOD   *85*

Brief Chapter Summary   *85*   • Learning Objectives   *86*   • Study Questions   *86*   • Ask Yourself   *95*   • Suggested Student Readings   *95*   • Puzzle 5.1   *96*   • Puzzle 5.2   *97*   • Practice Test #1   *98*   • Practice Test #2   *100*

CHAPTER 6   EMOTIONAL AND SOCIAL DEVELOPMENT IN INFANCY AND TODDLERHOOD   *103*

Brief Chapter Summary   *103*   • Learning Objectives   *104*   • Study Questions   *104*   • Ask Yourself   *115*   • Suggested Student Readings   *115*   • Puzzle 6.1   *116*   • Puzzle 6.2   *117*   • Practice Test #1   *118*   • Practice Test #2   *120*

**CHAPTER 7 PHYSICAL AND COGNITIVE DEVELOPMENT IN EARLY
              CHILDHOOD   123**

Brief Chapter Summary *123* • Learning Objectives *124* • Study Questions *125* •
Ask Yourself *138* • Suggested Student Readings *138* • Puzzle 7.1 *139* •
Puzzle 7.2 *140* • Practice Test #1 *141* • Practice Test #2 *143*

**CHAPTER 8 EMOTIONAL AND SOCIAL DEVELOPMENT IN EARLY
              CHILDHOOD   147**

Brief Chapter Summary *147* • Learning Objectives *148* • Study Questions *148* •
Ask Yourself *163* • Suggested Student Readings *163* • Puzzle 8.1 *164* •
Puzzle 8.2 *165* • Practice Test #1 *166* • Practice Test #2 *168*

**CHAPTER 9 PHYSICAL AND COGNITIVE DEVELOPMENT IN MIDDLE
              CHILDHOOD   171**

Brief Chapter Summary *171* • Learning Objectives *172* • Study Questions *172* •
Ask Yourself *189* • Suggested Student Readings *189* • Puzzle 9.1 *190* •
Puzzle 9.2 *191* • Practice Test #1 *192* • Practice Test #2 *194*

**CHAPTER 10 EMOTIONAL AND SOCIAL DEVELOPMENT IN MIDDLE
              CHILDHOOD   197**

Brief Chapter Summary *197* • Learning Objectives *197* • Study Questions *198* •
Ask Yourself *212* • Suggested Student Readings *212* • Puzzle 10.1 *213* •
Puzzle 10.2 *214* • Practice Test #1 *215* • Practice Test #2 *217*

CHAPTER 11 PHYSICAL AND COGNITIVE DEVELOPMENT IN ADOLESCENCE   221

Brief Chapter Summary *221* • Learning Objectives *222* • Study Questions *223* •
Ask Yourself *237* • Suggested Student Readings *237* • Puzzle 11.1 *238* •
Practice Test #1 *239* • Practice Test #2 *241*

CHAPTER 12 EMOTIONAL AND SOCIAL DEVELOPMENT IN ADOLESCENCE   245

Brief Chapter Summary *245* • Learning Objectives *245* • Study Questions *246* •
Ask Yourself *258* • Suggested Student Readings *258* • Puzzle 12.1 *259* •
Practice Test #1 *260* • Practice Test #2 *262*

**CHAPTER 13 PHYSICAL AND COGNITIVE DEVELOPMENT IN EARLY
              ADULTHOOD   265**

Brief Chapter Summary *265* • Learning Objectives *265* • Study Questions *266* •
Ask Yourself *278* • Suggested Student Readings *278* • Puzzle 13.1 *279* •
Practice Test #1 *280* • Practice Test #2 *282*

**CHAPTER 14   EMOTIONAL AND SOCIAL DEVELOPMENT IN EARLY
                ADULTHOOD   285**

Brief Chapter Summary *285* • Learning Objectives *286* • Study Questions *286* •
Ask Yourself *299* • Suggested Student Readings *299* • Puzzle 14.1 *300* •
Practice Test #1 *301* • Practice Test #2 *303*

**CHAPTER 15   PHYSICAL AND COGNITIVE DEVELOPMENT IN MIDDLE
                ADULTHOOD   307**

Brief Chapter Summary *307* • Learning Objectives *308* • Study Questions *308* •
Ask Yourself *320* • Suggested Student Readings *320* • Puzzle 15.1 *321* •
Practice Test #1 *322* • Practice Test #2 *324*

**CHAPTER 16   EMOTIONAL AND SOCIAL DEVELOPMENT IN MIDDLE
                ADULTHOOD   327**

Brief Chapter Summary *327* • Learning Objectives *328* • Study Questions *328* •
Ask Yourself *337* • Suggested Student Readings *337* • Puzzle 16.1 *338* •
Practice Test #1 *339* • Practice Test #2 *341*

**CHAPTER 17   PHYSICAL AND COGNITIVE DEVELOPMENT IN LATE
                ADULTHOOD   345**

Brief Chapter Summary *345* • Learning Objectives *346* • Study Questions *346* •
Ask Yourself *362* • Suggested Student Readings *362* • Puzzle 17.1 *363* •
Puzzle 17.2 *364* • Practice Test #1 *365* • Practice Test #2 *367*

**CHAPTER 18   EMOTIONAL AND SOCIAL DEVELOPMENT IN LATE
                ADULTHOOD   371**

Brief Chapter Summary *371* • Learning Objectives *372* • Study Questions *372* •
Ask Yourself *385* • Suggested Student Readings *385* • Puzzle 18.1 *386* •
Practice Test #1 *387* • Practice Test #2 *389*

CHAPTER 19   DEATH, DYING, AND BEREAVEMENT   393

Brief Chapter Summary *393* • Learning Objectives *394* • Study Questions *394* •
Ask Yourself *405* • Suggested Student Readings *405* • Puzzle 19.1 *406* •
Puzzle 19.2 *407* • Practice Test #1 *408* • Practice Test #2 *410*

CROSSWORD PUZZLE SOLUTIONS   *413*

ANSWERS TO PRACTICE TESTS   *429*

PREFACE

As you embark on the fascinating journey of studying human development, it is our hope that this workbook will help you master the material in your text, *Exploring Lifespan Development,* by Laura E. Berk. Our intention in preparing the workbook is to provide you with active practice in learning the content in your textbook and thought-provoking questions that help you clarify your own thinking. Each chapter in the workbook is organized into the following six sections:

CHAPTER SUMMARY

We begin with a brief summary of the material, mentioning major topics covered and general principles emphasized in text discussion. Each text chapter includes two additional summaries: an informal one at the beginning of the chapter, and a structured summary at the end of the chapter. Thus, the summary in the workbook will be your third review of the information covered in each chapter. It is intended to remind you of major points in the text before you embark on the remaining activities in the workbook.

LEARNING OBJECTIVES

We have organized the main points in each chapter into a series of objectives that indicate what you should be able to do once you have mastered the material. We suggest that you look over these objectives before you read each chapter. You may find it useful to take notes on information pertaining to objectives as you read. When you finish a chapter, try to answer the objectives in a few sentences or a short paragraph. Then check your answers against the text and revise your responses accordingly. Once you have completed this exercise, you will have generated your own review of chapter content. Because it is written in your own words, it should serve as an especially useful chapter overview that can be referred to when you prepare for examinations.

STUDY QUESTIONS

The main body of each chapter consists of study questions, organized according to major headings in the textbook, that assist you in identifying main points and grasping concepts and principles. Text pages on which answers can be found are indicated next to each entry. The study question section can be used in a number of different ways. You may find it helpful to answer each question as you read the chapter. Alternatively, try reading one or more sections and then testing yourself by answering the relevant study questions. Finally, use the study question section as a device to review for examinations. If you work through it methodically, your retention of chapter material will be greatly enhanced.

ASK YOURSELF

In each chapter of the textbook, critical thinking questions appear at the end of each major section. Three types of questions are included: Review questions, which assist with recall and comprehension of information in the text; Apply questions, which encourage application of your knowledge to controversial issues and problems; and Reflect questions, which help make the study of lifespan development personally meaningful by encouraging you to relate theory and research to your own life. Answering these questions will help you analyze important theoretical concepts and research findings. Each question is page-referenced to chapter material that will help you formulate a response. Model answers are found on the text's companion website.

SUGGESTED STUDENT READINGS

A list of three to five suggested readings complements each text chapter. The readings have been carefully selected for their interest value and readability; the majority are recently published. A brief description of the content of each suggested reading is provided.

CROSSWORD PUZZLES

To help you master the central vocabulary of the field, we have provided crossword puzzles that test your knowledge of important terms and concepts. Answers can be found at the back of the workbook. If you cannot think of the term that matches a clue in the puzzles, your knowledge of information related to the term may be insecure. Reread the material in the text chapter related to each item that you miss. Also, try a more demanding approach to term mastery: After you have completed each puzzle, cover the clues and write your own definitions of each term.

PRACTICE TESTS

Once you have thoroughly studied each chapter, find out how well you know the material by taking the two multiple choice practice tests. Then check your answers using the key at the back of the workbook. Each item is page-referenced to chapter content so you can look up answers to questions that you missed. If you answered more than a few items incorrectly, spend extra time rereading the chapter, writing responses to chapter objectives, and reviewing the study questions in this workbook.

Now that you understand how the workbook is organized, you are ready to begin using it to master *Exploring Lifespan Development*. We wish you a rewarding and enjoyable course of study.

Laura E. Berk
Trisha Mann
Sara Harris
Judy Ashkenaz
Pamela Barter

CHAPTER 1
HISTORY, THEORY, AND RESEARCH STRATEGIES

BRIEF CHAPTER SUMMARY

Human development is an interdisciplinary field of study devoted to understanding human constancy and change throughout the lifespan. Although great diversity exists among investigators who study human development, all have a single goal in common: the desire to describe and identify those factors that influence consistencies and transformations in people from conception to death.

Theories of human development take a stance on three basic issues: (1) Is development a continuous or discontinuous process? (2) Is there one course of development or many possible courses? (3) Is development determined primarily by nature or nurture, and is it stable or open to change? Many modern theories include elements from both sides of these debates. The lifespan perspective recognizes that great complexity exists in human change and the factors that underlie it. This perspective assumes (1) that development is lifelong; (2) that it is multidimensional and multidirectional; (3) that it is plastic, or flexible, at all ages; and (4) that it is influenced by multiple interacting forces.

After Charles Darwin constructed his theory of evolution in the nineteenth century, the scientific study of development evolved quickly. Sigmund Freud's psychosexual theory and Erik Erikson's psychosocial theory viewed development as discontinuous (occurring in stages), but Erikson added three adult stages to Freud's five stages of childhood.

The behaviorist perspective—rejecting the psychoanalytic concern with the unseen workings of the mind—focused on directly observable events: stimuli and responses. Albert Bandura's social learning theory, which expanded on the principles of conditioning, emphasizes modeling as a powerful source of development and is still influential today. Swiss cognitive theorist Jean Piaget, disagreeing with the behaviorists, developed his cognitive-developmental theory, based on the idea that children actively construct knowledge. Recent theoretical perspectives include information processing, which examines the human mind as a symbol-manipulating system; ethology and evolutionary developmental psychology, which are concerned with the adaptive value of behavior; Lev Vygotsky's sociocultural theory, which looks at the role of culture; and Urie Bronfenbrenner's ecological systems theory, which examines development in the context of a complex system of relationships.

Research in human development, like all scientific research, begins with a hypothesis, or prediction about behavior drawn from a theory. Research methods commonly used to study development include systematic observation, self-reports, clinical or case studies of single individuals, and ethnographies of the life circumstances of specific groups of people.

Investigators of human development generally choose either a correlational research design, which looks at relationships but cannot determine causality, or an experimental design, which uses dependent and independent variables to determine cause and effect. To study how individuals change over time, investigators use longitudinal, cross-sectional, and longitudinal-sequential designs. Each method and design has both strengths and limitations. Finally, conducting research with human subjects poses special ethical dilemmas, particularly for children and elderly people.

LEARNING OBJECTIVES

After reading this chapter, you should be able to:

1.1 Explain the importance of the terms *interdisciplinary* and *applied* as they help to define the field of human development. (pp. 4–5)

1.2 Explain the role of theories in understanding human development, and describe three basic issues on which major theories take a stand. (pp. 5–6)

1.3 Describe factors that sparked the emergence of the lifespan perspective, and explain the four assumptions that make up this point of view. (pp. 6–10)

1.4 Discuss the beginnings of scientific study of development in the late nineteenth and early twentieth centuries. (p. 11)

1.5 Describe theoretical perspectives that influenced human development research in the mid-twentieth century, and cite the contributions and limitations of each. (pp. 11–16)

1.6 Describe recent theoretical perspectives on human development, noting the contributions of major theorists. (pp. 16–21)

1.7 Identify the stand that each contemporary theory takes on the three basic issues presented earlier in this chapter. (p. 22)

1.8 Describe the research methods commonly used to study human development, citing the strengths and limitations of each. (pp. 21, 23–25)

1.9 Distinguish correlational and experimental research designs, and cite the strengths and limitations of each. (pp. 25–28)

1.10 Describe three research designs for studying development, noting the strengths and limitations of each. (pp. 29–31)

1.11 Discuss ethical issues related to lifespan research. (pp. 31–32)

STUDY QUESTIONS

Human Development as a Scientific, Applied, and Interdisciplinary Field

1. Human development is an interdisciplinary field. Explain what this means. (pp. 4–5)

Basic Issues

1. What are the three elements of a good theory? (p. 5)
   A. *describe*
   B. *explain*
   C. *predicts*

2. Cite two reasons why theories are important to the study of human development. (p. 5)
   A. *they provide organizing framework for our observations of people.*
   B. *theories that are verified by research provide a sound basis for practical act...*

3. **True** or False: Theories differ from opinion and belief in that they are subject to scientific verification. (p. 5)

4. Match each theoretical view with the appropriate description. (pp. 5–6)

   5 Views early traits as constant across the lifespan
   1 Views development as a process of gradually building on preexisting skills
   4 Regards the environment as the most important influence on development
   6 Regards human change as possible if new experiences support change
   2 Views development as a progression through a series of qualitatively distinct stages
   3 Views heredity as the most important influence on development

   1. Continuous development
   2. Discontinuous development
   3. Nature
   4. Nurture
   5. Stability
   6. Plasticity

5. True or False: Most modern theories of development take a strong position on controversial issues such as the nature–nurture debate. (p. 6)

The Lifespan Perspective: A Balanced Point of View

1. Explain how gains in average life expectancy have altered our view of human development. (p. 7)

   _____
   _____
   _____

2. Describe the lifespan perspective, noting four assumptions that make up this broader view of development. (p. 7)
   A. that development is life long
   B. multidimensional and multidirectional
   C. highly plastic
   D. influenced by multiple interacting forces

Development Is Lifelong

1. List the eight periods of human development covered in your text. (p. 7)
   A. prenatal
   B. infancy
   C. Early childhood
   D. Middle childhood
   E. Adolescence
   F. Early Adulthood
   G. Middle Adulthood
   H. Late adulthood

2. Cite the three broad domains of development in which change takes place across the lifespan. (p. 7)
   A. physical ~~cognitive~~   B. emotional / social
   C. cognitive

Development Is Multidimensional and Multidirectional

1. Explain how human development is both multidimensional and multidirectional. (pp. 7–8)

   Multidimensional: affected by an intricate blend of biological, psychological, social forces

   Multidirectional: At every period, development is a joint expression of growth and decline.

Development Is Plastic

1. True or False: Lifespan researchers emphasize that development is highly plastic at all ages. Briefly explain your response. (p. 8)

   _____
   _____

Biology and Environment: Resilience

1. What is *resilience*? (p. 9)

   _____
   _____

2. Briefly list and describe four broad factors that appear to offer protection from the damaging effects of stressful life events. (p. 9)

   A. _____
   _____

   B. _____
   _____

   C. _____
   _____

   D. _____
   _____

Development Is Influenced by Multiple, Interacting Forces

1. Events that are strongly related to age and therefore, fairly predictable in when they occur, and how long they last are called _____ -*graded influences*. (p. 8)

2. According to the lifespan perspective, development is influenced by what four factors? (p. 8)

   A. _____   B. _____
   C. _____   D. _____

3. _____ -*graded influences* explain why people born around the same time tend to be alike in ways that set them apart from people born at other times. Provide three examples of such influences. (p. 10)

   A. _____
   B. _____
   C. _____

4. What are *nonnormative influences*? (p. 10)

   _____
   _____
   _____

5. True or False: In contemporary adult development, nonnormative influences have become less powerful, while age-graded influences have become more so. (p. 10)

6. True or False: The lifespan perspective emphasizes multiple potential pathways and outcomes of development. (p. 10)

Scientific Beginnings

Darwin: Forefather of Scientific Child Study

1. Explain the two principles emphasized in Darwin's theory of evolution. (p. 11)

   A. _____

   _____

   B. _____

   _____

The Normative Period

1. _____ is regarded as the founder of the child study movement. (p. 11)

2. The _____ *approach* to child development uses age-related averages to represent typical development. (p. 11)

The Mental Testing Movement

1. Who constructed the first successful intelligence test? (p. 11)

   _____

2. A translated version of this test was developed for use with American children. What is the name of this instrument? (p. 11)

   _____

Mid-Twentieth-Century Theories

The Psychoanalytic Perspective

1. True or False: The psychoanalytic perspective emphasizes understanding the unique life history of each person. (p. 12)

2. Summarize the basic tenants of the *psychoanalytic perspective*. (p. 12)

   _____

   _____

   _____

3. Freud's _____ *theory* emphasized that how parents manage their child's sexual and aggressive drives in the first few years of life is crucial for healthy personality development. (p. 12)

4. Name and briefly describe the three components of personality outlined in Freud's theory. (p. 12)

    A. _____

    B. _____

    C. _____

5. Match each of the following stages of psychosexual development with the appropriate description. (p. 12)

    _____ During this stage, sexual instincts die down
    _____ Stage in which the infant desires sucking activities
    _____ Stage in which the Oedipal and Electra conflicts take place
    _____ Stage marked by mature sexuality
    _____ Stage in which toilet training becomes a major issue between parent and child

    1. Genital
    2. Anal
    3. Oral
    4. Latency
    5. Phallic

6. List criticisms of Freud's theory. (p. 12)

    _____
    _____
    _____
    _____

7. In what way did Erikson build upon and improve Freud's theory? (pp. 12–13)

    _____
    _____
    _____

8. Match each of Erikson's stages with the appropriate description. (p. 13)

    _____ Successful resolution of this stage depends on the adult's success at caring for other people and productive work
    _____ The primary task of this stage is the development of a sense of self and a sense of one's place in society
    _____ Successful resolution of this stage depends on a warm, loving relationship with the caregiver
    _____ In this stage, children experiment with adult roles through make-believe play
    _____ Successful resolution of this stage depends on parents granting the child reasonable opportunities for free choice
    _____ In this stage, successful resolution involves reflecting on life's accomplishments
    _____ The development of close relationships with others helps ensure successful resolution of this stage
    _____ Children who develop the capacity for cooperation and productive work will successfully resolve this stage

    1. Industry vs. inferiority
    2. Autonomy vs. shame and doubt
    3. Intimacy vs. isolation
    4. Identity vs. role confusion
    5. Basic trust vs. mistrust
    6. Generativity vs. stagnation
    7. Initiative vs. guilt
    8. Ego integrity vs. despair

9. Cite two contributions of psychoanalytic theory. (p. 13)

    A. _____

    B. _____

10. Why is psychoanalytic theory no longer in the mainstream of human development research? (p. 13)

Behaviorism and Social Learning Theory

1. True or False: Behaviorism focuses on the inner workings of the mind. (p. 14)

2. Watson's study of little Albert, an 11-month-old baby who was taught to fear a white rat by associating it with a loud noise, supported Pavlov's concept of _____. (p. 14)

3. Skinner, who proposed _____ *conditioning theory*, believed that behavior could be increased by following it with _____, such as food or praise, and decreased by following it with _____, such as disapproval or withdrawal of privileges. (p. 14)

4. Albert Bandura's *social learning theory* posits that children acquire both favorable and unfavorable behaviors through the process of _____, also known as imitation or observational learning. (p. 14)

5. Bandura's theory has been revised to include the importance of cognition, or thinking. Based upon this change, the theory is now referred to as a _____ *approach* rather than a social learning approach. Briefly explain this view of development. (p. 15)

    _____
    _____
    _____

6. What two procedures are combined in *behavior modification* in order to eliminate undesirable behaviors and increase socially acceptable ones? (p. 15)

    A. _____

    B. _____

7. Discuss two limitations of behaviorism and social learning theory. (p. 15)

    A. _____
    _____

    B. _____
    _____

Piaget's Cognitive-Developmental Theory

1. Summarize the basic principles of Piaget's *cognitive-developmental theory*. (p. 15)

    _____
    _____
    _____

2. Define Piaget's notion of adaptation. (p. 15)

    _____
    _____

3. Match each of Piaget's stages with the appropriate description. (p. 16)

   ____ During this stage, thought becomes more complex, and children develop the capacity for abstract reasoning.
   ____ This stage is characterized by the use of eyes, ears, and hands to explore the environment.
   ____ During this stage, children develop the capacity for abstract thought.
   ____ This stage is marked by the development of logical, organized reasoning skills.

   1. Sensorimotor
   2. Preoperational
   3. Concrete
   4. Formal operational

4. What was Piaget's chief method for studying child and adolescent thought? (p. 15)

   _____

5. Describe two major contributions of Piaget's theory. (pp. 15–16)

   A. _____

   B. _____

6. Describe three recent challenges to Piaget's theory. (p. 16)

   A. _____

   B. _____

   C. _____

Recent Theoretical Perspectives

Information Processing

1. Briefly describe the *information-processing* view of human development. (p. 17)

   _____

2. Information-processing theorists use _____ to map the precise steps that individuals use to solve problems and complete tasks. (p. 17)

3. In what basic way are information processing and Piaget's theory alike? In what basic way are they different? (p. 17)

   Alike: _____

   Different: _____

4. Cite one strength and two limitations of the information-processing approach. (p. 17)

   Strength: _____

   Limitation: _____

   Limitation: _____

5. A new area of research called _____ brings together multiple fields to study the relationship between changes in the brain and the developing person's cognitive processing and behavior patterns. (pp. 17–18)

Ethology and Evolutionary Developmental Psychology

1. *Ethology* is the study of _____. (p. 18)

2. Name the two European zoologists who laid the modern foundations of ethology. (p. 18)

   A. _____

   B. _____

3. Contrast the notion of a critical period with that of a sensitive period. (p. 18)

   Critical period: _____

   Sensitive period: _____

4. Explain how John Bowlby used the principles of ethology to understand the infant–caregiver relationship. (p. 18)

   _____
   _____
   _____
   _____

5. Briefly explain what is studied in the field of *evolutionary developmental psychology*. (pp. 18–19)

   _____
   _____
   _____

Vygotsky's Sociocultural Theory

1. Explain the importance of social interaction according to Vygotsky's *sociocultural theory*. (p. 19)

   _____
   _____
   _____

2. True or False: Because cultures select tasks for their members, individuals in every culture develop unique strengths not present in others. (p. 19)

3. Vygotsky's emphasis on culture and social experience led him to neglect _____ contributions to development. (p. 19)

Ecological Systems Theory

1. Briefly explain Bronfenbrenner's *ecological systems theory*. (p. 19)

   _____
   _____
   _____

2. Match each level of ecological systems theory with the appropriate description or example. (pp. 19–21)

   _____ Relationship between the child's home and school
   _____ The influence of cultural values
   _____ The parent's workplace
   _____ The child's interaction with parents

   1. Exosystem
   2. Microsystem
   3. Mesosystem
   4. Macrosystem

3. Provide examples of factors in each system that can enhance development. (pp. 20–21)

   Microsystem: _____

   Mesosystem: _____

   Exosystem: _____

   Macrosystem: _____

4. Describe Bronfenbrenner's notion of *bidirectional relationships* within the microsystem. (pp. 19–20)

   _____
   _____
   _____

5. Bronfenbrenner's _____ *system* refers to temporal changes that affect development, such as the timing of the birth of a sibling. (p. 21)

6. True or False: In ecological systems theory, development is controlled by the interaction of environmental circumstances and inner dispositions. (p. 19)

Comparing Theories

1. Identify the stand that each of the following theories takes on the three basic issues of childhood and child development: (p. 21)

Theory	One Course of Development verus Many Courses of Development	Continuous versus Discontinuous Development	Nature versus Nurture
Psychoanalytic perspective			
Behaviorism and social learning			
Piaget's cognitive-developmental theory			
Information processing			
Ethology			
Vygotsky's sociocultural theory			
Ecological systems theory			
Lifespan perspective			

Studying Development

1. Research usually begins with a _____, or a prediction about behavior drawn from a theory. (p. 21)

2. Distinguish between research methods and research designs. (p. 21)

    Research methods: _____

    _____

    Research designs: _____

    _____

Common Research Methods

1. Compare and contrast naturalistic and structured observation techniques, noting one strength and one limitation of each approach. (pp. 21–24)

    Naturalistic: _____

    _____

        Strength: _____

        Limitation: _____

    Structured: _____

    _____

        Strength: _____

        Limitation: _____

2. Explain how clinical interviews differ from structured interviews, and note the benefits of each technique. (p. 24)

    Clinical: _____

    _____

        Benefits: _____

    Structured: _____

    _____

        Benefits: _____

3. Summarize the limitations of the clinical interview technique. (p. 24)

    _____

    _____

4. True or False: Researchers can eliminate problems with inaccurate reporting (on the part of interviewees) by conducting structured interviews rather than clinical interviews. (p. 24)

    _____

5. Cite the primary aim of the *clinical method*. (p. 24)

    _____

6. The clinical method has been used to find out what contributes to the accomplishments of _____ extremely gifted children who attain the competence of an adult in a particular field before age 10. (p. 24)

7. Discuss the drawbacks of using the clinical method. (p. 24)

_____

_____

_____

8. _____ is a research method aimed at understanding a culture or distinct social group. This goal is achieved through _____, a technique in which the researcher lives with the cultural community and participates in all aspects of daily life. (p. 25)

9. Cite two limitations of the ethnographic method. (p. 25)

   A. _____

   _____

   B. _____

   _____

Cultural Influences: Immigrant Youths: Amazing Adaptation

1. True or False: Students who are first-generation (foreign-born) and second-generation (American-born with immigrant parents) achieve in school as well or better than do students of native-born parents. (p. 26)

2. Compared with their agemates, adolescents from immigrant families are (more / less) likely to commit delinquent and violent acts, use drugs and alcohol, and have early sex. (p. 26)

3. Discuss two ways in which family and community exert an influence on the academic achievement of adolescents from immigrant families. (p. 26)

   A. _____

   B. _____

General Research Designs

1. Describe the basic features of the *correlational design*. (pp. 25, 27)

2. True or False: The correlational design is preferred by researchers because it allows them to infer cause and effect. Explain your answer. (p. 27)

   _____

   _____

   _____

3. Investigators examine relationships among variables using a(n) _____, a number that describes how two measures, or variables, are associated with one another. (p. 27)

4. A *correlation coefficient* can range from _____ to _____. The magnitude of the number shows the (strength / direction) of the relationship between the two variables, whereas the sign indicates the (strength / direction) of the relationship. (p. 27)

5. For a correlation coefficient, a positive sign means that as one variable increases, the other (increases / decreases); a negative sign indicates that as one variable increases, the other (increases / decreases). (p. 27)

6. A researcher determines that the correlation between warm, consistent parenting and child delinquency is −.80. Explain what this indicates about the relationship between these two variables. (p. 27)

   _____
   _____

7. If the same researcher had found a correlation of +.45, what would this have indicated about the relationship between warm, consistent parenting and child delinquency? (p. 27)

   _____
   _____

8. What is the primary distinction between a *correlational design* and an *experimental design*? (p. 27)

   _____
   _____

9. The _____ *variable* is anticipated by the researcher to cause changes in the _____ *variable*. (p. 27)

10. What feature of an experimental design enables researchers to infer a cause-and-effect relationship between the variables? (p. 27)

    _____
    _____

11. By using _____ *assignment* of participants to treatment conditions, investigators are able to control for characteristics that could reduce the accuracy of their findings. (p. 28)

12. In _____ *experiments*, researchers randomly assign people to treatment conditions in natural settings. (p. 28)

13. True or False: Natural experiments differ from correlational research in that groups of participants are carefully chosen to ensure that their characteristics are as much alike as possible. (p. 28)

Designs for Studying Development

1. In a _____ *design*, a group of participants is studied repeatedly at different ages, and changes are noted as the participants mature. (p. 29)

2. List two strengths of the longitudinal design. (p. 29)

   A. _____
   B. _____

3. Describe three problems in conducting longitudinal research. (p. 29)

   A. _____
   _____

   B. _____
   _____

   C. _____
   _____

4. True or False: The term *cohort effect* refers to individuals born in different time periods who do not share similar historical and cultural conditions. (p. 29)

5. Describe the *cross-sectional design*. (p. 29)

6. In cross-sectional designs, researchers (do / do not) need to worry about participant dropout and practice effects. (p. 29)

7. Describe two problems associated with conducting cross-sectional research. (p. 30)

   A. _____

   B. _____

8. In the _____ design, researchers merge longitudinal and cross-sectional research strategies. List two advantages of this design. (p. 30)

   A. _____

   B. _____

Ethics in Lifespan Research

1. Describe participants' research rights. (p. 32)

   A. Protection from harm: _____

   B. Informed consent: _____

   C. Privacy: _____

   D. Knowledge of results: _____

   E. Beneficial treatments: _____

2. For children ___ years and older, their own informed consent should be obtained in addition to parental consent prior to participation in research. (p. 32)

3. True or False: Like children, most older adults require more than the usual informed consent procedures. (p. 32)

4. In _____, the investigator provides a full account and justification of research activities to participants in a study in which deception was used. (p. 32)

ASK YOURSELF...

For *Ask Yourself* questions for this chapter, please log on to the Companion Website at *www.ablongman.com/berk*.

1. Select the Companion Website for *Exploring Lifespan Development.*
2. Use the "Jump to" menu to go directly to this chapter.
3. From the menu on the left side of the screen, select "Ask Yourself."
4. Complete questions and choose "Submit answers for grading" or "Clear answers" to start over.

SUGGESTED STUDENT READINGS

Bronfenbrenner, U. (2004). *Making human beings human: Bioecological perspectives on human development.* London, England: Sage. An excellent resource for anyone interested in human development, psychology, sociology, education, family studies, or related fields, this book examines the complexity of human development, including one's ability to influence and be influenced by many layers of the environment.

Cabeza, R., Nyberg, L., & Park, D. (2005). *Cognitive neuroscience of aging: Linking cognitive and cerebral aging.* New York: Oxford University Press. Examines a new scientific discipline, known as the cognitive neuroscience of aging. Topics include: noninvasive measures of cerebral aging, the effects of cerebral aging on cognitive functions, and various theories of cognitive and cerebral aging.

Greene, S., & Hogan, D. (Eds.). (2005). *Researching children's experiences: Approaches and methods.* London, UK: Sage. Examines the various methods and designs for conducting research with children, including strengths, limitations, and ethical concerns.

Luthar, S. S., & Cichetti, D. (2003). *Resilience and vulnerability: Adaptation in the context of childhood adversities.* New York: Cambridge University Press. Presents an in-depth examination of childhood resilience, focusing on characteristics that distinguish resilient children from those who are overcome by adversity.

PUZZLE 1.1 TERM REVIEW

Across

2. _____ influences: events that are irregular in that they happen to one or a few people and do not follow a predictable timetable
4. _____-graded influences: events that are fairly predictable in when they occur and how long they last
8. _____-graded influences: explain why people born around the same time tend to be alike in ways that distinguish them from people born at other times
10. _____ development: field of study devoted to understanding constancy and change throughout the lifespan
11. Nature-_____ controversy: disagreement about whether genetic or environmental circumstances are more important determinants of development
12. _____ development: process of gradually augmenting the same types of skills that were there to begin with
14. _____ approach: age-related averages are computed to represent typical development
15. _____ perspective: approach to personality development introduced by Freud; assumes that children move through a series of stages in which they confront conflicts between biological and social expectations
16. Piaget's _____-developmental theory suggests that children actively construct knowledge as they manipulate and explore their world

Down

1. Approach that emphasizes the study of directly observable behavior
3. Genetically determined, naturally unfolding course of growth
5. _____ developmental psychology seeks to understand adaptive values of species-wide cognitive, emotional, and social competencies.
6. Freud's _____ theory emphasizes management of early sexual and aggressive drives.
7. Erikson's _____ theory of development focuses on resolution of psychological conflicts over the lifespan.
9. In ecological systems theory, temporal changes in children's environments
13. _____ perspective: assumes development is lifelong, multidimensional, highly plastic, and embedded in multiple contexts

PUZZLE 1.2 TERM REVIEW

Across
4. In ecological systems theory, connections between the child's immediate settings
6. In ecological systems theory, social settings that do not contain children but nevertheless affect their experiences in immediate settings
7. Effects of cultural-historical change on the accuracy of findings
8. A qualitative change in thinking, feeling, and behaving that characterizes a specific period of development
11. _____ learning theory: emphasizes the role of modeling in the development of behavior
12. Vygotsky's _____ theory focuses on how social interaction contributes to development.
13. _____ interview method: uses a flexible, conversational style
14. The ability to adapt effectively in the face of threats to development
15. An orderly, integrated set of statements that describes, explains, and predicts behavior

Down
1. _____ period: time that is optimal for certain capacities to emerge and in which the individual is especially responsive to environmental influences
2. Approach concerned with the adaptive value of behavior and its evolutionary history
3. Information _____: approach that views the human mind as a symbol-manipulating system through which information flows
5. In ecological systems theory, activities and interaction patterns in the child's immediate surroundings
6. _____ systems theory: views the child as developing within a complex system of relationships affected by multiple levels of the environment
9. Participant observation of a culture
10. In ecological systems theory, cultural values, laws, customs, and resources that influence experiences and interactions at inner levels of the environment

PUZZLE 1.3 TERM REVIEW

Across
1. Unique combinations of genetic and environmental circumstances that can result in markedly different paths of development
3. Interview method in which the researcher asks all participants the same questions in the same way
7. _____, or case study, method
8. Variable expected to be influenced by the experimental manipulations
10. _____-_____ design: groups of people differing in age are studied at the same point in time
12. _____ assignment: even-handed procedure for assigning participants to treatment conditions
13. Variable manipulated by the researcher
14. _____ designs: researchers conduct several similar cross-sectional or longitudinal studies at various times
15. _____ modification: procedures that combine conditioning and modeling to change behavior

Down
2. Design in which the researcher randomly assigns participants to two or more treatment conditions; permits inferences about cause and effect
4. Design in which the researcher gathers information without altering the participants' experience
5. Design in which one group of participants is studied repeatedly at different ages
6. Developmental Cognitive _____ brings together researchers from multiple fields to study the relationship between changes in the brain and cognitive processing and behavior patterns.
9. Structured _____: research method in which the researcher evokes the behavior of interest in a laboratory setting
10. A number describing how two variables are related is called a correlation _____.
11. _____ observation: researcher goes into the natural environment to observe behavior of interest

PRACTICE TEST #1

1. Contemporary theorists regard the contexts that shape development as (p. 6)
   a. rudimentary and easy to define.
   b. many-layered and complex.
   c. important only artificially.
   d. ambiguous and nearly impossible to define.

2. Which of the following is an example of nurture? (p. 6)
   a. Susan had red hair because her mother had red hair.
   b. John was six feet tall because his father was six feet tall.
   c. Kim hated the taste of broccoli just as her mother did when she was young.
   d. Gerald was polite because his father had always taught him to be polite.

3. Theorists who emphasize stability over plasticity generally (p. 6)
   a. stress the importance of heredity in development.
   b. give little importance to genetics.
   c. give great importance to the role society plays in development.
   d. believe that change is likely if new experiences support it.

4. According to the lifespan perspective, (p. 7)
   a. early childhood is the most critical period in human development.
   b. adolescent years have the greatest influence on the life course.
   c. early adulthood has the greatest effect on the remainder of life.
   d. no age period is supreme in its influence on the life course.

5. To say that development is plastic means that it (p. 8)
   a. is impacted by events that occur during each major period of the life course.
   b. remains flexible with advancing age.
   c. is a joint expression of growth and decline.
   d. is affected by a complex blend of biological, psychological, and social forces.

6. Age-graded and history-graded influences are normative because (p. 10)
   a. they are largely difficult for researchers to study.
   b. they occur individually and haphazardly.
   c. each affects large numbers of people in a similar way.
   d. they both enhance the multidirectionality of development.

7. Darwin's theory of evolution emphasized two principles: (p. 11)
   a. stage and maturation.
   b. natural selection and survival of the fittest.
   c. nature and nurture.
   d. behaviorism and social learning.

8. Before Sigmund Freud could construct his psychosexual theory, he first would (p. 12)
   a. study the genetic histories and hereditary traits of his patients.
   b. use his normative approach in studying others familiar to his patients.
   c. encourage his patients to talk freely about painful childhood events.
   d. observe his patients secretly in their daily lives.

9. A special strength of the psychoanalytic perspective is its emphasis on (p. 12)
   a. the individual's unique life history as worthy of study and understanding.
   b. nature rather than nurture.
   c. directly observable events.
   d. a genetically determined, naturally unfolding course of growth.

10. The correct order of stages in Piaget's cognitive-developmental theory is: (p. 16)
    a. sensorimotor, preoperational, concrete operational, formal operational
    b. preoperational, concrete operational, formal operational, sensorimotor
    c. formal operational, concrete operational, preoperational, sensorimotor
    d. sensorimotor, formal operational, concrete operational, preoperational

11. An ethologist would most likely study (p. 18)
    a. her patients' dream patterns.
    b. her patients' family histories and hereditary traits.
    c. the social world surrounding her patients.
    d. diverse animal species in their natural habitats.

12. In stating that all relationships are bidirectional, Urie Bronfenbrenner emphasizes that (p. 19)
    a. children are as likely to be affected by nature as they are by nurture.
    b. children must decide between two directions in life.
    c. children are more influenced by the macrosystem than by the microsystem.
    d. children are as likely to affect adult behavior as they are to have their behavior affected by adults.

13. According to Bronfenbrenner, the environment (p. 21)
    a. plays a far less important role in development than genetics.
    b. is not a static force that affects people in a uniform way.
    c. plays an important role in development only in the later years of life.
    d. is a constant, steady determinant of developmental change for many.

14. One major limitation of the clinical interview is (p. 24)
    a. that it does not allow people to display their thoughts in terms that are as close as possible to the way they think in everyday life.
    b. the inaccuracy with which people report their thoughts, feelings, and experiences.
    c. that it provides only a very small amount of information.
    d. that it is conducted over a very long period, usually several years.

15. The clinical research method is best suited to studying the development of (p. 24)
    a. a large group of kindergarteners.
    b. a family with strong hereditary traits.
    c. extremely gifted children.
    d. diverse animal species in their natural habitats.

16. Unlike the clinical method, ethnographic research (p. 25)
    a. is largely a descriptive, qualitative form of study.
    b. often takes only a few brief moments to complete.
    c. is not dependent on field notes or observations.
    d. is directed toward understanding a culture or social group through participant observation.

17. Which of the following correlation coefficients shows the strongest relationship between two variables? (p. 27)
    a. + .24
    b. + .09
    c. 0
    d. − .52

18. An experimental design permits inferences about cause and effect because (p. 27)
    a. the researcher controls changes in the independent variable.
    b. the researcher controls changes in the dependent variable.
    c. the researcher systematically assigns participants to specific treatment conditions based on their known characteristics.
    d. experimental studies are conducted in natural settings rather than laboratory settings.

19. Which of the following is a strength of the longitudinal design for studying development? (p. 29)
    a. It involves a relatively short study time.
    b. It permits investigators to examine relationships between early and later events.
    c. It allows researchers to gather information in a single setting.
    d. It is immune from any cohort effects.

20. Which of the following is the best example of a cohort effect? (p. 29)
    a. Compared to twenty years ago, today's children are much more likely to have computer skills.
    b. A dog's mouth waters after hearing a can opened.
    c. The sick children in the classroom are less active than the healthy ones.
    d. Three of the brothers inherited their father's baldness, but the fourth did not.

PRACTICE TEST #2

1. Our knowledge of human development is interdisciplinary. What does this mean? (pp. 4–5)
    a. Our knowledge of human development is based exclusively on research conducted by people in the field of human development.
    b. Human development is not recognized as a distinct field of study.
    c. Individuals from diverse fields have contributed to our knowledge of human development.
    d. Human development is part of a larger discipline known as developmental psychology.

2. If baby Charlie has the same types of skills his parents have, only not as fine-tuned, the change in his thinking as he matures would be considered (p. 5)
    a. continuous.
    b. discontinuous.
    c. psychosocial.
    d. psychoanalytic.

3. Lifespan researchers emphasize that development is (p. 8)
    a. plastic only after puberty.
    b. rigid at all ages.
    c. rigid after adolescence.
    d. plastic at all ages.

4. According to the lifespan perspective, starting school at around age 6 is an example of a(n) (pp. 8, 10)
    a. family-graded influence.
    b. social-graded influence.
    c. history-graded influence.
    d. age-graded influence.

5. In the normative approach to child study, researchers (p. 11)
    a. jot down day-to-day descriptions and impressions of a youngster's behavior beginning in early infancy.
    b. take measures of behavior in large numbers of children and then compute age-related averages to represent typical development.
    c. investigate children's cognitive development through the use of clinical interviews in which children describe their thinking.
    d. use flowcharts to map the precise steps that individuals take to solve problems and complete tasks.

6. G. Stanley Hall, one of the most influential American psychologists of the early twentieth century, is generally regarded as the founder of the (p. 11)
    a. theory of evolution.
    b. child study movement.
    c. psychosexual theory.
    d. lifespan perspective.

7. The first successful intelligence test, developed by Alfred Binet, was important because it (p. 11)
   a. resolved the nature versus nurture debate on human intelligence.
   b. increased interest in individual differences in development.
   c. was a culturally unbiased measure of intellectual ability.
   d. showed that intelligence is a poor predictor of school achievement.

8. Which of the following theories is noted for its focus on the unique developmental history of each individual? (p. 12)
   a. behaviorism
   b. social learning theory
   c. psychoanalytic theory
   d. information processing

9. During Piaget's _____ stage, children's reasoning becomes logical, and they develop the ability to organize objects into hierarchies of classes and subclasses. (p. 16)
   a. sensorimotor
   b. preoperational
   c. concrete operational
   d. formal operational

10. Which of the following theories is concerned with the adaptive value of behavior and its evolutionary significance? (p. 18)
    a. ethology
    b. ecological systems theory
    c. sociocultural theory
    d. bioecological theory

11. A sensitive period is a time in which an individual is (p. 18)
    a. especially responsive to environmental influences.
    b. nonresponsive to environmental influences.
    c. unable to determine which influences are environmental.
    d. lacking judgment due to a destructive event.

12. Evolutionary developmental psychology is the study of (p. 18)
    a. wide diversity in pathways of change.
    b. the adaptive value of specieswide cognitive, emotional, and social competencies as those competencies change over time.
    c. how culture is transmitted from one generation to the next.
    d. children's ability to adapt in the face of threats to development.

13. To understand human development at the level of the microsystem, one must keep in mind that all relationships are (p. 19)
    a. universal.
    b. unidirectional.
    c. predetermined.
    d. bidirectional.

14. Jennifer's mother volunteers as a room parent. This connection between home and school illustrates Bronfenbrenner's (p. 20)
    a. mesosystem.
    b. exosystem.
    c. microsystem.
    d. macrosystem.

15. The outermost level of Bronfenbrenner's model is the (pp. 20–21)
    a. exosystem.
    b. mesosystem.
    c. microsystem.
    d. macrosystem.

16. To study children's emotional reactions, an investigator creates a laboratory situation that evokes the behavior of interest so that each participant has an equal opportunity to exhibit the response. This research method is considered a (p. 23)
    a. structured observation.
    b. naturalistic observation.
    c. case study.
    d. clinical interview.

17. A researcher concludes that 5-year-olds in the 1950s learned more slowly than 5-year-olds today. Which of the following is responsible for this finding? (p. 29)
    a. biased sampling
    b. investigator bias
    c. cohort effects
    d. selective attrition

18. In a _____ design, groups of people differing in age are studied at the same point in time. (p. 29)
    a. longitudinal
    b. cross-sectional
    c. sequential
    d. microgenetic

19. A sequential design can identify cohort effects by comparing groups of people of (p. 30)
    a. differing ages who were born in the same year.
    b. the same age who were born in the same year.
    c. the same age who were born in different years.
    d. differing ages who were born in different years.

20. Which of the following is true of research rights involving informed consent? (p. 32)
    a. The right to informed consent applies to all research participants except young children and elderly people with mental impairments.
    b. In most cases, researchers need only obtain the child's assent; parental consent is not required.
    c. For children 7 years and older, their own informed consent should be obtained in addition to parental consent.
    d. Unless the research obviously risks harm to the participant, researchers are not required to obtain informed consent.

CHAPTER 2
BIOLOGICAL AND ENVIRONMENTAL FOUNDATIONS

BRIEF CHAPTER SUMMARY

This chapter examines the foundations of development: heredity and environment. The discussion begins at the moment of conception, an event that establishes the new individual's hereditary makeup. At conception, chromosomes containing genetic information from each parent combine to determine characteristics that make us human and also contribute to individual differences in appearance and behavior. Several different patterns of inheritance are possible, ensuring that each individual will be unique. Serious developmental problems often result from the inheritance of harmful recessive genes and by chromosomal abnormalities. Fortunately, genetic counseling and prenatal diagnostic methods make early detection of genetic problems possible.

Just as complex as heredity are the environments in which human development takes place. The family has an especially powerful impact on development, operating as a network of interdependent relationships in which members exert direct, indirect, and third-party influences on one another. Family functioning and individual well-being are influenced considerably by child-rearing practices, as well as by SES. Poverty and homelessness can pose serious threats to development, while children in affluent families may suffer from overscheduling and lack of emotional closeness. The availability of education of women in particular promotes a better quality of life for both parents and children.

Beyond the immediate family, quality of community life in neighborhoods, schools, towns, and cities also affects lifespan development. Cultural values—for example, the degree to which a society emphasizes collectivism versus individualism—combine with laws and government programs to shape experiences in all of these contexts. Public policies are needed to support the economic and social well-being of both children and the elderly.

Some researchers believe it is useful and possible to determine "how much" heredity and environment contribute to individual differences. Others think that the effects of heredity and environment cannot be clearly separated. Instead, they want to discover "how" these two major determinants of development work together in a complex, dynamic interplay.

LEARNING OBJECTIVES

After reading this chapter, you should be able to:

2.1 Explain the role and function of genes and how they are transmitted from one generation to the next. (p. 36)

2.2 Describe the genetic events that determine the sex of the new organism. (p. 37)

2.3 Identify two types of twins, and explain how each is created. (pp. 37–38)

2.4 Describe various patterns of genetic inheritance. (pp. 38–40)

2.5 Describe major chromosomal abnormalities, and explain how they occur. (pp. 40–41)

2.6 Explain how reproductive procedures can assist prospective parents in having healthy children. (pp. 41–42, 44)

2.7 Summarize research on adoption. (pp. 42–43)

2.8 Describe family functioning as a network of interdependent relationships, along with aspects of the environment that support family well-being and development. (pp. 45–46)

2.9 Discuss the impact of socioeconomic status and poverty on family functioning. (pp. 46–49)

2.10 Summarize the roles of neighborhoods, towns, and cities in the lives of children and adults. (pp. 49–50)

2.11 Explain how cultural values and practices, public policies, and political and economic conditions affect human development. (pp. 50–53)

2.12   Explain the various ways heredity and environment may combine to influence complex traits. (pp. 53–54)

2.13   Describe and evaluate methods researchers use to determine "how much" heredity and environment influence complex human characteristics. (pp. 54–56)

2.14   Describe concepts that indicate "how" heredity and environment work together to influence complex human characterisitcs. (pp. 54–56)

STUDY QUESTIONS

1. _____ are directly observable characteristics that depend in part on the individual's _____, the complex blend of genetic information that determines our species and influences all of our unique characteristics. (p. 36)

Genetic Foundations

1. Rodlike structures in the nucleus of a cell that store and transmit genetic information are called _____. (p. 36)

The Genetic Code

1. Chromosomes are made of a chemical substance called _____. It looks like a twisted ladder and is composed of segments called _____. (pp. 36–37)

2. A unique feature of DNA is that it can duplicate itself through a process called _____. (p. 37)

3. Genes send instructions for making a rich assortment of proteins to the _____, the area surrounding the cell nucleus. (p. 37)

4. True or False: Proteins are the biological foundation on which our characteristics are built. (p. 37)

The Sex Cells

1. New individuals are created when two special cells called _____, or _____ combine. (p. 37)

2. Gametes are formed through a cell-division process called _____, which ensures that a constant quantity of genetic material is transmitted from one generation to the next. (p. 37)

3. A _____ is the cell that results when a sperm and ovum unite at conception. (p. 37)

4. True or False: Sex cells are unique in that they contain only 23 chromosomes. (p. 37)

Boy or Girl?

1. The 22 matching pairs of chromosomes are called _____. The 23rd is made up of the _____ *chromosomes*. (p. 37)

Multiple Births

1. The following characteristics describe either identical or fraternal twins. Indicate your answer using "I" for identical or "F" for fraternal. (pp. 37–38)

   _____ The frequency of this type of multiple birth is about 1 out of every 285 births

   _____ The most common type of multiple birth

   _____ Genetically no more alike than ordinary siblings

   _____ Type of multiple birth created when a zygote duplicates and separates into two clusters of cells

   _____ Older maternal age, fertility drugs, and in vitro fertilization are associated with this type of multiple birth

2. True or False: Children of single births are often healthier and develop more rapidly than twins in the early years. (p. 38)

Patterns of Genetic Inheritance

1. If the alleles from both parents are alike, the child is _____ and will display the inherited trait. If they are different, then the child is _____, and relationships between the alleles determine the trait that will appear. (p. 38)

2. Give an example of a characteristic representing dominant–recessive inheritance. (p. 38) _____

3. One of the most frequently occurring recessive disorders is _____, which affects the way the body breaks down proteins contained in many foods. How do doctors identify this disorder? What is the most common intervention to prevent harmful aspects of the disease? (pp. 38–39)

    A. _____

    B. _____

4. _____ is a pattern of inheritance in which both alleles influence the individual's characteristics. Under what conditions is the sickle cell trait expressed by heterozygous individuals? (p. 39)

5. True or False: Males are more likely than females to be affected by X-linked inheritance. (p. 39)

6. Name two X-linked disorders. (p. 39)

    A. _____   B. _____

7. Describe *genetic imprinting*. (p. 39)
   _____
   _____

8. How are harmful genes created? (p. 40)
   _____

9. Cite an example of germline mutation and an example of somatic mutation. (p. 40)
   _____
   _____
   _____

10. Characteristics, such as height, weight, intelligence, and personality reflect _____, in which many genes determine the characteristic in question. (p. 40)

Chromosomal Abnormalities

1. _____, the most common chromosomal abnormality, often results from a defect in the 21st chromosome. (p. 40)

2. List the consequences of Down syndrome. (p. 40)
   _____
   _____

3. Describe popular beliefs about individuals with sex chromosome disorders, and explain whether or not research supports these beliefs. (p. 41)
   _____
   _____

Reproductive Choices

Genetic Counseling and Prenatal Diagnosis

1. What is the purpose of genetic counseling, and who is most likely to seek this service? (pp. 41–42)
   _____
   _____

2. What is the function of a pedigree in genetic counseling? (p. 42)
   _____
   _____

3. Which two prenatal diagnostic methods are frequently used with women of advanced maternal age? (p. 42)

   A. _____

   B. _____

4. What complications are frequently associated with prenatal diagnosis? (p. 42)
   _____
   _____
   _____

5. Advances in genetic _____ offer hope for correcting heredity defects. (p. 42)

6. List a condition in which symptoms have been successfully reduced through gene therapy. (p. 42)
   _____

Social Issues: The Pros and Cons of Reproductive Technologies

1. Explain the following reproductive technologies. (p. 44)

   Donor Insemination: _____
   _____
   _____

   In Vitro Fertilization: _____
   _____
   _____

2. The overall success rate of in vitro fertilization is about _____ percent. The success rate (increases / decreases) steadily with age. (p. 44)

3. Discuss some of the concerns surrounding the use of donor insemination and in vitro fertilization. (p. 44)
   _____
   _____
   _____

4. Cite at least two risks involved with surrogate motherhood. (pp. 44–45)

5. Describe how reproductive technologies are evolving, and explain ethical concerns regarding reproductive advances. (p. 45)

Adoption

1. List three possible reasons that adopted children have more learning and emotional difficulties than other children. (p. 42)

    A. _____

    B. _____

    C. _____

2. The decision to search for birth parents usually occurs during (adolescence / early adulthood). Why is the search more likely during this period of development? (p. 43)

3. True or False: Most adoptees appear well-adjusted as adults. (p. 43)

Environmental Contexts for Development

The Family

1. Distinguish between direct and indirect family influences. (pp. 45–46)

    Direct: _____

    Indirect: _____

2. Explain how important events and historical time period contribute to the dynamic, ever-changing nature of the family. (p. 46)

Socioeconomic Status and Family Functioning

1. What three interrelated variables define socioeconomic status (SES)? (p. 46)

    A. _____

    B. _____

    C. _____

2. How does SES affect the timing and duration of phases of the family life cycle? (pp. 46–47)

    _____
    _____
    _____

3. Describe the influence of SES on parenting practices and parent–child interaction. (p. 47)

    _____
    _____
    _____

A Lifespan Vista: Worldwide Education of Girls: Transforming Current and Future Generations

1. List two reasons why education of girls has a powerful impact on the welfare of families, societies, and future generations. (p. 48)

    A. _____

    B. _____

2. Years of schooling strongly predict women's preventive health behavior. How does education influence family health? (p. 48)

    _____
    _____
    _____

3. True or False: The empowerment that education provides women is associated with more equitable husband–wife relationships and a reduction in harsh disciplining of children. (p. 48)

Affluence

1. True or False: Affluent parents often engage in high levels of family interaction and parenting that promote favorable development. (p. 47)

2. Explain why affluent youth may be troubled or poorly adjusted. (p. 47)

    _____
    _____

Poverty

1. What two groups are hit hardest by poverty? (p. 47)

    A. _____   B. _____

2. True or False: The poverty rate is higher among children than any other age group. (p. 49)

3. List five outcomes children of poverty are more likely to suffer from than other children. (p. 49)

   A. _____
   B. _____
   C. _____
   D. _____
   E. _____

Beyond the Family: Neighborhoods, Towns, and Cities

1. Explain why neighborhood resources have a greater impact on economically disadvantaged than well-to-do children and adolescents. (p. 49)

   _____
   _____
   _____
   _____

2. Describe how neighborhoods affect adults' well-being. (p. 49)

   _____
   _____
   _____

3. Why do neighborhoods become increasingly important during late adulthood? (p. 49)

   _____
   _____

4. Summarize the benefits and drawbacks of living in a small town. (pp. 49–50)

   Benefits: _____
   _____

   Drawbacks: _____
   _____

The Cultural Context

1. Which central North American beliefs and values contribute to the public's slow endorsement of government support and benefits for all families? (p. 50)

   _____
   _____

2. What are *subcultures*? (p. 50)

   _____
   _____

3. In _____ societies, people define themselves as part of a group and stress group over individual goals. In _____ societies, people think of themselves as separate entities and are largely concerned with their own personal needs. (p. 50)

4. Collectivist societies value an _____ self, while individualistic societies value an _____ self. List three values of each. (pp. 50–51)

   A. _____   A. _____

   B. _____   B. _____

   C. _____   C. _____

5. What are public policies? How does the United States compare to other industrialized nations in terms of public policies designed to protect children and the elderly? (p. 51)

   A. _____

   B. _____

6. Why have attempts to help children through public policy been difficult to realize in the United States? (p. 51)

   _____

   _____

7. List the services that Area Agencies on Aging provide elderly individuals. (p. 52)

   _____

   _____

8. Explain why many senior citizens remain in dire economic conditions. (p. 52)

   _____

   _____

   _____

9. How has the number of aging poor changed since 1960, and how are the elderly in the United States faring in comparison to those in Australia, Canada, and Western Europe? (p. 52)

   _____

   _____

10. List the activities of the Children's Defense Fund. (p. 52)

    _____

    _____

    _____

11. List the activities of the American Association of Retired Persons. (pp. 52–53)

    _____

    _____

    _____

Understanding the Relationship Between Heredity and Environment

The Question, "How Much?"

1. Describe a method used to infer the role of heredity in complex human characteristics. (p. 53)

   _____
   _____

2. Heritability estimates are obtained from _____ *studies*, which compare characteristics of family members. (p. 53)

3. True or False: Among children and adolescents, heritability estimates for intelligence and personality are approximately .50, indicating that genetic makeup can explain half of the variance in these traits. (p. 54)

4. True or False: Unlike intelligence, heritability of personality does not increase over the lifespan. (p. 54)

5. List three limitations of heritability estimates. (p. 54)

   A. _____
   B. _____
   C. _____

The Question, "How?"

1. In range of reaction, heredity (limits / increases) responsiveness to varying environments. In canalization, heredity (restricts / expands) the development of certain behaviors. (p. 54)

2. Describe two important points that *reaction range* highlights. (p. 54)

   _____
   _____

3. Match the following types of genetic–environmental correlation with their appropriate descriptors. (p. 55)

   _____ Children increasingly seek out environments that fit their genetic tendencies (called niche-picking).
   _____ A child's style of responding influences others' responses, which then strengthen the child's original style.
   _____ Parents provide an environment consistent with their own heredity.

   1. Passive correlation
   2. Evocative correlation
   3. Active correlation

4. _____ means development resulting from ongoing, bidirectional exchanges between heredity and all levels of the environment. Researchers call this view of the relationship between heredity and environment the _____ framework. (p. 56)

5. What is the major reason that researchers are interested in the nature–nurture issue? (p. 56)

   _____
   _____

ASK YOURSELF...

For *Ask Yourself* questions for this chapter, please log on to the Companion Website at *www.ablongman.com/berk*.

1. Select the Companion Website for *Exploring Lifespan Development*.
2. Use the "Jump to" menu to go directly to this chapter.
3. From the menu on the left side of the screen, select "Ask Yourself."
4. Complete questions and choose "Submit answers for grading" or "Clear answers" to start over.

SUGGESTED STUDENT READINGS

Hogenboom, M. (2003). *Living with genetic syndromes associated with intellectual disability.* Encinitas, CA: Kingsley. An ecological approach to understanding genetic disorders, this book examines the impact of living with and caring for children with special needs.

Hudson, R. B. (Ed.). (2005). *The new politics of old age policy.* Danvers, MA: John Hopkins University Press. Presents a thorough overview of public policies for aging Americans, including demographic, economic, and political trends in government-funded programs.

McGee, G., & Malhorta, R. (2004). *The human cloning debate.* San Francisco, CA: Berkeley Hills. An interdisciplinary approach to understanding human cloning and its ethical implications, this book presents a straightforward explanation of cloning procedures, including pros and cons surrounding this highly controversial topic.

Segal, N. L. (2005). *Indivisible by two: Lives of extraordinary twins.* Cambridge, MA: Harvard University Press. A fascinating look into the lives of multiples, this book follows 12 sets of twins, triplets, and quadruplets. The author not only describes the unique experiences of multiples, but she also highlights the many challenges faced by the parents, friends, and spouses of these extraordinary individuals.

PUZZLE 2.1 TERM REVIEW

Across
1. Pattern of inheritance in which many genes determine the characteristic in question
4. Long, double-stranded molecules that make up chromosomes (abbr.)
7. Having two identical alleles at the same place on a pair of chromosomes
10. Directly observable characteristics
12. Having two different alleles at the same place on a pair of chromosomes
14. Pattern of inheritance in which a recessive gene is carried on the X chromosome
15. Rodlike structures in the cell nucleus that store and transmit genetic information
17. Genetic _____: alleles are chemically marked in such a way that one pair member is activated, regardless of its makeup
18. Pattern of inheritance in which, under heterozygous conditions, the influence of only one allele is apparent
20. Development resulting from ongoing bidirectional exchanges between heredity and all levels of the environment

Down
2. A segment of DNA along the length of the chromosome
3. Pattern of inheritance in which both alleles are expressed, resulting in a combined trait, or one that is intermediate between the two
5. Each form of a gene is called an _____
6. A sudden but permanent change in a segment of DNA
8. The complex blend of genetic information that determines our species and influences all our unique characteristics
9. The process of cell duplication
11. _____ chromosomes: the 23rd pair of chromosomes; XX in females, XY in males
13. The 22 matching chromosome pairs in each cell
16. Human sperm and ova
19. The process of cell division

PUZZLE 2.2 TERM REVIEW

Across
3. In _____ societies, people define themselves as part of a group and stress group over individual goals
6. The tendency to actively choose environments that complement our heredity (two words; hyph.)
7. Genetic-_____ correlation: idea that heredity influences the environment to which individuals are exposed
13. Each person's unique, genetically determined response to a range of environmental conditions (3 words)
14. _____ estimate: statistic that measures the extent to which individual differences in complex traits in a specific population are due to genetic factors
16. The tendency of heredity to restrict the development of some characteristics to just one or a few outcomes
17. Cell resulting from the union of the sperm and ova at conception

Down
1. _____ policies: laws and government programs aimed at improving current conditions
2. Twins that result when a zygote that has started to duplicate separates into two clusters of cells that develop into two individuals with the same genetic makeup; also known as monozygotic twins
4. In _____ societies, people think of themselves as separate entities and are largely concerned with their own personal needs
5. Group of people with beliefs and customs that differ from those of the larger culture
8. _____ diagnostic methods are medical procedures that permit detection of developmental problems before birth
9. _____ studies compare the characteristics of family members to determine the importance of heredity in complex human characteristics
10. In an _____-family household, the parent and child live with one or more adult relatives
11. Twins that result from the release and fertilization of two ova; genetically no more alike than ordinary siblings; also known as dizygotic twins
12. A measure of a family's social position and economic well-being (abbr.)
15. _____ counseling: helps couples assess the likelihood of giving birth to a baby with a hereditary disorder and to choose the best course of action in light of the risks and family goals
16. _____ studies compare the characteristics of family members to determine the importance of heredity in complex human characteristics

PRACTICE TEST #1

1. Chromosomes are made up of a chemical substance called (p. 36)
   a. deoxyribonucleic acid.
   b. meiosis.
   c. dizygotic.
   d. homozygous.

2. A molecule of DNA resembles (p. 37)
   a. a globe or sphere.
   b. a twisted ladder.
   c. either an X or a Y.
   d. no one knows what it looks like.

3. A unique feature of DNA is that it can duplicate itself through a process called (p. 37)
   a. meiosis.
   b. mitosis.
   c. imprinting.
   d. codominance.

4. The 23rd pair of chromosomes consists of (p. 37)
   a. autosomes.
   b. identical chromosomes.
   c. dominant chromosomes.
   d. sex chromosomes.

5. The case of PKU demonstrates that (p. 37)
   a. serious inherited disorders are more often due to dominant than to recessive genes.
   b. most inherited disorders are untreatable.
   c. even if we know the genetic makeup of the parents, it is difficult to predict the likelihood that children in a family will display a disorder.
   d. changes in the environment can alter the extent to which an inherited disorder influences a person's well-being.

6. How are harmful genes created? (p. 40)
   a. mutation
   b. mitosis
   c. meiosis
   d. imprinting

7. Which disorder of the sex chromosomes, caused by abnormal repetition of a sequence of DNA based on the X chromosome, results from genetic imprinting? (p. 40)
   a. PKU
   b. hemophilia
   c. Fragile X syndrome
   d. Turner syndrome

8. The most common chromosomal disorder, occurring in one out of every 800 live births, is (p. 40)
   a. Down syndrome.
   b. Klinefelter syndrome.
   c. Turner syndrome.
   d. XYY syndrome.

9. Except for _____, prenatal diagnosis should not be used routinely, as other methods pose some risk of miscarriage. (p. 42)
   a. fetoscopy
   b. maternal blood analysis
   c. chorionic villus sampling
   d. amniocentesis

10. Which of the following statements about adoption is true? (p. 42)
    a. Adopted children and adolescents fare as well as or better than children growing up with their biological parents.
    b. Children who are adopted later in life are better adjusted than children who are adopted in infancy and toddlerhood.
    c. Adopted children and adolescents have more learning and emotional difficulties than do other children.
    d. Adopted children are more similar in intelligence and personality to their adoptive parents than to their biological parents.

11. Which of the following is NOT a variable assessed as part of the socioeconomic status (SES) index? (p. 46)
    a. income
    b. marital status
    c. years of education
    d. skill required by one's job

12. Jonah is 3 years old and has been difficult to care for since birth. He cries often, throws tantrums, screams, and has unpredictable eating and sleeping habits. His mother often becomes upset with Jonah, responding to his behavior with anger and harshness, which causes Jonah to act out even more. Which of the following is being described in the example? (p. 45)
    a. third parties
    b. bidirectional influences
    c. dynamic influences
    d. extraneous variables

13. Approximately _____ percent of the population in the United States and Canada live in poverty. Which groups are hardest hit by poverty? (p. 47)
    a. 12; infants and teenagers
    b. 32; parents over age 40 with adolescent children and elderly people who reside in nursing homes
    c. 12; parents under age 25 with young children and elderly people who live alone
    d. 32; infants and the elderly

14. Compared to large cities, small towns are more likely to foster (p. 50)
    a. feelings of loneliness.
    b. limited social contact.
    c. participation in civic groups.
    d. more visits to museums and concerts.

15. A small group of people who hold a different faith from the vast majority of the population around them would be considered a(n) (p. 50)
    a. extended family.
    b. subculture.
    c. macrosystem.
    d. individualistic society.

16. In an individualistic society, (p. 50)
    a. people think of themselves as separate entities and are concerned with their own needs.
    b. people define themselves as part of a group and stress group goals.
    c. three or more generations usually live together.
    d. a small group of people hold different beliefs than those of the larger culture.

17. Kinship studies (p. 53)
    a. compare the characteristics of family members.
    b. look at many different ethnic and cultural groups.
    c. focus solely on religious groups and organizations.
    d. look at a large group of similarly aged individuals.

18. Which of the following statements represents a limitation of heritability estimates? (p. 54)
    a. They are only useful in studying fraternal twins.
    b. They neglect the role of biology in explaining human development.
    c. They can easily be misapplied, such as when they are used to suggest that ethnic differences in intelligence have a genetic basis.
    d. They are only useful in explaining personality traits.

19. Identical twins reared apart, who nevertheless have many psychological traits and lifestyle characteristics in common, illustrate a form of genetic–environmental correlation commonly called (p. 55)
    a. range of reaction.
    b. passive.
    c. niche-picking.
    d. evocative.

20. Maria provides her baby with plenty of age-appropriate stimulation, which increases brain growth and transforms gene expression. This series of interactions leads to new gene–environment exchanges, which further enhance brain growth and gene expression. This is an example of (p. 56)
    a. niche picking.
    b. evocative correlation.
    c. epigenesis.
    d. range of reaction.

PRACTICE TEST #2

1. A segment of DNA along the length of a chromosome is called a (p. 37)
    a. phenotype.
    b. genotype.
    c. gene.
    d. zygote.

2. The process of cell division, or _____, helps to explain why siblings differ from each other even though their genotypes come from the same pool of parental genes. (p. 37)
    a. autosomes
    b. mitosis
    c. meiosis
    d. dominance

3. New individuals are created when two special cells combine. These cells are called (p. 37)
    a. DNA.
    b. genes.
    c. zygotes.
    d. gametes.

4. When gametes form in males, the X and Y chromosomes (p. 37)
    a. separate into different sperm cells.
    b. combine with each other to form one chromosome.
    c. are destroyed by the chemical reaction.
    d. multiply to two sets of Xs and Ys.

5. Peter and Colin are twins. Genetically, they are no more alike than ordinary siblings. Peter and Colin are _____ twins. (pp. 37–38)
    a. monozygotic
    b. dizygotic
    c. identical
    d. homozygous

6. In a heterozygous pairing in which only one gene affects the child's characteristics, the pattern of genetic inheritance is called (p. 38)
   a. dominant–recessive.
   b. codominant.
   c. polygenic.
   d. mutagenic.

7. The sickle cell trait, a heterozygous condition present in many black Africans, is an example of (p. 39)
   a. incomplete dominance.
   b. X-linked inheritance.
   c. dominant–recessive inheritance.
   d. monogenic inheritance.

8. Which of the following explains why males are more likely than females to be affected by X-linked disorders? (p. 39)
   a. Males are more often homozygous for harmful recessive genes.
   b. Males are more likely than females to be born to women over the age of 35.
   c. Males' sex chromosomes do not match.
   d. Males tend to have fewer autosomes.

9. Mr. and Mrs. Chow would like to have a baby but are concerned about the presence of Down syndrome in their family. Which of the following would you recommend to help them determine their chances of giving birth to a baby with this disorder? (pp. 41–42)
   a. chorionic villus sampling
   b. genetic counseling
   c. ultrasound
   d. amniocentesis

10. Which of the following prenatal diagnostic procedures would be used if results were required very early in pregnancy? (p. 42)
    a. fetoscopy
    b. ultrasound
    c. chorionic villus sampling
    d. amniocentesis

11. Which of the following would be LEAST likely to put an adopted child at risk for learning and emotional difficulties in childhood? (pp. 42–43)
    a. a preadoptive history of conflict-ridden family relationships
    b. a biological mother who suffered from alcoholism or depression
    c. a disparity in intelligence and personality between adoptive parents and the child
    d. unresolved curiosity about the child's roots

12. Researchers view the family as (p. 45)
    a. a self-contained unit that is impervious to third party effects.
    b. a network of unidirectional influences.
    c. a system of interdependent relationships.
    d. a stable system that is resistant to change.

13. Which of the following is true with regard to socioeconomic influences on child-rearing? (pp. 46–47)
    a. Lower-SES people tend to marry and have children later than higher-SES people.
    b. Lower-SES parents tend to emphasize external characteristics, such as obedience, neatness, and cleanliness, whereas higher-SES parents emphasize psychological traits, such as curiosity, happiness, and self-direction.
    c. Lower-SES families use more warmth, explanation, and verbal praise, while higher-SES parents use more commands, criticism, and physical punishment.
    d. Education has little impact on SES differences in parenting.

14. Socioeconomic status consists of (p. 46)
    a. years of education, prestige and skill required of job, and income.
    b. years of education, neighborhood lived in, and cost of house.
    c. years at current job, prestige and skill required of job, and job title.
    d. size of bank savings account, stock portfolio, and income.

15. _____ is more common in neighborhoods where residents feel socially isolated. (p. 49)
    a. Child abuse and neglect
    b. Contact with relatives
    c. Church attendance
    d. Family cohesiveness

16. Laws and government programs aimed at improving current conditions are called (p. 51)
    a. charitable efforts.
    b. government bonds.
    c. statutory initiatives.
    d. public policies.

17. A statistic that measures the extent to which complex traits, such as intelligence and personality, can be traced to heredity is called a (p. 53)
    a. heritability estimate.
    b. kinship estimate.
    c. correlation coefficient.
    d. range of reaction.

18. The concept of range of reaction explains that children who are exposed to the same environmental conditions (p. 54)
    a. may respond to them differently because of their genetic makeup.
    b. will tend to show the same pattern of responses over time.
    c. tend to overcome their inheritance, so their genes have little effect.
    d. will become genetically more similar than other children are.

19. The well-coordinated, muscular teenager who spends more time at after-school sports is an example of (p. 55)
    a. active correlation.
    b. passive correlation.
    c. evocative correlation.
    d. disciplined correlation.

20. _____ refers to development resulting from ongoing, bidirectional exchanges between heredity and the environment. (p. 56)
    a. Genetic imprinting
    b. Heritability
    c. Epigenesis
    d. Niche-picking

CHAPTER 3
PRENATAL DEVELOPMENT, BIRTH, AND THE NEWBORN BABY

BRIEF CHAPTER SUMMARY

With conception, the story of prenatal development begins to unfold. The vast changes that take place during the 38 weeks of pregnancy are usually divided into three phases: (1) the period of the zygote, (2) the period of the embryo, and (3) the period of the fetus.

Although the prenatal environment is far more constant than the world outside the womb, many factors can affect the developing embryo and fetus. Various environmental agents, or teratogens, and other maternal factors can damage the developing organism, making the prenatal period a vulnerable time. For this reason, early and regular prenatal health care is vitally important to ensure the health of mother and baby.

Childbirth takes place in three stages: (1) dilation and effacement of the cervix, (2) delivery of the baby, and (3) birth of the placenta. Production of stress hormones during labor helps infants withstand oxygen deprivation, clear the lungs for breathing, and arouse them into alertness at birth. Doctors and nurses use the Apgar Scale to assess the infant's physical condition quickly after birth.

Childbirth practices are molded by the society of which the mother and baby are a part. Alternatives to traditional hospital childbirth include natural childbirth and delivery in a birth center or at home. When pregnancy and birth complications are likely, medical interventions help save the lives of many babies, but when used routinely, they may inaccurately identify infants as being in danger when they are not. Preterm and low-birth-weight infants are at risk for many problems. Interventions for preterm babies, such as special infant stimulation, can help these infants develop favorably.

Infants begin life with remarkable skills relating to their physical and social worlds. Reflexes are the newborn baby's most obvious organized patterns of behavior. Throughout the day and night, newborns move in and out of five different states of arousal. Rapid-eye-movement (REM) sleep seems to be especially critical, providing young infants with stimulation essential for central nervous system development. Crying is the first way babies communicate, letting parents know that they need food, comfort, and stimulation. The senses of touch, taste, smell, and sound are well developed at birth, while vision is the least mature of the newborn's senses.

After childbirth, all family members need to meet the challenges of living in the new family unit that has been created, but when parents support each other's needs, the stress remains manageable.

LEARNING OBJECTIVES

After reading this chapter, you should be able to:

3.1 List the three periods of prenatal development, and describe the major milestones of each (pp. 60–65)

3.2 Define the term *teratogen*, and summarize the factors that affect the impact of teratogens on prenatal development. (p. 65)

3.3 List agents known or suspected of being teratogens, and discuss evidence supporting the harmful impact of each. (pp. 65–70)

3.4 Discuss maternal factors other than exposure to teratogens that can affect the developing embryo or fetus. (pp. 70–71)

3.5 Explain the importance of early and regular health care during the prenatal period. (pp. 71–72)

3.6 Describe the three stages of childbirth. (pp. 73–74)

3.7 Discuss the baby's adaptation to labor and delivery. (p. 74)

3.8 Describe natural childbirth and home delivery, noting any benefits and concerns associated with each. (p. 75)

3.9 List common medical interventions during childbirth, circumstances that justify their use, and any dangers associated with each. (pp. 76–77)

3.10 Describe the risks associated with preterm and small-for-date births, along with factors that help infants who survive a traumatic birth recover. (pp. 77–80)

3.11 Describe the newborn baby's reflexes and states of arousal, including sleep characteristics and ways to soothe a crying baby. (pp. 80–85)

3.12 Describe the newborn's sensory capacities. (p. 85)

3.13 Summarize typical changes in the family after the birth of a new baby. (pp. 86–87)

3.14 Describe typical changes in the family after the birth of a new baby. (p. 86)

STUDY QUESTIONS

Prenatal Development

Conception

1. About once every 28 days, an ovum is released from one of a woman's two _____, and it is drawn into one of the two _____, which are long, thin structures that lead to the uterus. (p. 60)

Period of the Zygote

1. The period of the zygote lasts about _____ weeks. (p. 61)

2. Match the following terms with the appropriate descriptions. (p. 61)

    _____ Will provide protective covering and nourishment to the new organism
    _____ A hollow, fluid-filled ball that is formed by a tiny mass of cells four days after fertilization
    _____ Will become the new organism

    1. Blastocyst
    2. Embryonic disk
    3. Trophoblast

3. List two functions of the amniotic fluid. (p. 61)

    A. _____

    B. _____

4. True or False: As many as 30 percent of zygotes do not make it through the first two weeks after fertilization. (p. 62)

5. The _____ permits food and oxygen to reach the developing organism and waste products to be carried away. (p. 63)

6. The placenta is connected to the developing organism by the _____. (p. 63)

Period of the Embryo

1. True or False: The most rapid prenatal changes take place during the period of the embryo. (p. 63)

2. List the organs and structures that will be formed from each of the following layers of the embryonic disk. (p. 63)

    Mesoderm: _____

    _____

    Ectoderm: _____

    _____

    Endoderm: _____

    _____

3. Describe prenatal growth during the second month of pregnancy. Which one of the senses has already developed? (p. 63)

    A. _____

    _____

    _____

    B. _____

Period of the Fetus

1. The period of the fetus is sometimes referred to as the _____ phase. (p. 63)

2. Prenatal development is divided into _____, or three equal periods of time. (p. 64)

3. The white, cheese-like substance that completely covers the fetus to protect the skin from chapping in the amniotic fluid is called _____. (p. 64)

4. _____ is the white, downy hair that covers the entire body of the fetus. (p. 64)

5. What major milestone in brain development is reached at the end of the second trimester? (p. 64)

    _____

6. The age at which the baby can first survive if born early is called the *age of* _____. When does this typically occur? (p. 64)

    _____

7. Describe research findings on the relationship between fetal activity patterns and infant temperament. (p. 64)

    _____

    _____

    _____

8. List physical changes during the third trimester that permit increasing responsiveness to stimulation. (pp. 64–65)

    _____

    _____

    _____

Prenatal Environmental Influences

Teratogens

1. Define the term *teratogen*, and describe four factors that affect the impact of teratogens on prenatal development. (p. 65)

    Definition: _____

    A. _____

    B. _____

    C. _____

    D. _____

2. A _____ *period* is a limited time span in which a part of the body or a behavior is biologically prepared to develop rapidly and is especially vulnerable to its surroundings. (p. 65)

3. True or False: The fetal period is the time when teratogens are most likely to cause serious defects. (p. 65)

4. When taken by mothers 4 to 6 weeks after conception, _____, a sedative widely available in some countries during the early 1960s, produced deformities of the embryo's developing arms and legs, and less frequently, caused damage to the ears, heart, kidneys, and genitals. (p. 65)

5. A synthetic hormone called _____ was widely prescribed between 1945 and 1970 to prevent miscarriages. Cite the potential consequences of prenatal exposure to this medication. (p. 66)

    _____

6. A vitamin A derivative called _____, which is used to treat severe acne, is the most widely used, potent teratogen. Cite the potential consequences of early prenatal exposure to this medication. (p. 66)

    _____

7. True or False: Heavy caffeine intake during pregnancy is associated with low birth weight, miscarriage, and newborn withdrawal symptoms. (p. 66)

8. Describe the difficulties faced by babies who are prenatally exposed to heroin, cocaine, or methadone. (p. 67)

    _____

9. What are potential risks of prenatal marijuana exposure? (p. 67)

10. Summarize physical and behavioral effects of maternal smoking during the prenatal period. (p. 67)

11. True or False: If the mother stops smoking at any time during the pregnancy, even during the last trimester, she reduces the chances that her baby will be negatively impacted. (p. 67)

12. Explain the mechanisms through which smoking harms the fetus. (p. 67)

13. True or False: Passive smoking has not been linked with any adverse effects on the infant. (pp. 67–68)

14. Distinguish between *fetal alcohol syndrome* (FAS) and *fetal alcohol effects* (FAE). (p. 68)

15. List some physical and mental impairments typically associated with FAS. (p. 68)

16. True or False: The mental impairments seen in babies with FAS typically lessen by adolescence or early adulthood. (p. 68)

17. Explain how alcohol harms the fetus. (p. 68)

18. True or False: Fewer than 10 percent of American and Canadian mothers report drinking at some time during their pregnancies. (p. 68)

19. True or False: Even mild drinking, less than one drink per day, is associated with FAS-like facial features, reduced head size and body growth, and lower mental test scores. (p. 68)

20. True or False: Low doses of radiation exposure, such as through medical X-rays, are believed to be safe for the developing fetus and have not been linked to any negative outcomes. (p. 68)

21. Match each of the following environmental pollutants with its effect on development. (p. 69)

    _____ This teratogen, commonly found in paint chippings from old buildings and other industrial materials, is related to prematurity, low birth weight, brain damage, and physical defects.
    _____ This toxic compound, resulting from incineration, is linked to brain, immune system, and thyroid damage in babies and an increased incidence of breast and uterine cancer in women.
    _____ Women who ate fish contaminated with this substance gave birth to babies with slightly reduced birth weights, smaller heads, persisting attention and memory difficulties, and lower intelligence test scores in childhood.
    _____ This teratogen, formerly used to insulate electrical equipment, results in low birth weight, skin deformities, brain wave abnormalities, and delayed cognitive development.

    1. Mercury
    2. Lead
    3. PCBs
    4. Dioxins

22. _____, or 3-day measles, is a virus associated with eye cataracts; deafness; heart, genital, urinary, and intestinal abnormalities; and mental retardation. (p. 69)

23. True or False: Prenatal exposure to rubella increases risk of serious mental illness in adulthood. (p. 69)

24. When HIV-infected women become pregnant, they pass the deadly virus to the developing organism approximately _____ to _____ percent of the time. (p. 70)

25. True or False: Most infants prenatally exposed to the AIDS virus survive 8 to 10 years after the appearance of symptoms. (p. 70)

26. Pregnant women may become infected with _____, a parasitic disease found in many animals, from eating raw or undercooked meat or from contact with the feces of infected cats. (p. 70)

Other Maternal Factors

1. Summarize the behavioral and health problems of prenatally malnourished infants. (p. 70)

   _____
   _____
   _____
   _____

2. Why should women take a folic acid supplement around the time of conception and in the early weeks of pregnancy? (p. 70)

   _____
   _____

3. True or False: The U.S. Special Supplemental Food Program for Women, Infants, and Children (WIC) reaches about 90 percent of those who qualify, while the Canadian Prenatal Nutrition Program (CPNP) reaches only 10 percent of expectant mothers. What services do WIC and CPNP provide? (p. 70)

   _____
   _____
   _____

4. Describe the mechanisms through which maternal stress affects the developing organism, and note outcomes associated with severe emotional stress during pregnancy. (pp. 70–71)

   Mechanisms: _____
   _____
   _____

   Outcomes: _____
   _____
   _____

5. True or False: Stress-related prenatal complications are greatly reduced when mothers have husbands, other family members, and friends who offer social support. (p. 71)

6. Under what conditions can the Rh factor cause problems for the developing fetus? (p. 71)
   _____
   _____
   _____

7. The physical immaturity of teenage mothers (does / does not) lead to pregnancy complications. (p. 71)

The Importance of Prenatal Health Care

1. True or False: If untreated, toxemia can cause convulsions in the mother and fetal death. What is usually recommended to lower blood pressure to a safe level? (p. 72)
   _____

2. True or False: Seventeen percent of pregnant women in the United States receive late or no prenatal care. (p. 72)

3. Discuss some of the barriers to obtaining prenatal health care mentioned by expectant mothers who delay or never seek such care. (p. 72)
   _____
   _____
   _____

Childbirth

The Stages of Childbirth

1. Name and describe the three stages of labor. (pp. 73–74)
   A. _____
   B. _____
   C. _____

The Baby's Adaptation to Labor and Delivery

1. Cite the adaptive significance of high levels of cortisol and other stress hormones during childbirth. (p. 74)
   _____
   _____

Assessing the Newborn's Physical Condition: The Apgar Scale

1. List the five characteristics assessed by the Apgar Scale. (p. 74)

    A. _____

    B. _____

    C. _____

    D. _____

    E. _____

2. On the Apgar Scale, a score of _____ or better indicates that the infant is in good physical condition; a score between _____ and _____ indicates that the baby requires assistance in establishing breathing and other vital sign; a score of _____ or below indicates the infant is in serious danger and requires emergency medical attention. (p. 74)

Approaches to Childbirth

Natural, or Prepared, Childbirth

1. What is the goal of the natural childbirth approach? (p. 75)

    _____
    _____
    _____

2. List and describe three activities of a typical natural childbirth program. (p. 75)

    A. _____
    _____

    B. _____
    _____

    C. _____
    _____

3. Research suggests that social support (is / is not) an important part of the success of natural childbirth techniques. (p. 75)

Home Delivery

1. Home births are typically handled by certified _____, who have degrees in nursing and additional training in childbirth management. (p. 75)

2. True or False: For healthy women assisted by a trained professional, it is just as safe to give birth at home as in a hospital. (p. 75)

Medical Interventions

1. _____ refers to oxygen deprivation during labor and delivery. (p. 76)

2. Infants in the _____ position are turned in such a way that the buttocks or feet would be delivered first. (p. 76)

Fetal Monitoring

1. Explain the purpose of *fetal monitoring*. (p. 76)

2. True or False: Most U.S. hospitals require fetal monitoring, which is used in over 80 percent of American births. Canada reserves continuous fetal monitoring for at-risk babies. (p. 76)

3. Cite reasons why fetal monitoring is a controversial procedure. (p. 76)

Labor and Delivery Medication

1. True or False: Some form of medication is used in less than 80 percent of North American births. (p. 76)

2. Summarize potential problems associated with the use of labor and delivery medication. (p. 76)

Cesarean Delivery

1. What is a *cesarean delivery*? (p. 76)

2. Describe circumstances in which a cesarean delivery warranted. (pp. 76–77)

3. How can cesarean delivery affect the adjustment of the newborn baby and, consequently, the early infant–mother relationship? (p. 77)

Preterm and Low-Birth-Weight Infants

1. True or False: Birth weight is the best available predictor of infant survival and healthy development. (p. 77)

2. List the problems associated with low birth weight. (p. 77)

Preterm versus Small for Date

1. Distinguish between preterm and small-for-date babies. (p. 77)

    Preterm: _____
    _____

    Small for date: _____
    _____

2. Of the two types of babies, (preterm / small-for-date) infants usually have more serious problems. What difficulties do these babies have? (p. 77)

    _____
    _____

Consequences for Caregiving

1. Describe the characteristics of preterm infants, and explain how those characteristics may affect caregiving. (p. 77)

    _____
    _____
    _____
    _____

Interventions for Preterm Infants

1. Discuss several methods of stimulation used to foster the development of preterm infants. (p. 78)

    _____
    _____
    _____
    _____
    _____

2. Describe "kangaroo care," and list its benefits. (p. 78)

    A. _____

    B. _____

3. True or False: Research confirms that preterm babies and economically disadvantaged babies require intensive intervention to achieve lasting changes in their development. (p. 78)

Social Issues: A Cross-National Perspective on Health Care and Other Policies for Parents and Newborn Babies

1. _____ *mortality* refers to the number of deaths in the first year of life per 1,000 live births. (p. 79)

2. True or False: In the United States, African-American and Native-American infants are twice as likely as white infants to die in the first year of life. (p. 79)

3. True or False: Canada has achieved one of the lowest infant mortality rates in the world. (p. 79)

4. _____ *mortality,* the rate of death in the first month of life, accounts for 67 percent of the infant death rate in the United States and for 80 percent in Canada. (p. 79)

5. Which cause of neonatal mortality is mostly preventable? (p. 79)
   _____
   _____

6. List two factors largely responsible for the relatively high rate of infant mortality in the United States. (p. 79)
   A. _____
   B. _____

7. The United States ranks _____ in the world in infant survival, while Canada ranks _____. What do Canada and all the countries that outrank the United States provide its citizens that promotes infant survival and healthy growth? (p. 79)
   _____
   _____
   _____

8. True or False: Paid, job-protected employment leave is a vital societal intervention for new parents. Describe research findings on the length of childbirth leave for new parents. (p. 79)
   _____
   _____
   _____

Birth Complications, Parenting, and Resilience

1. Describe how the quality of the home environment affects the development of infants who experienced birth complications. (pp. 78, 80)
   _____
   _____

2. The influence of early biological risks often (increases / decreases) as the child's personal characteristics and social experiences increasingly contribute to their functioning. (p. 80)

The Newborn Baby's Capacities

Newborn Reflexes

1. What is a *reflex*? (p. 81)
   _____
   _____

2. List and briefly describe the reflexes presented in your text. Which ones have survival value? (p. 81)
   A. _____
   _____
   _____
   _____

B. _____

3. When do most newborn reflexes disappear? (p. 81)

4. Explain the importance of assessing newborn reflexes. (p. 81)

Newborn States

1. Name and describe the five infant *states of arousal.* (p. 82)

    A. _____

    B. _____

    C. _____

    D. _____

    E. _____

2. Describe how individual differences in infant's daily rhythms affect parents' attitudes toward and interaction with the baby. (p. 82)

3. Describe the characteristics of *REM* and *NREM* sleep. (p. 82)

    REM: _____

    NREM: _____

4. Why do infants spend more time in REM sleep than children, adolescents, and adults? (p. 82)

5. Describe sleep behavior of infants who are brain damaged or who have experienced serious birth trauma, and briefly explain possible consequences of this sleep behavior. (p. 82)

6. What is the most effective way to soothe a crying baby when feeding and diaper changing do not work? (p. 84)

7. How do the cries of brain-damaged babies and those who have experienced prenatal and birth complications differ from those of healthy infants, and how does this difference affect parental responding? (pp. 84–85)

Biology and Environment: The Mysterious Tragedy of Sudden Infant Death Syndrome

1. What is *Sudden Infant Death Syndrome (SIDS)*? (p. 83)

2. True or False: In industrialized countries, SIDS is the leading cause of infant mortality between 1 week and 12 months of age. (p. 83)

3. True or False: Researchers have recently determined the precise cause of SIDS. (p. 83)

4. Describe some early physical problems that are common among SIDS victims. (p. 83)

5. Explain how impaired brain functioning might cause SIDS. (p. 83)

6. Describe four environmental factors associated with SIDS. (p. 83)

   A.

   B.

   C.

   D.

7. Discuss several preventative measures that reduce the incidence of SIDS. (p. 83)

Sensory Capacities

1. True or False: Infants are born with a poorly developed sense of touch; consequently, they are not sensitive to pain. (p. 85)

2. During the prenatal period, which four areas of the body are first to become sensitive to touch? (p. 85)

   A. _____ B. _____

   C. _____ D. _____

3. True or False: Infants not only have taste preferences but also are capable of communicating these preferences through facial expressions. (p. 85)

4. True or False: Certain odor preferences are present at birth. (p. 85)

5. True or False: At 4 days of age, breastfed babies prefer the smell of their own mother's breast to that of an unfamiliar lactating mother. (p. 85)

6. True or False: Newborns prefer pure tones to complex sounds. (p. 86)

7. What evidence suggests that infants may have developed a preference for their mother's voice before birth? (p. 86)

   _____
   _____

8. Vision is the (most / least) mature of the newborn baby's senses. (p. 86)

9. Describe the newborn baby's visual acuity. (p. 86)

   _____
   _____

10. True or False: Infants have well-developed color vision at birth, and they are immediately capable of discriminating colors. (p. 86)

Adjusting to the New Family Unit

1. Describe birth-related hormonal changes in both the mother and father that prepare expectant parents for their new role. (p. 86)

   _____
   _____
   _____

2. Discuss several changes in the family system following the birth of a new baby. (pp. 86–87)

   _____
   _____
   _____
   _____

ASK YOURSELF...

For *Ask Yourself* questions for this chapter, please log on to the Companion Website at *www.ablongman.com/berk*.

1. Select the Companion Website for *Exploring Lifespan Development*.
2. Use the "Jump to" menu to go directly to this chapter.
3. From the menu on the left side of the screen, select "Ask Yourself."
4. Complete questions and choose "Submit answers for grading" or "Clear answers" to start over.

SUGGESTED STUDENT READINGS

Curtis, G. B. & Schuler, J. (2003). *Your pregnancy for the father-to-be*. New York: Perseus Publishing. Written for a general audience, this book provides information to expectant fathers about physical changes during pregnancy, medical tests and procedures, and the importance of providing the mother with social support during the pregnancy and after the baby arrives. Other topics include costs of having a baby, child-care expenses, planning for the future, and the impact of pregnancy on the couple's relationship.

Mifflin, P. C. (2004). *Saving very premature babies: Ethical issues.* London, UK: Butterworth-Heinemann. Examines the ethical and legal issues surrounding medical interventions for extremely premature babies. The author also addresses the challenges faced by parents of these babies, including the emotional and financial toll of long-term care.

Miller, M. W. (2006). *Brain development: Normal processes and the effects of alcohol and nicotine.* New York: Oxford University Press. Examines the effects of alcohol and nicotine on the developing nervous system. The author explores the immediate and long-term consequences of prenatal exposure to alcohol and nicotine, including research on brain plasticity and resilience.

Murkoff, H. E., Hathaway, S. E., & Eisenberg, A. (2003). *What to expect the first year*. New York: Workman Publishing. Explores the many milestones that occur during the first year of life. Other topics include infant crying and fussing, nutrition, sleep, common illnesses, and SIDS.

PUZZLE 3.1 TERM REVIEW

Across
2. Inner membrane that forms a protective covering around the prenatal organism that encloses it in amniotic fluid
4. Any environmental agent that causes damage during the prenatal period
9. Inadequate oxygen supply
10. Prenatal organism from 2 to 8 weeks after conception, during which time the foundation for all body structures and internal organs is laid down
11. Long cord connecting the prenatal organism to the placenta; delivers nutrients and removes waste products (2 words)
12. Prenatal organism from the beginning of the third month to the end of pregnancy, during which time completion of body structures and dramatic growth in size take place
14. White, cheese-like substance covering the fetus and preventing the skin from chapping in the amniotic fluid

Down
1. Organ that separates the mother's bloodstream from that of the fetus or embryo but permits exchange of nutrients and waste products
3. Attachment of the blastocyst to the uterine lining 7 to 9 days after fertilization
5. Outer membrane that forms a protective covering around the prenatal organism
6. Primitive spinal cord that develops from the ectoderm, the top of which swells to form the brain (2 words)
7. Three equal time periods in the prenatal period, each of which lasts three months
8. Fetal _____: electronic instruments that track the baby's heart rate during labor
13. White, downy hair that covers the entire body of the fetus

PUZZLE 3.2 TERM REVIEW

Across
2. _____ delivery: surgical delivery in which the doctor makes an incision in the mother's abdomen and lifts the baby out of the uterus
5. States of _____: different degrees of sleep and wakefulness
6. Childbirth approach designed to reduce pain and medical intervention
8. _____ mortality rate: the number of deaths in the first year of life per 1,000 live births
9. Set of defects that results when women consume large amounts of alcohol during most or all of their pregnancy (abbr.)
11. Infants born several weeks or more before their due date
13. Age of _____: age at which the fetus can survive if born early
14. An "irregular" sleep state in which brain wave activity is similar to that of the waking state (abbr.)

Down
1. Scale used to assess the newborn's physical condition immediately after birth
3. Infants whose birth weight is below normal when the length of the pregnancy is taken into account (3 words)
4. Condition of children who display some but not all of the defects of FAS (abbr.)
7. A "regular" sleep state in which the body is quiet and heart rate, breathing, and brain wave activity are slow and regular (abbr.)
10. Visual _____: fineness of visual discrimination
12. Inborn, automatic response to a particular form of stimulation

PRACTICE TEST #1

1. The period of the zygote lasts about (p. 61)
   a. two days.
   b. two weeks.
   c. eight weeks.
   d. six months.

2. What occurs between the seventh and ninth days after fertilization? (p. 61)
   a. the age of viability
   b. implantation
   c. the period of the fetus
   d. conception

3. The organ that brings the mother's and embryo's blood close together, without allowing them to mix directly, is called the (pp. 62–63)
   a. amnion.
   b. chorion.
   c. placenta.
   d. villi.

4. What covers the baby's skin and prevents it from chapping in the amniotic fluid? (p. 64)
   a. lanugo
   b. the amnion
   c. vernix
   d. the placenta

5. The period of the fetus (p. 63)
   a. typically lasts for only one week.
   b. occurs simultaneously with implantation.
   c. occurs during the second month.
   d. is the longest prenatal period.

6. The point at which the fetus can survive is called the (p. 64)
   a. age of viability.
   b. second trimester.
   c. period of the zygote.
   d. period of the embryo.

7. The term teratogen refers to (p. 65)
   a. the fluid within the placenta that helps feed the fetus.
   b. the blood that is passed from mother to child through the umbilical cord.
   c. any environmental agent that causes damage during the prenatal period.
   d. a perfect test score given to a newborn upon delivery.

8. The most well-known effect of smoking during pregnancy is (p. 67)
   a. low birth weight.
   b. infant death.
   c. childhood behavioral problems.
   d. long-term respiratory difficulties.

9. Mental retardation, slow physical growth, and facial abnormalities are typical effects of which of the following teratogens? (p. 68)
   a. caffeine
   b. cocaine
   c. alcohol
   d. marijuana

10. The AIDS virus (p. 70)
    a. is transmitted from infected mothers to their fetus approximately 80 percent of the time.
    b. most often results in illness in infants by age 18 months.
    c. progresses especially rapidly in infants.
    d. progresses more slowly in infants than in older children and adults.

11. A mother's emotional stress (p. 70)
    a. has no effect on her unborn child.
    b. can cause her baby to be at risk for a wide variety of difficulties.
    c. usually results in low birth weight.
    d. has similar effects as fetal alcohol syndrome.

12. Which of the following takes place during Stage 1 of childbirth? (p. 73)
    a. delivery of the baby
    b. prelabor
    c. dilation and effacement of the cervix
    d. birth of the placenta

13. What test is used to assess the physical condition of the newborn at 1 and 5 minutes after birth? (p. 74)
    a. Brazelton Neonatal Behavioral Assessment Scale
    b. Apgar Scale
    c. Bayley Scales of Infant Development
    d. Neonatal Reflex Inventory

14. Fetal monitors (p. 76)
    a. reduce the rate of infant brain damage and death in healthy pregnancies.
    b. save the lives of many babies in high-risk situations.
    c. reduce the rate of cesarean deliveries.
    d. are used in fewer than 40 percent of American births.

15. An infant born two months early but weighing an appropriate amount for the time spent in the uterus is called (p. 77)
    a. small-for-date.
    b. preterm.
    c. postterm.
    d. breech.

16. Small-for-date babies (p. 77)
    a. are often full-term.
    b. typically have fewer problems than preterm babies.
    c. are those born several weeks or more before their due date.
    d. probably experienced adequate nutrition before birth.

17. REM sleep (p. 82)
    a. accounts for a lower percentage of sleep time in infants than in children and adults.
    b. seems to fulfill young infants' need for stimulation because they spend so little time in an alert state.
    c. is a "regular" sleep state in which the body is almost motionless, and heart rate, breathing, and brain wave activity are slow and regular.
    d. is less frequent in the fetus and in preterm infants than in full-term infants.

18. Which of the following is true regarding SIDS? (p. 83)
    a. SIDS babies are more likely to sleep on their backs.
    b. SIDS is most likely between the ages of 10 and 12 months.
    c. Pacifier use increases the likelihood of SIDS tenfold.
    d. Maternal cigarette smoking, both during and after pregnancy, strongly predicts SIDS.

19. At birth, infants perceive objects at a distance of 20 feet about as clearly as adults do at (p. 86)
    a. 20 feet.
    b. 100 feet.
    c. 600 feet.
    d. 2000 feet.

20. Newborn infants (p. 86)
    a. prefer pure tones to complex sounds.
    b. are most attentive to low-pitched, monotonous patterns of sound.
    c. can discriminate almost all sounds in human languages.
    d. can discriminate only the speech sounds of their native language.

PRACTICE TEST #2

1. Typically, a woman's menstrual cycle lasts about (p. 60)
    a. 14 days.
    b. 28 days.
    c. six weeks.
    d. nine months.

2. A typical pregnancy usually lasts for about (p. 61)
    a. 24 weeks.
    b. 38 weeks.
    c. 52 weeks.
    d. 72 weeks.

3. The amniotic fluid (p. 61)
    a. produces blood cells until the developing liver, spleen, and bone marrow are mature enough to take over this function.
    b. permits oxygen and food to reach the developing organism.
    c. protects the fetus's skin from chapping.
    d. maintains a constant temperature in the womb and provides a cushion against jolts caused by the mother's movement.

4. How many layers of cells does the embryonic disk form during the first week of the period of the embryo? (p. 63)
    a. two
    b. three
    c. four
    d. five

5. The age of viability occurs sometime between (p. 64)
    a. 10 and 14 weeks.
    b. 16 and 20 weeks.
    c. 22 and 26 weeks.
    d. 28 and 32 weeks.

6. In which period are serious prenatal effects most likely to occur due to the effects of teratogens? (p. 65)
    a. the period of the zygote
    b. the embryonic period
    c. the fetal period
    d. the same level of risk is present during each of the prenatal stages

7. Infants who are prenatally exposed to cocaine (p. 67)
   a. rarely show addictions to the drug at birth.
   b. show few ill effects beyond the dangerous withdrawal period.
   c. typically have lasting difficulties.
   d. exhibit an easy temperament and are receptive to cuddling.

8. How much alcohol is required to produce Fetal Alcohol Effects (FAE)? (p. 68)
   a. maternal alcohol addiction
   b. more than two drinks per day
   c. as little as one ounce per day
   d. no amount is safe, so pregnant women should avoid alcohol entirely

9. When provided with enriched diets, fetal alcohol syndrome babies (p. 68)
   a. often experience poor physical health.
   b. catch up quickly in physical size during infancy.
   c. slowly catch up in physical size during later childhood.
   d. still fail to catch up in physical size during infancy and childhood.

10. Pregnant women who eat undercooked meat or clean a cat's litter box are at risk for (p. 70)
    a. toxoplasmosis.
    b. rubella.
    c. cytomegalovirus.
    d. tuberculosis.

11. Folic acid supplementation around the time of conception reduces the incidence of (p. 70)
    a. low birth weight.
    b. genetic disorders.
    c. neural tube defects.
    d. anoxia.

12. The most common cause of serious problems resulting from differing blood types in mother and baby is (p. 71)
    a. Rh factor incompatibility.
    b. spina bifida.
    c. anencephaly.
    d. toxoplasmosis.

13. The complication for mothers in which blood pressure increases sharply and the face, hands, and feet swell in the last half of pregnancy is called (p. 72)
    a. spina bifida.
    b. lanugo.
    c. cytomegalovirus.
    d. toxemia.

14. An Apgar score of _____ indicates that the infant is in good physical condition. (p. 74)
    a. 3 or below
    b. 4 to 6
    c. 5 or above
    d. 7 or above

15. Cesarean delivery (p. 77)
    a. emphasizes relaxation and breathing techniques.
    b. is rarely used in the United States except in extreme medical emergencies.
    c. may result in newborns who are sleepy and unresponsive.
    d. requires less recovery time than vaginal birth.

16. With respect to stimulation of preterm infants, massaging the baby several times a day in the hospital led to (p. 78)
    a. increased irritability.
    b. better mental and motor development.
    c. poor muscle tone.
    d. overly rapid weight gain.

17. Findings from the Kauai study revealed that (pp. 78, 80)
    a. postterm births are strongly associated with exposure to environmental pollution.
    b. newborn reflexes typically disappear in the first six months of life.
    c. biological risks far outweigh the impact of personal characteristics and social experiences on later development.
    d. in a supportive home environment, even children with serious birth problems can develop successfully.

18. The _____ reflex helps a breastfed baby find the mother's nipple. (p. 81)
    a. rooting
    b. sucking
    c. palmar grasp
    d. Moro

19. The most effective way to sooth a crying baby is to (p. 84)
    a. lift the baby to the shoulder and rock or walk.
    b. swaddle the baby.
    c. offer a pacifier.
    d. play rhythmic sounds.

20. Research on the sense of smell indicates that (p. 85)
    a. infants do not have a well-developed sense of smell until several months after birth.
    b. newborn infants recognize the smell of their own mother's breast.
    c. odor preferences are gradually developed through environmental exposure to a variety of scents.
    d. infants can distinguish pleasant and unpleasant odors but defend themselves from unpleasant odors by turning away.

CHAPTER 4
PHYSICAL DEVELOPMENT IN INFANCY AND TODDLERHOOD

BRIEF CHAPTER SUMMARY

During the first two years, children's body sizes increase dramatically—faster than at any other time after birth. Body fat is laid down quickly in the first 9 months, whereas muscle development is slow and gradual. As in all aspects of development, individual children differ in body size and muscle–fat makeup. The best way to estimate a child's physical maturity is by using skeletal age. Two growth patterns—cephalocaudal and proximodistal trends—describe changes in the child's body proportions.

At birth, the brain is nearer than any other physical structure to its adult size, and it continues to develop at an astounding pace throughout infancy and toddlerhood. Neurons, or nerve cells, that store and transmit information develop and form an elaborate communication system in the brain. As neurons form connections, stimulation becomes necessary for their survival. The cerebral cortex is the largest, most complex brain structure—accounting for 85 percent of the brain's weight, containing the greatest number of neurons and synapses, and responsible for the unique intelligence of our species. At birth, the two hemispheres of the cerebral cortex have already begun to specialize, a process called lateralization. However, the brain retains considerable plasticity during the first few years of life. Animal studies and research with orphanage children provide evidence for sensitive periods in brain development. Appropriate stimulation is key to promoting experience-expectant brain growth—the young brain's rapidly developing organization, which depends on ordinary experiences. Experience-dependent brain growth, in contrast, occurs throughout our lives as a result of specific learning experiences; there is no sensitive period for mastering such skills. Finally, rapid brain growth means that the organization of sleep and wakefulness changes substantially between birth and 2 years, and fussiness and crying also decline.

Physical growth, like other aspects of development, results from the continuous and complex interplay between genetic and environmental factors. Heredity, nutrition, and emotional well-being all affect early physical growth. Dietary diseases caused by malnutrition affect many children in developing countries. If allowed to continue, body growth and brain development can be permanently stunted. Breastfeeding provides many benefits to infants in the first year, especially for those in the developing world where safe, nutritious alternatives are not widely available. Babies who do not receive affection and stimulation may suffer from nonorganic failure to thrive, which has symptoms resembling those of malnutrition but has no physical cause.

Babies come into the world with built-in learning capacities that permit them to profit from experience immediately. Classical and operant conditioning, habituation and recovery, and imitation are all important mechanisms through which infants learn about their physical and social worlds.

Like physical development, motor development follows the cephalocaudal and proximodistal trends. Babies' motor achievements have a powerful effect on their social relationships. According to dynamic systems theory of motor development, each new motor skill is a joint product of central nervous system development, movement capacities of the body, goals the child has in mind, and environmental supports for the skill. Cultural differences in infant-rearing practices affect the timing of motor development.

Perception changes remarkably over the first year of life. Hearing and vision undergo major advances during the first two years as infants organize stimuli into complex patterns, improve their perception of depth and objects, and combine information across sensory modalities. From extensive everyday experience, babies gradually figure out how to use depth cues to detect the danger of falling. According to Eleanor and James Gibson's differentiation theory, perceptual development is a matter of detecting invariant features in a constantly changing perceptual world.

LEARNING OBJECTIVES

After reading this chapter, you should be able to:

4.1 Describe major changes in body growth over the first two years. (pp. 91–92)

4.2 Describe changes in brain development during infancy and toddlerhood, both at the level of individual brain cells and at the level of the cerebral cortex. (pp. 93–97)

4.3 Describe the development and functions of neurons and glial cells. (p. 93)

4.4 Describe the development of the cerebral cortex, and explain the concepts of brain lateralization and brain plasticity. (pp. 94–97)

4.5 Describe how both heredity and early experience contribute to brain organization. (pp. 96–97)

4.6 Summarize changes in the organization of sleep and wakefulness over the first two years. (p. 97)

4.7 Cite evidence that heredity, nutrition, affection, and stimulation contribute to early physical growth. (pp. 99–101)

4.8 Discuss the impact of severe malnutrition on the development of infants and toddlers, and cite two dietary diseases associated with malnutrition. (pp. 100–101)

4.9 Describe the growth disorder known as nonorganic failure to thrive, noting common symptoms and family circumstances surrounding it. (p. 101)

4.10 Describe infant learning capacities, the conditions under which they occur, and the unique value of each. (pp. 101–104)

4.11 Describe the general course of motor development during the first two years, along with factors that influence it. (pp. 104–105)

4.12 Explain dynamic systems theory of motor development, noting how cultural values and child-rearing customs contribute to early motor skills. (pp. 105–107)

4.13 Discuss changes in hearing, depth and pattern perception, and intermodal perception that occur during infancy. (pp.–107–112)

4.14 Explain differentiation theory of perceptual development. (p. 112)

STUDY QUESTIONS

Body Growth

Changes in Body Size and Muscle–Fat Makeup

1. Why do infants experience an increase in body fat during the first year of life? (p. 91)

   _____

   _____

2. Muscle tissue (increases / decreases) very slowly during infancy. (p. 91)

Individual and Group Differences

1. True or False: Boys and girls have an equal muscle-to-fat ratio during infancy. (p. 91)

2. True or False: Trends in body growth tend to be consistent cross-culturally. (pp. 91–92)

3. The best way to estimate a child's physical growth is to use _____, a measure of the development of the bones in the body. (p. 92)

4. When skeletal age is examined, (African-American / Caucasian) children and (boys / girls) tend to be slightly ahead. (p. 92)

Changes in Body Proportions

1. Briefly explain the *cephalocaudal* and *proximodistal* trends, which represent two growth patterns used to describe changes in body proportions. (p. 92)

   Cephalocaudal: _____

   _____

   Proximodistal: _____

   _____

Brain Development

Development of Neurons

1. What are *neurons*, and what is their function? (p. 93)

   A. _____

   _____

   B. _____

   _____

2. Between neurons, there are tiny gaps, or _____, across which messages pass. Neurons release chemicals called _____, which cross the synapse. (p. 93)

3. Explain the process of *synaptic pruning*. (p. 93)

   _____

   _____

   _____

4. About half of the brain's volume is made up of _____ *cells,* whose most important function is _____, the coating of neural fibers with an insulating fatty sheath that improves the efficiency of message transfer. (p. 93)

Development of the Cerebral Cortex

1. True or False: The cerebral cortex is the largest, most complex brain structure, accounting for 85 percent of the brain's weight and containing the greatest number of neurons and synapses. (p. 94)

2. Describe the different functions controlled by the left and right hemispheres of the brain. (p. 95)

   A. Left: _____

   B Right: _____

3. Explain the concepts of *lateralization* and *brain plasticity*, noting how the two are related. (p. 95)

   Lateralization: _____
   _____
   _____

   Brain plasticity: _____
   _____
   _____

   Relationship: _____
   _____
   _____

4. The brain is (more / less) plastic during the early years than during later years in life. (p. 95)

5. Among preschoolers with brain injuries sustained in the first year of life, deficits in _____ and _____ were milder than those observed in brain-injured adults. (p. 95)

Sensitive Periods in Brain Development

1. Describe the findings of natural experiments, in which children were victims of deprived early environments but were later exposed to stimulating sensitive care, as evidence for sensitive periods in development of the cerebral cortex. (p. 96)

   A. _____
   _____

   B. _____
   _____

2. True or False: Trying to prime infants with stimulation for which they are not ready, such as training with letter and number flash cards, can threaten their interest in learning. (pp. 96–97)

3. Distinguish between *experience-expectant* and *experience-dependent* brain growth, and cite experiences that promote each type of brain development. (p. 97)

   Experience-expectant: _____
   _____
   _____

   Experiences that foster experience-expectant brain development: _____
   _____
   _____

   Experience-dependent: _____
   _____
   _____

   Experiences that foster experience-dependent brain development: _____
   _____
   _____

Changing States of Arousal

1. Describe major changes in the organization of sleep and wakefulness during the first two years. (p. 97)

2. Describe how changing arousal patterns are affected by the social environment. (p. 97)

Cultural Influences: Cultural Variation in Infant Sleeping Arrangements

1. True or False: Although rare in North America, parent–infant cosleeping is common in many other countries around the world. (p. 98)

2. Explain the role of collectivist versus individualistic cultural values in infant sleeping arrangements. (p. 98)

3. Summarize several benefits of parent–infant cosleeping. (p. 98)

4. Discuss the criticisms and concerns surrounding parent–infant cosleeping. (p. 98)

Influences on Early Physical Growth

Heredity

1. True or False: When diet and health are adequate, height and rate of physical growth are largely determined by heredity. (p. 99)

2. What is *catch-up growth*? (p. 99)

Nutrition

1. Describe several nutritional and health benefits of breastfeeding. (p. 99)

   _____
   _____
   _____
   _____

2. Why is breastfeeding especially important in poverty-stricken regions of the world? (p. 99)

   _____
   _____
   _____

3. Breastfeeding has become (more / less) common in industrialized nations, especially among well-educated women. Today, _____ percent of American mothers and ____ percent of Canadian mothers breastfeed. (pp. 99)

4. True or False: In the United States and Canada, recommendations for breastfeeding include exclusive breastfeeding for the first 6 months. (p. 99)

5. In interviews with more than 3,000 U.S. parents of 4- to 24-month-olds, infants consumed _____ percent and toddlers _____ percent more calories than they needed. How many children ate no fruits or vegetables? (p.100)

   _____

Malnutrition

1. True or False: Recent evidence indicates that about one-quarter of the world's children suffer from malnutrition before age 5. (p. 100)

2. Describe the causes of *marasmus* and *kwashiorkor*, two dietary diseases associated with severe malnutrition, and summarize the developmental outcomes associated with these extreme forms of malnutrition. (pp. 100–101)

   Marasmus: _____
   _____

   Kwashiorkor: _____
   _____

   Outcomes: _____
   _____
   _____
   _____
   _____

3. Describe food insecurity, and identify groups in which it is especially high. (p. 101)

   A. _____

   B. _____

Emotional Well-Being

1. What is *nonorganic failure to thrive,* and what are some common symptoms? (p. 101)

   A. _____

   B. _____

2. Describe family circumstances surrounding nonorganic failure to thrive. (p. 101)

Learning Capacities

1. Define *learning*. (p. 101)

Classical Conditioning

1. Briefly explain how learning takes place through *classical conditioning*. (p. 101)

2. Why is classical conditioning of great value to infants? (p. 101)

3. Match the following terms to the appropriate definition. (pp. 101–102)

   _____ A neutral stimulus that leads to a new response after learning has occurred
   _____ A learned response exhibited toward a previously neutral stimulus
   _____ A reflexive response
   _____ A stimulus that automatically leads to a reflexive response

   1. Unconditioned stimulus (UCS)
   2. Conditioned stimulus (CS)
   3. Unconditioned response (UCR)
   4. Conditioned response (CR)

4. Using the definitions in question 3 as a guide, outline the three steps of classical conditioning. (p. 102)

   A. _____

   B. _____

   C. _____

5. In classical conditioning, if the CS is presented alone enough times without being paired with the UCS, the CR will no longer occur. This is referred to as _____. (p. 102)

Operant Conditioning

1. Briefly explain how learning takes place through *operant conditioning*. (p. 102)

2. Define the terms *reinforcer* and *punishment* as they relate to operant conditioning. (p. 102)

    Reinforcer: _____

    Punishment: _____

3. Describe how operant conditioning plays a vital role in the formation of social relationships. (p. 102)

Habituation

1. Define *habituation* and *recovery*. (p. 103)

    Habituation: _____

    Recovery: _____

2. Describe the changing meaning of novelty and familiarity preferences with lapse of time. What can be assessed using these preferences? (p. 103)

    A. _____

    B. _____

Imitation

1. What behaviors can most newborns imitate? (p. 103)

2. Summarize what infants are able to learn through imitation. (pp. 103–104)

Motor Development

The Sequence of Motor Development

1. Distinguish between *gross* and *fine motor development,* and provide examples of each. (pp. 104–105)

   Gross: _____

   _____

   Examples: _____

   Fine: _____

   _____

   Examples: _____

2. When should parents become concerned about a child's motor development? (p. 105)

   _____

Motor Skills as Dynamic Systems

1. According to the *dynamic systems theory of motor development,* mastery of motor skills involves acquisition of increasingly complex systems of action. Explain what this means. (p. 105)

   _____

   _____

   _____

   _____

2. List four factors that contribute to the development of each new motor skill. (p. 105)

   _____

   _____

   _____

   _____

3. True or False: In one study, researchers found that 8-week-olds violated the cephalocaudal trend by reaching for toys with their feet at least a month earlier than with their hands. (p. 106)

4. Give at least one example of how cultural variations in infant-rearing practices affect motor development. (p. 106)

   _____

   _____

   _____

5. The current Western practice of having babies sleep on their backs to protect against SIDS (advances / delays) gross motor milestones of rolling, sitting, and crawling. (p. 106)

Fine Motor Development: Reaching and Grasping

1. True or False: Of all motor skills, reaching may play the greatest role in infant cognitive development. (p. 106)

2. Match the following terms to the appropriate definition. (p. 106)

   _____ Well-coordinated movement in which infants use the thumb and forefinger opposably
   _____ Poorly coordinated swipes or swings toward an object
   _____ Clumsy motion in which the fingers close against the palm

   1. Prereaching
   2. Ulnar grasp
   3. Pincer grasp

Perceptual Development

Hearing

1. Describe changes in auditory perception over the first year that prepare infants to acquire language. (pp. 107–108)

Vision

1. What is *depth perception*, and why is it important in infant development? (p. 108)

   Definition: _____

   Importance: _____

2. Describe Gibson and Walk's findings using the visual cliff, and cite the limitations for understanding infant depth perception. (p. 108)

   Studies: _____

   Limitations: _____

3. Name and describe three cues for depth. (pp. 108–109)

   A. _____

   B. _____

   C. _____

4. Summarize the relationship between crawling and depth perception. (p. 109)

5. Newborn infants respond to (patterns as unified wholes / separate parts of a pattern). (p. 109)

6. True or False: Around 2 months of age, infants recognize their mothers' detailed facial features, and prefer her face to that of an unfamiliar woman. (p. 111)

Biology and Environment: Development of Infants with Severe Visual Impairments

1. True or False: Children with severe visual impairments show delays in motor, cognitive, language, and social development. (p. 110)

2. Discuss how severe visual impairments impact motor exploration and spatial understanding. (p. 110)

3. How do severe visual impairments affect the caregiver–infant relationship? (p. 110)

4. Explain how adults can help infants with minimal vision overcome early developmental delays. (p. 110)

Intermodal Perception

1. What is *intermodal perception*? (p. 111)

2. Babies perceive input from different sensory systems in a unified way by detecting _____ information that overlaps two or more sensory systems. Provide an example. (p. 111)

3. Explain how infants' intermodal sensitivity is crucial for perceptual development. (pp. 111–112)

Understanding Perceptual Development

1. Explain *differentiation theory* of perceptual development. (p. 112)

   _____
   _____
   _____
   _____

2. Explain how acting on the environment plays a vital role in perceptual differentiation. (p. 112)

   _____
   _____
   _____

ASK YOURSELF . . .

For *Ask Yourself* questions for this chapter, please log on to the Companion Website at *www.ablongman.com/berk*.

1. Select the Companion Website for *Exploring Lifespan Development*.
2. Use the "Jump to" menu to go directly to this chapter.
3. From the menu on the left side of the screen, select "Ask Yourself."
4. Complete questions and choose "Submit answers for grading" or "Clear answers" to start over.

SUGGESTED STUDENT READINGS

Gibson, E. J., & Pick, A. D. (2003). *An ecological approach to perceptual learning and development.* New York: Oxford University Press. Examines perceptual learning and development from birth to toddlerhood as they apply to early communication, perceiving and acting on objects and the environment, and locomotion.

Huttenlocher, P. R. (2002). *Neural plasticity: The effects of the environment on the development of the cerebral cortex.* Cambridge, MA: Harvard University Press. A compelling look at the positive and negative aspects of brain plasticity, including the brain's response to normal developmental processes and trauma, and the extent of plasticity beyond the first three years of life.

Zigler, E. F., Finn-Stevenson, M., & Hall, N. W. (2004). *The first three years and beyond: Brain development and social policy.* New Haven, CT: Yale University Press. Taking an interdisciplinary approach to understanding brain development, this book presents up-to-date research on the importance of early experiences for favorable development. Other topics include appropriate stimulation, the importance of breastfeeding and nutrition, and public policies for children and families.

PUZZLE 4.1 TERM REVIEW

Across
2. _____ cells are responsible for myelination of neural fibers
4. The gaps between neurons, across which messages are sent
9. A disease usually appearing in the first year of life, caused by a diet low in all essential nutrients
11. Experience-_____ brain growth: consists of additional growth and refinement of established brain structure as a result of specific learning experiences that vary widely across individuals and cultures
13. Neurons send messages to one another by releasing chemicals called _____, which cross the synapse
14. Synaptic _____ is the loss of connective fibers by seldom stimulated neurons
15. Nerve cells that store and transmit information to the brain
16. Experience-_____ brain growth: refers to the young brain's rapidly developing organization, which depends on ordinary experiences, such as opportunities to see and touch objects, to hear language and other sounds, and to move about and explore the environment

Down
1. _____ trend: pattern of growth that proceeds from head to tail
3. Specialization of functions of the two hemispheres of the cortex
5. _____ trend: pattern of growth that proceeds from the center of the body outward
6. A disease appearing between 1 and 3 years of age that is caused by a diet low in protein
7. Process in which neural fibers are coated with an insulating fatty sheath that improves the efficiency of message transfer
8. The largest structure of the human brain is the _____ cortex
10. Brain _____ refers to the ability of other parts of the brain to take over the functions of damaged regions
12. _____ failure to thrive: growth disorder caused by lack of affection and stimulation

PUZZLE 4.2 TERM REVIEW

Across
4. _____ conditioning: form of learning that involves associating a neutral stimulus with a stimulus that leads to a reflexive response
7. In operant conditioning, a stimulus that increases the occurrence of a response
8. _____ perception combines information from more than one sensory system.
11. In operant conditioning, removing a desirable stimulus or presenting an unpleasant one to decrease the occurrence of a response
13. A gradual reduction in the strength of a response due to repetitive stimulation

Down
1. _____ conditioning: form of learning in which a spontaneous behavior is followed by a stimulus that changes the probability that the behavior will occur again
2. Following habituation, an increase in responsiveness to a new stimulus
3. _____ theory: view that perceptual development involves detection of increasingly fine-grained, invariant features in the environment
5. In classical conditioning, a reflexive response that is produced by an UCS (abbr.)
6. In the differentiation theory of perceptual development, _____ features are those that remain stable in a constantly changing perceptual world
9. The _____ systems theory of motor development views new motor skills as reorganizations of previously mastered skills that lead to more effective ways of exploring and controlling the environment
10. In classical conditioning, a neutral stimulus that through pairing with an UCS leads to a new response (abbr.)
12. Learning by copying the behavior of another person
14. In classical conditioning, a stimulus that leads to a reflexive response (abbr.)

PRACTICE TEST #1

1. Which physical structure is closer to adult size at birth than any other? (p. 93)
   a. the heart
   b. the legs
   c. the brain
   d. the hands

2. Which growth pattern refers to growth that proceeds from head to tail? (p. 92)
   a. intermodal trend
   b. cephalocaudal trend
   c. proximodistal trend
   d. invariant trend

3. The process in which neural fibers are coated with an insulating fatty sheath that improves the efficiency of message transfer is called (p. 93)
   a. myelination.
   b. synaptic pruning.
   c. neural sheathing.
   d. brain plasticity.

4. Neurons that are seldom stimulated lose their synapses in a process called (p. 93)
   a. synaptic pruning.
   b. synaptic development.
   c. neurotransmission.
   d. stimulation.

5. Surrounding the brain is / are the (p. 94)
   a. glial cells.
   b. neural fibers.
   c. neurotransmitter.
   d. cerebral cortex.

6. Which of the following describes one of the ways the right hemisphere of the brain works? (p. 95)
   a. It is better at processing information in a sequential way.
   b. It is better at processing information in an analytic way.
   c. It deals better with verbal communication.
   d. It is ideal for making sense of spatial information.

7. Which of the following is true of breastfeeding during infancy? (p. 99)
   a. Breastfeeding is not recommended for women in developing countries because breast milk does not contain sufficient nutrients to protect against malnutrition and infection.
   b. Breastfeeding is rare among American mothers, and rates of breastfeeding have declined over the last two decades.
   c. Breastfeeding is essential for children's healthy psychological development.
   d. In poverty-stricken regions, breastfed infants are 6 to 14 times more likely to survive their first year of life.

8. Marasmus is caused by (p. 100)
   a. overeating during the first year of life.
   b. a severe iron deficiency.
   c. a diet low in protein.
   d. a diet low in all essential nutrients.

9. Which of the following is true of marasmus? (p. 100)
    a. It is never life-threatening to the baby.
    b. It is caused by an excess of vitamin A.
    c. It is a condition experienced by expectant mothers.
    d. It usually appears in the first year of life.

10. Nonorganic failure to thrive (p. 101)
    a. is associated with a known biological cause.
    b. is caused by a lack of stimulation and affection.
    c. results from an inadequate diet in early infancy.
    d. is associated with long-term deficits, even when treated early.

11. Nonorganic failure to thrive results from (p. 101)
    a. a lack of all essential nutrients.
    b. prenatal injuries.
    c. lack of parental love.
    d. excessive amounts of breast milk.

12. In classical conditioning, if the conditioned stimulus (CS) is presented alone enough times, without being paired with the unconditioned stimulus (UCS), the conditioned response (CR) will no longer occur. This is known as (p. 102)
    a. dishabituation.
    b. termination.
    c. extinction.
    d. disassociation.

13. In operant conditioning, a stimulus that increases the likelihood of a response is a (p. 102)
    a. punishment.
    b. reward.
    c. reinforcer.
    d. conditioned stimulus.

14. Among the learning capacities of infants is recovery, which refers to (p. 103)
    a. a gradual reduction in the strength of a response due to repetitive stimulation.
    b. the presentation of an unpleasant stimulus to decrease the occurrence of a response.
    c. a decrease in responsiveness to a new stimulus following previous interest in a similar stimulus.
    d. an increase in responsiveness to a new stimulus following previous loss of interest in an old stimulus.

15. Crawling, standing, and walking are examples of (pp. 104–105)
    a. fine motor development.
    b. gross motor development.
    c. coordinated motor development.
    d. dynamic motor development.

16. According to dynamic systems theory of motor development, (p. 105)
    a. mastery of motor skills involves blending separate abilities together.
    b. new skills are acquired independently of previously learned skills.
    c. motor development proceeds according to genetic coding and is unaffected by environmental influences.
    d. the pathways to motor skill acquisition are universal.

17. Over the first year of life, the greatest change in hearing that takes place is the ability to (p. 107)
    a. hear a wider range of tones.
    b. analyze complex sound patterns.
    c. turn the eyes and head in the direction of a sound.
    d. increasingly attend to the sounds of all human languages.

18. Infants have a sense of musical phrasing between (p. 107)
    a. 2 and 4 months.
    b. 4 and 7 months.
    c. 8 and 12 months.
    d. 12 and 18 months.

19. The capacity to perceive information from various sensory systems as unified wholes is called (p. 111)
    a. intermodal perception.
    b. sensory perception.
    c. systematic perception.
    d. integrative perception.

20. The Gibsons' theory that infants actively search for invariant features of the environment is called (p. 112)
    a. differentiation theory.
    b. environmental theory.
    c. intermodal theory.
    d. imposed meaning theory.

PRACTICE TEST #2

1. There are approximately how many neurons in the human brain? (p. 93)
    a. 10 to 20 million
    b. 100 to 200 million
    c. 10 to 20 billion
    d. 100 to 200 billion

2. Skeletal age is estimated by (p. 92)
    a. using the child's weight to estimate bone density.
    b. x-raying the child's long bones and determining the extent to which soft cartilage has hardened into bone.
    c. determining bone density through the use of ultrasound.
    d. examining the fontanels, or soft spots that separate the bones of the skull.

3. About half the brain's volume is made up of (p. 93)
    a. plastic cells.
    b. neural cells.
    c. glial cells.
    d. cortex cells.

4. Which is the largest, most complex brain structure containing the greatest number of neurons and synapses? (p. 94)
    a. frontal lobe
    b. cerebellum
    c. corpus callosum
    d. cerebral cortex

5. The left hemisphere of the brain is largely responsible for (p. 95)
    a. regulation of negative emotion.
    b. attention and complex thought.
    c. spatial abilities.
    d. verbal abilities.

6. A return to a genetically influenced growth path is referred to as (p. 99)
    a. normal growth.
    b. scheduled growth.
    c. catch-up growth.
    d. environmental growth.

7. The practice of isolating infants to promote sleep is (p. 97)
    a. rare outside the United States.
    b. more common in Europe than in the United States.
    c. always beneficial to the sleep patterns of babies.
    d. universally encouraged by health care professionals.

8. Breastfed babies in poverty-stricken regions of the world are (p. 99)
    a. less likely to survive the first year of life than non-breastfed babies.
    b. much less likely to be malnourished than non-breastfed babies.
    c. less protected against respiratory infections than bottle-fed babies.
    d. at higher risk for childhood overweight and obesity than bottle-fed babies.

9. Kwashiorkor results from a diet (p. 100)
    a. low in calcium.
    b. lacking in vitamins A and D.
    c. low in protein.
    d. high in fat.

10. When baby Sam sees his mother, he gazes at her and smiles. Sam's mother looks and smiles back, and then Sam looks and smiles again. This is an example of (p. 102)
    a. extinction.
    b. habituation.
    c. operant conditioning.
    d. classical conditioning.

11. After repeatedly listening to a particular tone for a period of time, an infant shows a gradual reduction in responding to this tone. When a new tone is introduced, the infant returns to a high level of responding. This increase in responsiveness to the new stimulus is known as (p. 103)
    a. habituation.
    b. recovery.
    c. differentiation.
    d. extinction.

12. Removing a desirable stimulus or presenting an unpleasant one to decrease the occurrence of a response is called (p. 102)
    a. habituation.
    b. reinforcement.
    c. punishment.
    d. imitation.

13. A gradual reduction in the strength of a response due to repetitive stimulation is referred to as (p. 103)
    a. habituation.
    b. reinforcement.
    c. punishment.
    d. imitation.

14. Memory for stimuli to which infants were exposed weeks or months earlier is (p. 103)
    a. habitual memory.
    b. remote memory.
    c. reinforced memory.
    d. imitated memory.

15. According to research, the average child walks alone between (p. 105)
    a. 8 and 9 months.
    b. 11 and 12 months.
    c. 13 and 14 months.
    d. 16 and 17 months.

16. In which sequence do infants develop reaching and grasping behaviors? (p. 106)
    a. pincer grasp, ulnar grasp, prereaching
    b. ulnar grasp, pincer grasp, prereaching
    c. prereaching, ulnar grasp, pincer grasp
    d. prereaching, pincer grasp, ulnar grasp

17. Newborns' uncoordinated swipes toward an object in front of them are called (p. 106)
    a. prereaching.
    b. proprioceptive reactions.
    c. arm reflexes.
    d. ulnar grasps.

18. By the end of the first year, infants use the thumb and index finger opposably in a well-coordinated (p. 106)
    a. pincer grasp.
    b. ulnar grasp.
    c. prereaching grasp.
    d. gross motor grasp.

19. Visual acuity reaches a near-adult level of about 20/20 at approximately (p. 108)
    a. 3 months of age.
    b. 6 months of age.
    c. 11 months of age.
    d. 18 months of age.

20. Research suggests that intermodal perception (p. 111)
    a. is a biologically primed capacity that is present at birth.
    b. emerges as a direct result of experience with the environment.
    c. develops as a result of independent locomotion.
    d. appears gradually over the first year of life.

CHAPTER 5
COGNITIVE DEVELOPMENT IN INFANCY AND TODDLERHOOD

BRIEF CHAPTER SUMMARY

According to Piaget, by acting directly on the environment, children move through four stages of cognitive development in which psychological structures, or schemes, change with age. The first stage, called the sensorimotor stage, spans the first two years of life and is divided into six substages. In this stage, infants make strides in intentional behavior and understanding of object permanence until, by the end of the second year, they become capable of mental representation, as seen in their sudden solutions to sensorimotor problems, mastery of object permanence problems involving hidden displacement, deferred imitation, and make-believe play. Recent research suggests that some sensorimotor capacities emerge earlier than Piaget believed, raising questions about the accuracy of his account of sensorimotor development.

Information-processing theorists, using computer-like flowcharts to describe the human cognitive system, focus on many aspects of thinking, from attention, memory, and categorization skills to complex problem solving. With age, infants attend to more aspects of the environment and take information in more rapidly. In the second year, as children become increasingly capable of intentional behavior, attention to novelty declines and sustained attention improves. As infants get older, they remember experiences longer and group stimuli into increasingly complex categories. Also, categorization shifts from a perceptual to conceptual basis. Information processing has contributed greatly to our view of young babies as sophisticated cognitive beings. However, its greatest drawback stems from its central strength—by analyzing cognition into its components, information processing has had difficulty putting them back together into a broad, comprehensive theory.

Vygotsky believed that complex mental activities have their origins in social interaction. Through joint activities with more mature members of their society, children come to master activities and think in ways that have meaning in their culture.

Infant intelligence tests primarily measure perceptual and motor responses and predict later intelligence poorly. Speed of habituation and recovery to visual stimuli, which tap basic cognitive processes, are better predictors of future performance. Home and child-care environments, as well as early intervention for at-risk infants and toddlers, exert powerful influences on mental development.

As perception and cognition improve during infancy, they pave the way for an extraordinary human achievement: language. The behaviorist perspective regards language development as entirely due to environmental influences, whereas nativism assumes that children are prewired with an innate language acquisition device to master the intricate rules of their language. The interactionist perspective maintains that language development results from interactions between inner capacities and environmental influences, such as social exchanges.

Babies begin cooing around 2 months, followed by babbling, which gradually reflects the sound and intonation patterns of the child's language community. First words appear around 12 months, and two-word utterances between 18 and 24 months. However, substantial individual differences exist in rate and style of early language progress. As toddlers learn words, they may apply them too narrowly (underextension) or too broadly (overextension), in part because their language comprehension develops ahead of their ability to produce language. Adults in many cultures speak to young children using child-directed speech, a simplified form of language that is well-suited to their learning needs. Deaf parents use a similar style of communication when signing to their deaf babies. Conversational give-and-take between adults and toddlers is one of the best predictors of early language development and academic competence during the school years.

LEARNING OBJECTIVES

After reading this chapter, you should be able to:

5.1 Describe how schemes change over the course of development. (pp. 116–117)

5.2 Identify Piaget's six sensorimotor substages, and describe the major cognitive achievements of the sensorimotor stage. (pp. 117–119)

5.3 Discuss recent research on sensorimotor development, noting its implications for the accuracy of Piaget's sensorimotor stage. (pp. 119–122)

5.4 Describe the information-processing view of cognitive development, noting the general structure of the information-processing system. (pp. 122–123)

5.5 Cite changes in attention, memory, and categorization during the first two years. (pp. 123–126)

5.6 Describe contributions and limitations of the information-processing approach, and explain how it contributes to our understanding of early cognitive development. (p. 126)

5.7 Explain how Vygotsky's concept of the zone of proximal development expands our understanding of early cognitive development. (pp. 126–127)

5.8 Describe the mental testing approach, the meaning of intelligence test scores, and the extent to which infant tests predict later performance. (pp. 127–129)

5.9 Discuss environmental influences on early mental development, including home, child care, and early intervention for at-risk infants and toddlers. (pp. 130–132)

5.10 Describe theories of language development, and indicate how much emphasis each places on innate abilities and environmental influences. (pp. 132–133)

5.11 Describe major language milestones, individual differences, and ways adults can support language development in the first two years. (pp. 134–136)

STUDY QUESTIONS

Piaget's Cognitive-Developmental Theory

1. During Piaget's _____ stage, which spans the first two years of life, infants and toddlers "think" with their eyes, ears, and hands. (p. 116)

Piaget's Ideas About Cognitive Change

1. According to Piaget, specific psychological structures, or organized ways of making sense of experience called _____, change with age. (p. 116)

2. Match the following terms with the appropriate description. (pp. 116–117)

   _____ Creating new schemes or adjusting old ones to produce a better fit with the environment
   _____ Taking new schemes, rearranging them, and linking them with other schemes to create an interconnected cognitive system
   _____ Using current schemes to interpret the external world
   _____ Building schemes through direct interaction with the environment

   1. Adaptation
   2. Accommodation
   3. Assimilation
   4. Organization

3. When children are not changing much, they assimilate more than they accommodate. Piaget called this a state of cognitive (disequilibrium / equilibrium). During rapid cognitive change, children are in a state of (disequilibrium / equilibrium), or cognitive discomfort. (p. 116)

The Sensorimotor Stage

1. True or False: According to Piaget, at birth babies already know a great deal about the world. (p. 117)

2. Explain the differences between primary, secondary, and tertiary circular reactions. (p. 118)

   Primary circular reaction: _____

   _____

   Secondary circular reaction: _____

   _____

   Tertiary circular reaction: _____

   _____

3. Match each of the following sensorimotor substages with the appropriate description. (pp. 117–119)

   _____ Infants' primary means of adapting to the environment is through reflexes.
   _____ Infants engage in goal-directed behavior and begin to attain object permanence.
   _____ Toddlers explore properties of objects by acting on them in novel ways and begin to imitate unfamiliar behaviors.
   _____ Infants display simple motor habits centered around their own body with limited anticipation of events.
   _____ Infants' actions are aimed at repeating interesting effects in the environment and imitation of familiar behaviors.
   _____ Toddlers gain the ability to create mental representations.

   1. Substage 1
   2. Substage 2
   3. Substage 3
   4. Substage 4
   5. Substage 5
   6. Substage 6

4. The understanding that objects continue to exist when out of sight is called _____. (p. 119)

5. What evidence suggests that 8- to 12-month-olds do not yet have a complete awareness of object permanence? (p. 118)

   _____

   _____

   _____

6. List three new capacities that result from the ability to create mental representations. (p. 119)

   A. _____

   B. _____

   C. _____

Follow-Up Research on Infant Cognitive Development

1. True or False: Recent studies suggest that Piaget overestimated infants' capacities. (p. 119)

2. Explain the *violation-of-expectation method*, which is often used by researchers to examine infants' grasp of object permanence and other aspects of physical reasoning. (p. 119)

   _____

   _____

   _____

3. True or False: Studies show that infants exhibit deferred imitation, a form of representation, as early as 6 weeks of age. (p. 120)

4. Describe how toddlers use *deferred imitation* to enrich their range of sensorimotor schemes. (p. 120)

_____
_____
_____

5. By 10 to 12 months, infants can solve problems by _____, meaning that they take a solution strategy from one problem and apply it to other relevant problems. (p. 121)

Evaluation of the Sensorimotor Stage

1. True or False: Recent research indicates that the cognitive attainments of infancy follow the neat, stepwise fashion that Piaget assumed. (p. 121)

2. According to the _____ perspective, babies are born with a set of innate knowledge systems, or core domains of thought. (p. 121)

3. Core knowledge theorists look at four domains of thought when assessing infants' cognitive knowledge. List these domains or types of knowledge. (pp. 121–122)

   A. _____   B. _____
   C. _____   D. _____

4. Cite Piaget's contributions to our knowledge of infant cognition. (p. 122)

_____
_____
_____

Information Processing

Structure of the Information-Processing System

1. Information-processing researchers assume we hold information in three parts of the mental system for processing. Name and describe each of these parts. (p. 123)

   A. _____
   _____

   B. _____
   _____

   C. _____
   _____

2. What is the *central executive*? (p. 123)

_____
_____
_____

3. True or False: Information-processing researchers believe that the basic structure of the mental system is similar throughout life. (pp. 123–124)

Attention

1. List two ways in which attention improves between 1 and 5 months of age. (pp. 123–124)

    A. _____

    B. _____

2. Summarize changes in attention from infancy to toddlerhood. (p. 124)

    _____
    _____

Memory

1. True or False: Both operant conditioning and habituation methods show that retention of visual events increases dramatically over infancy and toddlerhood. (p. 124)

2. Explain findings on operant conditioning and habituation research during infancy and toddlerhood. (p. 124)

    Operant Conditioning: _____
    _____
    _____

    Habituation / Recovery: _____
    _____
    _____

3. _____, the simplest form of memory, involves indicating whether a new experience is identical or similar to a previous one. _____, on the other hand, is much more challenging because it involves remembering something not present. (p. 124)

A Lifespan Vista: Infantile Amnesia

1. What is *infantile amnesia*? (p. 125)

    _____
    _____

2. Summarize two theories of infantile amnesia. (p. 125)

    A. _____

    B. _____

3. Describe the biological and social developments that contribute to the end of infantile amnesia. (p. 125)

    Biological developments: _____
    _____
    _____

    Social developments: _____
    _____
    _____

4. True or False: After age 3, children often participate in elaborate conversations, which help them encode autobiographical events in verbal form. (p. 125)

Categorization

1. The earliest categories are _____, or based on similar overall appearance or prominent object part. By the end of the first year, more categories are _____, or based on common function and behavior. (p. 126)

2. Briefly explain how the perceptual-to-conceptual change takes place. (p. 126)

_____
_____
_____

Evaluation of Information-Processing Findings

1. Information-processing research underscores the (continuity / discontinuity) of human thinking from infancy into adult life. (p. 126)

2. In what way does information-processing research challenge Piaget's view of early cognitive development? (p. 126)

_____
_____
_____

3. What is the greatest drawback of the information-processing approach to cognitive development? (p. 126)

_____
_____
_____

The Social Context of Early Cognitive Development

1. According to Vygotsky's sociocultural theory, how do children come to master activities and think in culturally meaningful ways? (p. 127)

_____
_____

2. Explain Vygotsky's concept of the *zone of proximal development,* emphasizing the role of adults in fostering children's cognition. (p. 127)

_____
_____
_____
_____

3. True or False: As early as the second year, cultural variations in social experience affect mental strategies. (p. 127)

4. Vygotsky adds to our understanding by emphasizing that many aspects of cognitive development are (physically / socially) mediated. (p. 127)

Cultural Influences: Caregiver–Toddler Interaction and Early Make-Believe Play

1. Briefly summarize Vygotsky's view of make-believe play. (p. 128)

2. Explain why adults' participation in toddlers' make-believe play is so important. (p. 128)

3. True or False: In some cultures, such as Indonesia and Mexico, older siblings are toddlers' first play partners. (p. 128)

Individual Differences in Early Mental Development

1. How does the mental testing approach differ from the cognitive theories discussed earlier in this chapter? (p. 127)

Infant and Toddler Intelligence Tests

1. What types of responses are tapped by most infant tests of intelligence? (p. 127)

2. One commonly used test is the _____ of *Infant Development*, designed for children between 1 month and 3½ years. (p. 127)

3. Describe how intelligence scores are computed. (p. 129)

4. True or False: When intelligence tests are standardized, the mean IQ is set at 100. (p. 129)

5. True or False: Scores on infant intelligence tests are excellent predictors of later intelligence. (p. 129)

6. How does the content of infant intelligence tests typically differ from intelligence tests given at later ages? (p. 129)

7. For what purpose are infant intelligence tests largely used? (p. 129)

8. Why does habituation and recovery predict later IQ more effectively than traditional infant tests? (p. 129)

   _____
   _____

Early Environment and Mental Development

1. List factors measured by the *Home Observation for Measurement of the Environment (HOME)*. (p. 130)

   _____
   _____
   _____

2. Cite ways in which both heredity and home environment contribute to mental test scores. (pp. 130)

   Heredity: _____

   Environment: _____

3. Today, more than _____ of North American mothers with children under age 2 are employed. (p. 130)

4. Discuss the impact of low- versus high-quality child care on mental development. (p. 131)

   Low-quality: _____
   _____

   High-quality: _____
   _____

5. True or False: In the United States and Canada, child-care standards are nationally regulated and funded to ensure their quality. (p. 131)

6. List and describe at least four signs of developmentally appropriate infant and toddler child care. (p. 131)

   A. _____
   _____

   B. _____
   _____

   C. _____
   _____

   D. _____
   _____

Early Intervention for At-Risk Infants and Toddlers

1. Describe the goals of center- and home-based interventions for low-SES infants and toddlers. (p. 132)

   Center-based: _____
   _____

   Home-based: _____
   _____

2. True or False: In most intervention programs, participating children score higher than untreated controls on mental tests by age 2. (p. 132)

3. List the main features of the Carolina Abecedarian Project. (p. 132)

   _____
   _____
   _____

4. Describe the long-term benefits of the Carolina Abecedarian project. (p. 132)

   _____
   _____
   _____
   _____

5. What is *Early Head Start*, and what did a recent evaluation reveal about its impact on participants? (p. 132)

   A. _____
   _____

   B. _____
   _____

Language Development

1. On average, children say their first word at _____ months of age. (p. 133)

Theories of Language Development

1. Match the following terms with the appropriate description. (p. 133)

   _____ A theory stating that children acquire language through operant conditioning, imitation, and reinforcement
   _____ A theory arguing that children are biologically primed to acquire language
   _____ A theory stating that language development reflects interactions between the child's inner capacities and environmental influences

   1. Interactionist perspective
   2. Behaviorist perspective
   3. Nativist perspective

2. True or False: Research supports the idea that there is a sensitive period for language acquisition. (p. 133)

Getting Ready to Talk

1. Around 2 months, babies begin to make vowel-like noises, called _____. Around 4 months, _____ appears, in which infants repeat consonant–vowel combinations in long strings. (p. 134)

2. What evidence indicates that experience contributes to the development of babbling? (p. 134)

   _____
   _____

3. Describe joint attention and indicate how it supports early language development. (p. 134)

   _____
   _____
   _____

4. True or False: Turn-taking games, such as pat-a-cake and peekaboo, contribute to infants' acquisition of language skills. (p. 134)

First Words

1. True or False: By the end of the second year, infants begin to understand word meanings. (p. 134)

2. When young children learn new words, they tend to make two errors. List and provide an example of each type of error. (pp. 134–135)

    A. _____

    B. _____

3. True or False: Children overextend many more words in comprehension than they do in production. (p. 135)

The Two-Word Utterance Phase

1. True or False: Recent evidence indicates that most toddlers show a steady, continuous increase in rate of word learning that continues through the preschool years. (p. 135)

2. Explain telegraphic speech. (p. 135)

    _____
    _____
    _____

Individual and Cultural Differences

1. True or False: Early language development of boys and girls proceeds at about the same rate. (p. 135)

2. Explain why the vocabularies of low-SES kindergartners are only one-fourth as large as those of their higher-SES peers? (p. 135)

    _____
    _____
    _____

3. Distinguish between *referential* and *expressive styles* of early language learning. Indicate which style is associated with faster vocabulary development. (p. 135)

    Referential: _____
    _____

    Expressive: _____
    _____

4. Cite factors that influence the development of referential and expressive styles. (p. 135)

    _____
    _____
    _____

Supporting Early Language Development

1. Describe the characteristics of child-directed speech (CDS), noting how it promotes language development. (p. 135)

   _____

   _____

   _____

2. True or False: Parent–toddler conversation strongly predicts language development and academic success during the school years. (p. 136)

3. Explain how CDS and parent–child conversation create a zone of proximal development. (p. 136)

   _____

   _____

ASK YOURSELF . . .

For *Ask Yourself* questions for this chapter, please log on to the Companion Website at *www.ablongman.com/berk*.

1. Select the Companion Website for *Exploring Lifespan Development.*
2. Use the "Jump to" menu to go directly to this chapter.
3. From the menu on the left side of the screen, select "Ask Yourself."
4. Complete questions and choose "Submit answers for grading" or "Clear answers" to start over.

SUGGESTED STUDENT READINGS

Bjorklund, D. F. (2004). *Children's thinking* (4th ed.). Belmont, CA: Wadsworth. Offers an overview of major research findings in areas such as development of perception, memory, conceptual understanding, language, and problem solving. The author also discusses major theories of cognitive development, including Piagetian, information processing, and sociocultural approaches.

Goldin-Meadow, S. (2003). *Hearing gesture: How our hands help us think.* Cambridge, MA: Harvard University Press. Presents up-to-date research on the meaning and importance of nonverbal behaviors in learning and communication. The author maintains that understanding children's gestures has significant implications for supporting their language development and other aspects of learning.

Lombardi, J., & Bogle, M. M. (Eds.). (2004). *The promise of Early Head Start for America's youngest children.* Washington, DC: Zero to Three. Provides a thorough overview of Early Head Start, including services offered to children and families, the importance of early learning experiences for infants and toddlers, and current research on early intervention.

Rakison, D. H., & Oakes, L. M. (Eds.). (2003). *Early category and concept development: Making sense of the blooming, buzzing confusion.* New York: Oxford University Press. Using up-to-date research on cognition, this book examines the importance and development of categorization and conceptualization abilities. A useful resource for anyone interested in cognitive development during infancy and toddlerhood.

PUZZLE 5.1 TERM REVIEW

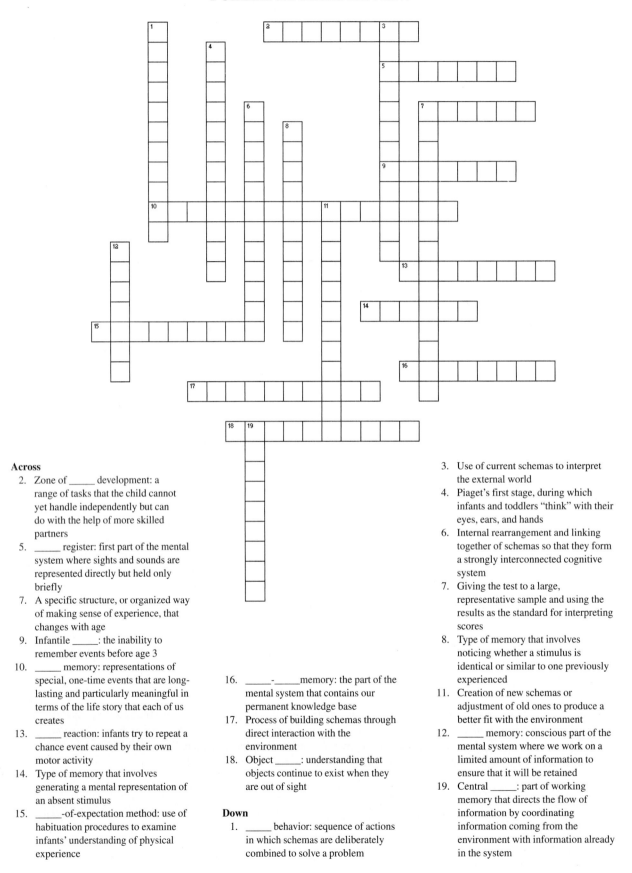

Across

2. Zone of _____ development: a range of tasks that the child cannot yet handle independently but can do with the help of more skilled partners
5. _____ register: first part of the mental system where sights and sounds are represented directly but held only briefly
7. A specific structure, or organized way of making sense of experience, that changes with age
9. Infantile _____: the inability to remember events before age 3
10. _____ memory: representations of special, one-time events that are long-lasting and particularly meaningful in terms of the life story that each of us creates
13. _____ reaction: infants try to repeat a chance event caused by their own motor activity
14. Type of memory that involves generating a mental representation of an absent stimulus
15. _____-of-expectation method: use of habituation procedures to examine infants' understanding of physical experience
16. _____-_____ memory: the part of the mental system that contains our permanent knowledge base
17. Process of building schemas through direct interaction with the environment
18. Object _____: understanding that objects continue to exist when they are out of sight

Down

1. _____ behavior: sequence of actions in which schemas are deliberately combined to solve a problem
3. Use of current schemas to interpret the external world
4. Piaget's first stage, during which infants and toddlers "think" with their eyes, ears, and hands
6. Internal rearrangement and linking together of schemas so that they form a strongly interconnected cognitive system
7. Giving the test to a large, representative sample and using the results as the standard for interpreting scores
8. Type of memory that involves noticing whether a stimulus is identical or similar to one previously experienced
11. Creation of new schemas or adjustment of old ones to produce a better fit with the environment
12. _____ memory: conscious part of the mental system where we work on a limited amount of information to ensure that it will be retained
19. Central _____: part of working memory that directs the flow of information by coordinating information coming from the environment with information already in the system

PUZZLE 5.2 TERM REVIEW

Across
5. Mental _____: learned procedures that operate on and tranform information
8. Perspective emphasizing that babies are born with knowledge systems (2 words)
9. _____ attention: infants gave in the same direction as adults, and adults follow the baby's line of vision and comment on what the infant sees, labelling the baby's environment
11. _____-_____ speech: form of speech marked by high-pitched, exaggerated expression, clear pronunciations, distinct pauses between speech segments, and repetition of new words
12. _____ speech: children's two-word utterances that leave out smaller and less important words
13. Early vocabulary error in which a word is applied too narrowly
14. Mental _____: an internal image of an absent object or past event
16. _____ quotient: a score that permits an individual's performance to be compared to the typical performance of same-age individuals
18. Repetition of consonant-vowel combinations in long strings, beginning around 4 months of age

Down
1. _____-_____ play: type of play in which children pretend, acting out everyday and imaginary activities
2. _____ distribution: bell-shaped distribution in which most scores cluster around the average when individual differences in large samples are measured
3. Pleasant vowel-like noises made by infants beginning around 2 months of age
4. Checklist for gathering information about the quality of children's home lives (abbr.)
6. In Chomsky's theory, an inborn system that permits children to speak in a rule-oriented fashion as soon as they learn enough words (abbr.)
7. _____ appropriate practice: set of standards devised by NAEYC that specify program characteristics that meet the developmental and individual needs of young children varying in age
10. _____ imitation: ability to remember and copy the behavior of models who are not immediately present
14. _____ style of language learning: toddlers use language mainly to label objects
15. Early vocabulary error in which a word is applied too broadly, to a wider collection of objects and events than is appropriate
17. _____ style of language learning: toddlers use language mainly to talk about people's feelings and needs

PRACTICE TEST #1

1. Piaget's sensorimotor stage spans (p. 116)
   a. the first 2 years of life.
   b. ages 2 and 3.
   c. ages 3 and 4.
   d. ages 6 through 8.

2. When children are not changing much, they assimilate more than they accommodate. Piaget called this a state of (p. 116)
   a. assimilation.
   b. accommodation.
   c. adaptation.
   d. equilibrium.

3. In Piaget's theory, which two processes account for changes in schemes? (p. 116)
   a. adaptation and assimilation
   b. adaptation and organization
   c. assimilation and organization
   d. assimilation and accommodation

4. Substage 5 spans (p. 118)
   a. 3 to 6 months.
   b. 6 to 12 months.
   c. 12 to 18 months.
   d. 18 to 24 months.

5. Internal depictions of information that the mind can manipulate are called (p. 119)
   a. mental representations.
   b. circular reactions.
   c. invisible displacements.
   d. deferred imitations.

6. To study infants' grasp of physical reality, researchers often use a violation-of-expectation method in which infants are (p. 119)
   a. habituated to a physical event and then researchers determine whether they recover faster to an expected or unexpected event.
   b. asked to seek an object after it has been moved from one hiding place to another.
   c. instructed to perform a response after seeing it modeled by an adult.
   d. asked to retrieve an object that has been hidden from their view.

7. Recent research on object permanence suggests that (p. 120)
   a. babies search for hidden objects only when those objects are toys.
   b. 10-month-olds may make the A-not-B search error because they have built a habit of reaching toward and looking at A.
   c. infants as young as 2 to 3 months of age can search for hidden objects.
   d. sensorimotor children lack the attention needed to remember where hidden objects have been placed.

8. Raegon's mother showed her how to obtain an out-of-reach toy by pulling a string. When encouraged to imitate her mother with a different-looking toy, Raegon successfully retrieved the toy. Raegon's behavior demonstrates that she (p. 121)
   a. can solve problems by analogy.
   b. has attained hypothetical thought.
   c. no longer exhibits the A-not-B search error.
   d. can engage in make-believe play.

9. According to the core knowledge perspective, studies of object permanence, object solidity, and gravity would test an infant's innate, prewired (p. 122)
   a. psychological knowledge.
   b. numerical knowledge.
   c. physical knowledge.
   d. linguistic knowledge.

10. The three parts of the information-processing system are (p. 123)
    a. sensation, perception, and interpretation.
    b. assimilation, accommodation, and equilibration.
    c. stimulus input, input manipulation, and response output.
    d. the sensory register, working memory, and long-term memory.

11. Sights and sounds are represented directly and stored briefly in (p. 123)
    a. working memory.
    b. the sensory register.
    c. short-term memory.
    d. long-term memory.

12. Which type of memory involves noticing whether a new experience is identical or similar to one previously experienced? (p. 124)
    a. recall
    b. recognition
    c. autobiographical
    d. retrospective

13. Based on similar overall appearance, babies' earliest categories are (p. 126)
    a. perceptual.
    b. conceptual.
    c. familial.
    d. sustained.

14. Which of the following statements accurately describes the prediction of IQ? (p. 129)
    a. Because infant tests measure cognitive skills similar to childhood tests, IQ scores remain relatively stable.
    b. IQ scores obtained in infancy accurately predict IQ in early childhood.
    c. Infant IQ scores do not reflect true abilities in distracted or fatigued infants.
    d. The younger the child at the time of the first testing, the better the prediction of later IQ.

15. Today, most infant intelligence tests are used for (p. 129)
    a. making long-term predictions about intelligence.
    b. identifying babies who may be at risk for developmental problems in the future.
    c. determining cognitive strengths.
    d. determining language delays.

16. By age 6, children have a vocabulary of about (p. 133)
    a. 1,000 words.
    b. 10,000 words.
    c. 100,000 words.
    d. 500,000 words.

17. Which of the following provides evidence that children are biologically primed to acquire language? (p. 133)
    a. Children's first word combinations do not appear to follow grammatical rules.
    b. Parental reinforcement results in rapid vocabulary acquisition.
    c. Children all over the world reach major language development milestones in a similar sequence.
    d. Children's progress in mastering many sentence constructions is steady and gradual.

18. The innate system that contains a set of rules common to all languages is called the (p. 133)
    a. Early Head Start.
    b. Chomsky device.
    c. Home Observation.
    d. language acquisition device (LAD).

19. One-year-old Fiona uses the word "doggie" to refer only to her family's pet dog and not to other dogs. Fiona's error is known as an (p. 134)
    a. underextension.
    b. overextension.
    c. underregularization.
    d. overregularization.

20. When first learning to talk, Alex used words mostly to label objects, such as "doggie," "ball," "car," and "book." Alex's style of language learning is best categorized as (p. 135)
    a. expressive.
    b. referential.
    c. concrete.
    d. attributional.

PRACTICE TEST #2

1. On a trip to a farm, 2-year-old Liam sees a horse for the first time. Noticing the horse's four legs, tail, and fur, Liam integrates it into his "dog" scheme. This is an example of (p. 116)
    a. accommodation.
    b. assimilation.
    c. organization.
    d. equilibrium.

2. According to Piaget, when children create new schemes or adjust old ones to produce a better fit with the environment, they are using (p. 116)
    a. overextension.
    b. recognition.
    c. accommodation.
    d. intentional behavior.

3. A child will eventually relate "dropping a ball" to "throwing a ball," which is an example of (pp. 116–117)
    a. organization.
    b. assimilation.
    c. accommodation.
    d. recognition.

4. In which substage do babies suck, grasp, and look in much the same way? (p. 118)
    a. Substage 1
    b. Substage 2
    c. Substage 3
    d. Substage 4

5. Tertiary circular reactions differ from primary and secondary circular reactions in that they are (p. 118)
    a. rich in mental representation.
    b. directed toward the environment.
    c. centered around the infant's own body.
    d. deliberately exploratory.

6. A child who is coordinating schemes deliberately to solve simple problems is engaging in (p. 118)
   a. intentional behavior.
   b. mental representation.
   c. deferred imitation.
   d. object permanence.

7. A toddler who can remember and copy the behavior of his mother when she is not present is engaging in (p. 119)
   a. circular reaction.
   b. invisible displacement.
   c. problem solving.
   d. deferred imitation.

8. Baby Gary's father playfully sticks his tongue out when changing Gary's diaper. The next day, the father notices Gary sticking his tongue out while waiting to have his diaper changed. Baby Gary is demonstrating (p. 119)
   a. make-believe play.
   b. a circular reaction.
   c. a reflex.
   d. deferred imitation.

9. Which of the following is the conscious part of our mental system, where we actively work on a limited amount of information? (p. 123)
   a. perceptual register
   b. sensory register
   c. working memory
   d. long-term memory

10. Our permanent knowledge base is our (p. 123)
    a. long-term memory.
    b. short-term memory.
    c. sensory register.
    d. working memory.

11. Which of the following best reflects changes in attention from infancy to toddlerhood? (p. 124)
    a. During the second year of life, children shift from thorough exploration of objects and patterns to unitary focus on high-contrast features.
    b. Toddlers have increasing difficulty disengaging their attention from interesting stimuli.
    c. With age, attraction to novelty declines and sustained attention improves.
    d. Because of their limited need for sustained attention, young children's efficiency at managing their attention changes very little from infancy to toddlerhood.

12. The greatest drawback of information-processing approach is that it (p. 126)
    a. fails to account for the continuity of human thinking from infancy into adulthood.
    b. regards infants and toddlers as passive beings who are acted on by their environment rather than acknowledging them as active, inquiring beings.
    c. explains cognitive development in terms of discrete stages.
    d. analyzes cognition in terms of its components but has difficulty putting the components back together into a comprehensive theory.

13. Vygotsky's theory emphasizes that individual differences in complex mental activities are mainly due to cultural differences in (p. 127)
    a. genetic makeup.
    b. social experiences.
    c. nutrition.
    d. infant physical care practices.

14. The Bayley Scales of Infant Development is suitable for children between (p. 127)
    a. 1 month and 6 months.
    b. 1 month and 3½ years.
    c. 6 months and 1½ years.
    d. 3 years and 5 years.

15. The checklist for gathering information about the quality of children's home lives through observation and interviews with parents is called (p. 130)
    a. the Bayley Scales of Infant Development.
    b. the Intelligence Quotient.
    c. the Home Observation for Measurement of the Environment.
    d. standardization.

16. Gains in IQ and academic achievement are greatest when intervention (p. 132)
    a. begins in the primary grades.
    b. includes home visits.
    c. begins early and is long lasting.
    d. is indirect, focusing on availability of community services rather than child and family functioning.

17. According to the nativist perspective, the early and rapid development of language in humans is due primarily to (p. 133)
    a. parental reinforcement of children's communication attempts.
    b. an innate system that contains a set of rules common to all languages.
    c. children's ability to imitate other people.
    d. parents' use of child-directed speech.

18. Research on babbling suggests that (p. 134)
    a. babies in industrialized countries begin babbling a few months before babies in nonindustrialized countries.
    b. sounds of infants' native language are incorporated into their babbling even in the absence of exposure to human speech.
    c. hearing-impaired infants do not babble.
    d. early babbling is due to maturation, since babies everywhere start babbling at about the same age and produce a similar range of early sounds.

19. "Mommy shoe" and "Baby go" are both examples of (p. 135)
    a. telegraphic speech.
    b. expressive style.
    c. overextension.
    d. underextension.

20. Child-directed speech (CDS) is a form of communication comprised of (p. 135)
    a. short sentences with high-pitched, exaggerated expression.
    b. vocabularies made up mainly of words that refer to objects.
    c. vocabularies made up of words that refer to objects, plus many pronouns and social formulas.
    d. two-word utterances.

CHAPTER 6
EMOTIONAL AND SOCIAL DEVELOPMENT IN INFANCY AND TODDLERHOOD

BRIEF CHAPTER SUMMARY

Although Freud's psychoanalytic theory is no longer in the mainstream of human development research, his emphasis on the importance of the parent–child relationship was accepted and elaborated by other theorists, notably Erik Erikson. Erikson believed that the psychological conflict of the first year of life is basic trust versus mistrust, and that a healthy outcome depends on the quality of the parent–child relationship. During toddlerhood, the conflict of autonomy versus shame and doubt is resolved favorably when parents provide appropriate guidance and reasonable choices. If children emerge from the first few years without sufficient trust in caregivers, and without a healthy sense of individuality, the seeds are sown for adjustment problems.

All humans and other primates experience basic emotions—happiness, interest, surprise, fear, anger, sadness, and disgust—that can be inferred from similar facial expressions in diverse cultures. Emotions play powerful roles in organizing social relationships, exploration of the environment, and discovery of the self. Cognitive and motor development, caregiver–infant communication, and cultural factors all affect the development and expression of emotions.

Infants' emotional expressions are closely tied to their ability to interpret the emotional cues of others. As toddlers become aware of the self as a separate, unique individual, self-conscious emotions—guilt, shame, embarrassment, envy, and pride—appear. Toddlers also begin to use emotional self-regulation strategies to manage their emotions. Rapid development of the cerebral cortex, sensitive caregiving, and growth in representation and language contribute to the development of self-regulation.

Infants vary widely in temperament, including both reactivity (quickness and intensity of emotional arousal, attention, and motor activity) and self-regulation (strategies for modifying reactivity). Research findings have inspired a growing body of research on temperament, examining its stability, biological roots, and interaction with child-rearing experiences. The goodness-of-fit model explains how temperament and environment can together produce favorable outcomes by creating child-rearing environments that recognize each child's temperament while encouraging more adaptive functioning.

Attachment refers to the strong affectionate tie we have with special people in our lives that leads us to feel pleasure when we interact with them and to be comforted by their nearness in times of stress. By the second half of the first year, infants have become attached to familiar people who have responded to their needs. Today, ethological theory of attachment, which recognizes the infant's emotional tie to the caregiver as an evolved response that promotes survival, is the most widely accepted view. By the end of the second year, children develop an enduring affectionate tie to the caregiver that serves as an internal working model, a guide for future close relationships. Attachment security is influenced by opportunity for attachment, quality of caregiving, infant characteristics, and parents' internal working models. Babies form attachments to a variety of familiar people in addition to mothers—fathers, siblings, grandparents, and professional caregivers. Mounting evidence indicates that continuity of caregiving determines whether attachment security in early life is linked to later development; the effects of early attachment security depend on the quality of the baby's future relationships.

During the first two years, knowledge of the self as a separate, permanent identity emerges, beginning with self-recognition—awareness of the self's physical features. Self-awareness is associated with the beginnings of empathy—the ability to understand another person's emotional state and to respond emotionally in a similar way. Self-awareness also contributes to effortful control—the extent to which children can inhibit impulses, manage negative emotion, and behave in socially acceptable ways. Self-control begins with compliance, including the ability to delay gratification.

LEARNING OBJECTIVES

After reading this chapter, you should be able to:

6.1 Discuss personality changes that occur during Erikson's psychosocial stages of basic trust versus mistrust and autonomy versus shame and doubt. (pp. 140–141)

6.2 Describe changes in happiness, anger, and fear over the first year, noting the adaptive function of each. (pp. 141–142)

6.3 Summarize changes during the first two years in understanding others' emotions, expression of self-conscious emotions, and emotional self-regulation. (pp. 142–145)

6.4 Describe temperament, and identify the three temperamental styles elaborated by Thomas and Chess. (p. 145)

6.5 Compare Thomas and Chess's model of temperament with that of Rothbart. (p. 146)

6.6 Explain how temperament is assessed, and distinguish inhibited, or shy, children from uninhibited, or sociable, children. (p. 146)

6.7 Discuss the role of heredity and environment in the stability of temperament, including the goodness-of-fit model. (pp. 146–149)

6.8 Describe Bowlby's ethological theory of attachment, and trace the development of attachment during the first two years. (pp. 149–150)

6.9 Describe the Strange Situation, along with the four patterns of attachment that have been identified using this procedure. (pp. 151–152)

6.10 Discuss the factors that affect attachment security, including opportunity for attachment, quality of caregiving, infant characteristics, and parents' internal working models. (pp. 152–154)

6.11 Describe infants' attachment to fathers and siblings. (pp. 154–156)

6.12 Describe and interpret the relationship between secure attachment in infancy and later development. (pp. 156–157)

6.13 Trace the emergence of self-awareness, and explain how it influences early emotional and social development, categorization of the self, and development of self-control. (pp. 157–159)

STUDY QUESTIONS

Erikson's Theory of Infant and Toddler Personality

Basic Trust versus Mistrust

1. How did Erikson expand and enrich Freud's view of the importance of the parent–infant relationship during the first year? (p. 140)

   _____

   _____

2. Based on Erikson's theory, summarize the psychological conflict of the first year, *basic trust versus mistrust,* and explain how it can be positively resolved. (pp. 140–141)

   A. _____

   _____

   B. _____

   _____

Autonomy versus Shame and Doubt

1. In what way did Erikson expand on Freud's view of development during the second year? (p. 141)
   _____
   _____

2. Explain how the psychological conflict of toddlerhood, *autonomy versus shame and doubt,* is resolved favorably. (p. 141)
   _____
   _____

Emotional Development

Development of Some Basic Emotions

1. Define the term *basic emotions,* and provide several examples. (p. 141)

   A. _____
   _____

   B. _____
   _____

2. True or False: At birth, infants are able to express all of the basic emotions. (p. 141)

3. What is the *social smile,* and when does it develop? (p. 141)
   _____
   _____
   _____

4. Laughter, which appears around _____ to _____ months, reflects (faster / slower) processing of information than smiling. (p. 141)

5. How do expressions of happiness change between early infancy and the middle of the first year? (p. 141)
   _____
   _____

6. The frequency and intensity of infants' angry reactions (increases / decreases) with age. (pp. 141–142)

7. Fear reactions (increase / decrease) during the second half of the first year. (p. 142)

8. The most frequent expression of fear in infancy is, to unfamiliar adults, a response called _____ *anxiety.* (p. 142)

9. Explain how the rise in fear after 6 months of age is adaptive. (p. 142)
   _____
   _____

10. What factors contribute to a decline in stranger anxiety in late toddlerhood? (p. 142)
    _____
    _____

A Lifespan Vista: Parental Depression and Children's Development

1. Approximately _____ to _____ percent of women experience chronic depression—mild to severe feelings of sadness and withdrawal that continue for months or years. (p. 143)

2. Describe characteristics of *postpartum depression*. (p. 143)

3. Discuss how depression affects the mother's interactions with her infant. (p. 143)

4. Explain how persistent maternal depression and associated parenting behaviors affect the development of the child. (p. 143)

5. List behavior problems that infants of depressed fathers may develop in the preschool years. (p. 143)

6. True or False: At older ages, parental depression is linked to frequent father–child conflict. (p. 143)

7. True or False: Early treatment of parental depression is vital to prevent the disorder from interfering with the parent–child relationship. (p. 143)

Understanding and Responding to the Emotions of Others

1. Early on, babies detect others' emotions through the fairly automatic process of *emotional* _____; that is, they tend to feel happy or sad when they sense these emotions in others. (p. 142)

2. Define *social referencing,* and explain the functions it serves for infants and toddlers. (pp. 142, 144)

    A. _____

    B. _____

3. True or False: By the middle of the second year, children appreciate that others' emotional reactions may differ from their own. (p. 144)

Emergence of Self-Conscious Emotions

1. What are *self-conscious emotions*? (p. 144)

2. Self-conscious emotions appear between ____ and ____ months of age. (p. 144)

3. Describe two factors that contribute to the development of self-conscious emotions. (p. 144)

    A. _____

    B. _____

4. True or False: The situations in which adults encourage children's expressions of self-conscious emotions are very similar from culture to culture. (p. 144)

Beginnings of Emotional Self-Regulation

1. Define *emotional self-regulation*. (p. 144)

2. Describe developments during the first year of life that contribute to infants' ability to regulate their emotions. (p. 144)

3. Explain how a caregiver's responses to an infant's emotional cues affect the infant's developing capacity for self-regulation. (pp. 144–145)

4. By the end of the second year, gains in language lead to new ways of regulating emotion. Explain how this occurs. (p. 145)

Temperament and Development

1. Define *temperament*. (p. 145)

2. Cite two important findings from the New York Longitudinal Study of temperament. (p. 145)

    A. _____

    B. _____

The Structure of Temperament

1. Match each type of temperament with the appropriate description. (p. 145)

    _____ Quickly establishes regular routines in infancy, is generally cheerful, and adapts easily to new experiences
    _____ Is inactive, shows mild, low-key reactions to environmental stimuli, is negative in mood, and adjusts slowly to new experiences
    _____ Is irregular is daily routines, is slow to accept new experiences, and tends to react negatively and intensely

    A. Slow-to-warm-up child
    B. Easy child
    C. Difficult child

2. True or False: All children fit into one of the three categories of temperament described above. (p. 145)

3. List the five dimensions of reactivity described in Rothbart's model of temperament. (p. 146)

    A. _____
    B. _____
    C. _____
    D. _____
    E. _____

4. What is *effortful control*? (p. 146)

    _____
    _____

Measuring Temperament

1. Discuss the advantages and disadvantages of using parent reports to assess children's temperament. (p. 146)

    Advantages: _____
    _____
    _____

    Disadvantages: _____
    _____
    _____

2. Parental ratings are (strongly / moderately) related to observational measures of children's behavior. (p. 146)

3. Most physiological assessments of temperament have focused on _____ children, who react negatively to and withdraw from novel stimuli, and _____ children, who display positive emotion to and approach novel stimuli. (p. 146)

Biology and Environment: Development of Shyness and Sociability

1. According to Kagan, differences in arousal of the _____, an inner brain structure that controls avoidance reactions, contributes to contrasting temperamental styles. (p. 147)

2. List and briefly describe four physiological responses that distinguish shy versus sociable children. (p. 147)

   A. _____

   B. _____

   C. _____

   D. _____

3. Explain how child-rearing practices affect the chances that an emotionally reactive baby will become a fearful child. (p. 147)

   _____

Stability of Temperament

1. True or False: Temperamental stability from one age period to the next is generally low to moderate. (p. 146)

2. Long-term predictions about early temperament are best achieved after age ____, when styles of responding are better established. (p. 148)

Genetic Influences

1. Research shows that identical twins (are / are not) more similar than fraternal twins in temperament and personality. (p. 148)

2. True or False: Lack of consistent ethnic and sex differences in early temperament have called into question the role of heredity. (p. 148)

Environmental Influences

1. Describe how parental behaviors contribute to ethnic and sex differences in temperament. (p. 148)

   Ethnic differences: _____

   Sex differences: _____

2. True or False: Research indicates that parents often regard siblings as having more distinct temperaments than observers do. Provide an example to support your answer. (p. 148)

   _____

Temperament and Child Rearing: The Goodness-of-Fit Model

1. Describe the *goodness-of-fit* model. (p. 148)

2. Briefly summarize parenting practices that sustain the difficult child's irritable, conflict-ridden style. (pp. 148–149)

3. Provide an example of how life conditions can affect parenting. (p. 149)

4. Describe parental behaviors that benefit difficult and shy children. (p. 149)

5. True or False: Whereas reserved, inactive toddlers benefit from highly stimulating maternal behavior, the same parental behavior has a negative impact on active children. (p. 149)

Development of Attachment

1. Define *attachment*. (p. 149)

2. True or False: Both psychoanalytic and behaviorist theories emphasize feeding as the central context in which infants and caregivers build a close emotional bond. (p. 149)

3. How did research on rhesus monkeys challenge the idea that attachment depends on hunger satisfaction? (p. 150)

Ethological Theory of Attachment

1. True or False: The ethological theory of attachment is the most widely accepted view of the infants' emotional tie to the caregiver. (p. 150)

2. Summarize the ethological theory of attachment. (p. 150)

3. Match each phase of attachment with the appropriate description. (p. 150)

_____ Infants display separation anxiety and use the familiar caregiver as a secure base.
_____ Built-in signals help bring newborn babies into close contact with other humans, who comfort them.
_____ Separation anxiety declines as children gain an understanding of the parent's comings and goings and can predict his / her return.
_____ Infants start to respond differently to a familiar caregiver than to a stranger.

1. Preattachment phase
2. "Attachment-in-the making"
3. "Clear-cut" attachment phase
4. Formation of a reciprocal relationship

4. According to Bowlby, children construct an *internal working model* based on their experiences during the four phases of attachment. Define and explain this term. (p. 150)

_____
_____
_____

Measuring the Security of Attachment

1. The _____, designed by Mary Ainsworth, is the most widely used technique for measuring the quality of attachment between 1 and 2 years of age. (p. 151)

2. Match each of the following attachment classifications with the appropriate description. (p. 151)

_____ Before separation, these infants seek closeness to the parent and fail to explore. When she returns, they display angry behaviors, may continue to cry after being picked up, and cannot be easily comforted.
_____ Before separation, these infants use the parent as a base from which to explore. They are upset by the parent's absence, and they seek contact and are easily comforted when she returns.
_____ Before separation, these infants seem unresponsive to the parent. When she leaves, they react to the stranger in much the same way as to the parent. Upon her return, they are slow to greet her.
_____ When the parent returns, these infants show confused, contradictory behaviors, such as looking away while being held.

1. Secure
2. Avoidant
3. Resistant
4. Disorganized / Disoriented

Stability of Attachment

1. Summarize SES differences in patterns of attachment. (p. 152)

_____
_____
_____

2. True or False: Insecurely attached infants maintain their attachment status more often than securely attached infants. (p. 152)

3. Which pattern of insecure attachment remains highly stable over time? (p. 152)

_____

Cultural Variations

1. How do German and Japanese infants differ from American infants in attachment patterns? (p. 152)

   German infants: _____

   _____

   Japanese infants: _____

   _____

2. True or False: The secure pattern is the most common attachment quality in all societies studied. (p. 152)

Factors That Affect Attachment Security

1. List four important influences on attachment security. (pp. 152–153)

   A. _____

   B. _____

   C. _____

   D. _____

2. True or False: Research on adopted children indicates that children can develop a first attachment bond as late as 4 to 6 years of age. (p. 153)

3. Describe several adjustment problems associated with a lack of opportunity to develop attachment bonds during infancy and early childhood. (p. 153)

   _____

   _____

   _____

4. Describe differences in the sensitivity of caregiving experienced by securely attached and insecurely attached infants. (p. 153)

   Securely attached: _____

   _____

   Insecurely attached: _____

   _____

5. How does the parental care experienced by securely attached infants differ from that experienced by avoidant and resistant infants? (p. 153)

   _____

   _____

   _____

   _____

6. Among maltreated infants, _____ attachment is especially high. (p. 153)

7. Why are infant characteristics only weakly related to attachment quality? (p. 153)

   _____

   _____

   _____

8. Explain how family circumstances, such as job loss, a failing marriage, or financial difficulties, can affect infant attachment. (p. 154)

9. Describe how parents' internal working models affect infants' attachment quality. (p. 154)

10. True or False: The way parents view their childhood experiences is more influential than their actual experiences in determining how they rear their own children. (p. 154)

Social Issues: Does Child Care in Infancy Threaten Attachment Security and Later Adjustment?

1. True or False: North American infants placed in full-time child care before 12 months of age are far more likely than infants who remain at home to display insecure attachments. (p. 155)

2. Summarize two factors that influence the relationship between child care and attachment quality. (p. 155)

   A.

   B.

   C.

3. According to the findings of the NICHD study, what child-care characteristics promote positive child–caregiver interactions and favorable child development? (p. 155)

   A.

   B.

   C.

Multiple Attachments

1. True or False: When both parents are present and infants are anxious, unhappy, or distressed, they prefer to be comforted by their mother. (p. 154)

2. Describe how mothers and fathers in many cultures differ in the way they interact with infants. (p. 154)

3. How have parental roles in relating to infants changed in response to women's workforce participation? (pp. 154, 156)

4. When a new baby arrives, how is a preschool sibling likely to respond? Include both negative and positive reactions in your answer. (p. 156)

   Negative: _____

   Positive: _____

Attachment and Later Development

1. True or False: Research consistently shows that secure infants show more favorable development than insecure infants. (p. 156)

2. Evidence suggests that *continuity of caregiving* determines whether attachment is linked to later development. Briefly explain this relationship. (p. 156)

Self-Development During the First Two Years

Self-Awareness

1. Babies' capacity for _____ perception supports the beginnings of self-awareness. (p. 157)

2. Define self-recognition, and provide an example of this ability. (p. 157)

   A. _____

   B. _____

3. Describe two ways in which self-awareness supports emotional and social development. (p. 158)

   A. _____

   B. _____

Categorizing the Self

1. Describe categorizations of the self that appear in toddlerhood, and cite an example of how children use this knowledge to organize their behavior. (p. 158)

   A. _____

   B. _____

Self-Control

1. Between ___ and ___ months, toddlers first become capable of compliance. Opposition is far (less common / more common) than compliance. (p. 158)

2. True or False: Children who are advanced in development of attention and language tend to have greater difficulty delaying gratification. (p. 158)

3. Describe ways that parents can help toddlers develop compliance and self-control. (p. 158)

_____
_____
_____

ASK YOURSELF . . .

For *Ask Yourself* questions for this chapter, please log on to the Companion Website at *www.ablongman.com/berk*.

1. Select the Companion Website for *Exploring Lifespan Development*.
2. Use the "Jump to" menu to go directly to this chapter.
3. From the menu on the left side of the screen, select "Ask Yourself."
4. Complete questions and choose "Submit answers for grading" or "Clear answers" to start over.

SUGGESTED STUDENT READINGS

Crittenden, P. M., & Claussen, A. H. (Eds.). (2003). *Organization of attachment relationships: Maturation, culture, and context.* Cambridge, England: Cambridge University Press. Examines the development and importance of attachment from infancy to early adulthood, including cross-cultural findings on attachment.

Holinger, P. C., & Doner, K. (2003). *What babies can say before they can talk.* New York: Simon & Schuster. Using research on basic and self-conscious emotions, the author examines the diverse meanings of infant signals. Because babies' understanding of the world reflects experiences with parents and caregivers, understanding and responding to infant cues is essential for healthy development.

Kagan, J., & Snidman, N. (2004). *The long shadow of temperament.* Cambridge, MA: Harvard University Press. Using results from over two decades of longitudinal research, this book explores the relationship between temperament and psychological development.

Lamb, M. E. (Ed.). (2004). *The role of the father in child development* (4th ed.). Hoboken, NJ: Wiley. Examines the diverse and enduring contributions of father involvement to child development. An excellent resource for students, educators, mental health professionals, and anyone interested in working with children and families.

PUZZLE 6.1 TERM REVIEW

Across
3. _____ control: the capacity to suppress a dominant response in order to plan and execute a more adaptive response
7. Identification of the self as a physically unique being
10. A child who reacts negatively to and withdraws from novel stimuli
11. Emotions that can be directly inferred from facial expressions
12. Temperament style characterized by establishment of regular routines in infancy, general cheerfulness, and easy adaptation to new experiences
15. A child who reacts positively to and approaches novel stimuli
18. Stable, individual differences in quality and intensity of emotional reaction, activity level, attention, and emotional self-regulation

Down
1. _____-_____ emotions involve injury to or enhancement of the sense of self.
2. Temperament style characterized by inactivity, mild, low-key reactions to environmental stimuli, negative mood, and slow adjustment to new experiences (4 words, hyph.)
4. _____ self: between 18 and 30 months children develop the capacity to categorize themselves and others on the basis of age, sex, physical characteristics, and goodness versus badness
5. Social _____ involves reliance upon another's emotional reaction to appraise uncertain situations
6. Emotional _____ - _____ : strategies for adjusting our emotional state to a comfortable level of intensity
8. Delay of _____ : waiting for an appropriate time and place to engage in a tempting act
9. Basic trust versus _____ : Erikson's psychological conflict of the first year
13. Attachment _____ : an alternative method of measuring the security of attachment through observation
14. _____ versus shame and doubt: Erikson's psychological conflict of toddlerhood
16. Temperament style characterized by irregular daily routines; slow acceptance of new experiences; and negative, intense reactions
17. Ability to understand another's emotional state and feel with that person

PUZZLE 6.2 TERM REVIEW

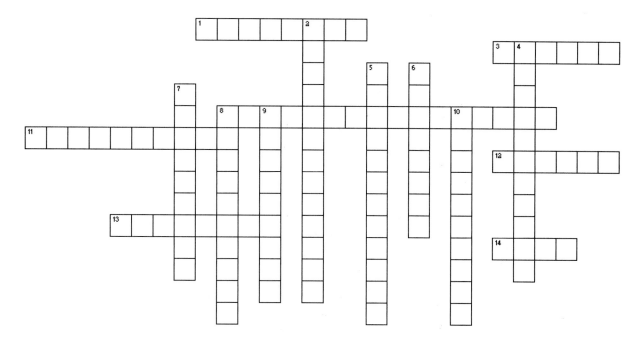

Across
1. _____ anxiety: infant's expressions of fear in response to unfamiliar adults
3. Attachment style characterizing infants who are distressed at parental separation and easily comforted upon parental return
8. Procedure involving brief separations from and reunions with the parent that assesses the quality of the attachment bond (2 words)
11. Voluntary obedience to requests and commands
12. The _____ smile is evoked by the stimulus of the human face.
13. Attachment style characterizing infants who are not distressed by parental separation and who avoid the parent when she returns
14. Infants use the caregiver as a secure _____ from which to explore, returning for emotional support

Down
2. Model of attachment that states that an effective match between child-rearing practices and a child's temperament leads to favorable adjustment (3 words, hyph.)
4. _____ theory of attachment views the infant's emotional tie to the caregiver as an evolved response that promotes survival
5. Attachment style characterizing infants who respond in a confused, contradictory fashion when reunited with the parent (a.k.a. disoriented attachment)
6. _____ working model: set of expectations derived from early caregiving experiences
7. _____ caregiving involves prompt, consistent, and appropriate responding to infant signals
8. _____ anxiety refers to an infant's distressed reaction to the departure of a familiar caregiver
9. Attachment style characterizing infants who remain close to the parent prior to separation and display angry behavior upon reunion
10. The strong affectional ties that humans feel toward special people in their lives

PRACTICE TEST #1

1. According to Erikson's theory, a healthy outcome during infancy depends on the (p. 140)
   a. amount of food the child receives.
   b. amount of oral stimulation the child receives.
   c. quality of caregiving the child receives.
   d. genes the child has inherited.

2. Emotions that can be directly inferred from facial expressions are referred to as (p. 141)
   a. social emotions.
   b. self-conscious emotions.
   c. basic emotions.
   d. referential emotions.

3. Between 6 and 10 weeks, the human face evokes a broad grin called the (p. 141)
   a. social smile.
   b. happy face.
   c. playful grin.
   d. infant smirk.

4. Early on, infants detect others' emotions through a fairly automatic process of (p. 142)
   a. stranger anxiety.
   b. emotional contagion.
   c. social referencing.
   d. emotional self-regulation.

5. When an unfamiliar adult offers Heather a toy, she hesitates and looks at her mother, who smiles and nods. Heather then reaches out and takes the toy. This is an example of (p. 142)
   a. self-control.
   b. social referencing.
   c. emotional contagion.
   d. compliance.

6. Which of the following are self-conscious emotions? (p. 144)
   a. happiness and sadness
   b. fear and anger
   c. interest and surprise
   d. shame and embarrassment

7. The capacity to adjust one's emotional state to a comfortable level of intensity is known as (p. 144)
   a. affective monitoring.
   b. emotional self-regulation.
   c. emotional self-control.
   d. emotive self-referencing.

8. Research on the stability of temperament shows that (p. 146)
   a. temperament is highly stable from infancy to adulthood.
   b. temperament is low to moderately stable from one age period to the next.
   c. temperament is not at all stable from one age period to the next.
   d. temperament stabilizes in late childhood and is consistent after that time.

9. The notion that an effective match between child-rearing practices and a child's temperament will lead to favorable outcomes is known as (p. 148)
   a. secure base.
   b. goodness-of-fit.
   c. an internal working model.
   d. sensitive caregiving.

10. The first of Bowlby's four attachment phases is (p. 150)
    a. attachment-in-the-making.
    b. clear-cut attachment.
    c. preattachment.
    d. formation of a reciprocal relationship.

11. When baby Zoey becomes upset when her mother leaves a room, she is displaying (p. 150)
    a. effortful control.
    b. separation anxiety.
    c. emotional self-regulation.
    d. social referencing.

12. Formation of a reciprocal relationship usually occurs between (p. 150)
    a. 6 and 9 months.
    b. 9 months and 1 year.
    c. 1 year and 18 months.
    d. 18 months and 2 years, and beyond.

13. When placed in the Strange Situation, infants who seek closeness to their mother before separation but display angry behavior when she returns are classified as having which pattern of attachment? (p. 151)
    a. secure
    b. avoidant
    c. resistant
    d. disorganized / disoriented

14. Research on the relationship between caregiving and attachment style shows that (p. 153)
    a. sensitive caregiving distinguishes securely from insecurely attached infants.
    b. disorganized/disoriented infants typically receive overly stimulating, intrusive care.
    c. resistant infants tend to have mothers who are minimally involved in caregiving and unresponsive to infant signals.
    d. children who experience abuse and neglect are no more likely than other children to develop insecure attachments.

15. In caring for and interacting with infants, fathers are more likely than mothers to (p. 154)
    a. devote more time to physical care.
    b. devote more time to expressing affection.
    c. engage in conventional games like pat-a-cake.
    d. engage in highly arousing physical play.

16. When do babies identify the self as a physically unique being? (p. 157)
    a. at birth
    b. 6 months
    c. 1 year
    d. 2 years

17. The ability to understand another's emotional state and feel with that person is called (p. 158)
    a. basic trust.
    b. self-recognition.
    c. empathy.
    d. self-awareness.

18. The beginnings of self-awareness are grounded in (p. 158)
    a. gains in perspective taking.
    b. theory of mind.
    c. infants' recognition that their actions cause objects and people to react in predictable ways.
    d. infants' conscious awareness of the self's physical features.

19. Self-awareness strengthens the capacity to resist an impulse to engage in socially disapproved behavior, exhibiting (p. 158)
    a. self-regulation.
    b. self-control.
    c. compliance.
    d. perspective taking.

20. When 3-year-old Harry resists taking a toy from his baby sister, he is showing (p. 158)
    a. self-regulation.
    b. self-control.
    c. compliance.
    d. perspective taking.

PRACTICE TEST #2

1. According to Erikson's theory, a mother who provides suitable guidance and reasonable choices is fostering her child's sense of (p. 141)
    a. attachment.
    b. autonomy.
    c. trust.
    d. self.

2. Research on happiness indicates that (p. 141)
    a. infants do not begin to smile until around 3 months of age.
    b. by 3 months of age, infants smile more often when they see a dynamic, eye-catching object than when they interact with people.
    c. smiling reflects faster processing of information than laughing.
    d. infants smile and laugh when they achieve new skills.

3. The social smile typically appears (p. 141)
    a. at birth.
    b. between 6 and 10 weeks.
    c. at 3 to 4 months.
    d. between 12 and 18 months.

4. Infants' expression of fear toward unfamiliar adults during the second half of the first year is called (p. 142)
    a. separation anxiety.
    b. the strange situation.
    c. stranger anxiety.
    d. avoidant attachment.

5. Babies use the familiar caregiver as a point from which to explore, called a(n) (p. 142)
    a. secure base.
    b. comfort zone.
    c. emotional contagion.
    d. social reference.

6. Guilt, shame, and embarrassment appear in children between the ages of (p. 144)
    a. 12 and 18 months.
    b. 18 and 24 months.
    c. 24 and 30 months.
    d. 30 and 36 months.

7. Which of the following is the best example of an infant engaging in social referencing? (pp. 142, 144)
   a. looking for home while riding in a stroller
   b. crying loudly when hungry at mealtime
   c. taking a toy back from an older sibling
   d. searching for mother's face in a crowded market

8. The capacity to voluntarily suppress a dominant response in order to plan and execute a more adaptive response is known as (p. 146)
   a. effortful control.
   b. emotional control.
   c. emotional contagion.
   d. compliance.

9. In the measurement of temperament, (p. 146)
   a. parental reports have been found to be the most unbiased source of information.
   b. behavior ratings by pediatricians and teachers are the measures most often used.
   c. direct observations by researchers have been emphasized because of their convenience.
   d. physiological assessments have been successful in differentiating shy children from sociable children.

10. Research on genetic and environmental influences on temperament shows that (p. 148)
    a. identical twins are no more alike than fraternal twins across a wide range of temperament traits.
    b. about half of the individual differences in temperament and personality can be traced to differences in genetic makeup.
    c. findings on ethnic and sex differences have failed to reveal distinct patterns, suggesting that temperament is entirely attributable to genetic foundations.
    d. environmental factors appear to be solely responsible for the development of temperament.

11. In which of Bowlby's attachment phases will a baby display separation anxiety? (p. 150)
    a. attachment-in-the-making
    b. clear-cut attachment
    c. preattachment
    d. formation of a reciprocal relationship

12. Which of the following patterns of attachment is linked to extremely negative caregiving and is highly stable over the second year? (p. 152)
    a. secure
    b. resistant
    c. avoidant
    d. disorganized / disoriented

13. If Maria responds promptly, consistently, and appropriately to her baby daughter and she holds her tenderly and carefully, she is exhibiting (p. 153)
    a. clear-cut attachment.
    b. sensitive caregiving.
    c. empathy.
    d. separation anxiety.

14. Studies of institutionalized infants indicate that (p. 153)
    a. infants fail to form close emotional bonds with caregivers when adopted after the first year of life.
    b. when infants are adopted in early childhood, they easily form strong attachments to caregivers and cease to exhibit further social and emotional problems.
    c. children adopted as late as 4 to 6 years of age are able to form a first attachment bond, although they continue to display emotional and social problems.
    d. institutionalized children experience fully normal development, even in the absence of close attachment relationships.

15. Which attachment pattern is especially high among maltreated infants? (p. 153)
    a. avoidant
    b. resistant
    c. secure
    d. disorganized / disoriented

16. During the Strange Situation, baby Emmanuel seeks closeness to his mother and fails to explore. When his mother returns, Emmanuel cries and displays angry, aggressive behavior. Emmanuel most likely receives what kind of care from his mother? (pp. 151, 153)
    a. inconsistent
    b. overstimulating
    c. unresponsive
    d. neglectful

17. Toddlers become consciously aware of the self's physical features (p. 157)
    a. during the first 6 months.
    b. between 6 and 12 months.
    c. during the second year.
    d. after the second year.

18. When Sarah shows clear awareness of her mother's wishes and expectations and can obey simple requests and commands, she has become capable of (p. 158)
    a. resistance.
    b. compliance.
    c. avoidance.
    d. attachment.

19. Ronald waited for his parents to leave the room before he opened the jar to get a cookie. Ronald is exhibiting (p. 158)
    a. delay of gratification.
    b. compliance.
    c. attachment.
    d. avoidance.

20. As soon as children develop the ability to categorize themselves, they tend to show an increase in (p. 158)
    a. their capacity to resist an impulse to engage in socially disapproved behavior.
    b. their ability to understand another's emotional state.
    c. sociable play with peers.
    d. gender-stereotyped behaviors.

CHAPTER 7
PHYSICAL AND COGNITIVE DEVELOPMENT IN EARLY CHILDHOOD

BRIEF CHAPTER SUMMARY

While body growth slows during early childhood, the brain continues to grow faster than any other body structure. Lateralization increases, and handedness develops. Myelination continues, and connections between parts of the brain increase, supporting motor and cognitive development. Heredity influences physical growth by controlling the release of hormones, but environmental factors also play important roles. Malnutrition can interfere with physical development, and illness can interact with malnutrition to undermine children's growth. In industrialized countries, unintentional injuries are the leading cause of childhood mortality.

In early childhood, an explosion of new motor skills occurs, with each building on the simpler movement patterns of toddlerhood. As the child's center of gravity shifts toward the trunk and balance improves, gross motor skills are performed with greater speed and endurance. Fine motor skills, including self-help skills such as shoe-tying, also advance dramatically as control of the hands and fingers improves. Drawing begins in the toddler years with scribbling and progresses to representational forms and then to more complex, realistic drawings at age 5 or 6. Both gross and fine motor skills are influenced by a combination of heredity and environment.

The beginning of Piaget's preoperational stage is marked by an extraordinary increase in representational, or symbolic, activity, including language, which is the most flexible means of mental representation. Make-believe play is another example of the development of representation. By age 2½, children engage in sociodramatic play—make-believe with others—which increases rapidly over the next few years as children display growing awareness that make-believe is a representational activity. As adults point out similarities between models and real-world spaces, young children gain a grasp of symbol–real world relations—the understanding that an object can stand for another.

Piaget described preschool children in terms of their limitations compared with the capabilities of older children—for example, their egocentrism, animistic thinking, inability to conserve, irreversibility, and lack of hierarchical classification. Research has challenged this view, indicating that on simplified tasks based on familiar experiences, preschoolers do show the beginnings of logical thinking. A more flexible stage notion better describes the unique qualities of early childhood thinking. In contrast to Piaget, Vygotsky's sociocultural theory, which emphasizes the social context of cognitive development, regarded language as the foundation for all higher cognitive processes. As adults and skilled peers provide children with verbal guidance on challenging tasks, children incorporate these dialogues into their own self-directed, or private, speech. In this view, children learn within a zone of proximal development, attempting tasks too difficult to do alone but possible with the help of adults and more skilled peers. Vygotsky saw make-believe play as the ideal social context for fostering cognitive development in early childhood. Guided participation, an expansion of Vygotsky's concept of scaffolding, refers to shared endeavors between more expert and less expert participants, allowing for variations across situations and cultures.

Information-processing theorists focus on children's use of mental strategies; during early childhood, advances in representation and children's ability to guide their own behavior lead to more efficient ways of attending, manipulating information, and solving problems. Preschoolers also become better at planning. Although young children's recognition memory is very accurate, their recall for listlike information is much poorer than that of older children and adults, mostly because preschoolers use memory strategies less effectively. Like adults, young children remember everyday experiences in terms of scripts. As children's cognitive and conversational skills improve, their descriptions of special events become better organized, detailed, and related to the larger context of their own lives. Improvements in representation, memory, and problem solving contribute to the young child's theory of mind, or metacognition. Through informal experiences with written symbols, preschoolers engage in emergent literacy, making active efforts to understand how these symbols, as well as math concepts, convey meaning.

Children with warm, affectionate parents who stimulate language and academic knowledge and who make reasonable demands for mature behavior score higher on mental tests, especially when they also have access to educational toys and books. At-risk children show long-term benefits from early intervention and high-quality child care. In contrast, poor-quality child care undermines the development of all children. Exposure to educational media—both television and computers—is extremely common in industrialized nations, and both media can have value for emergent literacy and other aspects of cognitive development. The content of much entertainment programming has a controversial impact on social and emotional development.

Language development, including both word learning and grammar, proceeds rapidly in early childhood and is supported by conversational give-and-take. By the end of the preschool years, children have an extensive vocabulary, use most grammatical constructions competently, and are effective conversationalists.

LEARNING OBJECTIVES

After reading this chapter, you should be able to:

7.1 Describe major trends in body growth during early childhood. (p. 165)

7.2 Discuss brain development in early childhood, including handedness and changes in the cerebellum and the corpus callosum. (pp. 165–167)

7.3 Explain how heredity influences physical growth by controlling the production of hormones. (p. 168)

7.4 Describe the effects of nutrition and infectious disease on physical development. (pp. 168–169)

7.5 Summarize factors that increase the risk of unintentional injuries, and cite ways childhood injuries can be prevented. (pp. 169–170)

7.6 Cite major milestones of gross and fine-motor development in early childhood, including individual and sex differences. (pp. 171–173)

7.7 Describe advances in mental representation during the preschool years. (pp. 173–175)

7.8 Describe limitations of preoperational thought, and summarize the implications of recent research for the accuracy of the preoperational stage. (pp. 175–179)

7.9 Contrast Piaget's and Vygotsky's views on the development and significance of children's private speech, along with related evidence. (pp. 179–180)

7.10 Summarize challenges to Vygotsky's ideas. (pp. 180–181)

7.11 Describe changes in attention and memory during early childhood. (pp. 182–183)

7.12 Describe the young child's theory of mind. (pp. 183–184)

7.13 Summarize children's literacy and mathematical knowledge during early childhood. (pp. 184–186)

7.14 Describe early childhood intelligence tests and the impact of home, educational programs, child care, and media on mental development in early childhood. (pp. 187–190)

7.15 Trace the development of vocabulary, grammar, and conversational skills in early childhood. (pp. 190–192)

7.16 Cite factors that support language learning in early childhood. (pp. 192–193)

STUDY QUESTIONS

Physical Development

Body Growth

1. On the average, children add _____ inches in height and about _____ pounds in weight each year. (p. 165)

2. Between ages 2 and 6, approximately 45 new _____, or growth centers in which cartilage hardens into bone, emerge in various parts of the skeleton. (p. 165)

3. Explain how heredity and environment influence the age at which children lose their primary, or "baby," teeth. (p. 165)

   _____
   _____

4. An estimated _____ percent of North American 5-year-olds have tooth decay, a figure that rises to _____ percent by age 18. List three factors that increase the likelihood of tooth decay. (p. 165)

   A. _____
   B. _____
   C. _____

Brain Development

1. Between 2 and 6 years of age, the brain increases from _____ to _____ percent of its adult weight. (p. 165)

Changes in the Cerebral Cortex

1. The (right / left) hemisphere is especially active between 3 and 6 years of age and then levels off; in contrast, activity in the (right / left) hemisphere increases steadily throughout early and middle childhood. This helps explain the pattern of development of what two skills? (pp. 165–166)

   A. _____   B. _____

Handedness

1. A strong hand preference reflects the greater capacity of one side of the brain, or the _____, to carry out skilled motor action. (p. 167)

2. True or False: For right-handed people, language is housed with hand control in the left hemisphere of the brain. (p. 167)

3. For left-handers, language is typically shared between both hemispheres, which indicates that their brains tend to be (less / more) strongly lateralized than those of right-handers. (p. 167)

4. List three possible influences on handedness. (p. 167)

   A. _____
   _____

   B. _____
   _____

   C. _____
   _____

Other Advances in Brain Development

1. For each of the following brain structures, describe developmental changes in early childhood, and indicate their impact on children's physical and cognitive skills. (pp. 167–168)

   Cerebellum

   Changes: _____

   _____

   Impact: _____

   _____

   Corpus Callosum

   Changes: _____

   _____

   Impact: _____

   _____

Influences on Physical Growth and Health

Heredity and Hormones

1. The _____, located at the base of the brain, plays a critical role by releasing two hormones that induce growth. (p. 168)

2. Without *growth hormone (GH)*, children reach an average mature height of only about _____. (p. 168)

3. How does treatment with injections of GH influence growth in GH-deficient children? (p. 168)

   _____

4. _____ stimulates the release of thyroxin, which is necessary for normal development of the nerve cells of the brain and for GH to have its full impact on body size. (p. 168)

Nutrition

1. True or False: During early childhood, many children become picky eaters. (p. 168)

2. Why does appetite decline in early childhood? Explain why preschoolers' wariness of new foods is adaptive. (p. 168)

   A. _____

   B. _____

3. Cite two factors that influence young children's food preferences. (p. 168)

   A. _____

   B. _____

Infectious Disease

1. Describe the relationship between infectious disease and malnutrition. (p. 169)

   _____
   _____
   _____

2. Most growth retardation and deaths due to diarrhea can be prevented with a nearly cost-free _____, a glucose, salt, and water solution that quickly replaces fluids the body loses. (p. 169)

3. Overall, _____ percent of American preschoolers lack essential immunizations, a rate that rises to _____ percent for poverty-stricken preschoolers. Fewer than _____ percent of preschoolers lack immunizations in Canada, Great Britain, the Netherlands, and Sweden. (p. 169)

4. What are some causes of inadequate immunization in the United States? (p. 169)

   _____
   _____

5. True or False: Large-scale studies show no association between the measles-mumps-rubella vaccine and the rise in the number of children diagnosed with autism. (p. 169)

Childhood Injuries

1. What is the leading cause of childhood mortality in industrialized countries? (p. 169)

   _____

2. List the three most common injuries during the early childhood years. (p. 169)

   A. _____ B. _____

   C. _____

3. Because of their higher activity level and greater willingness to take risks, (boys / girls) are 1.5 times more likely to be injured than (boys / girls). (p. 170)

4. Describe family characteristics associated with injury. (p. 170)

   _____
   _____
   _____

5. Provide reasons for the high childhood injury rates in the United States and Canada. (p. 170)

   _____
   _____
   _____

6. True or False: About 10 percent of Canadian parents and 40 percent of American parents fail to place their preschoolers in car safety seats. (p. 170)

7. Briefly describe three factors that can help prevent childhood injuries. (p. 170)

   A. _____

   B. _____

   C. _____

Motor Development

Gross Motor Development

1. As children's bodies become more streamlined and less top-heavy, their center of gravity shifts downward, and as a result, _____ improves greatly, paving the way for new motor skills involving the large muscles of the body. (p. 171)

2. Briefly summarize advances in gross motor development during the preschool years. (p. 171)

   _____
   _____
   _____

Fine Motor Development

1. Fine motor development is most apparent in what two areas? (p. 171)

   A. _____   B. _____

2. List and briefly describe the sequence in which drawing develops in early childhood. (pp. 171–172)

   A. _____
   B. _____
   C. _____

3. True or False: From the beginning, children distinguish writing from drawing. (p. 172)

4. True or False: Between ages 4 and 6, children begin to realize that writing stands for language. (p. 172)

Individual Differences in Motor Skills

1. Describe sex differences in motor development during early childhood. (p. 172)

   _____
   _____
   _____

2. Provide an example of how social pressures might exaggerate small, genetically based sex differences in motor skills. (p. 172)

   _____
   _____

3. True or False: Preschoolers exposed to formal lessons in motor skills are generally ahead in motor development. (p. 172)

4. How does the social climate created by adults affect preschoolers' motor development? (pp. 172–173)

   _____
   _____
   _____

Cognitive Development

Piaget's Theory: The Preoperational Stage

1. As children move from the sensorimotor to the *preoperational stage,* the most obvious change is an extraordinary increase in _____. (p. 173)

Mental Representation

1. According to Piaget, _____ is the most flexible means of mental representation. (p. 173)

2. True or False: Piaget believed that language plays a major role in cognitive development. (p. 173)

Make-Believe Play

1. List and provide an example of three important changes in make-believe play that take place in early childhood. (pp. 173–174)

    A. _____

    Example: _____

    B. _____

    Example: _____

    C. _____

    Example: _____

2. Summarize contributions of make-believe play to children's cognitive and social development. (p. 174)

    _____

    _____

    _____

Symbol–Real World Relations

1. Around age 3, children begin to understand _____, or the ability to view a symbolic object as both an object in its own right and a symbol. (p. 175)

2. Explain how children grasp the dual representation of symbolic objects. (p. 175)

    _____

    _____

    _____

Limitations of Preoperational Thought

1. Piaget described preschoolers in terms of what they (can / cannot) understand. (p. 175)

2. According to Piaget, young children are not capable of _____, or mental actions that obey logical rules. (p. 175)

3. For Piaget, the most fundamental deficiency of preoperational thinking is _____, or failure to distinguish the symbolic viewpoints of others from one's own. (p. 175)

4. The belief that inanimate objects have lifelike qualities, such as thoughts, wishes, and intentions is called _____. (p. 175)

5. Explain the meaning of *conservation*. (p. 175)

6. Match each of the following features of preoperational thought with the appropriate description. (pp. 175–176)

   _____ Cannot mentally go through a series of steps and then return to the starting point
   _____ Treats initial and final states as unrelated events
   _____ Focuses on one aspect of a situation to the neglect of other features

   1. Centration
   2. Focus on states, not dynamic transformations
   3. Irreversibility

7. Preschoolers' performance on Piaget's class inclusion problem illustrates their difficulty with _____. (p. 176)

Follow-Up Research on Preoperational Thought

1. True or False: Current research supports Piaget's account of a cognitively deficient preschooler. (pp. 176–177)

2. Cite an example of a nonegocentric response in preschoolers' everyday interactions. (p. 177)

3. Between ages 4 and 8, as familiarity with physical events and principles increases, children's magical beliefs (increase / decline). (p. 177)

4. When preschoolers are given tasks that are simplified and relevant to their everyday lives, they do better than Piaget might have expected. Provide an example illustrating this point. (p. 177)

5. By the _____ year of life, children easily move back and forth between basic-level categories and superordinate categories, such as "furniture." (p. 177)

6. How can adults help guide children's inferences about categories? (p. 177)

7. Explain why preschoolers have difficulty distinguishing appearance from reality. (p. 178)

Evaluation of the Preoperational Stage

1. Provide an example that illustrates preschoolers' gradual understanding of logical operations. (p. 179)

2. Some neo-Piagetian theorists combine Piaget's stage approach with the information-processing emphasis on task-specific change. Briefly describe this viewpoint. (p. 179)

Vygotsky's Sociocultural Theory

1. Vygotsky's sociocultural theory stresses the _____ context of cognitive development. (p. 179)

Private Speech

1. Contrast Piaget's view of children's self-directed speech with that of Vygotsky. (p. 179)

    Piaget: _____

    _____

    Vygotsky: _____

    _____

2. Most research findings have supported (Piaget's / Vygotsky's) view of children's private speech. (p. 179)

3. Under what circumstances are children likely to use private speech? (p. 179)

    _____

    _____

Social Origins of Early Childhood Cognition

1. Vygotsky believed that children's learning takes place within a *zone of proximal development*. Explain what this means, and provide an example. (pp. 179–180)

    A. _____

    B. _____

2. _____ involves adjusting the support offered during a teaching session to fit the child's current level of performance. (p. 180)

Vygotsky's View of Make-Believe Play

1. According to Vygotsky, how is make-believe play an ideal social context for cognitive development in early childhood? (p. 180)

    _____

    _____

2. Pretending is rich in _____, a finding that supports its role in helping children bring action under the control of thought. (p. 180)

Evaluation of Vygotsky's Theory

1. True or False: Vygotsky's theory underscores the vital role of teaching in cognitive development. (p. 180)

2. _____, a broader concept than scaffolding, accounts for children's diverse ways of learning through involvement with others. (p. 181)

3. Discuss the limitations of Vygotsky's theory regarding the development of basic cognitive processes. (p. 181)

    _____

    _____

    _____

Cultural Influences: Children in Village and Tribal Cultures
Observe and Participate in Adult Work

1. Describe differences in the daily lives of children in the two U.S. middle-SES suburbs compared to the Efe and Mayan children. (p. 181)

   U.S.: _____

   _____

   Efe and Mayan: _____

   _____

2. Explain how Mayan parents interact with their children. What skills do Mayan children have that are not commonly observed in Western children? (p. 181)

   A. _____

   _____

   B. _____

   _____

Information Processing

Attention

1. What two abilities contribute to steady gains in preschoolers' capacity to sustain attention? (p. 182)

   A. _____

   B. _____

2. Under which conditions are preschoolers able to generate and follow a plan? (p. 182)

   _____

   _____

3. Provide examples of activities that support and encourage preschoolers' developing ability to plan. (p. 182)

   _____

   _____

Memory

1. True or False: Preschoolers' recognition memory is much better than their recall memory. (p. 182)

2. What explains preschoolers' deficiency in recall? (pp. 182–183)

   _____

3. Explain why young children seldom use memory strategies. (p. 183)

   _____

   _____

4. Like adults, preschoolers remember familiar experiences in terms of _____, general descriptions of what occurs and when it occurs in a particular situation. (p 183)

5. Describe the importance of preschoolers' use of scripts. (p. 183)

6. Adults use two styles for prompting children's autobiographical narratives. List and briefly describe them. (p. 183)

   A. _____

   B. _____

The Young Child's Theory of Mind

1. A theory of mind, also called _____, is a coherent set of ideas about mental activities. (p. 183)

2. Describe children's developing awareness of mental life during the following preschool years. (p. 184)

   By age 3: _____

   Age 4 and on: _____

3. True or False: Across diverse cultural and SES backgrounds, false-belief understanding strengthens between ages 4 and 6, and becomes a good predictor of social skills. (p. 184)

4. List four factors that contribute to preschoolers' theory of mind. (p. 184)

   A. _____
   B. _____
   C. _____
   D. _____

5. Discuss limitations in preschoolers' awareness of mental activities. (p. 184)

Biology and Environment: "Mindblindness" and Autism

1. The term *autism* means _____. (p. 185)

2. Cite three core areas of functioning that are deficient in children with autism. (p. 185)

   A. _____
   B. _____
   C. _____

3. True or False: Researchers agree that autism stems from abnormal brain functioning, usually due to genetic or prenatal environmental conditions. (p. 185)

4. Children with autism have (an efficient / a deficient) theory of mind. Explain what this means. (p. 185)

_____
_____
_____

5. What deficits do children with autism display in the development of understanding mental life? (p. 185)

_____
_____
_____

6. How does impairment in executive processing affect children with autism? (p. 185)

_____
_____
_____

Early Childhood Literacy

1. True or False: Preschoolers understand a great deal about written language long before they are able to read and write. (p. 184)

2. What is *emergent literacy*? (p. 185)

_____
_____

3. List ways adults can foster young children's literacy development. (p. 186)

_____
_____

Young Children's Mathematical Reasoning

1. List four steps in the development of preschoolers' mathematical reasoning that correspond with the following general age ranges. (p. 186)

    Between 14 and 16 months: _____

    Between 2½ and 3½ years: _____

    Between 3½ and 4 years: _____

    Around 4 years: _____

2. Provide examples of ways adults can promote preschoolers' mathematical skills. (p. 186)

_____
_____

Individual Differences in Mental Development

1. Why do low-SES and certain ethnic minority preschoolers often do poorly on intelligence tests? What steps can be taken to help improve their performance? (p. 187)

    A. _____

    B. _____

2. Intelligence tests (do / do not) sample all human abilities, and performance (is / is not) affected by cultural and situational factors. (p. 187)

3. Despite their flaws, intelligence test scores remain important. Explain why. (p. 187)

    _____
    _____
    _____

Home Environment and Mental Development

1. Describe characteristics of homes that foster young children's intellectual growth. (p. 187)

    _____
    _____
    _____
    _____

2. True or False: When low-SES parents manage, despite daily pressures, to obtain high HOME scores, their preschoolers perform substantially better on intelligence tests. (p. 187)

Preschool, Kindergarten, and Child Care

1. Over the past several decades, the number of young children in preschool or child care has steadily increased, reaching nearly _____ percent in the United States and in some Canadian provinces. (p. 187)

2. Describe the difference between child-centered preschool programs and academic preschool programs. (p. 187)

    Child-centered: _____
    _____

    Academic: _____
    _____

3. How do formal academic programs undermine preschooler's motivation and emotional well-being? (pp. 187–188)

    _____
    _____
    _____

4. Describe the features of *Project Head Start* and Canada's *Aboriginal Head Start*. (p. 188)

    A. _____
    _____

    B. _____
    _____

5. Briefly summarize the long-term benefits of preschool intervention. (p. 188)

6. True or False: Research suggests that gains in IQ and achievement scores from attending Head Start and other interventions are maintained across the school years. (p. 188)

7. Discuss the long-term benefits to children who participated in the High/Scope Perry Preschool Project. (p. 188)

8. Describe the outcomes for children in substandard child care versus high-quality child care. (p. 189)

    Substandard: _____

    High quality: _____

Educational Media

1. Describe the benefits of watching *Sesame Street*. (p. 190)

2. The average North American 2- to 6-year-old watches TV for _____ hours a day. _____ children are more frequent viewers, perhaps because few alternative forms of entertainment are available in their neighborhoods or affordable for their parents. (p. 190)

3. What does research reveal about the effects of heavy TV viewing on children's cognitive development? (p. 190)

4. How do computer word-processing programs support emergent literacy? (p. 190)

5. True or False: Computer programming experiences using simplified computer languages lead to gains in preschoolers' problem-solving skills and metacognition. (p. 190)

Language Development

Vocabulary

1. True or False: Preschoolers learn an average of five new words each day, increasing their vocabulary from 200 words at age 2 to 10,000 at age 6. (p. 190)

2. A process called _____ contributes to children's rapid vocabulary growth over the preschool years. (p. 191)

3. What explains Chinese-, Japanese-, and Korean-speaking children's especially rapid acquisition of verbs? (p. 191)

4. When young preschoolers assume that words refer to entirely separate categories, they are applying the principle of _____. (p. 191)

5. What do preschoolers do to differentiate objects that have more than one name? (p. 191)

6. When are preschoolers most successful at figuring out new word meanings? (p. 191)

Grammar

1. True or False: All English-speaking children master grammatical markers in a regular sequence. (p. 192)

2. Once children acquire grammatical markers, they apply them so consistently that they occasionally overextend the rules to words that are exceptions, a type of error called _____. (p. 192)

3. Briefly describe the predictable errors preschoolers make in forming questions and demonstrating their understanding of the passive voice. (p. 192)

   Questions: _____

   Passive voice: _____

4. True or False: By the end of the preschool years, children have mastered most of the grammatical constructions of their language. (p. 192)

Conversation

1. The practical, social side of language is called _____. (p. 192)

2. Cite evidence that at the beginning of early childhood, children are already skilled conversationalists. (p. 192)

3. By age 4, children (do / do not) adjust their speech to fit the age, sex, and social status of the listener. (p. 192)

Supporting Language Development in Early Childhood

1. Describe two techniques adults use to promote early language skills. (p. 193)

    A. _____

    B. _____

2. Adults provide subtle, indirect feedback about grammar using two strategies. List and briefly describe these strategies. (p. 193)

    A. _____

    B. _____

ASK YOURSELF . . .

For *Ask Yourself* questions for this chapter, please log on to the Companion Website at *www.ablongman.com/berk*.

1. Select the Companion Website for *Exploring Lifespan Development*.
2. Use the "Jump to" menu to go directly to this chapter.
3. From the menu on the left side of the screen, select "Ask Yourself."
4. Complete questions and choose "Submit answers for grading" or "Clear answers" to start over.

SUGGESTED STUDENT READINGS

De Haan, M., & Johnson, M. H. (Eds.). (2003). *The cognitive neuroscience of development*. New York: Psychology Press. Examines the influence of biology and environment on cognitive development. Topics include attention and memory development, language development, the importance of early childhood experiences, and methods used to study cognitive development.

Golomb, C. (2004). *The child's creation of a pictorial world* (2nd ed.). Mahwah, NJ: Erlbaum. Using a developmental framework, this book examines the emergence of artistic skills in young children. The author combines theoretical perspectives with research on average, emotionally disturbed, and exceptional children.

Paley, V. G. (2005). *A child's work: The importance of fantasy play*. Chicago, IL: University of Chicago Press. A collection of chapters highlighting the developmental importance of play in childhood, including strategies for parents and educators on how to incorporate play into a child's daily routine.

Schneider, W., Schumann-Hengsteler, R., & Sodian, B. (2004). *Young children's cognitive development: Interrelationships among executive functioning, working memory, verbal ability, and theory of mind*. Mahwah, NJ: Erlbaum. Using research by leading experts in the field, this book examines how advances in information processing contribute to young children's cognitive development.

PUZZLE 7.1 TERM REVIEW

Across
6. The tendency to focus on one aspect of a situation to the exclusion of other important features
8. Inability to mentally go through a series of steps in a problem and then reverse direction, returning to the starting point
10. _____ stimulating hormone: pituitary hormone that stimulates the thyroid gland to produce thyroxine
12. Brain structure that aids in balance and control of body movements
13. _____ thinking: belief that inanimate objects have lifelike qualities
14. The _____ cerebral hemisphere is the hemisphere of the brain responsible for skilled motor action

Down
1. Piaget's second stage in which rapid development of representation takes place
2. The _____ gland, located near the base of the brain, releases hormones affecting physical growth
3. Dual _____: viewing a symbolic object as both an object in its own right and a symbol
4. The understanding that certain physical properties of objects remain the same, even when their outward appearance changes
5. _____ play: make-believe play with others
7. _____ classification: organization of objects into classes and subclasses based on similarities and differences
9. The tendency to focus on one's own viewpoint and ignore others' perspectives
11. _____ hormone is a pituitary hormone that affects the development of almost all body tissues
12. Corpus _____: large bundle of fibers that connects the two hemispheres of the brain

PUZZLE 7.2 TERM REVIEW

Across
1. _____ Head Start: program initiated in Canada that provides low-income children with preschool education and nutritional and health services
6. Adult responses that elaborate on children's speech, increasing its complexity
7. Principle specifying order relationships between quantities
8. Connecting a new word with an underlying concept after only a brief encounter (2 words, hyph.)
10. Changing quality of support over a teaching session in which adults adjust the assistance they provide to fit the child's current level of performance
11. Mathematical principle that the last number in a counting sequence indicates the quantity of items in the set
15. Preschools in which teachers provide a wide variety of activities from which the children select and most of the day is devoted to free play (2 words, hyph.)
16. Thinking about thought; awareness of mental activities
18. _____ strategies: deliberate mental activities that improve the likelihood of remembering

Down
2. Application of regular grammatical rules to words that are exceptions
3. The practical, social side of language that is concerned with how to engage in effective and appropriate communication with others
4. _____ speech: self-directed speech that children use to plan and guide their own behavior
5. General descriptions of what occurs and when it occurs in a particular situation
9. _____ participation refers to shared endeavors between more expert and less expert participants, without specifying the precise features of communication
12. Project _____ is a federally funded program that provides low-income children with a year or two of preschool, as well as encouraging parent involvement in children's development. (2 words)
13. _____ programs: preschools in which teachers structure the program, training children in academic skills through repetition and drill
14. Adult responses that restructure children's incorrect speech into a more mature form
17. _____ literacy: attempt to figure out how written symbols convey meaning

PRACTICE TEST #1

1. Individual differences in body size are most apparent in (p. 165)
   a. infancy.
   b. toddlerhood.
   c. early childhood.
   d. middle childhood.

2. How is lateralization different for right-handers versus left-handers? (p. 167)
   a. Language skills are housed in the right hemisphere for right-handers and in the left hemisphere for left-handers.
   b. Language skills are shared between both hemispheres for right-handers.
   c. Language skills are shared between both hemispheres for left-handers.
   d. The research is inconclusive on hemispheric control related to handedness.

3. As baby Susie is learning to walk, the area of her brain that is most helpful in her balance and the control of her body is the (p. 167)
   a. cerebellum.
   b. corpus callosum.
   c. frontal lobe.
   d. dominant cerebral hemisphere.

4. The pituitary gland plays a critical role in growth by releasing which two hormones? (p. 168)
   a. growth hormone and estrogen
   b. growth hormone and thyroid-stimulating hormone
   c. thyroid-stimulating hormone and testosterone
   d. thyroxine and thyroid-stimulating hormone

5. Of the following nations, which has the LOWEST percentage of fully immunized preschoolers? (p. 169)
   a. Canada
   b. Great Britain
   c. Sweden
   d. United States

6. Boys are 1.5 times more likely to be injured than girls because (p. 170)
   a. there are 1.5 times as many boys as girls.
   b. boys' bodies are less suited to physical strain.
   c. boys display higher activity levels and greater willingness to take risks.
   d. girls tend to complain less and more injuries go unnoticed.

7. The leading cause of death among children over 1 year of age is (p. 169)
   a. motor vehicle collisions.
   b. infectious diseases.
   c. drowning.
   d. choking.

8. Which of the following children is most at-risk for experiencing a serious injury? (p. 170)
   a. Keri, a 6-year-old girl who lives in a middle-class neighborhood
   b. Sam, a 3-year-old boy whose father is a teacher and mother is a stay-at-home mom
   c. Winston, a 5-year-old boy living in the inner city with his unemployed mother and five siblings
   d. Valencia, a 6-year-old girl who lives with her father and older sister in a small, rural town with most of her extended family living nearby

9. Gross motor development involves improvement in the child's ability to (p. 171)
   a. put puzzles together.
   b. build with small blocks.
   c. cut and paste.
   d. throw and catch a ball.

10. Sex differences in motor skills are apparent in early childhood. Boys have an edge in (p. 172)
    a. gross motor skills that require balance.
    b. fine motor skills.
    c. precision of movement.
    d. skills that emphasize power.

11. The preoperational stage of child development spans the years of (p. 173)
    a. 1 to 4.
    b. 2 to 7.
    c. 5 to 10.
    d. 9 to 13.

12. Dante's mother has recently noticed some significant changes in his play. For example, she saw him using the television remote as a telephone, holding it up to his ear and talking into it. Dante's play illustrates which of the following changes in symbolic mastery? (pp. 173–174)
    a. Over time, play increasingly detaches from real-life conditions associated with it.
    b. Play becomes less self-centered with age.
    c. Play gradually includes more complex scheme combinations.
    d. Play remains egocentric throughout early childhood.

13. Viewing a symbolic object as both an object in its own right and a symbolic object is referred to as (p. 175)
    a. centration.
    b. animistic thinking.
    c. dual representation.
    d. make-believe play.

14. Piaget's famous class inclusion problem demonstrated the difficulty preschoolers have with (p. 176)
    a. egocentrism.
    b. conservation.
    c. centration.
    d. hierarchical classification.

15. Vygotsky challenged Piaget's theory with his (p. 179)
    a. education theory.
    b. sociocultural theory.
    c. preoperational theory.
    d. motor development theory.

16. According to Vygotsky's theory, the force that drives a child's cognitive development is (p. 180)
    a. joint activities with adults or more competent peers.
    b. interaction with the physical environment.
    c. the biological unfolding of genetic structures.
    d. the physical world acting on the child.

17. When asked the question, "Can you tell me what happens when you go to the doctor's office?" Yvonne answers, "The nurse gives you a shot, the doctor checks your heart, you get a lollipop, and then you go home." This is an example of a(n) (p. 183)
    a. verbatim memory.
    b. autobiographical memory.
    c. script.
    d. semantic memory.

18. In North America, the typical 2- to 6-year-old watches TV (p. 190)
    a. for less than an hour a day.
    b. from 1½ to 2 hours a day.
    c. for 3½ hours a day.
    d. for more than 4 hours a day.

19. Research shows that children are able to build their vocabularies quickly through a process called (pp. 190–191)
    a. metacognition.
    b. fast-mapping.
    c. scripting.
    d. ordinality.

20. Pragmatics refers to (p. 192)
    a. restructuring inaccurate speech into correct form.
    b. the ability to connect new words with their underlying concepts after only a brief encounter.
    c. elaborating on children's speech, increasing its complexity.
    d. the practical, social side of language.

PRACTICE TEST #2

1. Which of the following suggests that the two hemispheres of the brain continue to lateralize throughout childhood and adolescence? (p. 166)
    a. Language skills increase at an astonishing pace in early childhood, whereas spatial skills develop gradually over childhood and adolescence.
    b. Children experiment with their right and left hands, eventually developing a strong hand preference in middle childhood.
    c. For most children, language is shared between the two hemispheres.
    d. Mathematical skills develop more slowly than language skills.

2. Handedness reflects the greater capacity of one side of the brain, often referred to as the individual's (p. 167)
    a. greater cerebellum.
    b. corpus callosum.
    c. dominant hierarchical classification.
    d. dominant cerebral hemisphere.

3. Stephen might only grow to four feet, four inches if he lacks (p. 168)
    a. growth hormone.
    b. thyroid-stimulating hormone.
    c. corpus callosum.
    d. pituitary hormone.

4. Dramatic gains in motor control at the end of the preschool years can be attributed to completed myelinization of the fibers linking the (p. 167)
    a. left and right hemispheres.
    b. corpus callosum and cerebellum.
    c. cerebellum and cerebral cortex.
    d. cerebral cortex and corpus callosum.

5. Why must children born with a thyroxine deficiency receive it at once? (p. 168)
    a. Thyroxine is necessary for brain development and growth. Its absence results in mental retardation and stunted growth.
    b. Thyroxine controls heart rate. Its absence results in cardiac distress.
    c. Thyroxine is necessary for the air sacs in the lungs to function properly. Its absence causes anoxia.
    d. Children with thyroxine deficiencies are at-risk for developing an insufficient central nervous system and abnormal genitals.

6. Bailey's parents often eat rice and seafood. Research on nutrition in early childhood suggests that Bailey will (p. 168)
    a. reject these foods.
    b. eat rice but not seafood.
    c. likely develop an allergy to these foods.
    d. also prefer rice and seafood.

7. As children move from the sensorimotor to the preoperational stage, the most obvious change is (p. 173)
    a. an increase in the child's use of senses and movements to explore the world.
    b. development of the capacity for abstract, scientific reasoning.
    c. an increase in representational, or symbolic, activity.
    d. more logical, flexible, and organized thought.

8. As 3-year-old Garry begins make-believe play with others, he is engaging in (p. 174)
    a. sociodramatic play.
    b. self-centered play.
    c. preoperational play.
    d. egocentric play.

9. Research on the benefits of make-believe play indicates that (p. 174)
    a. play contributes to certain mental abilities, such as attention and memory, but does little to support children's social skills.
    b. children who spend more time in make-believe are rated as more socially competent by their teachers.
    c. the benefits only apply to children living in middle-income homes.
    d. children who spend a great deal of time playing are more intelligent than their peers but often interact with others in an immature, make-believe manner.

10. The 2½-year-old who has trouble viewing a symbolic object as both an object in its own right and as a symbol is not yet capable of (p. 175)
    a. sociodramatic play.
    b. preoperational imaging.
    c. dual representation.
    d. egocentrism.

11. Three-year-old Grace, who explains that it rains when the clouds are sad and crying, is demonstrating (p. 175)
    a. egocentrism.
    b. animistic thinking.
    c. reversibility.
    d. centration.

12. For Piaget, the most fundamental deficiency of preoperational thinking is (p. 175)
    a. irreversibility.
    b. egocentrism.
    c. centration.
    d. hierarchical classification.

13. When Lily coddles her doll after it falls on the floor, then tells her mother that the doll is sad, she is displaying (p. 175)
    a. animistic thinking.
    b. illogical thought.
    c. centration.
    d. irreversibility.

14. Current research on preoperational thought indicates that when preschoolers are presented with familiar objects, they (p. 177)
    a. continue to give egocentric responses.
    b. show clear awareness of others' viewpoints.
    c. show the beginnings of logical operations.
    d. perform worse than when unfamiliar objects are used.

15. Over the past three decades, almost all studies have (p. 179)
    a. maintained a Piagetian approach to language and learning.
    b. supported the egocentric speech theory.
    c. supported Vygotsky's perspective on private speech.
    d. rejected both Piaget and Vygotsky's theories.

16. Research on planning indicates that (p. 182)
    a. the ability to generate and follow plans emerges during the elementary school years.
    b. even when young children design effective plans, they often forget to implement important steps.
    c. the development of planning is not directly related to changes in other cognitive processes.
    d. when children use rehearsal, it has little impact on performance.

17. As memory and problem solving improve, children start to reflect on their own thought processes. This understanding is called (p. 183)
    a. metacognition.
    b. scripting.
    c. scaffolding.
    d. ordinality.

18. As 4-year-old Christian begins to figure out how written symbols convey meaning, he is displaying (p. 185)
    a. metacognition.
    b. scaffolding.
    c. emergent literacy.
    d. scripting.

19. By age 3½ to 4, most children grasp the vital principle of cardinality, which means they understand that (p. 186)
    a. there is an order relationship between quantities, such that three is more than two.
    b. written symbols convey meaning.
    c. the last number in a counting sequence indicates the quantity of items in a set.
    d. both beliefs and desires determine behavior.

20. Young Xiao Chu says, "I go school, too." Her mother says, "Yes, you are going to school, too." Her mother's response would be classified as (p. 193)
    a. repetition and correction.
    b. correction and reflection.
    c. rejection and restatement.
    d. expansion and recast.

CHAPTER 8
EMOTIONAL AND SOCIAL DEVELOPMENT IN EARLY CHILDHOOD

BRIEF CHAPTER SUMMARY

Erikson identified the psychological conflict of the preschool years as initiative versus guilt. Through play, children practice using new skills and cooperating to achieve common goals. Conscience development prompts children to feel guilt for disobeying society's standards; excessive guilt interferes with initiative.

As they begin to view themselves as having both physical and psychological attributes, preschoolers develop a self-concept, which is initially based on observable characteristics but soon expands to include typical emotions and attitudes. Through conversations with adults, children develop autobiographical memory—a sense of the self in relation to the social context. By age 4, children develop several separate self-judgments based on performance in different areas; together, these make up self-esteem, which affects long-term psychological adjustment.

Between ages 2 and 6, children make gains in emotional competence, experiencing the self-conscious emotions of pride and shame, as well as empathy. By age 4 or 5, children can correctly judge the causes of many basic emotions and understand that thinking and feeling are related. Emotional outbursts decline as children use effortful control to achieve emotional self-regulation. Temperament plays a role; so do children's observations of adult strategies for handling their own feelings. To induce adaptive levels of shame and pride, parents should focus on how to improve performance and should avoid labeling the child.

The capacity for empathy, an important motivator of prosocial behavior, increases as children develop the ability to take another's perspective. Preschoolers form first friendships with peers and move from nonsocial activity to parallel play and then to social interaction. The beginnings of moral development are evident by age 2, when children can evaluate behavior as good or bad. Conscience gradually comes to be regulated by inner standards. Children whose parents discipline with physical punishment or withdrawal of affection tend to misbehave more often and feel little guilt. A more effective disciplinary approach is induction, in which an adult supports conscience formation and encourages empathy and sympathy by pointing out the effects of misbehavior on others.

According to social learning theory, morality is acquired through reinforcement and modeling—observing and imitating people who behave appropriately. Harsh punishment is an ineffective disciplinary tactic, promoting momentary compliance but no lasting change. Positive alternatives, such as time out and withdrawal of privileges, are more effective. Unfortunately, use of corporal punishment is common in North America.

All children occasionally display aggression. Instrumental aggression occurs when a child wants something and attacks a person who is in the way, while hostile aggression, intended to hurt another person, can take several forms: physical, verbal, or relational. A conflict-ridden family atmosphere and exposure to media violence promote aggressive behavior, leading children to see the world from a violent perspective. Treatment for aggressive children should break the cycle of hostilities between family members and promote effective ways of relating to others, while also teaching parents effective techniques for interacting with an aggressive child.

Gender typing develops rapidly in the preschool years. Heredity, through prenatal hormones, contributes to boys' higher activity level and overt aggression and to children's preference for same-sex playmates. At the same time, parents, teachers, peers, and the broader social environment encourage many gender-typed responses. Masculine and androgynous identities are linked to better psychological adjustment. Neither cognitive-developmental theory nor social learning theory provides a complete account of the development of gender identity. Gender schema theory is an information-processing approach to gender typing that combines social learning and cognitive developmental features. It emphasizes that both environmental pressures and children's cognition combine to affect gender-role development. Parents and teachers help children avoid gender stereotyping by modeling and providing alternatives to traditional gender roles.

Child-rearing styles can be distinguished on the basis of three features: acceptance and involvement, control, and autonomy granting. The most successful style is authoritative child rearing, which combines high acceptance and involvement, adaptive control techniques, and appropriate autonomy granting. Authoritarian child rearing is low in acceptance, involvement, and autonomy granting, and high in coercive control. The permissive style is warm and accepting, but uninvolved. Uninvolved parenting is low in acceptance, involvement, and control; at the extreme, it can be considered neglect.

Child maltreatment, which can take the form of physical, sexual, or emotional abuse, is the result of factors at the family, community, and cultural levels. Interventions at all of these levels are essential for preventing it.

LEARNING OBJECTIVES

After reading this chapter, you should be able to:

8.1 Describe major personality changes that take place during Erikson's stage of initiative versus guilt. (pp. 198–199)

8.2 Discuss preschool children's self-development, including characteristics of self-concepts and the emergence of self-esteem. (pp. 199–200)

8.3 Cite changes in understanding and expression of emotion during early childhood, along with factors that influence those changes. (p. 200)

8.4 Explain how language and temperament contribute to the development of emotional self-regulation during the preschool years. (pp. 200-201)

8.5 Discuss the development of self-conscious emotions, empathy, sympathy, and prosocial behavior during early childhood, noting the influence of parenting. (p. 201)

8.6 Describe advances in peer sociability and in friendship in early childhood, along with parental influences on early peer relations. (pp. 201–204)

8.7 Compare psychoanalytic, social learning, and cognitive-developmental approaches to moral development, and cite child-rearing practices that support or undermine moral understanding. (pp. 204–209)

8.8 Describe the development of aggression in early childhood, noting the influences of family and television, and cite strategies for controlling aggressive behavior. (pp. 209–211)

8.9 Discuss genetic and environmental influences on preschoolers' gender-stereotyped beliefs and behavior. (pp. 211–214)

8.10 Describe and evaluate the accuracy of major theories of gender identity, including ways to reduce gender stereotyping in young children. (pp. 214–215)

8.11 Describe the impact of child-rearing styles on children's development, explain why authoritative parenting is effective, and note cultural variations in child-rearing beliefs and practices. (pp. 215–218)

8.12 Discuss the multiple origins of child maltreatment, its consequences for development, and effective prevention. (pp. 218–219)

STUDY QUESTIONS

Erikson's Theory: Initiative versus Guilt

1. Define *initiative,* and describe how it is exhibited in preschoolers. (p. 198)

_____
_____
_____

2. Explain why Erikson regarded play as the central means through which children learn about themselves and their social world. (p. 199)

___

3. According to Erikson, what leads to a negative resolution of initiative versus guilt? (p. 199)

___

Self-Understanding

Foundations of Self-Concept

1. Preschoolers' self-concepts are very (abstract / concrete). (p. 199)

2. Describe preschoolers' developing understanding of emotions and attitudes. (p. 199)

___

3. Explain the link between preschoolers' self-development and their possessiveness of objects. Given this information, how can adults promote friendly peer interaction? (p. 199)

___

Emergence of Self-Esteem

1. Cite an example of a common self-judgment in early childhood. (p. 200)

___

2. True or False: When making self-evaluations, preschoolers tend to rate their own ability as extremely low and often overestimate task difficulty. (p. 200)

3. List three ways adults can avoid promoting low self-esteem and self-defeating reactions in preschoolers. (p. 200)

A. ___

B. ___

C. ___

Emotional Development

1. List three developmental gains that support emotional development in early childhood. (p. 200)

    A. _____

    B. _____

    C. _____

Understanding Emotions

1. Preschoolers' explanations of basic emotions tend to emphasize (external / internal) factors over (external / internal) states, a balance that changes with age. (p. 200)

2. Preschoolers (do / do not) realize that thoughts and feelings are interconnected. (p. 200)

3. True or False: In situations with conflicting cues about how a person is feeling, preschoolers can easily reconcile this differing information. (p. 200)

4. How can parents increase children's emotional understanding? (p. 200)

    _____

    _____

5. Describe how make-believe play contributes to children's emotional understanding. (p. 200)

    _____

    _____

    _____

Emotional Self-Regulation

1. True or False: Language contributes to preschoolers' improved emotional self-regulation. (p. 200)

2. List three strategies that preschoolers use to control their emotions. (p. 200)

    A. _____

    B. _____

    C. _____

3. What is *effortful control,* and how does it help preschoolers manage emotion? (p. 200)

    _____

    _____

    _____

4. Explain how parents influence the development of emotional self-regulation in early childhood. (p. 200)

    _____

    _____

5. Temperament (does / does not) play a role in emotional self-regulation. (pp. 200–201)

Self-Conscious Emotions

1. True or False: By age 3, self-conscious emotions are clearly linked to self-evaluation; however, preschoolers rely on adults' messages for information on when to feel proud, ashamed, or guilty. (p. 201)

2. Explain the role of parental feedback in the development of shame and pride. (p. 201)
   _____
   _____
   _____

3. Among Western children, intense (guilt / shame) is associated with feelings of personal inadequacy. In contrast, (guilt / shame), as long as it occurs in appropriate circumstances, is related to good adjustment, perhaps because it helps children resist harmful impulses. (p. 201)

Empathy

1. Empathy serves as an important motivator of _____ behavior, or actions that benefit another person without any expected reward for the self. (p. 201)

2. True or False: In some children, empathizing with an upset peer or adult escalates into personal distress. (p. 201)

3. Distinguish between *empathy* and *sympathy*. (p. 201)
   _____

4. Describe the role of temperament in children's empathy and sympathy. (p. 201)
   _____
   _____
   _____

5. Explain how parenting affects empathy and sympathy. (p. 201)
   _____
   _____

Peer Relations

Advances in Peer Sociability

1. Match each of Parten's stages of social development with its appropriate description. (p. 202)

   _____ When children engage in separate activities but exchange toys and comment on one another's behavior
   _____ A more advanced type of interaction in which children orient toward a common goal
   _____ A child plays near other children with similar materials but does not try to influence their behavior
   _____ Unoccupied, onlooker behavior and solitary play

   A. Cooperative play
   B. Nonsocial activity
   C. Associative play
   D. Parallel play

2. True or False: Longitudinal research shows that Parten's play types emerge in a developmental sequence, with later-appearing ones replacing earlier ones. (p. 202)

3. True or False: The *type,* rather than the *amount,* of solitary and parallel play changes during early childhood. (p. 202)

4. What types of nonsocial activity in preschoolers are cause for concern? (p. 202)

5. True or False: Most preschoolers with low rates of peer interaction are not socially anxious. Instead, they prefer to play by themselves. (p. 202)

6. True or False: Peer sociability takes essentially the same form in collectivist and individualistic cultures. (p. 202)

7. Provide an example of how cultural beliefs influence early peer associations. (p. 203)

First Friendships

1. Summarize preschoolers' understanding of the uniqueness of friendship. (p. 203)

2. Describe the unique qualities of preschoolers' interactions with friends. (p. 203)

Parental Influences on Early Peer Relations

1. Explain how parents directly influence children's peer sociability. (pp. 203–204)

2. How does attachment security promote peer sociability? (p. 204)

Foundations of Morality

1. Cite three points on which all major theories of moral development agree. (p. 204)

    A. _____

    B. _____

    C. _____

2. Match each of the following theories of moral development with its appropriate description. (pp. 204–205)

   _____ Emotional side of conscience development, with emphasis on identification and guilt as motivators for good conduct
   _____ Thinking, specifically children's ability to reason about justice and fairness
   _____ Moral behavior, learned through reinforcement and modeling

   A. Social learning theory
   B. Psychoanalytic theory
   C. Cognitive-developmental theory

The Psychoanalytic Perspective

1. Briefly summarize Freud's psychoanalytic theory of moral development. (p. 205)

   _____
   _____
   _____

2. True or False: Most researchers agree with Freud's assertion that fear of punishment and loss of parental love motivates conscience formation. (p. 205)

3. Research indicates that a special type of discipline called _____ supports conscience development in the following three ways: (p. 205)

   A. _____

   B. _____

   C. _____

4. How does a child's temperament influence his or her responsiveness to induction? (p. 205)

   _____
   _____
   _____

5. True or False: Recent research shows that Freud was incorrect in his assertion that guilt is an important motivator of moral action. (p. 205)

Social Learning Theory

1. Why is operant conditioning insufficient for children to acquire moral responses? (pp. 205–206)

   _____
   _____

2. Social learning theorists believe that children learn to behave morally largely through _____—observing and imitating adults who demonstrate appropriate behavior. (p. 206)

3. Models are most influential during the (preschool / elementary school) years. (p. 206)

4. True or False: Punishment promotes momentary compliance but does not produce long-lasting changes in children's behavior. (p. 206)

5. List five undesirable side effects of harsh punishment. (p. 206)

   A. _____   B. _____

   C. _____   D. _____

   E. _____

6. Describe two alternatives to harsh punishment. (p. 206)

   A. _____

   B. _____

7. Describe three ways that parents can increase the effectiveness of punishment. (pp. 206–207)

   A. _____

   B. _____

   C. _____

8. List three ways parents can effectively encourage good conduct, reducing the need for punishment. (pp. 207–208)

   A. _____

   B. _____

   C. _____

Cultural Influences: Ethnic Differences in the Consequences of Physical Punishment

1. True or False: Use of physical punishment is highest among low-SES ethnic minority parents. (p. 207)

2. How is physical punishment in early and middle childhood related to adolescent outcomes in Caucasian- and African-American families? (p. 207)

   Caucasian-American: _____

   African-American: _____

3. How do Caucasian-American and African-American beliefs about physical punishment differ? (p. 207)

   Caucasian-American: _____

   African-American: _____

The Cognitive-Developmental Perspective

1. In what major way does the cognitive-developmental perspective of morality differ from the psychoanalytic and behaviorist approaches? (p. 208)

   _____
   _____
   _____

2. Preschoolers are able to distinguish _____ *imperatives,* which protect people's rights and welfare, from two other forms of action: _____ *conventions,* or customs determined solely by consensus, such as table manners and dress style, and *matters of* _____, which do not violate rights or harm others, are not socially regulated, and therefore are up to the individual. (p. 208)

3. Cite factors that support preschoolers' moral understanding. (pp. 208–209)

   _____
   _____

The Other Side of Morality: Development of Aggression

1. Match each type of aggression with its appropriate description. (p. 209)

   _____ Aggression in which children want an object, privilege, or space and, in trying to get it, push, shout at, or otherwise attack a person in their way
   _____ Aggression meant to hurt another person
   _____ Aggression meant to harm others through physical injury—pushing hitting, kicking, punching others, or destroying another's property
   _____ Aggression that damages another's peer relationships through social exclusion, malicious gossip, or friendship manipulation
   _____ Aggression that harms others through threats of physical aggression, name-calling, or hostile teasing

   A. Relational aggression
   B. Verbal aggression
   C. Instrumental aggression
   D. Hostile aggression
   E. Physical aggression

2. In early childhood, (physical / verbal) aggression is gradually replaced by (physical / verbal) aggression. (p. 209)

3. In early childhood, instrumental aggression (declines / increases), while hostile aggression (declines / increases). (p. 209)

4. Describe sex differences in aggression during the late preschool years. (p. 209)

   Boys: _____
   _____

   Girls: _____
   _____

5. Describe child-rearing practices linked to aggression from early childhood through adolescence in children of both sexes and in many cultures. (p. 210)

   _____
   _____
   _____

6. (Boys / Girls) are more likely to be targets of harsh, inconsistent discipline. (p. 210)

7. True or False: Of all TV programs, children's cartoons are the least violent. (p. 210)

8. Describe the lasting negative consequences of childhood exposure to violent television. (p. 210)

   _____
   _____
   _____
   _____

9. True or False: TV violence hardens children to aggression, making them more willing to tolerate it in others. Briefly explain your answer. (p. 210)

   _____
   _____

10. Describe how Canada and the United States have intervened to regulate children's television programming. Are these interventions effective? Explain. (p. 210)

    Canada: _____
    _____

    United States: _____
    _____

    Effectiveness: _____
    _____

11. To reduce children's aggression, list several ways of intervening with both parents and children. (p. 211)

    Parents:
    A. _____
    B. _____
    C. _____

    Children:
    A. _____
    B. _____

Gender Typing

1. Define *gender typing*. (p. 211)

   _____
   _____
   _____

Gender-Stereotyped Beliefs and Behavior

1. True or False: Preschoolers associate toys, clothing, tools, household items, games, occupations, and colors (pink or blue) with one sex or the other. (p. 211)

2. Describe gender differences in the development of personality traits. (p. 211)

   Boys: _____

   Girls: _____

3. In early childhood, children's gender-stereotyped beliefs become (stronger / weaker), operating more like blanket rules than as flexible guidelines. (p. 211)

Genetic Influences on Gender Typing

1. How does the evolutionary perspective explain gender typing? (pp. 211–212)

2. Describe Eleanor Maccoby's argument that hormonal differences between males and females have important consequences for gender typing, including play styles in early childhood. (p. 212)

A Lifespan Vista: David: A Boy Who Was Reared as a Girl

1. Explain how David Reimer's development confirms the impact of genetic sex and prenatal hormones on a person's sense of self as male or female. (p. 213)

2. What does David Reimer's childhood reveal about the importance of environmental influences on gender typing? (p. 213)

Environmental Influences on Gender Typing

1. How do parents encourage gender-stereotyped beliefs and behaviors in their children? (p. 212)

2. Of the two sexes, (boys / girls) are clearly more gender-typed. Why might this be so? (p. 212)

3. Discuss ways teachers promote gender typing within the classroom, noting effects on children's social behaviors. (p. 212)

4. Peer rejection is greater for (girls / boys) who frequently engage in "cross-gender" activities. (p. 213)

5. Discuss the different styles of social influence within gender-segregated peer groups. (p. 214)

   Boys: _____

   Girls: _____

6. As boys and girls separate, _____, or more positive evaluations of members of one's own gender, becomes another factor that sustains the separate social worlds of boys and girls. (p. 214)

Gender Identity

1. Define *gender identity,* and indicate how it is measured. (p. 214)

2. _____ refers to a type of gender identity in which the person scores high on both masculine and feminine personality characteristics. (p. 214)

3. Contrast social learning and cognitive-developmental accounts of the emergence of gender identity. (p. 214)

   Social Learning: _____

   Cognitive-Developmental: _____

4. Gender _____ refers to the understanding that sex is biologically based and remains the same even if clothing, hairstyles, and play activities change. (p. 214)

5. Cite evidence supporting the notion that cognitive immaturity is largely responsible for preschoolers' difficulty grasping the permanence of sex. (p. 214)

6. Is gender constancy responsible for children's gender-typed behavior? Why or why not? (p. 214)

7. Briefly describe *gender schema theory*. (pp. 214–215)

8. What are *gender schemas*? (p. 215)

9. Provide an example of how young children endorse gender-typed views. (p. 215)

10. True or False: When children see others behaving in "gender inconsistent" ways, they often cannot remember the information or distort it to make it "gender-consistent." (p. 215)

Reducing Gender Stereotyping in Young Children

1. Explain how biology affects young children's gender typing. (p. 215)

2. How do cognitive limitations contribute to preschoolers' gender typing? (p. 215)

3. Cite several ways that adults can reduce gender stereotyping in young children. (p. 215)

Child Rearing and Emotional and Social Development

Child-Rearing Styles

1. Using research findings of Baumrind and others, cite three features that consistently differentiate a competent, authoritative parenting style from less effective authoritarian and permissive styles. (p. 215)

    A. _____

    B. _____

    C. _____

2. Match each style of parenting with the appropriate description. (pp. 215–217)

    _____ Involves high acceptance and involvement, adaptive control techniques, and appropriate autonomy granting

    _____ Involves warmth and acceptance but is uninvolved, overindulgent, or inattentive

    _____ Involves low acceptance and involvement with little control and general indifference for autonomy granting

    _____ Involves low acceptance and involvement, but is high in coercive control and low in autonomy granting

    A. Uninvolved child-rearing style
    B. Authoritative child-rearing style
    C. Permissive child-rearing style
    D. Authoritarian child-rearing style

3. Summarize child outcomes associated with each of the following styles of parenting: (pp. 215–217)

    Authoritative: _____

    _____

    _____

    Authoritarian: _____

    _____

    _____

    Permissive: _____

    _____

    _____

    Uninvolved: _____

    _____

    _____

4. In addition to unwarranted direct control, authoritarian parents engage in a more subtle type called _____, in which they intrude on and manipulate children's verbal expression, individuality, and attachment to parents. (p. 216)

5. At its extreme, uninvolved parenting is a form of child maltreatment called _____. (p. 217)

6. Which child-rearing style is most effective? (pp. 215, 217)

    _____

What Makes Authoritative Child Rearing Effective?

1. How does authoritative child rearing create an emotional context for positive parental influence? (p. 217)

    A. _____

    B. _____

    C. _____

    D. _____

Cultural Variations

1. Describe parenting practices of each of the following cultural groups: (p. 217)

    Chinese: _____
    _____
    _____

    Hispanic and Asian Pacific Island: _____
    _____
    _____

    African-American: _____
    _____
    _____

Child Maltreatment

1. Match the following descriptions with the type of child maltreatment. (p. 218)

    _____ Social isolation, repeated unreasonable demands, ridicule, humiliation, intimidation, or terrorizing
    _____ Fondling, intercourse, exhibitionism, commercial exploitation through prostitution or production of pornography
    _____ Failure to meet a child's basic needs for food, clothing, medical attention, or supervision
    _____ Assaults on children, such as kicking, biting, shaking, punching, or stabbing, that inflict physical injury

    A. Neglect
    B. Physical abuse
    C. Sexual abuse
    D. Emotional abuse

2. True or False: Parents commit more than 80 percent of abusive incidents. (p. 218)

3. Which types of child maltreatment are more often committed by mothers, and which by fathers? (p. 218)

    Mothers: _____

    Fathers: _____

4. True or False: Researchers have identified a single "abusive personality type." (p. 218)

5. List parent, child, and family-environment characteristics associated with an increased likelihood of abuse. (pp. 218–219)

   Parent: _____

   _____

   _____

   Child: _____

   _____

   _____

   Family environment: _____

   _____

6. Cite two reasons why most abusive parents are isolated from supportive ties to their communities. (p. 219)

   A. _____

   B. _____

7. Societies that view violence as an appropriate way to solve problems set the stage for child abuse. These conditions (do / do not) exist in the United States or Canada. (p. 219)

8. True or False: Laws in both the United States and Canada allow school corporal punishment. (p. 219)

9. List examples of negative outcomes of child maltreatment. (p. 219)

   A. _____

   B. _____

   C. _____

   D. _____

   E. _____

10. True or False: Repeated child abuse has no effect on the central nervous system. (p. 219)

11. What is the most important factor in preventing mothers with childhood histories of abuse from repeating the cycle with their own children? (p. 219)

    _____

12. List several strategies for preventing child maltreatment. (p. 219)

    _____

    _____

    _____

ASK YOURSELF...

For *Ask Yourself* questions for this chapter, please log on to the Companion Website at *www.ablongman.com/berk*.

1. Select the Companion Website for *Exploring Lifespan Development.*
2. Use the "Jump to" menu to go directly to this chapter.
3. From the menu on the left side of the screen, select "Ask Yourself."
4. Complete questions and choose "Submit answers for grading" or "Clear answers" to start over.

SUGGESTED STUDENT READINGS

Gibbs, J. C. (2003). *Moral development and reality: Beyond the theories of Kohlberg and Hoffman.* Thousand Oaks, CA: Sage. Provides an extensive overview of moral development in childhood. The author also describes his EQUIP program, which was designed to teach antisocial children moral and prosocial behavior.

Hartup, W. W., & Tremblay, R. E. (2005). *Developmental origins of aggression.* New York: Guilford. Examines the biological and environmental correlates of childhood aggression, including longitudinal research on the developmental trajectories of children who display aggression early in life. The authors also describe sex differences in adaptive and maladaptive aggression.

Hines, M. (2005). *Brain gender.* New York: Oxford University Press. Examines both biological and environmental factors that contribute to sex differences in human behavior. Topics include sex differences in play, mathematical and verbal ability, aggression, and the development of gender identity.

Olfman, S. (Ed.). (2005). *Childhood lost: How American culture is failing our kids.* New York: Guilford. A collection of chapters by authors from diverse disciplines that address the negative impact of various aspects of American culture on children. Chapters address such topics as why parenting matters, lack of societal supports for child rearing, the consequences of children developing sexual awareness at younger and younger ages, and what can happen when television and computers replace family time.

PUZZLE 8.1

Across
5. _____ aggression is intended to harm another person.
6. Self-_____: set of attributes, abilities, attitudes, and values that an individual believes defines who he/she is
8. _____ control: type of control used by authoritarian parents, in which they intrude on and manipulate children's verbal expression, individuality, and attachment to parents
9. _____ aggression is aimed at obtaining an object, privilege, or space with no deliberate intent to harm another person
10. _____ aggression is a form of hostile aggression that damages another's peer relationships
11. _____ versus guilt: Erikson's psychological conflict of the preschool years
14. Type of discipline in which the effects of the child's behavior on others are communicated to the child
15. Actions that protect people's rights and welfare (2 words)
16. Matters of _____ choice: actions which do not violate rights, are not socially regulated, and are up to the individual

Down
1. Self-_____: refers to judgments that we make about our own worth and the feelings associated with those judgments
2. _____, or altruistic, behavior: actions that benefit another without any expected reward for the self
3. Feelings of concern or sorrow for another's plight
4. _____ aggression: harms others through physical injury
7. Customs determined solely by consensus, such as table manners (2 words)
12. Form of punishment in which children are removed from the immediate setting until they are ready to act appropriately (2 words)
13. _____ aggression: harms others through threats of physical aggression

PUZZLE 8.2

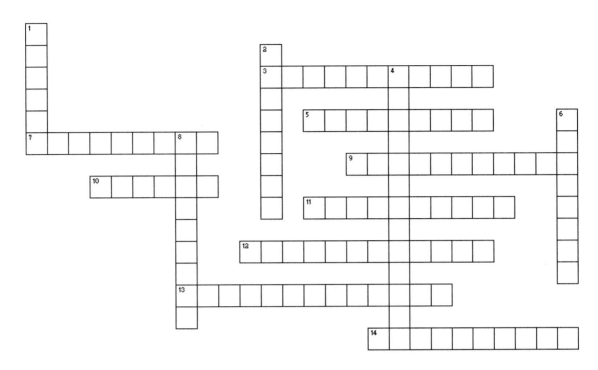

Across

3. _____ play: form of true social participation in which children engage in separate activities but interact by exchanging toys and commenting on one another's behavior
5. Gender _____: understanding that sex is biologically based and remains the same even if clothing, hairstyle, and play activities change
7. Type of gender identity in which a person scores high on both masculine and feminine characteristics
9. _____ play: form of true social participation in which children's actions are directed toward a common goal
10. Gender _____: the process of developing gender-linked beliefs, gender roles, and a gender-role identity
11. _____ style of child rearing: high in acceptance but overindulging and inattentive, low in control, lax rather than appropriate autonomy granting
12. _____-rearing styles: constellations of parenting behaviors that occur over a wide range of situations
13. _____ style of child rearing: high in acceptance and involvement, emphasizes firm control with explanations, includes gradual, appropriate autonomy granting
14. _____ style of child rearing: low acceptance and involvement, little control or effort to grant autonomy, minimal commitment to parenting

Down

1. Gender _____ theory is an information processing approach to gender typing that combines social learning and cognitive-developmental features
2. _____ play: the child plays near other children, with similar materials, but does not interact or try to influence their behavior
4. _____ style of child rearing: low in acceptance and involvement, high in coercive control, restricts rather than grants autonomy
6. Gender _____: the perception of oneself as relatively masculine or feminine in characteristics
8. _____ activity: unoccupied, onlooker behavior and solitary play

PRACTICE TEST #1

1. Preschoolers' self-concepts are (p. 199)
   a. concrete, typically focused on observable characteristics.
   b. abstract, usually centered on their unique psychological characteristics.
   c. internalized, since they cannot yet talk about their own subjective experiences.
   d. based on stable personality traits.

2. When 4-year-old Harvey begins to inhibit his impulses for emotional outbursts, he is showing early signs of (p. 200)
   a. gender identity.
   b. modeling.
   c. altruistic behavior.
   d. effortful control.

3. Noah is playing with blocks near his classmate. Though his classmate is also playing with blocks, the two are not interacting. This type of play is termed (p. 202)
   a. nonsocial.
   b. parallel.
   c. associative.
   d. cooperative.

4. Recent research on peer interaction indicates that (p. 202)
   a. it is the type, rather than the amount, of play that changes in early childhood.
   b. Parten's play types emerge in a developmental sequence, with later-appearing ones replacing earlier ones.
   c. nonsocial activity among preschoolers is a sign of maladjustment.
   d. most preschoolers with low rates of peer interaction are socially anxious.

5. Functional play is particularly common during (p. 203)
   a. during the first year of life.
   b. during the first two years of life.
   c. between 2 and 6 years.
   d. between 3 and 6 years.

6. Four- to 7-year-olds regard friendship as (p. 203)
   a. based on mutual trust.
   b. capable of enduring through most disputes.
   c. pleasurable play and sharing of toys.
   d. sharing of toys and intimate feelings.

7. By pointing out to Johnny how his bad behavior affects his younger sister, Johnny's mother is practicing (p. 205)
   a. induction.
   b. time out.
   c. positive discipline.
   d. relational aggression.

8. According to Freud, children obey the superego to avoid (p. 205)
   a. punishment.
   b. conflict.
   c. guilt.
   d. injury.

9. Social learning theorists believe that children learn to behave morally by observing and imitating people who demonstrate appropriate behavior. This process is known as (p. 206)
   a. induction.
   b. modeling.
   c. identifying.
   d. mimicking.

10. Adults whose parents used corporal punishment are (p. 206)
    a. less accepting of such discipline.
    b. more accepting of such discipline.
    c. unable to discipline their children through any means.
    d. very unlikely to have children of their own.

11. The most effective form of discipline is (p. 207)
    a. withdrawal of privileges.
    b. time out.
    c. encouraging good conduct.
    d. punishment.

12. By the early preschool years, the most common type of aggression is (p. 209)
    a. instrumental aggression.
    b. physical aggression.
    c. verbal aggression.
    d. relational aggression.

13. TV violence (p. 210)
    a. hardens children to aggression, making them more willing to tolerate it in others.
    b. teaches children that violence is socially unacceptable and has harsh negative consequences.
    c. is unlikely to increase violent behavior, even among highly aggressive children.
    d. is uncommon in children's programming, particularly cartoons.

14. Which of the following correctly represents Maccoby's view of gender typing? (p. 212)
    a. Beginning at birth, parents have different expectations of sons than of daughters.
    b. Same-sex peers positively reinforce one another for "gender-appropriate" play.
    c. Teachers encourage girls to participate in adult-structured activities, and use more controlling discipline with boys.
    d. Hormones affect human play styles, leading to rough, noisy movements among boys and calm, gentle actions among girls.

15. Research on familial influences on gender typing shows that (p. 213)
    a. from birth, parents hold similar perceptions and expectations of their sons and daughters.
    b. parents espouse similar child-rearing values for sons and daughters.
    c. of the two sexes, boys are more gender-stereotyped than girls.
    d. mothers are less tolerant of cross-gender behavior in their children than are fathers.

16. Individuals who are androgynous (p. 214)
    a. display highly gender-stereotyped behavior.
    b. demonstrate mostly cross-gender behaviors.
    c. score high in both masculine and feminine personality characteristics.
    d. have a poorly developed gender identity.

17. Gender schema theory (pp. 214–215)
    a. stresses genetic influences on gender typing.
    b. emphasizes development of gender-stereotyped beliefs through identification with the same-sex parent.
    c. focuses on the role of modeling and reinforcement in gender identity development.
    d. emphasizes how environmental pressures and children's cognitions work together to shape gender-role development.

18. The type of child rearing that is marked by low acceptance and involvement, high coercive control, and low autonomy granting is (p. 216)
    a. authoritarian.
    b. permissive.
    c. uninvolved.
    d. authoritative.

19. The most successful approach to child rearing is (p. 215)
    a. the authoritative child-rearing style.
    b. the authoritarian child-rearing style.
    c. the uninvolved child-rearing style.
    d. psychological control.

20. Child maltreatment is (p. 219)
    a. rare in large, industrialized nations and has declined in recent years.
    b. rooted in adult psychological disturbance and, therefore, abusers demonstrate an easily identifiable abusive personality type.
    c. best understood from a social learning perspective.
    d. associated with peer difficulties, academic failure, depression, substance abuse, and delinquency.

PRACTICE TEST #2

1. The high self-esteem characteristic of most preschoolers contributes to their developing sense of (p. 200)
    a. initiative.
    b. empathy.
    c. altruism.
    d. androgyny.

2. As 4-year-old Sofia begins to develop a set of attributes, abilities, attitudes, and values that she believes defines who she is, she is developing (p. 199)
    a. a self-concept.
    b. gender identity.
    c. instrumental aggression.
    d. moral imperatives.

3. Children have the capacity to correctly judge the causes of many basic emotions by age (p. 200)
    a. 2 to 3.
    b. 4 to 5.
    c. 6 to 7.
    d. 8 to 9.

4. According to Parten, the first form of true social interaction to develop during early childhood is (p. 202)
    a. cooperative play.
    b. associative play.
    c. parallel play.
    d. onlooker behavior.

5. Most children first acquire skills for interacting with peers (p. 203)
    a. within the family.
    b. at child care.
    c. at preschool.
    d. in kindergarten.

6. Most theories of moral development agree that (p. 204)
    a. at first, a child's morality is regulated by inner standards.
    b. over time, a child's morality becomes externally controlled.
    c. conscience starts to form in middle childhood.
    d. truly moral individuals have developed principles of good conduct.

7. Modeling of prosocial behavior (p. 206)
    a. is less effective than reinforcement in helping children acquire moral responses.
    b. has no long-term effects on children's behavior.
    c. exerts the greatest influence on children's behavior during the preschool years.
    d. is equally effective regardless of the model's characteristics.

8. Harsh discipline, such as yelling at, slapping, or spanking children for misbehavior, (p. 206)
    a. is never justified.
    b. promotes lasting changes in children's behavior.
    c. has been linked with increases in adaptive behavior and academic performance.
    d. often has undesirable side effects, including modeling of aggressive behavior.

9. Preschoolers consider choice of friends and color of clothing to be (p. 208)
    a. social conventions.
    b. matters of personal choice.
    c. moral violations.
    d. moral imperatives.

10. While talking to a group of classmates, Alexis says, "Don't play with Maggie, she's a nerd." This is an example of (p. 209)
    a. relational aggression.
    b. emotional aggression.
    c. overt aggression.
    d. instrumental aggression.

11. Preschool and young school-age children tend to reason (p. 208)
    a. freely.
    b. rigidly.
    c. maturely.
    d. infrequently.

12. The process of developing gender-linked preferences and behaviors valued by the larger society is called gender (p. 211)
    a. typing.
    b. intensification.
    c. identification.
    d. constancy.

13. Eleanor Maccoby's research on hormonal influences on play indicates that (p. 212)
    a. preference for same-sex playmates is rarely found in cultures outside of the United States, suggesting that hormones exert little influence on play behavior.
    b. hormonal differences lead boys to prefer rough, noisy play and girls to prefer calm, gentle actions.
    c. preference for same-sex playmates declines during the preschool years.
    d. hormonal differences lead girls to prefer large group activities, while boys prefer to play in pairs.

14. In nontraditional homes where fathers devote as much time to caregiving as mothers, children tend to (p. 214)
    a. show a greater frequency of overt aggression.
    b. be less gender-typed in emotional style.
    c. display a greater sense of moral imperatives.
    d. be more rigid.

15. At the end of the preschool years, when children understand that their sex is a permanent characteristic of the self, they have developed (p. 214)
    a. gender constancy.
    b. sexual stability.
    c. gender identity.
    d. gender neutrality.

16. Four-year-old Gisele's mother often tells her that "cars and trucks are for boys." According to gender schema theory, Gisele is likely to (p. 215)
    a. avoid playing with cars and trucks.
    b. ask her father to play cars and trucks with her.
    c. be resentful when she sees other girls playing with cars and trucks.
    d. seek out opportunities to play with boys who are playing with cars and trucks.

17. What do permissive and uninvolved parenting styles have in common? (p. 217)
    a. Both are overindulgent.
    b. Both are indifferent to the child's decision making.
    c. Both make few or no demands.
    d. Both are emotionally detached.

18. The permissive child-rearing style is warm and accepting, (p. 217)
    a. but uninvolved.
    b. but psychologically controlling.
    c. but authoritarian.
    d. and proven successful.

19. Within the family, children whose characteristics make them more of a challenge to rear are (p. 218)
    a. at increased risk for abuse.
    b. at decreased risk for abuse.
    c. more likely to have authoritative parents.
    d. more likely to have permissive parents.

20. Parents Anonymous combats child maltreatment by providing (p. 219)
    a. access to health care.
    b. social supports.
    c. clean, uncrowded living conditions.
    d. low-cost, high-quality child care.

CHAPTER 9
PHYSICAL AND COGNITIVE DEVELOPMENT IN MIDDLE CHILDHOOD

BRIEF CHAPTER SUMMARY

Physical growth during the school years continues at the slow, regular pace of early childhood. Bones of the body lengthen and broaden, and primary teeth are replaced with permanent teeth.

Although most children appear to be at their healthiest in middle childhood, a variety of health problems do occur, especially in children who live in poverty. Over the past several decades, a rise in overweight and obesity has occurred in many Western nations, putting many children at risk for lifelong health problems. Children experience a somewhat higher rate of illness during the first two years of elementary school than they will later, because of exposure to sick children and an immune system that is still developing. Gains in flexibility, balance, agility, and force contribute to school-age children's advances in gross motor development. Steady gains in reaction time also occur. Fine motor development improves over the school years, and sex differences in motor skills that appeared in the preschool years continue and, in some instances, become more pronounced in middle childhood. School-age boys' genetic advantage in muscle mass is not sufficient to account for their gross-motor superiority; the social environment plays a larger role. Games with rules become common in the school years, as does rough-and-tumble play. High-quality physical education classes that focus on individual exercise rather than competitive sports help ensure that all children have access to the benefits of regular exercise and play.

During Piaget's concrete operational stage, children's thought becomes far more logical, flexible, and organized than in early childhood. A limitation of concrete operational thought is that children's mental operations work poorly with abstract ideas. Specific cultural and school practices affect children's mastery of Piagetian tasks. Some neo-Piagetian theorists argue that the development of operational thinking can best be understood in terms of gains in information-processing speed rather than a sudden shift to a new stage.

In contrast to Piaget's focus on overall cognitive change, the information-processing perspective examines separate aspects of thinking. Brain development contributes to an increase in information-processing speed and capacity and gains in cognitive inhibition. In addition, attention becomes more selective, adaptable, and planful. As attention improves, so do memory strategies. School-age children's theory of mind, or metacognition, expands, as does their understanding of sources of knowledge and of false belief. However, they are not yet good at cognitive self-regulation. Fundamental discoveries about the development of information processing have been applied to children's learning of reading and mathematics.

Around age 6, IQ becomes more stable than it was at earlier ages, and it correlates well with academic achievement. Intelligence tests provide an overall score (the IQ), which represents general intelligence, as well as an array of scores measuring specific mental abilities. Sternberg's triarchic theory of successful intelligence identifies three broad, interacting intelligences: analytical intelligence, creative intelligence, and practical intelligence. Gardner's theory of multiple intelligences defines eight independent intelligences in terms of distinct sets of processing operations. SES accounts for some, but not all, of the black–white IQ difference, and many experts acknowledge that IQ scores can underestimate the intelligence of culturally different children.

Vocabulary and grammar and pragmatics continue to develop in middle childhood, although less obviously than at earlier ages. In addition, school-age children develop language awareness. Many children throughout the world grow up bilingual; as with first-language development, a sensitive period for second-language development exists. Research shows that bilingualism has positive consequences for development, but the question of how to educate bilingual children continues to be hotly debated.

Schools are vital forces in children's cognitive development, with educational philosophies and teacher–student relationships playing important roles. Teaching children with learning disabilities, as well as those with special gifts and talents, presents unique challenges. A great many factors, both within and outside schools, affect children's learning, including societal values, school resources, quality of teaching, and parental encouragement.

LEARNING OBJECTIVES

After reading this chapter, you should be able to:

9.1 Describe major trends in body growth during middle childhood. (p. 225)

9.2 Describe the causes and consequences of serious nutritional problems in middle childhood, giving special attention to obesity. (pp. 226–228)

9.3 Identify factors that contribute to illness during the school years, and describe ways to reduce these health problems. (pp. 228)

9.4 Cite major changes in motor development and play during middle childhood, including sex differences and the importance of physical education. (pp. 228–231)

9.5 Describe major characteristics of concrete operational thought. (pp. 231–232)

9.6 Discuss recent research on concrete operational thought, noting the importance of culture and schooling. (pp. 232–234)

9.7 Cite basic changes in information processing, and describe the development of attention and memory in middle childhood. (pp. 234–237)

9.8 Describe the school-age child's theory of mind and capacity to engage in self-regulation. (p. 237)

9.9 Discuss current controversies in teaching reading and mathematics to elementary school children. (pp. 237–239)

9.10 Describe major approaches to defining and measuring intelligence. (pp. 239–242)

9.11 Describe evidence indicating that both heredity and environment contribute to intelligence. (pp. 242–244)

9.12 Summarize changes in school-age children's vocabulary, grammar, and pragmatics, and cite advantages of bilingualism. (pp. 245–247)

9.13 Explain the impact of educational philosophies and teacher–student interaction on children's motivation and academic achievement. (pp. 248–249)

9.14 Explain the conditions that contribute to successful placement of children with mild mental retardation and learning disabilities in regular classrooms. (p. 250)

9.15 Describe the characteristics of gifted children, including creativity and talent, and current efforts to meet their educational needs. (pp. 250–251)

9.16 Compare the academic achievement of North American children with children in other industrialized nations. (pp. 252–253)

STUDY QUESTIONS

Physical Development

Body Growth

1. During middle childhood, children add about _____ inches in height and _____ pounds in weight each year. (p. 225)

2. True or False: Between ages 6 and 8, girls are slightly shorter and lighter than boys; by age 9, this trend reverses. (p. 225)

3. List two factors that account for unusual flexibility of movement in middle childhood. (p. 225)

   A. _____

   B. _____

4. Between the ages of _____ and _____, all primary teeth are lost and replaced by permanent teeth. (p. 225)

Health Issues

1. List factors that lead many children from advantaged homes to be at their healthiest in middle childhood. (p. 226)

   _____

   _____

2. True or False: During the school years, poverty is no longer a powerful predictor of ill health. (p. 226)

Nutrition

1. The percentage of children eating dinner with their families (rises / drops) sharply between ages 9 and 14 years. (p. 226)

2. List four ways that prolonged malnutrition affects school-age children. (p. 226)

   A. _____

   B. _____

   C. _____

   D. _____

Obesity

1. About _____ percent of Canadian children and _____ percent of American children are obese. (p. 227)

2. Why are obesity rates increasing rapidly in developing countries? (p. 227)

3. How do both heredity and environment contribute to childhood obesity? (p. 227)

   Heredity: _____

   _____

   Environment: _____

   _____

4. More than _____ percent of obese children become overweight adults. Cite four lifelong health problems associated with obesity. (p. 227)

   A. _____

   B. _____

   C. _____

   D. _____

5. Summarize the consequences of childhood obesity on emotional and social development. (p. 227)

   _____

   _____

   _____

6. The most effective interventions for childhood obesity focus on the (family / individual). Cite evidence to support your answer. (pp. 227–228)

___

Illnesses

1. What accounts for the somewhat higher rate of illness during the first two years of elementary school than in the later school years? (p. 228)

___

2. The most common chronic illness, representing the most frequent cause of school absence and childhood hospitalization, is _____. (p. 228)

3. Cite five factors that place children at-risk for developing asthma. (p. 228)

    A. ___
    B. ___
    C. ___
    D. ___
    E. ___

4. Which environmental factors contribute to the higher rate and greater severity of asthma among African-American and poverty-stricken children? (p. 228)

    A. ___
    B. ___
    C. ___

5. Why are chronically ill children at-risk for academic, emotional, and social difficulties? (p. 228)

___

6. Briefly describe effective interventions for chronically ill children and their families. (p. 228)

___

Motor Development and Play

Gross Motor Development

1. Improvements in motor skills over middle childhood reflect gains in what four basic motor capacities? (p. 228)

    A. ___
    B. ___
    C. ___
    D. ___

174

2. Body growth, as well as more efficient _____, plays a vital role in improved motor performance in middle childhood. (p. 228)

Fine Motor Development

1. Describe typical gains in writing and drawing during middle childhood. (p. 229)

   Writing: _____

   _____

   Drawing: _____

   _____

Sex Differences

1. Summarize sex differences in motor skills during middle childhood. (p. 229)

   _____

   _____

   _____

2. True or False: School-age boys' genetic advantage in muscle mass is great enough to account for their superiority in most gross motor skills. (p. 229)

3. How do social experiences contribute to sex differences in motor development during middle childhood? (p. 229)

   _____

   _____

   _____

4. List two strategies for increasing girls' participation, self-confidence, and sense of fair treatment in athletics. (p. 229)

   A. _____

   B. _____

Games with Rules

1. What cognitive capacity permits the transition to rule-oriented games in middle childhood? (p. 229)

   _____

2. Briefly describe how child-organized games contribute to emotional and social development. (pp. 229–230)

   _____

   _____

   _____

3. List two reasons why today's children devote less time to informal outdoor play. (p. 230)

   A. _____

   B. _____

4. Explain how adults can ensure that athletic leagues provide positive learning experiences for children. (p. 230)

Shadows of Our Evolutionary Past

1. What is *rough-and-tumble play*? (p. 230)

2. Why was rough-and-tumble play important in our evolutionary past? (p. 230)

3. Explain how rough-and-tumble play changes from middle childhood to adolescence. (p. 230)

Physical Education

1. List three ways physical activity and games support children's development. (p. 230)

    A. _____
    B. _____
    C. _____

2. The average American school-age child gets only _____ minutes of physical education a week, while the average Canadian child gets about _____ hours a week. (p. 231)

3. How can physical education programs reach the least physically fit children? (p. 231)

4. Cite four long-term benefits of physical fitness in childhood. (p. 231)

    A. _____
    B. _____
    C. _____
    D. _____

Cognitive Development

Piaget's Theory: The Concrete Operational Stage

Concrete Operational Thought

1. During Piaget's *concrete operational stage*, thought is far more _____, _____, and _____ than it was during early childhood. (p. 231)

2. Match each of the following terms with its appropriate description. (pp. 231–232)

   _____ Ordering items along a quantitative dimension, such as length or weight
   _____ Awareness of classification hierarchies and the ability to focus on relations between a general and two specific categories at the same time
   _____ Focusing on several aspects of a problem and relating them rather than centering on just one
   _____ Thinking through a series of steps and then mentally reversing irection, returning to the starting point

   A. Seriation
   B. Decentration
   C. Reversibility
   D. Classification

3. Describe *transitive inference,* and provide an example of this ability. (p. 232)

   Transitive inference: _____

   Example: _____

4. What evidence did Piaget use to conclude that school-age children have a more accurate understanding of space than preschoolers? (p. 232)

   _____
   _____
   _____
   _____

Limitations of Concrete Operational Thought

1. Cite the major limitation of concrete operational thought. (p. 232)

   _____
   _____

2. True or False: School-age children master Piaget's concrete operational tasks all at once, not step by step. (p. 232)

Follow-Up Research on Concrete Operational Thought

1. Cite two examples that illustrate how culture and schooling contribute to children's mastery of conservation and other Piagetian problems. (pp. 232–233)

   A. _____

   B. _____

2. True or False: The forms of logic required by Piagetian tasks appear to emerge spontaneously during childhood and are not heavily influenced by training, context, or cultural conditions. (p. 233)

3. Some neo-Piagetian theorists argue that the development of operational thinking can best be understood in terms of gains in _____ speed rather than a sudden shift to a new stage. (p. 233)

4. Define central conceptual structures, and explain how these structures help school-age children master Piagetian tasks. (p. 233)

   A. _____

   B. _____

5. True or False: Compared with Piaget's, Case's theory better accounts for the unevenness in cognitive development. (p. 233)

Evaluation of the Concrete Operational Stage

1. Cite two types of change that researchers believe may be involved in the school-age child's approach to Piagetian problems. (pp. 233–234)

   A. _____

   B. _____

Information Processing

1. Summarize two basic changes in information processing that facilitate diverse aspects of thinking. (p. 234)

   A. _____

   B. _____

Attention

1. Describe three ways that attention changes in middle childhood. (p. 234)

   A. _____

   B. _____

   C. _____

Biology and Environment: Children with Attention-Deficit Hyperactivity Disorder

1. (Boys / Girls) are three to nine times more likely to be diagnosed with ADHD than children of the other sex. (p. 235)

2. Describe characteristics of children with ADHD. (p. 235)

   _____
   _____
   _____
   _____

3. True or False: All children with ADHD exhibit hyperactive symptoms. (p. 235)

4. According to one view with substantial research support, two related deficits underlie ADHD symptoms: (p. 235)

   A. _____

   B. _____

5. Cite evidence that ADHD is influenced by both genetic and environmental factors. (p. 235)

   Heredity: _____

   _____

   Environmental: _____

   _____

6. The most common treatment for ADHD is _____. List two additional interventions for children with ADHD. (p. 235)

   A. _____

   B. _____

7. ADHD is a lifelong disorder. Provide evidence to support this assertion. (p. 235)

   _____

   _____

Memory Strategies

1. List and define two memory strategies that develop in middle childhood, in the order that they typically appear. (pp. 234, 236)

   A. _____

   _____

   B. _____

   _____

2. Define *elaboration*, and explain why this memory strategy develops later than other memory strategies. (p. 236)

   A. _____

   B. _____

   _____

3. Because organization and elaboration combine items into _____, they permit children to hold on to much more information. (p. 236)

The Knowledge Base and Memory Performance

1. Explain how extensive knowledge and use of memory strategies support one another by the end of the school years. (p. 236)

   _____

   _____

   _____

2. How does motivation contribute to children's strategic memory processing? (p. 236)

Culture and Memory Strategies

1. True or False: People in non-Western cultures who have no formal schooling are likely to use and benefit from instruction in memory strategies. (p. 236)

2. How do cultural circumstances influence the development of memory strategies? (pp. 236–237)

The School-Age Child's Theory of Mind

1. Compared to preschoolers, how do school-age children view the mind? (p. 237)

2. School-age children realize that people can extend their knowledge not only by directly observing events and talking to others, but also by making _____. (p. 237)

3. How does schooling contribute to the school-age child's theory of mind? (p. 237)

Cognitive Self-Regulation

1. Although metacognition expands, school-age children are not yet good at _____, the process of continuously monitoring progress toward a goal, checking outcomes, and redirecting unsuccessful efforts. (p. 237)

2. Explain why cognitive self-regulation develops gradually. (p. 237)

3. How can adults foster self-regulation during middle childhood? (p. 237)

Applications of Information Processing to Academic Learning

1. Cite information-processing skills that contribute to reading. (pp. 237–238)

2. What is *phonological awareness,* and how does it contribute to reading achievement? (pp. 237–238)

   A. _____

   B. _____

3. Summarize the debate over how to teach beginning reading. (p. 238)

   Whole Language Approach: _____

   Phonics Approach: _____

4. What evidence suggests that children learn best with a mixture of whole language and phonics instruction? (p. 238)

5. True or False: If practice in basic reading skills is overemphasized, children may lose sight of the goal of reading. (p. 238)

6. School-age children acquire basic math facts through a combination of what types of activities? (p. 238)

   A. _____

   B. _____

   C. _____

7. Summarize the arguments about how to teach mathematics. What approach is most beneficial? (p. 238)

8. Describe factors that support the acquisition of mathematical knowledge in Asian countries. (pp. 238–239)

Individual Differences in Mental Development

1. Around age _____, IQ becomes (less / more) stable than it was at earlier ages, and it correlates moderately well with academic achievement. (p. 239)

Defining and Measuring Intelligence

1. Distinguish between group-administered and individually administered IQ tests. (p. 239)

    A. _____

    B. _____

2. In addition to general intelligence, list the five intellectual factors measured by the *Stanford-Binet Intelligence Scales (SB-IV)*. (p. 240)

    A. _____

    B. _____

    C. _____

    D. _____

    E. _____

3. List the four broad factors measured by the *Wechsler Intelligence Scale for Children (WISC-IV)*. (p. 240)

    A. _____

    B. _____

    C. _____

    D. _____

    E. _____

4. The (Stanford-Binet Intelligence Scale / Wechsler Intelligence Scale for Children) was the first test to be standardized on children representing the total population of the United States, including ethnic minorities. It has also been adapted for and standardized in Canada. (p. 240)

Recent Efforts to Define Intelligence

1. What is *componential analyses,* and why is it used? (p. 240)

    _____

    _____

    _____

2. Cite evidence that speed of processing is related to IQ. (p. 240)

    _____

    _____

    _____

3. What is one major shortcoming of the componential approach? (p. 240)

4. Briefly describe the three interacting intelligences identified in Sternberg's *Triarchic Theory of Successful Intelligence.* (p. 240)

   A. _____

   B. _____

   C. _____

5. How does Sternberg's theory help explain cultural differences in IQ? (p. 241)

6. True or False: Gardner dismissed the idea of general intelligence. (p. 241)

7. List Gardner's eight independent intelligences. (p. 241)

   A. _____   B. _____
   C. _____   D. _____
   E. _____   F. _____
   G. _____   H. _____

Explaining Individual and Group Differences in IQ

1. How does SES relate to IQ? What do these findings reveal about the black–white IQ gap? (p. 242)

   A. _____

   B. _____

2. What do kinship studies reveal about the role of heredity in IQ? (p. 242)

3. What do adoption studies reveal about the contribution of environmental factors to IQ? (p. 242)

4. A controversial question about ethnic differences in IQ has to do with whether they result from _____, or unfair measure. (pp. 242–243)

5. Explain why some experts reject the idea that intelligence tests are biased. (p. 243)

_____
_____

6. Describe ways ethnic minority families foster unique communication skills that do not match the expectations of most classrooms and testing situations. (p. 243)

_____
_____
_____
_____
_____

7. Describe the difference between collaborative and hierarchical styles of communication. (p. 243)

   A. _____
   _____

   B. _____
   _____

8. True or False: Because low-income ethnic minority children grow up in "object-oriented" homes, they often lack opportunities to use games and objects that promote certain intellectual skills. (p. 243)

9. The fear of being judged on the basis of a negative stereotype, or _____, can trigger anxiety that interferes with performance. (p. 243)

10. Why is assessment of adaptive behavior especially important for minority children? (p. 243)

_____
_____

11. _____ is a culturally relevant testing procedure that enhances minority children's test performance. This approach is consistent with Vygotsky's zone of proximal development. (p. 244)

Social Issues: High-Stakes Testing

1. Explain how the U.S. No Child Left Behind Act has promoted high-stakes testing in schools. (p. 245)

_____
_____
_____

2. List the potential benefits of high-stakes testing. (p. 245)

_____
_____
_____

3. Evidence indicates that high-stakes testing (undermines / upgrades) the quality of education. (p. 245)

4. Describe two concerns about high-stakes testing. (p. 245)

   A. _____

   B. _____

5. True or False: High-stakes testing has led to an increased emphasis on teaching for deeper understanding. (p. 245)

Language Development

Vocabulary and Grammar

1. Describe ways school-age children add new words to their vocabulary. (pp. 245–246)

2. Provide an example that illustrates the school-age child's ability to appreciate the multiple meanings of words. (p. 246)

3. Cite two grammatical achievements of middle childhood. (p. 246)

   A. _____

   B. _____

Pragmatics

1. Define *pragmatics*. How do the pragmatic skills of school-age children differ from those of preschoolers? (p. 246)

   A. _____

   B. _____

2. Describe cultural differences in children's narrative styles. (p. 246)

Learning Two Languages at a Time

1. List two ways that children can become bilingual. (p. 247)

   A. _____

   B. _____

2. True or False: Children of bilingual parents who teach them both languages in early childhood acquire normal native ability in their first language and good-to-native ability in the second language. (p. 247)

3. True or False: A sensitive period for second-language development exists; mastery must begin sometime in childhood for most second-language learners to attain full proficiency. (p. 247)

4. List some positive consequences of bilingualism. (p. 247)
   _____
   _____
   _____

5. Describe Canada's language immersion programs. (p. 247)
   _____
   _____

6. Summarize the current debate in the United States regarding how best to educate ethnic minority children with limited English proficiency. (p. 247)
   _____
   _____
   _____

7. True or False: In the United States, current public opinion and educational practice favor English-only instruction. (p. 247)

Learning in School

Educational Philosophies

1. Match the type of classroom with the appropriate description. (pp. 248–249)

   _____ Encourages students to construct their own knowledge. Many are grounded in Piaget's theory, which views children as active agents. Students are evaluated by considering their progress in relation to their own prior development.

   _____ The teacher is the sole authority for knowledge, rules, and decision making and does most of the talking. Students are relatively passive. Progress is evaluated by how well they keep pace with a uniform set of standards for their grade.

   _____ Children participate in a wide range of challenging activities with teachers and peers, with whom they jointly construct understandings. Grounded in Vygotsky's theory.

   A. Traditional classroom
   B. Social-constructivist classroom
   C. Constructivist classroom

2. Cite several benefits associated with constructivist classrooms. (p. 248)
   _____
   _____
   _____

3. Cite three educational themes inspired by Vygotsky's sociocultural theory. (pp. 248–249)
   A. _____
   B. _____
   C. _____

4. What is *reciprocal teaching*? Briefly discuss its positive effects. (p. 249)

   A. _____

   B. _____

Teacher–Student Interaction

1. List three characteristics of elementary school teachers that are positively associated with student learning. (p. 249)

   A. _____

   B. _____

   C. _____

2. How does teacher interaction with well-behaved, high-achieving students differ from teacher interaction with unruly students? (p. 249)

   A. _____

   B. _____

3. Define *educational self-fulfilling prophecies,* and explain what type of student is most likely to be affected by them. (p. 249)

   A. _____

   B. _____

Teaching Children with Special Needs

1. True or False: Both American and Canadian legislation mandates that schools place children who require special supports for learning in the "least restrictive" environments that meet their educational needs. (p. 250)

2. Explain the difference between *mainstreaming* and *full inclusion.* (p. 250)

   _____

3. Describe characteristics of students who have *mild mental retardation.* (p. 250)

   _____

4. A large number of mainstreamed students have _____, or great difficulty with one or more aspects of learning, usually reading. As a result, their achievement is considerably behind what would be expected on the basis of their IQ. (p. 250)

5. Using research to support your answer, how effective are mainstreaming and full inclusion? (p. 250)

   _____

187

6. Under which two classroom conditions do children with mild to moderate learning disabilities do best? (p. 250)

   A. _____

   B. _____

7. What special steps can be taken to promote peer acceptance of mainstreamed and fully included children? (p. 250)

   _____

8. List characteristics of *gifted* children. (p. 250)

   _____

9. Match each of the following terms with its appropriate description. (pp. 250–251)

   _____ Outstanding performance in a specific field
   _____ The ability to produce work that is original yet appropriate
   _____ Involves arriving at a single correct answer and is emphasized on intelligence tests
   _____ The generation of multiple and unusual possibilities when faced with a task or problem

   A. Creativity
   B. Divergent thinking
   C. Convergent thinking
   D. Talent

10. Cite parental characteristics that help nurture talented children. (p. 251)

    _____

11. Describe negative social consequences for children with extreme giftedness. (p. 251)

    _____

12. Briefly summarize the debate regarding the effectiveness of programs for the gifted. (p. 251)

    _____

How Well-Educated Are North American Children?

1. Cite four factors, both within and outside schools, that affect children's learning. (p. 252)

   A. _____

   B. _____

   C. _____

   D. _____

2. Explain why U.S. children fall behind in academic accomplishment. (p. 252)

_____

_____

_____

3. List four social forces that combine to foster a strong commitment to learning in Asian families and schools. (pp. 252–253)

   A. _____

   B. _____

   C. _____

   D. _____

ASK YOURSELF...

For *Ask Yourself* questions for this chapter, please log on to the Companion Website at *www.ablongman.com/berk*.

1. Select the Companion Website for *Exploring Lifespan Development*.
2. Use the "Jump to" menu to go directly to this chapter.
3. From the menu on the left side of the screen, select "Ask Yourself."
4. Complete questions and choose "Submit answers for grading" or "Clear answers" to start over.

SUGGESTED STUDENT READINGS

Champion, T. B. (2003). *Understanding storytelling among African-American children: A journey from Africa to America.* Mahwah, NJ: Erlbaum. A useful resource for teachers, researchers, and professionals working with African-American children, this book explores the unique communication style of black children, including the structure of their storytelling and its impact on learning and achievement.

Critser, G. (2003). *Fat land: How Americans became the fattest people in the world.* Boston: Houghton Mifflin. Explores how multiple aspects of American life—class, politics, culture, and economics—have contributed to the obesity epidemic. Also presents up-to-date research on childhood obesity, marketing tactics of fast-food chains, and adult-onset diabetes resulting from poor eating habits and includes suggestions for how American society should go about tackling this growing epidemic.

Jensen, P. S. (2004). *Making the system work for your child with ADHD.* New York: Guilford. Provides an extensive overview of ADHD, including diagnostic criteria, health care, resources, and problem-solving strategies to help parents effectively advocate for school services.

Sternberg, R. J., & Pretz, J. E. (Eds.). (2005). *Cognition and intelligence: Identifying the mechanisms of the mind.* Cambridge, England: Cambridge University Press. Written by leading experts, this book presents an extensive overview of research on cognition and intelligence, including current theories, up-to-date research, and future directions.

PUZZLE 9.1

Across
3. Transitive _____: the ability to seriate mentally
8. _____-_____ classroom: children participate in a wide range of challenging activities with teachers and peers, with whom they jointly construct understanding
10. Phonological _____: the ability to reflect on and manipulate the sound structure of spoken language, as indicated by sensitivity to changes in sounds within words and to incorrect pronunciation
11. _____ operational stage: Piaget's third stage, during which thought becomes more logical, flexible, and organized than it was during early childhood
12. Memory strategy of repeating the information
13. Ability to order items along a quantitative dimension
14. Cognitive _____: the ability to control internal and external distracting stimuli
15. Greater than 20 percent increase over average body weight, based on an individual's age, sex, and physical build
16. Memory strategy of creating a relationship between two or more pieces of information that are not members of the same category

Down
1. Ability to mentally go through a series of steps and then reverse direction, returning to the starting point
2. Memory strategy of grouping related items together
4. _____ classroom: encourages students to construct their own knowledge
5. Beginning reading view that children should be given simplified reading materials and should be coached on the basic rules for translating written text into sounds (2 words)
6. _____-_____ approach: beginning reading approach that parallels natural language and keeps reading materials whole and meaningful
7. Child's mental representation of familiar large-scale spaces, such as neighborhood or school (2 words)
8. Cognitive _____-_____: process of continually monitoring progress toward a goal, checking outcomes, and redirecting unsuccessful efforts
9. The fear of being judged on the basis of a negative stereotype, which can trigger anxiety that interferes with performance (2 words)

PUZZLE 9.2

Across

6. _____ teaching: a teacher and two to four students form a cooperative group and take turns leading dialogues on the content of a text passage
9. Displaying exceptional intellectual strengths
11. _____ thinking: generation of multiple and unusual possibilities when faced with a task or problem
13. _____-_____-_____ play: children's friendly chasing and play-fighting
14. Outstanding performance in a specific field
15. Full _____: refers to placement of students with learning difficulties in regular classrooms for the entire school day
16. _____ disabilities: great difficulty with one or more aspects of learning that results in poor school achievement, despite average to above-average IQ

Down

1. _____ assessment: individualized teaching is introduced into the testing situation to see what the child can attain with social support
2. Sternberg's _____ theory of successful intelligence states that information-processing skills, prior experience with tasks, and contextual factors combine to influence intelligent behavior.
3. _____ mental retardation: a condition that characterizes children whose IQs fall between 55 and 70, and who also show problems in adaptive behavior
4. _____ classroom: children are regarded as passive learners who acquire information presented by teachers
5. Educational _____-_____ prophecy: idea that students may adopt teachers' positive and negative attitudes toward them and start to live up to these views
7. Placement of students with learning difficulties in regular classrooms for part of the school day
8. _____ thinking: generation of a single correct answer for a problem
10. Ability to produce work that is original yet appropriate
12. _____ hierarchy: a stable ordering of group members that predicts who will win when conflict arises
17. Childhood disorder involving inattentiveness, impulsivity, and excessive motor activity (abbr.)

PRACTICE TEST #1

1. Retarded physical growth, low intelligence scores, poor motor coordination, and inattention are associated with (p. 226)
    a. otitis media.
    b. obesity.
    c. malnutrition.
    d. rapid development of the immune system.

2. The percentage of obese children who later become overweight adults is roughly (p. 227)
    a. 80 percent.
    b. 60 percent.
    c. 40 percent.
    d. 20 percent.

3. Dodging opponents in tag and soccer best exemplifies which of the following gross motor skills? (p. 228)
    a. balance
    b. agility
    c. force
    d. flexibility

4. During middle childhood, body growth and more efficient information processing contribute to (p. 228)
    a. sex differences in motor skills.
    b. improved motor performance.
    c. children's desire to play sports.
    d. gradual improvements in writing and drawing.

5. Gains in perspective taking permit the transition to (p. 229)
    a. training in competitive sports.
    b. gender-stereotyped games.
    c. participation and self-confidence in sports.
    d. rule-oriented games.

6. School-age boys (p. 229)
    a. continue to lag behind girls in other gross motor skills, such as throwing and kicking.
    b. have less confidence in their athletic abilities than school-age girls.
    c. have a genetic advantage in muscle mass that fully accounts for their gross-motor superiority.
    d. outperform girls in all gross motor skills except skipping, jumping, and hopping.

7. Piaget's concrete operational stage extends from about (p. 231)
    a. 3 to 5 years.
    b. 6 to 9 years.
    c. 7 to 11 years.
    d. 10 to 15 years.

8. Nine-year-old Billy understands transitive inference. This means he can (p. 232)
    a. draw an accurate map.
    b. seriate mentally.
    c. count by 10s to 1,000.
    d. recite the alphabet backwards.

9. In middle childhood, school-age children acquire networks of concepts and relations that permit them to think more effectively about a wide range of situations. Neo-Piagetian theorists call these networks (p. 233)
    a. cognitive maps.
    b. a continuum of acquisitions.
    c. transitive inference.
    d. central conceptual structures.

10. Gains in cognitive inhibition help school-age children (p. 234)
    a. prevent their minds from straying to irrelevant thoughts.
    b. retrieve information from long-term memory.
    c. retrieve information from short-term memory.
    d. understand their own mental processes.

11. Quentin needs to remember the words "tree" and "toaster." If he uses the memory strategy of elaboration, he will (p. 236)
    a. think of words that rhyme with both.
    b. imagine a tree with toasters growing out of it.
    c. write the words several times on a piece of paper.
    d. say the words over and over to himself.

12. In academic learning, some researchers believe that children should be taught to read using the whole-language approach. In this method, children should be (p. 238)
    a. taught to identify incorrect punctuation and changes in sounds, so they can manipulate the sound structure of spoken language.
    b. exposed to stories, poems, and letters in their complete form, so they can identify the basic rules of grammar.
    c. exposed to stories, poems, and letters in their complete form, so they can appreciate the communicative function of written language.
    d. exposed to simplified versions of stories, poems, and letters, so they can master the rules for translating written symbols into sounds.

13. The three broad, interacting intelligences identified by Sternberg's triarchic theory of successful intelligence are (p. 240)
    a. analytical intelligence, creative intelligence, and practical intelligence.
    b. analytical intelligence, mathematical intelligence, and imaginative intelligence.
    c. theoretical intelligence, creative intelligence, and inquisitive intelligence.
    d. theoretical intelligence, artistic intelligence, and practical intelligence.

14. In his theory of multiple intelligences, Gardner dismisses the idea of (p. 241)
    a. practical intelligence.
    b. general intelligence.
    c. spatial intelligence.
    d. culturally valued activities.

15. Eleven-year-old Sarah's performance on her state's standardized test is adversely affected by her worries that she, as an African-American student, is not expected to do well on the test. The anxiety she feels is known as (p. 243)
    a. dynamic assessment.
    b. test performance blocker.
    c. stereotype threat.
    d. cultural negativity.

16. When asked which shirt he wanted to wear, 9-year-old Vaughn said, "the blue shirt with the baseball on the sleeve." Vaughn's description illustrates which of the following language developments in middle childhood? (p. 246)
    a. vocabulary
    b. grammar
    c. a reflective approach to language
    d. pragmatics

17. Which of the following statements is true of bilingual development? (p. 247)
    a. When bilingual parents try to teach their children both languages during early childhood, the children often experience severe problems in language development.
    b. Parents and teachers should not be concerned if children learning two languages display inadequate proficiency in both languages.
    c. Recent research refutes the notion of a sensitive period for second language learning.
    d. Bilingual children are advanced in cognitive development.

18. In language immersion programs, (p. 247)
    a. only the second language being learned is used in the classroom.
    b. the second language being learned is gradually introduced.
    c. the second language being learned is not spoken in the classroom.
    d. the second language being learned is used equally with the native language.

19. Louisa has an above average IQ but is failing math. Louisa may have (p. 250)
    a. mild mental retardation.
    b. a learning disability.
    c. difficulty with divergent thinking.
    d. a lack of talent.

20. In international studies of reading, mathematics, and science achievement, children in the United States generally perform (p. 252)
    a. above children in Hong Kong, Korea, and Japan.
    b. far below the international average.
    c. far above the international average.
    d. at the international average.

PRACTICE TEST #2

1. During the school years, physical growth (p. 225)
    a. is most evident in the upper body, which is growing fastest.
    b. adds about 2 to 3 inches in height and 5 pounds in weight each year.
    c. quickly outpaces the slow growth of early childhood.
    d. is less for girls, who remain slightly shorter and lighter than boys for the duration of middle childhood.

2. What role does heredity play in child obesity? (p. 227)
    a. It is the leading cause.
    b. It plays no role.
    c. It accounts only for a tendency to gain weight.
    d. Children with obese parents are always obese themselves.

3. Obese children (p. 227)
    a. rarely become obese adults.
    b. eat more than their normal-weight peers but maintain a high level of physical activity.
    c. are more responsive to external stimuli associated with food and less responsive to internal hunger cues than their normal-weight peers.
    d. are no more likely to become depressed than their normal-weight peers.

4. By far the most common chronic disease or condition in North American children is (p. 228)
    a. asthma.
    b. diabetes.
    c. obesity.
    d. glaucoma.

5. Jillian and Justin are in the third grade. Which of the following statements best illustrates their motor skills? (p. 229)
    a. Both Jillian and Justin do well at skills requiring balance and agility, such as skipping and jumping.
    b. Jillian is ahead of Justin in drawing skills but lags behind in skipping, jumping, and hopping.
    c. Justin is able to throw and kick a ball farther than Jillian but is unable to write and draw as well as Jillian.
    d. Both Jillian and Justin do well on fine and gross motor tasks. Sex differences in motor skills don't become evident until adolescence.

6. As children reach puberty, individual differences in strength become apparent, and (p. 230)
   a. rough-and-tumble play declines.
   b. rough-and-tumble play begins.
   c. rough-and-tumble play increases.
   d. rough-and-tumble play disappears.

7. In first grade, Caleb began collecting baseball cards. Now that he's older, Caleb spends a great deal of time sorting his cards, arranging them by team, and putting them into albums. Which of Piaget's concepts is Caleb demonstrating? (p. 232)
   a. conservation
   b. centration
   c. classification
   d. spatial reasoning

8. The ability to order items along a quantitative dimension, such as length or weight, is called (p. 232)
   a. division.
   b. classification.
   c. conservation.
   d. seriation.

9. As 9-year-old Nancy repeats the state capitals to herself over and over again before a test, she is using the (p. 234)
   a. studying memory strategy.
   b. organization memory strategy.
   c. rehearsal memory strategy.
   d. planning memory strategy.

10. Parents and teachers can foster self-regulation by (p. 237)
    a. allowing children to figure out task demands independently.
    b. encouraging children to use ineffective strategies first and then providing them with more effective strategies.
    c. pointing out the special demands of tasks and suggesting effective strategies.
    d. forcing children to use strategies until they effectively apply them across settings.

11. In first grade, teaching that includes phonics (p. 238)
    a. is overwhelming for young children and can result in low reading achievement scores.
    b. only boosts reading achievement scores for children in high-SES homes.
    c. boosts reading achievement scores, especially for children from low-SES backgrounds who are at-risk for reading difficulties.
    d. has no empirical benefits over the whole-language approach.

12. The test that measures general intelligence and four broad factors (verbal reasoning, perceptual reasoning, working memory, and processing speed) and that is widely used for 6- through 16-year-olds is the (p. 240)
    a. Wechsler Intelligence Scale for Children.
    b. Stanford-Binet Intelligence Scale.
    c. Sternberg Triarchic Intelligence Scale.
    d. Piagetian Practical Intelligence Scale for Children.

13. Gardner defines intelligence in terms of (p.241)
    a. three broad interacting intelligences.
    b. 180 unique intellectual factors organized along three dimensions.
    c. a pyramid with "general intelligence" at the top.
    d. eight independent intelligences that are based on distinct sets of processing operations.

14. Adoption studies reveal that (p. 242)
    a. children of low-IQ biological mothers rarely benefit from being adopted by higher income families.
    b. children of low-IQ biological mothers show a steady decline in IQ over middle childhood.
    c. heredity is a more powerful predictor of IQ test performance than environmental factors.
    d. IQ test performance can be greatly improved by an advantaged home life.

15. Dynamic assessment (p. 244)
    a. shows no transfer effects to new test items.
    b. often underestimates the IQs of ethnic minority children.
    c. presents fewer challenges to children than traditional assessments.
    d. introduces purposeful teaching to find out what the child can attain with social support.

16. During the elementary school years, vocabulary increases (p. 245)
    a. twofold.
    b. threefold.
    c. fourfold.
    d. fivefold.

17. What percentage of American children speak a language other than English at home? (p. 246)
    a. 5 percent
    b. 15 percent
    c. 25 percent
    d. 45 percent

18. The time in which children can most readily learn to speak one, two, or more languages is known as a (p. 247)
    a. sensitive period.
    b. period of awareness.
    c. learning period.
    d. lingual period.

19. Students would be most likely to passively listen, respond only when called upon, and complete teacher-assigned tasks in (p. 248)
    a. reciprocal teaching.
    b. a social-constructivist classroom.
    c. a traditional classroom.
    d. a constructivist classroom.

20. Researchers newly distinguish children who are gifted from children with talent. Those in the latter category (p. 251)
    a. display exceptional intellectual strengths.
    b. display outstanding performance in a specific field.
    c. are able to produce original yet appropriate work.
    d. are able to generate unusual possibilities when faced with a task.

CHAPTER 10
EMOTIONAL AND SOCIAL DEVELOPMENT IN MIDDLE CHILDHOOD

BRIEF CHAPTER SUMMARY

According to Erikson, the combination of adult expectations and children's drive toward mastery sets the stage for the psychosocial conflict of middle childhood—industry versus inferiority—which is resolved positively when experiences lead children to develop a sense of competence at useful skills and tasks. Psychological traits and social comparisons appear in children's self-concepts, and a hierarchically organized self-esteem emerges. Greater self-awareness and social sensitivity support emotional development in middle childhood. Changes take place in experience of self-conscious emotions, emotional understanding, and emotional self-regulation. Cognitive maturity and experiences in which adults and peers encourage children to take note of another's viewpoint support gains in perspective-taking. An expanding social world, the capacity to consider more information when reasoning, and perspective taking lead moral understanding to advance greatly in middle childhood.

By the end of middle childhood, children form peer groups, which give them insight into larger social structures. One-to-one friendships strengthen, contributing to the development of trust and sensitivity. During the school years, friendship becomes more complex and psychologically based. Peer acceptance becomes a powerful predictor of current and future psychological adjustment.

School-age children extend the gender-stereotyped beliefs they acquired in early childhood. Boys' masculine gender identities strengthen, whereas girls' identities become more flexible. Cognitive and social forces influence these trends.

In middle childhood, the amount of time children spend with parents declines dramatically. Child rearing shifts toward coregulation as parents grant children more decision-making power. Sibling rivalry tends to increase in middle childhood, and, in response, siblings often strive to be different from one another. When children experience divorce—often followed by entry into blended families as a result of remarriage—child, parent, and family characteristics all influence how well they fare. Growing up in dual-earner families can have many benefits for school-age children, particularly when mothers enjoy their work, when work settings are flexible, and when high-quality child care is available, including appropriate after-school activities for school-age children.

Fears and anxieties in middle childhood are directed toward new concerns, including physical safety, media events, academic performance, parents' health, and peer relations. Child sexual abuse has devastating consequences for children and is especially difficult to treat. Personal characteristics of children, a warm, well-organized family life, and social supports outside the immediate family are related to the development of resilience: the ability to cope with stressful life conditions.

LEARNING OBJECTIVES

After reading this chapter, you should be able to:

10.1 Describe Erikson's stage of industry versus inferiority, noting major personality changes in middle childhood. (p. 257)

10.2 Describe school-age children's self-concept and self-esteem, and discuss factors that affect their achievement-related attributions. (pp. 257–260)

10.3 Cite changes in understanding and expression of emotion in middle childhood, including the importance of problem-centered coping and emotion-centered coping for managing emotion. (pp. 260–261)

10.4 Trace the development of perspective taking, and discuss the relationship between perspective taking and social skills. (pp. 261–262)

10.5 Describe changes in moral understanding during middle childhood. (pp. 262–263)

10.6 Summarize changes in peer sociability during middle childhood, including characteristics of peer groups and friendships. (pp. 264–265)

10.7 Describe four categories of peer acceptance, noting how each is related to social behavior, and discuss ways to help rejected children. (pp. 265–266)

10.8 Describe changes in gender-stereotyped beliefs and gender identity during middle childhood, including cognitive and social influences. (pp. 266–268)

10.9 Discuss changes in parent–child communication and sibling relationships in middle childhood, and describe the adjustment of only children. (pp. 268–270)

10.10 Discuss factors that influence children's adjustment to divorce and remarriage, highlighting the importance of parent and child characteristics as well as social supports within the family and surrounding community. (pp. 270–273)

10.11 Discuss the impact of maternal employment and life in dual-earner families on school-age children's development, noting the influence of social supports within the family and surrounding community, including child care for school-age children. (pp. 273–274)

10.12 Cite common fears and anxieties in middle childhood, with particular attention to school phobia. (p. 274)

10.13 Discuss factors related to child sexual abuse, and describe consequences for children's development. (pp. 274–276)

10.14 Cite factors that foster resilience in middle childhood. (pp. 276–277)

STUDY QUESTIONS

Erikson's Theory: Industry versus Inferiority

1. According to Erikson, what two factors set the stage for *industry versus inferiority*? (p. 257)
   A. _____
   B. _____

2. In industrialized nations, the beginning of _____ marks the transition to middle childhood. (p. 257)

3. List two factors that contribute to a sense of inferiority during middle childhood. (p. 257)
   A. _____
   B. _____

4. Erikson's sense of industry combines the following four developments: (p. 257)
   A. _____   B. _____
   C. _____   D. _____

Self-Understanding

1. List three ways that self-understanding changes in middle childhood. (p. 257)
   A. _____
   B. _____
   C. _____

Self-Concept

1. True or False: In middle childhood, children's self-descriptions emphasize competencies instead of specific behaviors. (p. 257)

2. How do older children differ from younger children in social comparisons? (p. 257)

3. Describe factors that are responsible for revisions in self-concept during middle childhood. (pp. 257–258)

4. Discuss the relationship between perspective-taking skills and the development of self-concept. (pp. 257–258)

5. True or False: Beginning in middle childhood, self-descriptions include frequent reference to social groups. (p. 258)

Development of Self-Esteem

1. List four broad self-evaluations that develop by the age of 6 to 7. (p. 258)

   A. _____ B. _____

   C. _____ D. _____

2. True or False: During middle childhood and adolescence, perceived physical appearance correlates more strongly with overall self-worth than any other self-esteem factor. (p. 258)

3. For most children, self-esteem (declines / increases) during the first few years of elementary school and then (declines / increases) from fourth to sixth grade. (p. 258)

Influences on Self-Esteem

1. True or False: From middle childhood on, individual differences in self-esteem become increasingly unstable. (p. 258)

2. Chinese and Japanese children score (lower / higher) in self-esteem than North American children. Briefly explain this finding. (p. 258)

3. Why do girls score slightly lower than boys in overall sense of self-worth? (pp. 258–259)

4. Compared to Caucasian children, African-American children tend to have slightly (higher / lower) self-esteem. Briefly explain this finding. (p. 259)

   _____
   _____

5. Describe child-rearing practices associated with high and low self-esteem in middle childhood. (p. 259)

   High self-esteem: _____
   _____

   Low self-esteem: _____
   _____

6. What is the best way to foster a positive, secure self-image in school-age children? (p. 259)

   _____
   _____

7. _____ are common, everyday explanations for the causes of behavior. (p. 259)

8. Distinguish between mastery-oriented attributions and learned helplessness, noting differences between children who possess these attributional styles. (pp. 259–260)

   Mastery-oriented attributions: _____
   _____
   _____

   Learned-helplessness: _____
   _____
   _____

9. True or False: Over time, the ability of learned-helpless children no longer predicts their performance. Explain your response. (p. 260)

   _____
   _____
   _____

10. How does adult communication contribute to the different attributions of mastery-oriented and learned-helpless children? (p. 260)

    _____
    _____
    _____
    _____

11. True or False: Girls and low-income ethnic minority children are especially vulnerable to negative adult feedback. (p. 260)

12. _____ is an intervention that encourages learned-helpless children to believe that they can overcome failure by exerting more effort. Briefly describe this technique. (p. 260)

    _____
    _____
    _____

Emotional Development

Self-Conscious Emotions

1. Describe changes in how children experience pride and guilt during middle childhood. (p. 261)

    Pride: _____

    _____

    _____

    Guilt: _____

    _____

    _____

Emotional Understanding

1. Describe how school-age children's ability to appreciate mixed emotions contributes to their emotional understanding. (p. 261)

    _____

    _____

2. What factors lead to a rise in empathy during middle childhood? (p. 261)

    _____

    _____

Emotional Self-Regulation

1. Describe two general strategies for managing emotion in middle childhood. (p. 261)

    Problem-centered coping: _____

    _____

    _____

    Emotion-centered coping: _____

    _____

    _____

2. True or False: In middle childhood, children tend to use internal strategies to regulate negative emotions. (p. 261)

3. Distinguish characteristics of emotionally well-regulated children versus children with poor emotional self-regulation. (p. 261)

    Well-regulated: _____

    _____

    _____

    Poorly regulated: _____

    _____

    _____

Understanding Others: Perspective Taking

1. Match each of Selman's stages of perspective taking with the appropriate description. (pp. 261–262)

   _____ Understands that third-party perspective taking can be influenced by larger societal values
   _____ Recognizes that self and others can have different perspectives, but confuse the two
   _____ Understands that different perspectives may be due to access to different information
   _____ Can imagine how the self and others are viewed from the perspective of an impartial third person
   _____ Can view own thoughts, feelings, and behavior from others' perspective

   A. Undifferentiated
   B. Social-informational
   C. Self-reflective
   D. Third-party
   E. Societal

2. Cite two factors that contribute to children's perspective taking. (p. 262)

   A. _____
   B. _____

Moral Development

Learning About Justice Through Sharing

1. Define *distributive justice,* and provide an example. (pp. 262–263)

   A. _____

   B. _____

2. Using Damon's three-step sequence, trace the development of distributive justice over early and middle childhood. (p. 263)

   A. _____

   B. _____

   C. _____

3. True or False: Peer interaction is particularly important in the development of distributive justice. (p. 263)

Moral and Social-Conventional Understanding

1. Describe two changes in moral and social-conventional understanding during middle childhood. (p. 263)

   A. _____

   B. _____

2. True or False: Children in Western and non-Western cultures reason similarly about moral and social-conventional concerns. (p. 263)

Understanding Individual Rights

1. How do notions of personal choice enhance children's moral understanding? (p. 263)

2. Describe changes in the understanding of individual choice among older school-age children. (p. 263)

3. True or False: Prejudice usually increases over middle childhood. (p. 263)

Peer Relations

Peer Groups

1. What is a *peer group*? (p. 264)

2. Describe the function of "peer culture," and discuss positive influences of group identity. (p. 264)

    A.

    B.

3. True or False: Most school-age children believe it is wrong to exclude a child from a peer group. (p. 264)

4. What are the outcomes for school-age children who are socially excluded from a peer group? (p. 264)

Friendships

1. Describe children's view of friendship in middle childhood. (p. 264)

2. True or False: School-age children are less selective in their choice of friends than they were at younger ages. (p. 264)

3. In what ways do school-age friends resemble one another? (p. 264)

    A.

    B.

4. Describe the qualities of aggressive children's friendships. (p. 265)

Aggressive girls: _____

_____

_____

Aggressive boys: _____

_____

_____

Peer Acceptance

1. Define *peer acceptance,* noting how it differs from friendship. (p. 265)

_____

_____

_____

2. Name and define the four categories of peer acceptance. (p. 265)

   A. _____ B. _____

   C. _____ D. _____

3. True or False: All school-age children fit into one of the categories of peer acceptance described in Question 2. (p. 265)

4. Cite several consequences of peer rejection in middle childhood. (p. 265)

_____

_____

_____

5. What two early influences largely explain the link between peer acceptance and adjustment? (p. 265)

   A. _____

   B. _____

6. Match the following subtypes of popular and rejected children to the appropriate description. (pp. 265–266)

   _____ Shows high rates of conflict, physical and relational aggression, and hyperactivity, inattention, and impulsive behavior
   _____ Combines academic and social competence, performing well in school and communicating with peers in sensitive, friendly, and cooperative ways
   _____ Includes "tough" boys who are athletically skilled but poor students who cause trouble and defy adult authority
   _____ Includes timid children who are passive and socially awkward

   A. Popular-prosocial children
   B. Rejected-aggressive children
   C. Rejected-withdrawn children
   D. Popular-antisocial children

7. True or False: Controversial children are hostile and disruptive but also engage in high rates of positive, prosocial acts. (p. 266)

8. True or False: Neglected children are more poorly adjusted and display less socially competent behavior than their "average" counterparts. (p. 266)

9. Most interventions aimed at improving the peer relations and psychological adjustment of rejected children involve _____, _____, and _____. (p. 266)

10. True or False: Interventions that focus primarily on the rejected child may not be effective. Explain your answer. (p. 266)

Biology and Environment: Bullies and Their Victims

1. What is *peer victimization*? (p. 267)

2. Describe characteristics of bullies. (p. 267)

3. Describe biologically based traits and family characteristics of victimized children. (p. 267)

    Biological:

    Family:

4. List adjustment difficulties associated with peer victimization. (p. 267)

5. Briefly describe characteristics of effective interventions for rejected children. (p. 267)

Gender Typing

Gender-Stereotyped Beliefs

1. Describe ways that children extend their gender-stereotyped beliefs during middle childhood. (p. 266)

2. Explain how adult treatment of boys and girls contributes to children's gender-stereotyped beliefs. (p. 266)

3. List academic subjects and skills that children stereotype as either masculine or feminine. (p. 266)

   Masculine: _____

   _____

   Feminine: _____

   _____

4. True or False: As school-age children extend their knowledge of gender stereotypes, they become more closed-minded about what males and females can do. (p. 266)

Gender Identity and Behavior

1. Contrast the gender identity development of girls and boys during middle childhood. (p. 267)

   Girls: _____

   _____

   Boys: _____

   _____

2. List and define three self-evaluations that make up school-age children's gender identity. (p. 268)

   A. _____

   B. _____

   C. _____

3. Gender-typical and gender-contented children (increase / decline) in self-esteem in middle childhood. In contrast, gender-atypical and gender-discontented children (increase / decline). (p. 268)

Family Influences

Parent–Child Relationships

1. True or False: In middle childhood, the amount of time that children spend with parents declines dramatically. (p. 268)

2. During the school years, child rearing becomes easier for those parents who established a(n) _____ parenting style during the early years. (p. 268)

3. What is *coregulation* and how does it foster a cooperative relationship between parent and child? (pp. 268–269)

   A. _____

   _____

   B. _____

   _____

4. Describe differences in mother and father involvement during the school years. (p. 269)

   Mother involvement: _____

   _____

   Father involvement: _____

   _____

Siblings

1. In middle childhood, sibling rivalry tends to (increase / decrease). (p. 269)

2. Cite sibling characteristics associated with frequent parental comparisons, noting the impact of these comparisons on development. (p. 269)

   Sibling characteristics: _____

   _____

   _____

   Impact: _____

   _____

   _____

3. What do children often do to reduce sibling rivalry? (p. 269)

   _____

   _____

Only Children

1. True or False: Research indicates that sibling relationships are essential for healthy development. (p. 269)

2. True or False: Research supports the commonly held belief that only children are spoiled and selfish. (p. 269)

3. Discuss the developmental advantages and disadvantages of being an only child. (p. 269)

   Advantages: _____

   _____

   Disadvantages: _____

   _____

Divorce

1. True or False: The United States has the highest divorce rate in the world, while Canada has the sixth highest. (p. 270)

2. True or False: About two-thirds of divorced parents marry again, and about half of those marriages end in divorce. (p. 270)

3. Summarize ways that divorce has an immediate impact on the home environment. (pp. 270–271)

   _____

   _____

   _____

4. Explain how younger and older children react to divorce. (p. 271)

   Younger: _____

   _____

   _____

   Older: _____

   _____

   _____

5. Summarize sex differences in children's reactions to divorce. (p. 271)

   Boys: _____

   _____

   _____

   Girls: _____

   _____

   _____

6. In mother-custody families, (girls / boys) typically experience more serious adjustment problems. (p. 271)

7. Most children show improved adjustment by _____ years after their parents' divorce. (p. 271)

8. True or False: For both sexes, divorce is linked to problems with adolescent sexuality and development of intimate ties. (p. 271)

9. What is the overriding factor in children's positive adjustment following parental divorce? (p. 271)

   _____

10. Explain why a good father–child relationship is important for both boys and girls following a parental divorce. (p. 271)

    Boys: _____

    _____

    _____

    Girls: _____

    _____

    _____

11. True or False: Transitioning to a low-conflict, single-parent household is better for children than staying in a high-conflict, intact family. (p. 271)

12. Describe *divorce mediation,* and explain why it is beneficial for children. (p. 271)

    A. _____

    _____

    B. _____

    _____

13. In _____, the court grants the mother and father equal say in important decisions regarding the child's upbringing. (p. 271)

14. True or False: All U.S. states and Canadian provinces have procedures for withholding wages from parents who fail to make child support payments. (p. 271)

Blended Families

1. List two reasons why blended families present adjustment difficulties for most children. (p. 272)

   A. _____

   _____

   B. _____

   _____

2. (Older / Younger) children and (girls / boys) have the hardest time adjusting to a blended family. (p. 272)

3. The most frequent form of blended family is a (father-stepmother / mother-stepfather) arrangement. Contrast boys' and girls' adjustment in this type of family. (pp. 272–273)

   Boys: _____

   _____

   Girls: _____

   _____

4. Explain why older children and adolescents of both sexes living in mother-stepfather families display more irresponsible, acting out, and antisocial behavior than their agemates. (p. 273)

   _____

   _____

   _____

5. Remarriage of noncustodial fathers often leads to (reduced / increased) contact with children. (p. 273)

6. Cite two alternative reasons why children tend to react negatively to the remarriage of custodial fathers. (p. 273)

   A. _____

   B. _____

7. (Girls / Boys) have an especially hard time getting along with stepmothers. Briefly explain your response. (p. 273)

   _____

   _____

8. Explain how family life education and therapy can help parents and children in blended families adapt to the complexities of their new circumstances. (p. 273)

   _____

   _____

   _____

Maternal Employment and Dual-Earner Families

1. True or False: Single mothers are far more likely than their married counterparts to enter the workforce. (p. 273)

2. Describe potential benefits of maternal employment for school-age children, noting the circumstances under which positive outcomes are achieved. (p. 273)

   _____

   _____

   _____

   _____

3. True or False: Maternal employment leads fathers to take on greater child-rearing responsibilities. (p. 273)

4. Discuss the risks of stressful maternal employment on child adjustment. (p. 273)

   _____

   _____

5. True or False: Self-care increases with age and also with SES. (p. 273)

6. Describe self-care children's adjustment, and provide reasons for variations in adjustment. (p. 273)

   A. _____

   B. _____

7. Before age _____ or _____, children need supervision because they are not yet competent to handle emergencies. (p. 273)

Some Common Problems of Development

Fears and Anxieties

1. List new fears and anxieties that emerge in middle childhood. (p. 274)

2. What is the most common source of children's fears in Western nations? (p. 274)

3. Describe the symptoms of *school phobia*. (p. 274)

4. Most cases of school phobia appear around age ___ to ___. List common causes of school phobia during this time. (p. 274)

A Lifespan Vista: Children of War

1. Discuss children's adjustment to war and social crises, noting differences between situations involving temporary crises and those involving chronic danger. (p. 275)

2. What is the best safeguard against lasting problems? (p. 275)

3. Discuss some interventions used to help children from Public School 31 in Brooklyn, New York, in the wake of the September 11 attack on the World Trade Center. (p. 275)

Child Sexual Abuse

1. Sexual abuse is committed against children of both sexes, but more often against (girls / boys). (p. 276)

2. List typical characteristics of sexual abusers. (p. 276)

3. What type of children do abusers often target? (p. 276)

4. Discuss the adjustment problems of sexually abused children, noting differences between younger children and adolescents. (p. 276)

   Younger children: _____

   Adolescents: _____

5. Describe common behavioral characteristics of sexually abused girls as they move into early adulthood. (p. 276)

6. Why is it difficult to treat victims of child sexual abuse? (p. 276)

7. Discuss the role of educational programs in preventing child sexual abuse. (p. 276)

Fostering Resilience in Middle Childhood

1. List four broad factors that help children cope with stress and protect against maladjustment. (p. 277)

    A. _____

    B. _____

    C. _____

    D. _____

2. True or False: Resilience is a preexisting attribute. Explain your answer. (p. 277)

    _____

    _____

ASK YOURSELF . . .

For *Ask Yourself* questions for this chapter, please log on to the Companion Website at *www.ablongman.com/berk*.

1. Select the Companion Website for *Exploring Lifespan Development*.
2. Use the "Jump to" menu to go directly to this chapter.
3. From the menu on the left side of the screen, select "Ask Yourself."
4. Complete questions and choose "Submit answers for grading" or "Clear answers" to start over.

SUGGESTED STUDENT READINGS

Bierman, K. L. (2005). *Peer rejection: Developmental processes and intervention strategies.* New York: Guilford. Presents an extensive overview of research on peer rejection, including causes and correlates, characteristics of bullies and their victims, long-term consequences, and intervention strategies for parents and educators.

Dunn, J. (2004). *Children's friendships: The beginnings of intimacy.* Oxford, U.K.: Blackwell. Explores the nature and significance of children's friendships, age-related changes in concepts of friendship, and suggestions for parents and teachers on how to handle friendship difficulties and bullying.

Hetherington, E. M., & Kelly, J. (2003). *For better or worse: Divorce reconsidered.* New York: Norton. A longitudinal approach to understanding the effects of divorce on children, this book presents the nature and consequences of divorce in American culture.

Krippner, S., & McIntyre, T. M. (Eds.). (2003). *The psychological impact of war trauma on civilians: An international perspective.* Westport, CT: Praeger. A collection of chapters highlighting both the short- and long-term effects of war on individuals throughout the world. Although this book does not exclusively focus on the impact of war on children, several chapters thoroughly examine children's reactions to war, including therapeutic efforts for treating traumatized children.

PUZZLE 10.1

Across
1. Distributive _____ refers to beliefs about how to divide material goods fairly.
7. Children with _____-_____ attributions credit their successes to ability and their failures to insufficient effort or the difficulty of the task.
9. Divorce _____ attempts to settle disputes of divorcing couples while avoiding legal battles that intensify family conflict.
10. _____ versus inferiority: Erikson's psychological crisis of middle adulthood

Down
2. Supervision in which parents exercise general oversight but permit children to manage moment-to-moment decisions
3. Social _____: judging one's appearance, abilities, and behavior in relation to those of others
4. Children who develop learned _____ attribute failures, but not successes, to ability.
5. In _____ custody, the court grants both parents equal say in important decisions about the child's upbringing.
6. _____-taking: the capacity to imagine what other people may be thinking and feeling
8. _____-_____ children regularly look after themselves during after-school hours.

PUZZLE 10.2

Across
1. _____ children get a large number of positive and negative votes on sociometric measures of peer acceptance
3. Popular-_____ children: subgroup of popular children largely made up of "tough" boys who are athletically skilled, highly aggressive, defiant of adult authority, and poor students
4. Rejected-_____ children: subgroup of rejected children who engage in high rates of conflict, hostility, and hyperactive, inattentive, and impulsive behavior
5. Peer _____: peers who form a social unit by generating unique values and standards of behavior and a social structure of leaders and followers
7. Peer _____ refers to likability, the extent to which a child is viewed by agemates as a worthy social partner
9. _____ children are seldom chosen, either positively or negatively, on sociometric measures of peer acceptance
11. An intense, unmanageable fear
12. Peer _____: destructive form of peer interaction in which certain children become frequent targets of verbal and physical attacks or other forms of abuse
13. _____-_____ coping: refers to adaptive coping in which the situation is appraised, the difficulty is identified, and a decision is made
14. Rejected-_____ children: subgroup of rejected children who are passive and socially awkward

Down
2. _____-_____ coping: internal, private coping aimed at controlling distress when little can be done about an outcome
6. _____ children are actively disliked and get many negative votes on sociometric measures of peer acceptance.
8. _____, or reconstituted, families: family structure comprised of the parent, stepparent, and children
10. _____ children get many positive votes on sociometric measures of peer acceptance
11. Popular-_____ children: subgroup of popular children who combine academic and social competence

PRACTICE TEST #1

1. Ten-year-old Sandra has begun to compare her performance level to more than one other student. Sandra has begun making (p. 258)
   a. peer comparisons.
   b. social comparisons.
   c. peer judgments.
   d. social judgments.

2. Over the first few years of elementary school, children's level of self-esteem (p. 258)
   a. declines.
   b. stabilizes.
   c. slowly increases.
   d. emerges.

3. In overall sense of self-worth, (p. 258)
   a. boys score slightly lower than girls.
   b. girls score slightly lower than boys.
   c. girls score dramatically lower than boys.
   d. boys and girls score the same.

4. Children who develop mastery-oriented attributions (p. 259)
   a. persist on tasks when they succeed but experience an anxious loss of control when they are given a difficult task.
   b. attribute failures to lack of ability, which they regard as a fixed trait.
   c. believe they can succeed at challenging tasks by increasing their effort.
   d. tend to have parents who use an authoritarian style of child rearing.

5. Attribution retraining (p. 260)
   a. encourages learned-helpless children to attribute their success, but not their failures, to external factors.
   b. provides children with easy tasks in order to prevent failure and negative attributions.
   c. teaches low-effort children to focus less on learning and more on grades.
   d. encourages children to view their successes as due to both ability and effort rather than chance events.

6. During which of Selman's stages of perspective taking can children "step into another person's shoes" and view their own feelings and behavior from the other person's perspective? (p. 262)
   a. self-reflective perspective taking
   b. third-party perspective taking
   c. societal perspective taking
   d. undifferentiated perspective taking

7. Most 5- to 6-year-olds' ideas about sharing focus on (p. 263)
   a. merit.
   b. strict equality.
   c. equity and benevolence.
   d. "everything for me."

8. Which of the following is true of school-age children's peer groups? (p. 264)
   a. Peer groups organize on the basis of shared values and morals.
   b. Once children begin to form peer groups, relational and overt aggression toward "outgroup" members declines dramatically.
   c. Peer groups often direct their hostilities toward no longer "respected" children within their own group.
   d. Formal group ties (e.g., scouting, 4-H) are ineffective for meeting school-age children's desire for group belonging.

9. Research on peer acceptance indicates that (p. 265)
    a. all children fit into one of the four categories of peer acceptance—popular, rejected, neglected, or controversial.
    b. rejected children, in particular, are at risk for poor school performance, absenteeism, dropping out, and antisocial behavior.
    c. peer status during the school years is unrelated to later adjustment.
    d. controversial children have few friends and are typically unhappy with their peer relationships.

10. Research on social behavior indicates that (p. 266)
    a. neglected children are usually well-adjusted.
    b. rejected-withdrawn children display a blend of positive and negative social behaviors.
    c. controversial children are at high risk for social exclusion.
    d. popular-prosocial children are often "tough" boys who are athletically skilled but poor students.

11. In general, school-age boys feel more competent than school-age girls at (p. 266)
    a. reading.
    b. language arts.
    c. art.
    d. math and science.

12. A transitional form of supervision in which parents exercise general oversight while permitting children to be in charge of moment-by-moment decision making is called (pp. 268–269)
    a. permissive parenting.
    b. cooperative parenting.
    c. coregulation.
    d. self-regulation.

13. During middle childhood, sibling rivalry (p. 269)
    a. tends to decrease.
    b. tends to increase.
    c. is very rare.
    d. is most common when siblings are far apart in age.

14. Compared with agemates who have siblings, only children (pp. 269–270)
    a. exhibit higher rates of hyperactive, inattentive, and impulsive behavior.
    b. tend to be more well-accepted by peers.
    c. are less socially competent.
    d. do better in school and attain higher levels of education.

15. Children of divorce live, on average, in a single-parent home for (p. 270)
    a. 2 years.
    b. 5 years.
    c. 10 years.
    d. 15 years.

16. What percentage of children in divorced families display severe problems? (p. 271)
    a. 10–12 percent
    b. 15–20 percent
    c. 20–25 percent
    d. 30–40 percent

17. Research suggests that, in the long run, divorce (p. 271)
    a. is better for children than remaining in a high-conflict intact family.
    b. has no impact on children's behavior and adjustment.
    c. is often associated with serious difficulties that persist into adulthood.
    d. is more detrimental for girls than for boys.

18. How can divorced parents BEST increase the chances that their children will grow up competent, stable, and happy? (p. 271)
    a. by supporting one another in their child-rearing roles
    b. by moving far enough away from each other to mask the conflict
    c. by not interacting with one another unless absolutely necessary
    d. by battling in court for joint custody

19. Because Suzie is at home after school for several hours by herself, she is a (p. 274)
    a. home-alone child.
    b. self-care child.
    c. stay-at-home child.
    d. self-aware child.

20. Research on child sexual abuse indicates that (p. 276)
    a. both boys and girls are equally likely to be sexually abused.
    b. reported cases are highest in early childhood and adolescence.
    c. the abuser is most often a parent or someone the child knows well.
    d. most sexually abused children experience only a single incident of abuse.

PRACTICE TEST #2

1. Erikson believed that the combination of _____ and _____ sets the stage for the conflict of industry versus inferiority in middle childhood (p. 257)
    a. parental responsiveness; child-rearing practices
    b. children's sense of purposefulness; adults' willingness to help
    c. adult expectations; children's drive toward mastery
    d. children's drive toward mastery; child-rearing practices

2. Which of the following is true of the cultural and familial influences on self-esteem? (p. 259)
    a. Because of their higher academic achievement, Chinese and Japanese children have higher self-esteem than North American children.
    b. Girls tend to have higher self-esteem than boys.
    c. Caucasian children typically have higher self-esteem than African-American children.
    d. Children whose parents adopt an authoritative style of childrearing have especially high self-esteem.

3. Children who attribute their failures, not their successes, to ability have developed (p. 260)
    a. learned helplessness.
    b. mastery-oriented attributions.
    c. self-esteem.
    d. a social comparison.

4. Children who develop learned helplessness (p. 260)
    a. think that ability can be changed through increased effort.
    b. do not develop the metacognitive and self-regulatory skills necessary for high achievement.
    c. often persevere on difficult tasks in an effort to gain a sense of mastery and competence.
    d. have parents who set unusually low standards.

5. By age 10, most children shift adaptively between two general strategies for managing emotion: (p. 261)
    a. self-efficacy and self-awareness.
    b. self-regulation and self-control.
    c. problem-centered coping and emotion-centered coping.
    d. goal-oriented management and process-oriented management.

6. As Marcus, Andy, Karen, and Jane decide how to divide up eleven marbles, they are partaking in (pp. 262–263)
    a. distributive justice.
    b. problem-centered coping.
    c. self-efficacy.
    d. mastery-oriented distribution.

7. Damon's sequence of distributive justice reasoning is as follows: (p. 263)
    a. merit, equality, and benevolence.
    b. equality, merit, and benevolence.
    c. benevolence, equality, and merit.
    d. merit, benevolence, and equality.

8. By the end of middle childhood, children display a strong desire for group belonging. They form collectives that generate unique values and standards for behavior and a social structure of leaders and followers. These collectives are called (p. 264)
    a. niche circles.
    b. friendship trusts.
    c. emotion-centered groups.
    d. peer groups.

9. Most school-age children believe that excluding a peer from a group is (p. 264)
    a. justified in most cases.
    b. always acceptable.
    c. wrong.
    d. funny.

10. Rejected-aggressive children (pp. 265–266)
    a. make up the smallest subgroup of rejected children.
    b. are deficient in perspective taking and regulation of emotion.
    c. are passive and socially awkward.
    d. are hostile and disruptive but also engage in positive, prosocial acts.

11. The degree to which a child feels similar to others of the same gender is called gender (p. 268)
    a. behavior.
    b. typicality.
    c. contentedness.
    d. influence.

12. Sibling rivalry tends to be especially strong (p. 269)
    a. among siblings who are close in age.
    b. when siblings strive to be different from one another.
    c. among other-sex siblings.
    d. when parents fail to make comparisons between children.

13. Sibling relationships bring many benefits, (p. 269)
    a. and they are essential for healthy development.
    b. but they are, overall, detrimental to healthy development.
    c. and no detrimental issues to healthy development.
    d. but they are not essential for healthy development.

14. Immediately following a divorce, (p. 270)
    a. family conflict declines.
    b. discipline becomes more consistent and reasonable.
    c. children have frequent contact with noncustodial fathers.
    d. mothers experience high rates of stress, depression, and anxiety, which typically leads to a disorganized family situation.

15. After a parental divorce, most children show improved adjustment by (p. 271)
    a. 4 to 6 weeks.
    b. 6 months.
    c. 2 years.
    d. 5 years.

16. Divorce mediation (p. 271)
    a. involves a series of meetings between divorcing adults and a trained professional aimed at reducing family conflict.
    b. encourages both parents to remain involved by granting the mother and father equal say in important decisions about the child's upbringing.
    c. involves court mandated counseling to help divorcing couples resolve their differences.
    d. has been shown to increase out-of-court settlements, although compliance with these agreements and cooperation between parents is low.

17. The new family formed between parent, stepparent, and new siblings is called the (p. 272)
    a. post-divorce family.
    b. joint family.
    c. blended family.
    d. step family.

18. Of the following reconstituted family arrangements, the one most likely to work out well is a (p. 272)
    a. girl in a mother-stepfather family.
    b. boy in a mother-stepfather family.
    c. girl in a father-stepmother family.
    d. boy in a father-stepmother family.

19. Child self-care is (p. 274)
    a. consistently linked with adjustment problems, including low self-esteem, antisocial behavior, and poor academic achievement.
    b. associated with worse outcomes for older children than for younger children.
    c. inappropriate for children who are not yet competent to handle emergencies.
    d. associated with positive outcomes for children who have a history of permissive parenting.

20. Sexual offenders tend to select child victims who are (p. 276)
    a. physically attractive.
    b. popular and outgoing.
    c. hostile and aggressive.
    d. physically weak, emotionally deprived, and socially isolated.

CHAPTER 11
PHYSICAL AND COGNITIVE DEVELOPMENT IN ADOLESCENCE

BRIEF CHAPTER SUMMARY

The beginning of adolescence is marked by puberty: biological changes leading to physical and sexual maturity. Modern research has shown that adolescence is a product of biological, psychological, and social forces.

Genetically influenced hormonal processes regulate pubertal growth. On average, girls reach puberty two years earlier than boys. As the body enlarges, girls' hips and boys' shoulders broaden, girls add more fat, and boys add more muscle. Puberty is accompanied by steady improvement in gross motor performance, but whereas girls' gains are slow and gradual, leveling off by age 14, boys show a dramatic spurt in strength, speed, and endurance that continues through the teenage years.

Menarche, or first menstruation, occurs late in the girl's sequence of pubertal events, following the rapid increase in body size. Among boys, spermarche (first ejaculation) occurs around age 13½, as the sex organs and body enlarge and pubic and underarm hair appears. Heredity, nutrition, and overall health contribute to the timing of puberty. A secular trend in pubertal timing reflects the role of physical well-being. Brain development continues in adolescence, supporting cognitive advances as well as more intense reactions to stimuli.

Puberty is related to a rise in parent–child conflict, but this is usually mild. Parent–child distancing seems to be a modern substitute for the physical departure of young people in nonindustrialized cultures and among nonhuman primates. Reactions to pubertal changes are influenced by prior knowledge, support from family members, and cultural attitudes toward puberty and sexuality. Puberty is related to increased moodiness and a mild rise in parent–child conflict. Early-maturing boys and late-maturing girls, whose appearance closely matches cultural standards of physical attractiveness, have a more positive body image and usually adjust well in adolescence. In contrast, early-maturing girls and late-maturing boys experience emotional and social difficulties.

The arrival of puberty is accompanied by new health issues related to the young person's striving to meet physical and psychological needs. As the body grows, nutritional requirements increase. Eating disorders, sexually transmitted diseases, adolescent pregnancy and parenthood, and substance abuse are some of the most serious health concerns of the teenage years.

During Piaget's formal operational stage, young people develop the capacity for systematic, scientific thinking, arriving at new, more general logical rules through internal reflection. Piaget believed that adolescents become capable of hypothetico-deductive reasoning, in which they begin with a hypothesis, or prediction, from which they deduce logical inferences. Piaget used the term *propositional thought* to refer to adolescents' ability to evaluate the logic of verbal statements without referring to real-world circumstances. Recent research indicates that adolescents are capable of a much deeper grasp of scientific principles than are school-age children. However, even well-educated adults have difficulty with formal operational reasoning, indicating that Piaget's highest stage is affected by specific, school-learning opportunities. Information-processing theorists agree with the broad outlines of Piaget's description of adolescent cognition. But they refer to a variety of specific mechanisms for cognitive change, with metacognition regarded as central to adolescent cognitive development. By coordinating theories with evidence, adolescents develop advanced scientific reasoning skills.

The development of formal operations leads to dramatic revisions in the way adolescents see themselves, others, and the world in general. Using their new cognitive powers, teenagers become more argumentative, idealistic, and critical. Although they show gains in self-regulation, adolescents often have difficulty making decisions in everyday life.

School transitions create adjustment problems for adolescents, especially girls. Teenagers who must cope with added stresses are at greatest risk for adjustment problems following school change. Enhanced support from parents, teachers, and peers eases the strain of school transition.

Adolescent achievement is the result of a long history of cumulative effects. Early on, positive educational environments, both family and school, lead to personal traits that support achievement. The dropout rate in the United States and Canada is particularly high among low-SES ethnic minority youths and is affected by family and school experiences.

LEARNING OBJECTIVES

After reading this chapter, you should be able to:

11.1 Explain how conceptions of adolescence changed over the past century. (pp. 283–284)

11.2 Describe pubertal changes in body size, proportions, motor performance, and sexual maturity. (pp. 284–287)

11.3 Cite factors that influence the timing of puberty. (p. 287)

11.4 Describe brain development in adolescence. (pp. 287–288)

11.5 Discuss adolescents' reactions to the physical changes of puberty, including sex differences, and describe the influence of family and culture. (pp. 288–290)

11.6 Discuss the impact of maturational timing on adolescent adjustment, noting sex differences. (pp. 290–291)

11.7 Describe the nutritional needs, and cite factors related to serious eating disturbances during adolescence. (pp. 291–292)

11.8 Discuss social and cultural influences on adolescent sexual attitudes and behavior. (pp. 292–294)

11.9 Describe factors involved in the development of homosexuality, and discuss the unique adjustment problems of gay and bisexual youths. (pp. 294–296)

11.10 Discuss factors related to sexually transmitted diseases and to teenage pregnancy and parenthood, including interventions for adolescent parents. (pp. 296–298)

11.11 Cite personal and social factors that contribute to adolescent substance use and abuse, and describe prevention and treatment programs. (pp. 298–299)

11.12 Describe the major characteristics of formal operational thought. (pp. 300–301)

11.13 Discuss recent research on formal operational thought and its implications for the accuracy of Piaget's formal operational stage. (pp. 301–302)

11.14 Explain how information-processing researchers account for cognitive change in adolescence, emphasizing the development of scientific reasoning. (pp. 302–303)

11.15 Describe cognitive and behavioral consequences of adolescents' newfound capacity for advanced thinking. (pp. 303–305)

11.16 Discuss the impact of school transitions on adolescent adjustment, and cite ways to ease the strain of these changes. (pp. 305–306)

11.17 Discuss the influence of family, peer, and classroom learning experiences on academic achievement during adolescence. (pp. 306–308)

11.18 Describe personal, family, and school factors related to dropping out, and cite ways to prevent early school leaving. (pp. 308–310)

STUDY QUESTIONS

Physical Development

Conceptions of Adolescence

1. Describe G. Stanley Hall's view of adolescence. (p. 283)

   _____
   _____

2. True or False: Contemporary research shows that the storm-and-stress notion of adolescence is exaggerated. (p. 283)

3. Describe Margaret Mead's view of adolescent development. (p. 283)

   _____
   _____
   _____

4. Cite three factors that combine to influence adolescent development. (pp. 283–284)

   A. _____
   B. _____
   C. _____

5. True or False: The demands and pressures of adolescence are similar across cultures. Explain your answer. (p. 284)

   _____
   _____

Puberty: The Physical Transition to Adulthood

Hormonal Changes

1. Secretions of _____ and _____ increase during puberty, leading to tremendous gains in body size and attainment of skeletal maturity. (p. 284)

2. Cite ways that estrogens and androgens contribute to pubertal growth in both sexes. (p. 284)

   Estrogens: _____

   Androgens: _____

3. Pubertal changes can be divided into two broad types. (p. 284)

   A. _____   B. _____

Body Growth

1. The first outward sign of puberty is the rapid gain in height and weight known as the _____. (p. 284)

2. On average, the adolescent *growth spurt* is underway for North American girls shortly after age _____ and for boys around age _____. (p. 284)

3. True or False: During adolescence, the cephalocaudal growth trend of infancy and childhood reverses. (p. 284)

4. Briefly describe sex differences in body proportions and muscle-fat makeup during adolescence. (pp. 284–285)

Boys: _____

_____

Girls: _____

_____

Motor Development and Physical Activity

1. How does motor development differ between adolescent girls and boys? (p. 285)

    Adolescent girls: _____

    _____

    Adolescent boys: _____

    _____

2. Among (boys / girls) athletic competence is (modestly / strongly) related to peer admiration and self-esteem. (p. 285)

3. Describe adolescents' use of performance-enhancing drugs, noting the side effects of anabolic steroids. (p. 285)

    _____

    _____

    _____

4. Cite the benefits of sports and exercise in adolescence. (p. 286)

    _____

    _____

    _____

Sexual Maturation

1. Distinguish between *primary* and *secondary sexual characteristics*. (p. 286)

    Primary: _____

    Secondary: _____

2. _____, or first menstruation, typically happens around age _____ for North American girls and age _____ for European girls. Around age _____ boys experience _____ or first ejaculation. (p. 287)

Individual Differences in Pubertal Growth

1. Cite evidence that heredity contributes to the timing of puberty. What roles do nutrition and exercise play? (p. 287)

    A. _____

    B. _____

2. True or False: Explain how early family experiences contribute to the timing of puberty. (p. 287)

    _____

    _____

5. Discuss the long-term consequences of early and late maturation. (pp. 290–291)

   Early maturation: _____
   _____
   _____

   Late maturation: _____
   _____
   _____

Health Issues

Nutritional Needs

1. True or False: Of all age groups, adolescents are the most likely to skip breakfast, consume empty calories, and eat on the run. (p. 291)

2. List two factors that are associated with consumption of high-fat foods and soft drinks. (p. 291)

   A. _____
   B. _____

3. What factor strongly predicts healthy eating in teenagers? (p. 291)
   _____

Eating Disorders

1. What three factors put adolescents at high risk for serious eating problems? (p. 291)

   A. _____
   B. _____
   C. _____

2. Describe characteristics of *anorexia nervosa*. (p. 291)
   _____
   _____
   _____

3. Cite forces within the person, the family, and the larger culture that give rise to anorexia nervosa. (pp. 291–292)

   Individual: _____
   _____

   Family: _____
   _____

   Culture: _____
   _____

4. Why is treating anorexia nervosa so difficult? (p. 292)
   _____
   _____
   _____

5. Describe characteristics of *bulimia nervosa*. (p. 292)

   _____
   _____
   _____

6. True or False: Bulimia is far less common than anorexia nervosa. (p. 292)

7. How are bulimics similar to anorexics? How are they different? (p. 292)

   Similar: _____

   Different: _____

Sexual Activity

1. Explain how hormonal changes contribute to an increased sex drive in adolescence. (p. 292)

   _____
   _____
   _____

2. Why do many parents avoid meaningful discussions about sex? (p. 293)

   _____
   _____

3. True or False: Adolescents tend to receive contradictory messages about sex from their parents and the media. Explain your answer. (p. 293)

   _____
   _____
   _____

4. Describe trends in the sexual behavior of adolescents in the United States and Canada. (pp. 293–294)

   _____
   _____
   _____

5. True or False: American youths tend to begin sexual activity at a younger age than their Canadian and Western European counterparts. (p. 293)

6. Cite at least six factors that are linked to early and frequent teenage sexual activity. (p. 294)

   A. _____
   B. _____
   C. _____
   D. _____
   E. _____
   F. _____

7. Why do many sexually active adolescents fail to use contraception consistently? (p. 294)

8. What factors increase the likelihood that teenagers will use birth control? (p. 294)

9. Explain how heredity might contribute to homosexuality. (p. 296)

10. True or False: Most gay, lesbian, and bisexual youths are "gender deviant" in dress or behavior, meaning they dress and behave quite differently than their heterosexual peers. (p. 296)

Social Issues: Gay, Lesbian, and Bisexual Youths: Coming Out to Oneself and Others

1. True or False: In North America, homosexuals are rarely stigmatized. (p. 295)

2. Describe the three-phase sequence adolescents go through in coming out to themselves and others. (p. 295)

    A. _____

    B. _____

    C. _____

3. For most gay and lesbian individuals, a first sense of their sexual orientation appears between the ages of _____ and _____. In what context does this commonly occur? (p. 295)

4. What are some potential outcomes for adolescents who are extremely troubled or guilt-ridden about their sexual orientation? (p. 295)

5. What factors increase the likelihood that gay and lesbian youths will reach self-acceptance? (p. 295)

6. Explain how coming out can enhance development of gay and lesbian adolescents. (p. 295)

Sexually Transmitted Diseases

1. True or False: Adolescents have the highest rates of sexually transmitted diseases (STDs) of all age groups. (p. 296)

2. What are the consequences of untreated STDs? (p. 296)

3. By far, the most serious STD is _____. (p. 296)

4. True or False: It is at least twice as easy for a female to infect a male with any STD, including AIDS, as it is for a male to infect a female. (p. 296)

Adolescent Pregnancy and Parenthood

1. True or False: The adolescent pregnancy rate in Canada is nearly double that of the United States. (p. 296)

2. List three factors that heighten the incidence of adolescent pregnancy. (p. 296)

   A. _____
   B. _____
   C. _____

3. Why is teenage pregnancy a much greater problem today than it was 35 years ago? (pp. 296–297)

4. Describe common background characteristics of teenage parents. (p. 297)

5. Summarize the consequences of adolescent parenthood in the following areas: (p. 297)

   Educational attainment: _____

   Marital patterns: _____

   Economic circumstances: _____

6. Cite a birth complication that is common among babies of teenage mothers. (p. 297)

7. List three common characteristics of children born to adolescent mothers. (p. 297)

   A. _____
   B. _____
   C. _____

8. What factors protect adolescent parents and their children from long-term difficulties? (p. 297)

   _____
   _____
   _____

9. List three components of effective sex education programs. (p. 297)

   A. _____
   B. _____
   C. _____

10. Cite the most controversial aspect of adolescent pregnancy prevention. (p. 297)

    _____

11. Efforts to prevent adolescent pregnancy and parenthood must go beyond improving sex education to build _____ and _____. (p. 298)

12. What are some characteristics of effective interventions for adolescent parents? (p. 298)

    _____
    _____
    _____
    _____

13. Nearly half of young fathers visit their children during the first few years after birth, and contact usually (diminishes / increases) over time. (p. 298)

Substance Use and Abuse

1. By tenth grade, _____ percent of U.S. young people have tried cigarette smoking, _____ percent drinking, and _____ percent at least one illegal drug. Canadian rates of teenage alcohol and drug use are (similar / much lower). (p. 298)

2. Cite factors that may explain recent trends in adolescent substance use. (p. 298)

   _____
   _____
   _____

3. True or False: Teenagers who experiment with alcohol, tobacco, and marijuana are headed for a life of addiction. (p. 298)

4. How do experimenters differ from drug abusers? (p. 298)

   _____
   _____

5. What environmental factors are associated with adolescent drug abuse? (p. 299)

   _____
   _____
   _____

6. List three lifelong consequences of adolescent drug abuse. (p. 299)

   A. _____

   B. _____

   C. _____

7. List three characteristics of successful drug prevention programs. (p. 299)

   A. _____

   B. _____

   C. _____

Cognitive Development

Piaget's Theory: The Formal Operational Stage

1. Summarize the basic differences between concrete and formal operational reasoning. (p. 300)

   _____
   _____
   _____

Hypothetico-Deductive Reasoning

1. What is *hypothetico-deductive reasoning*? (p. 300)

   _____
   _____
   _____

2. Describe adolescents' performance on Piaget's *pendulum problem*. (pp. 300–301)

   _____
   _____

Propositional Thought

1. Define *propositional thought,* and provide an example. (p. 301)

   A. _____

   B. _____

2. True or False: Piaget maintained that language plays a more central role in children's than in adolescents' cognitive development. (p. 301)

Follow-Up Research on Formal Operational Thought

1. Cite examples illustrating that school-age children show signs of *hypothetico-deductive reasoning* and *propositional thought* but are not as competent as adolescents. (p. 301)

   Hypothetico-deductive reasoning: _____

   _____

   Propositional thought: _____

   _____

2. True or False: Hypothetico-deductive reasoning and propositional thought appear suddenly, around the time of puberty. (p. 301)

3. What is one reason why many adults are not fully formal operational? (p. 301)

___

4. True or False: In many villages and tribal societies, formal operational tasks are not mastered at all. Explain your answer. (pp. 301–302)

___

An Information-Processing View of Adolescent Cognitive Development

1. List mechanisms of cognition change according to information-processing theorists. (p. 302)

   A. ___
   B. ___
   C. ___
   D. ___
   E. ___
   F. ___
   G. ___

2. Which mechanism is central to adolescent cognitive development? (p. 302)

   ___

Scientific Reasoning: Coordinating Theory with Evidence

1. How does scientific reasoning change from childhood into adolescence and adulthood? (p. 302)

   ___

How Scientific Reasoning Develops

1. Identify three factors that support adolescents' skill at coordinating theory with evidence. (p. 302)

   A. ___
   B. ___
   C. ___

2. Scientific reasoning is (strongly / weakly) influenced by years of schooling. (p. 302)

3. True or False: Like Piaget, information-processing theorists maintain that scientific reasoning results from an abrupt, stagewise change. Briefly explain your response. (p. 303)

   ___

Consequences of Adolescent Cognitive Changes

Self-Consciousness and Self-Focusing

1. What developmental changes contribute to adolescents' ability to think more about themselves? (p. 303)

2. Describe two distorted images of the self and others that appear during adolescence. (pp. 303–304)

    Imaginary audience: _____

    Personal fable: _____

3. When are the imaginary audience and personal fable the strongest? (p. 304)

4. How do gains in perspective taking contribute to adolescents' distorted visions of the self? (p. 304)

Idealism and Criticism

1. How are *idealism* and *criticism* advantageous to teenagers? (p. 304)

Decision Making

1. List four components of decision making. (p. 304)

    A. _____
    B. _____
    C. _____
    D. _____

2. True or False: When making decisions, adolescents, more often than adults, fall back on well-learned, intuitive judgments. (p. 304)

3. Why is decision making so challenging for adolescents? (pp. 304–305)

Learning in School

School Transitions

1. With each school change, adolescents' grades (decline / increase). Why is this so? (p. 305)

2. Cite adjustment problems that can occur with school transitions. (p. 305)

3. Which adolescents are at greatest risk for developing self-esteem and academic difficulties during school transitions? (p. 305)

4. List four environmental changes during school transitions that fit poorly with adolescents' developmental needs. (p. 305)

   A.
   B.
   C.
   D.

5. Discuss ways that parents, teachers, and peers can ease the strain of school transitions. (p. 306)

Academic Achievement

1. How do authoritative, authoritarian, permissive, and uninvolved child-rearing styles contribute to adolescent academic achievement? Which style is the most effective, and why? (p. 306)

   Authoritative:
   Authoritarian:
   Permissive:
   Uninvolved:
   Most effective:

2. How do parent–school partnerships foster academic achievement? (pp. 306–307)

3. What role do peers play in academic achievement? (p. 307)

4. How does the surrounding peer climate and social order influence ethnic minority youths' academic achievement? (p. 307)

___

5. Compare the academic progress of students who are assigned to a college preparatory track with those who are assigned to a vocational or general education track. (pp. 307–308)

   College: ___

   Vocational/General Education: ___

6. True or False: Among the industrialized countries, only the United States and Canada assign high school students into academic and vocational tracks. (p. 308)

Dropping Out

1. List two consequences of dropping out of school. (p. 308)

   A. ___

   B. ___

2. Cite characteristics of students who are at risk for dropping out of high school. (p. 308)

___

3. How does family background contribute to dropping out of school? (p. 308)

___

4. List four strategies for helping teenagers who are at risk for dropping out of high school. (pp. 308–309)

   A. ___
   B. ___
   C. ___
   D. ___

5. Over the past half century, the percentage of American and Canadian adolescents completing high school has (increased / decreased) steadily. (p. 310)

> ### A Lifespan Vista:
> ### Extracurricular Activities: Contexts for Positive Youth Development

1. What types of extracurricular activities promote diverse academic and social skills and have a lasting positive impact on adjustment? (p. 309)

   _____
   _____

2. Cite benefits of extracurricular involvement that extend into adult life. (p. 309)

   _____
   _____

3. True or False: Adolescents who spend many afternoons and evenings engaged in unstructured activities resemble adolescents who engage in structured, goal-oriented activities in adjustment outcomes. (p. 309)

4. Which teenagers are especially likely to benefit from extracurricular participation? (p. 309)

   _____

ASK YOURSELF . . .

For *Ask Yourself* questions for this chapter, please log on to the Companion Website at *www.ablongman.com/berk*.

1. Select the Companion Website for *Exploring Lifespan Development*.
2. Use the "Jump to" menu to go directly to this chapter.
3. From the menu on the left side of the screen, select "Ask Yourself."
4. Complete questions and choose "Submit answers for grading" or "Clear answers" to start over.

SUGGESTED STUDENT READINGS

Brown, J. D., Steele, J. R., & Walsh-Childers, K. (Eds.). (2002). *Sexual teens, sexual media.* Mahwah, NJ: Erlbaum. Examines the influence of the media on adolescent sexual attitudes, gender roles, sexual orientation, standards of beauty, and romantic relationships.

Carskadon, M. A. (2003). *Adolescent sleep patterns: Biological, social, and psychological influences.* New York: Cambridge University Press. A collection of chapters focusing on adolescent wake and sleep patterns, including the role of sleep deprivation in risky driving behavior, the effects of school and work on sleep habits, severe disturbances in adolescent sleep cycles, and benefits of starting school later in the day.

Hayward, C. (Ed.). (2003). *Gender differences at puberty.* New York: Cambridge University Press. An ecological examination of the effects of puberty, this book focuses on the impact of puberty on physical, social, and psychological development. Other topics include changes in body image, aggression, sexual abuse, and romantic relationships.

Ogbu, J. U. (2003). *Black American students in an affluent suburb: A study of academic disengagement.* Mahwah, NJ: Erlbaum. Explores factors that contribute to academic disengagement in black students of all socioeconomic backgrounds, including the impact of school race relations, discipline, culture, language, and peer relations.

PUZZLE 11.1

Across
1. First menstruation
3. _____ sexual characteristics: features visible on the outside of the body that serve as signs of sexual maturity but do not involve reproductive organs
5. Growth _____: rapid gain in height and weight during adolescence
6. Personal _____: adolescents' belief that they are special and unique and that others cannot understand their thoughts and feelings
8. _____ nervosa: eating disorder in which individuals go on eating binges followed by deliberate vomiting, other purging techniques, and strict dieting
9. _____ nervosa: eating disorder in which individuals starve themselves because of a compulsive fear of getting fat
11. _____ thought: type of formal operational reasoning in which adolescents evaluate the logic of verbal statements without referring to real-world circumstances
13. In Piaget's _____ operational stage, adolescents develop the capacity for abstract, scientific thinking.
14. _____ trend: change in body size and rate of growth from one generation to the next

Down
2. _____-deductive reasoning: formal operational problem-solving strategy in which adolescents begin with a general theory of all possible factors that could affect an outcome and deduce specific hypotheses, which they test systematically
4. Period of development in which the individual crosses the dividing line between childhood and adulthood
5. First ejaculation of seminal fluid
7. _____ audience: adolescents' belief that they are the focus of everyone else's attention and concern
10. Body _____: conception of and attitude toward one's physical appearance
11. _____ sexual characteristics: physical features that involve the reproductive organs
12. Biological changes at adolescence that lead to an adult-sized body and sexual maturity

238

3. Describe the secular trend in pubertal timing in industrialized nations. What factors have likely contributed to this trend? (p. 287)

   A. _____

   B. _____

Brain Development

1. Describe major changes in the brain during adolescence. (pp. 287–288)

   _____

2. True or False: During adolescence, sensitivity of neurons to certain chemicals increases, resulting in more intense reactions to stressful events and pleasurable stimuli. (p. 288)

3. True or False: Adolescents need much less sleep than school-age children. (p. 288)

4. List three consequences of sleep deprivation in adolescence. (p. 288)

   A. _____

   B. _____

   C. _____

The Psychological Impact of Pubertal Events

Reactions to Pubertal Changes

1. Cite factors that contribute to girls' and boys' psychological reactions to reaching puberty. (p. 288)

   Girls: _____

   _____

   Boys: _____

   _____

2. Overall, (boys / girls) get much less social support for the physical changes of puberty. (p. 288)

3. How does cultural context influence the experience of puberty? (pp. 288–289)

   _____

Pubertal Change, Emotion, and Social Behavior

1. Research shows that adolescents report (more / less) favorable moods than school-age children and adults. (p. 289)

2. Compared with adults' moods, those of younger adolescents are (less / more) stable. (p. 289)

3. Cite factors associated with high and low points in mood during adolescence. (p. 289)

   High points: _____

   Low points: _____

4. How might parent–child conflict during adolescence be adaptive? (p. 289)

   _____

5. True or False: Parent–child disputes are often severe in adolescence. (pp. 289–290)

Pubertal Timing

1. Describe the effects of maturational timing on the following groups of adolescents. (p. 290)

   Early-maturing boys: _____

   Late-maturing boys: _____

   Early-maturing girls: _____

   Late-maturing girls: _____

2. Cite two factors that contribute to boys' and girls' adjustment to early versus late pubertal maturation. (p. 290)

   A. _____

   B. _____

3. What is *body image*? How does pubertal timing affect body image? (p. 290)

   A. _____

   B. _____

4. Describe the importance of physical status in relation to peers for early and late maturers. (p. 290)

   Early maturers: _____

   Late maturers: _____

PRACTICE TEST #1

1. The beginning of adolescence is marked by (p. 283)
   a. the tenth birthday.
   b. becoming a teenager.
   c. puberty.
   d. adulthood.

2. The first outward sign of puberty is the rapid gain in height and weight known as the (p. 284)
   a. growing phase.
   b. adolescent surge.
   c. expansion stage.
   d. growth spurt.

3. Girls, who have been advanced in physical maturity since the prenatal period, reach puberty, on average, (p. 284)
   a. two years earlier than boys.
   b. six years earlier than boys.
   c. at the same time as boys.
   d. two years later than boys.

4. Physical growth in adolescence (p. 285)
   a. occurs at a slow, steady pace.
   b. follows the cephalocaudal trend that is also characteristic of infancy and childhood.
   c. leads to large differences in the body proportions of boys and girls.
   d. causes boys to add more fat, while girls add more muscle.

5. Nature delays sexual maturity in girls until (p. 287)
   a. pubic and underarm hair appears.
   b. the girl's body is large enough for childbearing.
   c. the secular trend has taken place.
   d. the stage of menopause.

6. Changes in the brain during adolescence (p. 288)
   a. are less extensive than were previously believed.
   b. play a role in teenagers' drive for novel experiences.
   c. allow teenagers to get along with very little sleep.
   d. cause a decrease in the ability to experience pleasurable stimuli, which in turn leads to moodiness.

7. Adolescent moodiness is generally (p. 289)
   a. strongly linked to higher pubertal hormonal levels.
   b. the result of alcohol or drug abuse.
   c. no different from moodiness in adults.
   d. linked to negative life events.

8. Beneath most parental–adolescent disputes about mundane, day-to-day matters lie parental efforts to (p. 290)
   a. protect teenagers from harm.
   b. control teenagers' unruly behavior.
   c. initiate psychological distancing.
   d. develop teenagers' powers of reasoning.

9. In contrast to those with anorexia, adolescents with bulimia nervosa (p. 292)
   a. do not have a pathological fear of getting fat.
   b. feel guilty about their eating habits.
   c. are afraid of becoming too thin.
   d. do not want help for their problem.

10. Which of the following factors is linked to increased contraceptive use among sexually active adolescents? (p. 294)
    a. Having sexual contact with multiple partners
    b. Imitating the sexually responsible role models seen in many prime-time TV shows
    c. Being able to talk openly with parents about sex and contraceptives
    d. Participating in sex education courses

11. Why do adolescents have higher rates of STDs than any other age group? (p. 296)
    a. Most teens have limited understanding of many STDs and are poorly informed about how to protect themselves.
    b. Teenagers are biologically ill-equipped to fight off many of these aggressive diseases.
    c. Only a very small percentage of high school students are aware of basic facts about AIDS.
    d. Contraceptives are not available to most teenagers.

12. Adolescent mothers (p. 297)
    a. are just as likely as other adolescent girls to finish high school.
    b. usually have a good understanding of child development.
    c. tend to have children who achieve poorly in school and who engage in disruptive social behavior.
    d. rarely experience complications of pregnancy or birth.

13. Research on adolescent drug use and abuse shows that (p. 298)
    a. the majority of adolescents completely abstain from using drugs and alcohol.
    b. many adolescents who engage in limited experimentation with drugs and alcohol are psychologically healthy, sociable, and curious individuals.
    c. experimentation with drugs often leads to long-term abuse and dependency.
    d. parents and teachers should not worry about drug experimentation because it is a normal part of adolescent development.

14. A researcher hides a poker chip in her hand and asks participants to indicate whether the following statement is true, false, or uncertain: "Either the chip in my hand is green or it is not green." An adolescent responds by using _____ to conclude that the "either-or" statement must be true. (p. 301)
    a. hypothetico-deductive reasoning
    b. propositional thought
    c. concrete operational reasoning
    d. relativistic reasoning

15. The adolescent capacity for scientific reasoning (p. 302)
    a. develops as an abrupt, stagewise change, similar to earlier Piagetian stages.
    b. results from an increase in working-memory capacity, regardless of years of schooling or other experiences.
    c. develops out of many specific experiences that require children and adolescents to match theories against evidence and evaluate their thinking.
    d. is a purely cognitive attainment that is unrelated to the individual's personality.

16. Thirteen-year-old Peter has become extremely self-conscious because he believes he is the focus of everyone else's attention and concern. Peter's distorted view is called (p. 303)
    a. the imaginary audience.
    b. the personal fable.
    c. propositional thought.
    d. metacognitive reasoning.

17. Adolescent idealism often leads teenagers to be (p. 304)
    a. more cooperative at home.
    b. better students at school.
    c. more realistic in their evaluations of others.
    d. more critical of parents and siblings.

18. Students are at especially great risk for academic and social difficulties after a school transition if they (p. 305)
    a. move from a larger school to a smaller one.
    b. had very high grades in their old school.
    c. have to cope with additional life transitions at the same time.
    d. come from a K–8 school.

19. A(n) _____ parenting style predicts higher grades for adolescents of varying SES. (p. 306)
    a. uninvolved
    b. permissive
    c. authoritarian
    d. authoritative

20. Approximately _____ of school dropouts return to finish their secondary education within a few years. (p. 310)
    a. one-quarter
    b. one-third
    c. 50 percent
    d. 65 percent

PRACTICE TEST #2

1. Margaret Mead was the first researcher to demonstrate that adolescent adjustment is greatly influenced by (p. 283)
    a. the age at which children reach puberty.
    b. social and cultural forces.
    c. diet and exercise.
    d. biological predispositions.

2. Side effects of steroid use include (p. 285)
    a. lack of body hair.
    b. low blood pressure.
    c. passive behavior.
    d. mood swings.

3. In boys, the first sign of puberty is (p. 287)
    a. enlargement of the penis.
    b. emergence of facial and body hair.
    c. enlargement of the testes.
    d. deepening of the voice.

4. Delayed menarche in poverty-stricken regions of the world reflects (p. 287)
    a. the role of physical well-being in pubertal development.
    b. the effects of emotional stress.
    c. a secular change in pubertal timing.
    d. the effects of overweight and obesity due to an unhealthy diet.

5. Compared to school-age children and adults, adolescents (p. 289)
    a. experience decreased moodiness.
    b. report less favorable moods.
    c. have more stable moods.
    d. are more likely to report negative mood during times of a day spent with friends.

6. Many studies show that puberty is related to a rise in parent–child (p. 289)
   a. conflict.
   b. interaction.
   c. closeness.
   d. interdependency.

7. Parent–adolescent conflicts typically focus on (p. 290)
   a. substance abuse.
   b. mundane, day-to-day matters such as driving or curfews.
   c. early sexual activity.
   d. long-term goals such as college or vocational training.

8. Compared with their on-time and late-maturing agemates, early-maturing girls usually report (p. 290)
   a. a more positive body image.
   b. a less positive body image.
   c. an indifferent attitude toward their body.
   d. a healthier outlook on puberty.

9. Which of the following statements about anorexia and bulimia is true? (p. 292)
   a. Bulimia is more common than anorexia nervosa.
   b. Individuals with bulimia rarely feel depressed or guilty about their eating habits.
   c. Neither anorexia nor bulimia is influenced by heredity.
   d. Most individuals with anorexia only worsen their health by refusing to exercise.

10. Mothers of girls with anorexia tend to be (p. 292)
    a. obese.
    b. overprotective and controlling.
    c. uninvolved.
    d. uninterested in physical appearance.

11. Which of the following statements about adolescent sexual activity is true? (p. 294)
    a. Adolescent contraceptive use has increased in recent years.
    b. A recent trend toward liberal sexual attitudes has resulted in a greater frequency of premarital sex.
    c. Females tend to have their first sexual intercourse earlier than males.
    d. Income level is unrelated to amount or type of adolescent sexual activity.

12. In North America, which of the following risky behaviors is engaged in by the highest percentage of students at the end of high school? (p. 298)
    a. heavy drinking during the past two weeks
    b. ingestion of at least one highly addictive and toxic substance
    c. regular cigarette smoking
    d. experimentation with illegal drugs

13. In Piaget's famous *pendulum problem,* children at the concrete operational stage (p. 300)
    a. perform better than either older or younger children.
    b. cannot separate the effects of each variable.
    c. usually notice variables that are not immediately suggested by the concrete materials of the task.
    d. do not acknowledge the difference in string lengths.

14. The thinking of many college students and adults is not fully formal operational because (p. 301)
    a. they lack the types of experiences necessary for solving formal operational tasks.
    b. they are not motivated to solve formal operational tasks.
    c. only the most intelligent people reach the formal operational stage.
    d. they are more interested in socializing than thinking.

15. Which of the following statements reflects the imaginary audience? (p. 303)
    a. "I don't care if my new haircut is bad. I'm going to the party anyway."
    b. "I can't go to the party with a huge pimple on my cheek! Everyone will make fun of me!"
    c. "My parents don't understand how hard school is for me!"
    d. "No one will care if I can't afford a new dress for the prom. I'll just wear the same one I wore last year."

16. In decision making, adolescents (p. 304)
    a. outperform adults, making good use of their newly developed ability to think rationally and evaluate various alternatives.
    b. are more likely than adults to suggest seeking advice in solving a real-world problem.
    c. are more likely than adults to fall back on well-learned intuitive judgments.
    d. are especially good at predicting potential outcomes because of their growing capacity to think about possibilities.

17. When schools minimize competition and differential treatment based on ability, (p. 306)
    a. many otherwise competitive students develop a feeling of ineptitude.
    b. their orderly atmosphere is replaced with a feeling of anarchy.
    c. students in middle and junior high school are less likely to feel angry and depressed.
    d. those with greater abilities are stifled, leading to a decline in their abilities.

18. Which of the following supports academic achievement in adolescence? (p. 307)
    a. authoritarian parenting
    b. reduced parental involvement in school-related issues
    c. having close friends who value school achievement
    d. large, departmentalized secondary schools

19. Typically, parents of students who drop out of school (p. 308)
    a. encourage achievement but just aren't successful.
    b. completed high school themselves.
    c. have serious emotional problems.
    d. show little involvement in their teenagers' education.

20. Among adolescents, the most powerful influence on involvement in extracurricular activities is (p. 309)
    a. small school size.
    b. academic achievement.
    c. level of SES.
    d. a mentoring program.

CHAPTER 12
EMOTIONAL AND SOCIAL DEVELOPMENT IN ADOLESCENCE

BRIEF CHAPTER SUMMARY

Erikson was the first to recognize identity as the major personality achievement of adolescence and as a crucial step toward becoming a productive, happy adult. Young people who successfully resolve the psychological conflict of identity versus role confusion construct a solid self-definition based on self-chosen values and goals. During adolescence, cognitive changes transform the young person's vision of the self into a more complex, well-organized, and consistent picture. For most young people, self-esteem rises over the teenage years, influenced by factors in the family, at school, and in the larger social environment.

Adolescents' well-organized self-descriptions and differentiated sense of self-esteem provide the cognitive foundation for identity development. Researchers have derived four identity statuses that reflect adolescents' progress toward developing a mature identity. Two of these—identity achievement and moratorium—are adaptive, associated with positive personality characteristics. Adolescents who remain in one of the other statuses—identity foreclosure or identity diffusion—tend to have adjustment difficulties.

Lawrence Kohlberg, continuing the research of Piaget, identified six distinct stages of moral development. According to Kohlberg, moral development is a gradual process that extends into adulthood as the individual actively grapples with moral issues and achieves gains in perspective taking, which lead to more effective ways of resolving moral conflicts. Child-rearing practices, schooling, peer interaction, and culture all contribute to moral development. As individuals advance through Kohlberg's stages, moral reasoning becomes more closely related to behavior.

Biological, social, and cognitive factors all play a role in making early adolescence a period of gender intensification—increased gender stereotyping of attitudes and behavior, and movement toward a more traditional gender identity, especially for girls. Development at adolescence involves striving for autonomy—a sense of oneself as a separate, self-governing individual. Over the adolescent years, relationships with parents and siblings change as teenagers strive to establish a healthy balance between connection to and separation from the family. As adolescents spend more time with peers, intimacy and loyalty become central features of friendship. Adolescent peer groups are organized into tightly knit groups called cliques; as teenagers become interested in dating, several cliques come together to form a crowd.

Although most young people move through adolescence with little difficulty, some encounter major disruptions, such as premature parenthood, substance abuse, and school failure. The most common psychological problem of the teenage years, depression, is influenced by a diverse combination of biological and environmental factors. The suicide rate increases dramatically at adolescence. Many teenagers become involved in some delinquent activity, but only a few are serious or repeat offenders. Family, school, peer, and neighborhood factors are related to delinquency.

LEARNING OBJECTIVES

After reading this chapter, you should be able to:

12.1 Discuss Erikson's theory of identity development. (pp. 314–315)

12.2 Describe changes in self-concept and self-esteem during adolescence. (pp. 315–316)

12.3 Describe the four identity statuses, the adjustment outcomes of each status, and factors that promote identity development. (pp. 316–318)

12.4 Describe Kohlberg's theory of moral development and evaluate its accuracy. (pp. 319–321)

12.5 Summarize research on Gilligan's claim that Kohlberg underestimated the moral maturity of females. (pp. 321–322)

12.6 Describe influences on moral reasoning and its relationship to moral behavior. (pp. 322–324)

12.7 Explain why early adolescence is a period of gender intensification. (p. 324)

12.8 Discuss changes in parent–child and sibling relationships during adolescence. (pp. 325–326)

12.9 Describe adolescent friendships, peer groups, and dating relationships and their consequences for development. (pp. 326–329)

12.10 Discuss factors related to adolescent depression and suicide, along with approaches for prevention and treatment. (pp. 330–331)

12.11 Summarize factors related to delinquency, and describe strategies for prevention and treatment. (pp. 331–333)

STUDY QUESTIONS

Erikson's Theory: Identity versus Role Confusion

1. Explain how adolescents construct an identity. (p. 314)

2. Discuss Erikson's notion of *identity crisis*. (p. 314)

3. Current theorists (do / do not) agree with Erikson that the process of identity development constitutes a "crisis." (p. 314)

4. What did Erikson describe as the negative outcome of adolescence? Explain how this develops. (pp. 314–315)

   A. _____

   B. _____

Self-Understanding

Changes in Self-Concept

1. True or False: Young adolescents often provide contradictory self-descriptions—for example, describing themselves as both shy and outgoing. (p. 315)

2. Compared to school-age children, teenagers place (more / less) emphasis on social virtues, such as being friendly, considerate, kind, and cooperative. Why is this so? (p. 315)

Changes in Self-Esteem

1. List three new dimensions of self-evaluation that are added during adolescence. (p. 315)

    A. _____

    B. _____

    C. _____

2. Except for temporary declines after _____, self-esteem rises for most young people. (p. 315)

3. Differentiate factors associated with high versus low self-esteem in adolescence. (pp. 315–316)

    High: _____

    _____

    Low: _____

    _____

Paths to Identity

1. Match each of the following identity statuses with its appropriate description. (p. 316)

    _____ Committed to values and goals without taking time to explore alternatives

    _____ Have not yet made definite commitments and are still exploring alternatives

    _____ Committed to self-chosen values and goals after having already explored alternatives

    _____ Lack clear direction; are not committed to values and goals and are not actively seeking them

    1. Identity achievement
    2. Moratorium
    3. Identity foreclosure
    4. Identity diffusion

2. Most adolescents start out at "lower" identity statuses, such as _____ and _____, but by the time they reach their twenties, they have moved toward "higher" statuses, including _____ and _____. (p. 316)

Identity Status and Psychological Well-Being

1. True or False: Research supports the conclusion that identity achievement and moratorium are psychologically healthy routes to a mature self-definition, whereas identity foreclosure and identity diffusion are maladaptive. (p. 316)

2. How do adolescents in moratorium resemble identity-achieved individuals? (pp. 316–317)

    _____

    _____

3. Long-term (diffused / foreclosed) individuals are the least mature in identity development. Explain your answer. (p. 317)

    _____

    _____

Factors Affecting Identity Development

1. Match the following identity statuses with the appropriate description. Descriptions may apply to more than one identity status. (p. 317)

    _____ Assumes that absolute truth is always attainable
    _____ Lacks confidence in the prospect of ever knowing anything with certainty
    _____ Appreciates that they can use rational criteria to choose among alternatives
    _____ Feels attached to parents but are also free to voice their own opinions
    _____ Has close bonds with parents but lack healthy separation
    _____ Reports the lowest levels of warm, open communication at home
    _____ Fostered by classrooms that promote high-level thinking, as well as extracurricular and community activities that permit teens to take on responsible roles

    1. Identity achievement
    2. Moratorium
    3. Identity foreclosure
    4. Identity diffusion

2. How do peers help adolescents explore their identity options? (p. 317)

3. How can schools foster adolescent identity development? (p. 317)

Cultural Influences: Identity Development among Ethnic Minority Adolescents

1. What is an *ethnic identity*? (p. 318)

2. What unique problems do ethnic-minority adolescents experience during identity development? (p. 318)

3. Explain the special challenges faced by young people with parents of different ethnicities. (p. 318)

4. List three ways society can help minority adolescents to resolve identity conflicts constructively. (p. 318)

    A. _____
    B. _____
    C. _____

5. What is a *bicultural identity,* and how does it benefit minority adolescents? (p. 318)

   A. _____

   B. _____

Moral Development

Kohlberg's Theory of Moral Development

1. What are *moral dilemmas,* and what do they reveal about moral reasoning? (p. 319)

   _____

2. True or False: Kohlberg emphasized that *the way an individual reasons* about a dilemma, not *the content of the response,* determines moral maturity. (p. 319)

3. List two factors that both Piaget and Kohlberg believed promoted moral understanding. (p. 320)

   A. _____

   B. _____

4. Explain the basic characteristics of moral reasoning at each of Kohlberg's three levels. (p. 320)

   Preconventional: _____

   Conventional: _____

   Postconventional or Principled: _____

5. Match each of the following moral orientations with its appropriate description. (pp. 320–321)

   _____ Laws must be obeyed under all circumstances; rules must be enforced in the same even-handed manner for everyone, and each member of society has a personal duty to uphold them

   _____ Right action is defined by self-chosen ethical principals of conscience that are valid for all humanity, regardless of law and social agreement

   _____ Ignores people's intentions and focuses on fear of authority and avoidance of punishment as reasons for behaving morally

   _____ Obeys rules because they promote social harmony

   _____ Regards rules and laws as flexible and emphasizes fair procedures for interpreting and changing the law in order to protect individual rights and the interests of the majority

   _____ Views right action as flowing from self-interest; reciprocity is understood as equal exchange of favors

   1. Punishment and obedience orientation
   2. Instrumental purpose orientation
   3. "Good boy–good girl" orientation
   4. Social-order-maintaining orientation
   5. Social contract orientation
   6. Universal ethical principle orientation

6. True or False: Longitudinal research suggests that individuals do not move through the stages of moral development in the order in which Kohlberg suggested. (p. 321)

7. True or False: Few people move beyond Kohlberg's Stage 4, the social-order-maintaining orientation. Briefly explain your response. (p. 321)

8. Moral maturity can be found in a revised understanding of Stages 3 and 4, which require profound moral constructions. Describe what those are. (p. 321)

9. Moral reasoning about real-life problems tends to fall (above / below) a person's actual moral capacity. Explain your answer. (p. 321)

10. True or False: Kohlberg's stages develop in a neat, stepwise fashion. (p. 321)

Are There Sex Differences in Moral Reasoning?

1. Carol Gilligan believes that feminine morality emphasizes an ethic of care that is devalued in Kohlberg's model. Explain what she means by this. (p. 321)

2. True or False: Research supports Gilligan's claim that Kohlberg's approach underestimates females' moral maturity. (pp. 321–322)

3. True or False: Females tend to emphasize care, whereas males either stress justice or focus equally on justice and care. (p. 322)

Coordinating Personal Choice with Morality

1. True or False: In diverse Western and non-Western cultures, teenagers express great concern with matters of personal choice. (p. 322)

2. By tenth grade, young people indicate that exclusion of another peer is "OK." How do adolescents justify this exclusion? (p. 322)

3. Teenagers display more subtle thinking than school-age children on certain issues. Describe two of these issues. (p. 322)

   A. _____

   B. _____

Influences on Moral Reasoning

1. Describe child-rearing practices that promote gains in moral understanding. (p. 322)

   _____

   _____

   _____

2. True or False: Years of schooling is one of the most powerful predictors of moral maturity. (p. 322)

3. Cite two aspects of peer discussions that stimulate moral development. (p. 322)

   A. _____

   B. _____

4. True or False: Cross-cultural research shows that individuals in industrialized nations move through Kohlberg's stages more quickly and advance to higher levels than individuals in village societies. Briefly explain your answer. (p. 323)

   _____

   _____

   _____

Moral Reasoning and Behavior

1. A (weak / modest / strong) relationship exists between advanced moral reasoning and action. (p. 323)

2. Besides cognition, what factors influence moral behavior in adolescence? (p. 323)

   _____

   _____

3. What is *moral self-relevance*? (p. 323)

   _____

4. How can close relationships and schools foster adolescents' sense of moral self-relevance? (p. 323)

   Close relationships: _____

   _____

   Schools: _____

   _____

Religious Involvement and Moral Development

1. In recent national polls, nearly _____ of Americans and about _____ of Canadians reported being religious. As adolescents search for a personally meaningful identity, formal religious involvement (declines / increases). (pp. 323–324)

2. How do religious communities promote adolescents' moral values and behaviors? (p. 324)

   _____

   _____

   _____

Gender Typing

1. What is *gender intensification*? (p. 324)

   _____

2. Gender intensification is stronger for (boys / girls). (p. 324)

3. Cite biological, social, and cognitive factors associated with gender intensification. (p. 324)

   Biological: _____

   Social: _____

   Cognitive: _____

4. Gender intensification (declines / increases) during middle to late adolescence. (p. 324)

5. (Androgynous / Gender-typed) adolescents tend to be psychologically healthier. (p. 324)

The Family

1. During adolescence, _____—establishing oneself as a separate, self-governing individual—becomes a salient task. (p. 325)

Parent–Child Relationships

1. Describe parenting practices that foster adolescent autonomy. (p. 325)

   _____

2. What is a major reason that many parents find rearing teenagers to be stressful? (p. 325)

   _____

3. True or False: The quality of the parent–child relationship is the most consistent predictor of mental health throughout adolescence. (p. 325)

4. Explain how mild parent–child conflict is beneficial during adolescence. (p. 325)

   _____

Family Circumstances

1. True or False: Maternal employment or a dual-earner family reduces the amount of time that parents spend with their teenagers and is harmful to adolescent development. Explain your response. (p. 326)

2. What factors promote resilience in adolescents who have seriously troubled relationships with their families? (p. 326)

Siblings

1. During adolescence, teenagers invest (more / less) time and energy in siblings. Explain your answer. (p. 326)

2. Sibling relationships become (more / less) intense during adolescence, in both positive and negative feelings. (p. 326)

3. True or False: In adolescence, mild sibling differences in perceived parental affection no longer trigger jealousy but, instead, predict increasing sibling warmth. (p. 326)

Peer Relations

Friendships

1. Cite the two characteristics of adolescent friendship. (p. 326)

    A. _____

    B. _____

2. List ways in which adolescent friends are likely to resemble one another. (p. 326)

3. Adolescents are (less / more) possessive of their friends than they were in childhood. (p. 327)

4. Briefly summarize sex differences in adolescents' close friendships. (p. 327)

5. When can closeness in friendship be problematic? (p. 327)

6. How do adolescents use the Internet to build and support relationships? (p. 327)

7. Cite four reasons why adolescent friendships are related to psychological health and competence into early adulthood. (pp. 327–328)

   A.

   B.

   C.

   D.

Cliques and Crowds

1. Differentiate between cliques and crowds, noting the characteristics of each. (p. 328)

   Cliques:

   Crowds:

2. Provide some examples of typical high school crowds. (p. 328)

3. True or False: Peer group values are often an extension of values learned in the home. Explain your answer. (p. 328)

4. Describe the function of mixed-sex cliques in early adolescence. (pp. 328–329)

5. True or False: Crowds increase in importance from early to late adolescence. (p. 329)

Dating

1. Differentiate younger and older adolescents' reasons for dating. (p. 329)

    Younger: _____

    Older: _____

2. How do experiences with parents influence the quality of adolescents' friendships and romantic relationships? (p. 329)

3. True or False: Early dating is positively associated with social maturity. (p. 329)

4. What factors increase the likelihood of dating violence? (p. 329)

5. Describe the unique challenges faced by homosexual adolescents in initiating and maintaining visible romances. (p. 329)

6. Describe the benefits of close romantic relationships among older teenagers. (p. 329)

Problems of Development

Depression

1. True or False: Depression is the most common psychological problem of adolescence. (p. 330)

2. About _____ to _____ percent of U.S. teenagers have experienced one or more depressive episodes, and _____ to _____ percent are chronically depressed. (p. 330)

3. List three events that might spark depression in a vulnerable young person. (p. 330)

    A. _____

    B. _____

    C. _____

4. Biological changes associated with puberty (can / cannot) account for sex differences in depression. Explain your answer. (p. 330)

5. Explain how the gender intensification of early adolescence can contribute to higher rates of depression in girls. (p. 330)

Suicide

1. True or False: Suicide is currently the leading cause of death among young people in the United States and Canada. (p. 330)

2. True or False: Adolescent suicide rates are roughly equivalent in all industrialized countries. (p. 330)

3. Discuss sex differences in adolescent suicide. (pp. 330–331)

4. Compared with their Caucasian peers, African-American and Hispanic adolescents have (lower / higher) suicide rates. (p. 331)

5. True or False: Gay, lesbian, and bisexual youth are three times more likely than other adolescents to attempt suicide. (p. 331)

6. Describe two types of young people who tend to commit suicide. (p. 331)

   A.

   B.

7. Describe the family backgrounds of suicidal teenagers. (p. 331)

8. Why does suicide increase in adolescence? (p. 331)

9. What types of treatments are available for depressed and suicidal adolescents? (p. 331)

10. True or False: Teenage suicides often take place in clusters. Explain your answer. (p. 331)

Delinquency

1. Explain why delinquency rises over adolescence, then declines into young adulthood. (p. 331)

2. For most adolescents, a brush with the law (does / does not) forecast long-term antisocial behavior. (p. 332)

3. Describe gender differences in delinquent and aggressive behavior. (p. 332)

    Males: _____

    Females: _____

4. List personal, family, neighborhood, and school factors associated with delinquency. (p. 332)

    Personal: _____

    Family: _____

    Neighborhood: _____

    School: _____

5. Describe characteristics of effective treatment programs for adolescent delinquency. (p. 332)

A Lifespan Vista: Two Routes to Adolescent Delinquency

1. Persistent adolescent delinquency follows two paths of development, one with an onset of _____ problems in childhood, the second with an onset in _____. Longitudinal research reveals that the (early / late) onset type is far more likely to lead to a life course pattern of aggression and criminality. (p. 333)

2. Describe characteristics that distinguish early-onset from late-onset delinquent youth. (p. 333)

   Early-onset: _____
   _____
   _____

   Late-onset: _____
   _____
   _____

ASK YOURSELF . . .

For *Ask Yourself* questions for this chapter, please log on to the Companion Website at *www.ablongman.com/berk*.

1. Select the Companion Website for *Exploring Lifespan Development*.
2. Use the "Jump to" menu to go directly to this chapter.
3. From the menu on the left side of the screen, select "Ask Yourself."
4. Complete questions and choose "Submit answers for grading" or "Clear answers" to start over.

SUGGESTED STUDENT READINGS

Kruger, J. (2005). *Identity in adolescence: The balance between self and other.* New York: Routledge. Presents a thorough overview of identity development in adolescence, including theories of identity development, the process of forming an identity, and up-to-date research.

Ladd, G. W. (2005). *Children's peer relations and social competence: A century of progress.* New Haven: Yale University Press. Using over a century's worth of research, this book examines the importance of peer relations for healthy child and adolescent development. Topics include early research on peer relations, friendship, the origins of social competence, and the role of gender, emotion, and culture in peer relationships.

Marcovitz, H. (2004). *Teens and family issues.* Folcroft, PA: Mason Crest Publishers. Based on results from the Gallup Youth Study, which surveys U.S. teenagers' perspectives on family, peers, school, social issues, and other relevant topics, this book examines the importance of family relationships for healthy development.

Underwood, M. (2003). *Social aggression among girls.* New York: Guilford. A collection of chapters highlighting the development and unique features of aggression in girls. The author also includes up-to-date research on the consequences of girls' aggression and approaches to intervention.

PUZZLE 12.1

Across

3. _____ identity: identity constructed by adolescents who explore and adopt values from both their subculture and the dominant culture
7. Identity status of individuals who are exploring alternatives in an effort to find values and goals to guide their life
10. Kohlberg's highest level of moral development; individuals define morality in terms of abstract principles and values that apply to all situations and societies
11. _____ identity: sense of ethnic group membership and the attitudes and feelings associated with that membership
12. _____ self-relevance: the degree to which morality is central to self-concept
13. A well-organized conception of the self, made up of values, beliefs, and goals to which the individual is solidly committed
14. A large, loosely organized peer group in which membership is based on reputation and stereotype
15. A sense of oneself as a separate, self-governing individual
16. A small group of about five to seven peers who are friends
17. Identity _____: identity status of individuals who do not have firm commitments to values and goals and are not actively trying to reach them

Down

1. _____ morality: Piaget's second stage of moral development in which children view rules as flexible, socially agreed-upon principles that can be revised to suit the will of the majority
2. Identity versus role _____: Erikson's psychological conflict of adolescence
4. Kohlberg's second level of moral development; moral understanding is based on conforming to social rules to ensure positive relationships and social order
5. Identity _____: identity status of individuals who have accepted ready-made values and goals that authority figures have chosen for them
6. _____ morality: Piaget's first stage of moral development in which children view rules as permanent and unchangeable
8. Identity _____: identity status of individuals who have explored and committed themselves to self-chosen values and goals
9. Gender _____: increased stereotyping of attitudes and behavior; movement toward a more traditional gender identity
10. Kohlberg's first level of moral development; moral understanding is based on rewards, punishment, and the power of authority figures

PRACTICE TEST #1

1. According to Erikson, young people have trouble finding ideals to have faith in when they reach adolescence with a weak sense of (p. 314)
   a. humor.
   b. trust.
   c. hope.
   d. ideals.

2. In adolescence, young people add _____ as a new dimension of their self-concept. (p. 315)
   a. close friendship
   b. membership in social groups
   c. individual interests
   d. personal preferences

3. Individuals who have difficulty realizing their occupational goals because of lack of training or vocational choices are likely to be at risk for (p. 316)
   a. identity achievement.
   b. identity moratorium.
   c. identity diffusion.
   d. identity foreclosure.

4. Research on identity construction indicates that (p. 316)
   a. most adolescents experience a serious identity crisis.
   b. adolescents typically retain the same identity status across adolescence and early adulthood.
   c. adolescents in high school make more progress toward identity formation than college students.
   d. adolescents who go to work after high school settle on an identity status earlier than do college-bound youths.

5. Kieran has followed the religious path of his family without exploring alternatives and tends to be defensive when his teenage friends bring up the subject. Kieran is (p. 317)
   a. identity foreclosed.
   b. identity diffused.
   c. in moratorium.
   d. identity achieved.

6. According to Kohlberg, moral maturity is determined is determined by (p. 319)
   a. adherence to laws.
   b. whether an individual understands a moral dilemma.
   c. the way an individual reasons about a moral dilemma.
   d. the content of the response to a moral dilemma.

7. Which of the following is true, based on research on Kohlberg's stage sequence? (p. 321)
   a. By early adulthood, Stage 5 is the typical response.
   b. Stages 3 and 4 require a profound understanding of ideal reciprocity.
   c. Postconventional morality is less mature than originally thought.
   d. People rely only on cognition to resolve moral dilemmas.

8. When individuals are faced with real-life, as opposed to hypothetical, moral dilemmas, their moral reasoning tends to (p. 321)
   a. become more mature.
   b. become less mature.
   c. remain at the same level of maturity.
   d. follow no predictable pattern.

9. Yolanda's greater propensity to get involved in community service than her agemates' (though she does not differ from them in moral reasoning) is an example of (p. 323)
   a. moral development.
   b. moral behavior.
   c. moral self-relevance.
   d. moral involvement.

10. During early adolescence, gender intensification is (p. 324)
    a. stronger for boys.
    b. stronger for girls.
    c. equally strong for both boys and girls.
    d. not yet an important issue.

11. Teenagers who are encouraged to explore non-gender-typed options and to question the value of gender stereotypes for themselves and society are more likely to build a(n) _____ gender identity. (p. 324)
    a. erroneous
    b. androgynous
    c. intensified
    d. gender-specific

12. Which of the following fosters adolescent autonomy? (p. 325)
    a. parents who are assertive enough to use psychological control
    b. teenagers' unquestioning admiration of their parents
    c. parents who are warm, supportive, and permit teenagers to explore ideas
    d. parents who delay granting certain privileges, such as driving and dating

13. Throughout adolescence, the most consistent predictor of mental health is (p. 325)
    a. the quality of the parent–child relationship.
    b. development of positive peer relationships.
    c. popularity and social status.
    d. success in academic efforts.

14. During adolescence, siblings (p. 326)
    a. have a more unequal relationship, with younger siblings showing greater willingness to accept direction from older siblings.
    b. devote more time to each other.
    c. have less intense interactions.
    d. experience a decline in the quality of their relationship.

15. John, Gerry, Samuel, Suzanne, and Karen spent much of their free time in and out of school together. They often did things together on weekends, and even began to dress alike. The closely knit group they formed would be considered a (p. 328)
    a. clique.
    b. crowd.
    c. bunch.
    d. pact.

16. The assortment of teenagers into cliques and crowds is influenced by (p. 328)
    a. teacher preference.
    b. parenting style.
    c. stress of school transition.
    d. desire to date.

17. In early adolescence, dating (p. 329)
    a. is done for recreational purposes, as well as to achieve status among agemates.
    b. is focused on psychological intimacy, shared interests, and the search for a good permanent partner.
    c. fosters social maturity.
    d. protects teens against drug use, delinquency, and poor school performance.

18. Studies on the effects of depression on adolescents show that adolescent girls (p. 330)
    a. almost never report persistent depression.
    b. are much less likely than boys to report persistent depression.
    c. are just as likely as boys to report persistent depression.
    d. are twice as likely as boys to report persistent depression.

19. Youth crime (p. 331)
    a. has declined over the past decade.
    b. accounts for a minimal proportion of police arrests—less than 5 percent.
    c. is most often serious in nature.
    d. forecasts a long-term pattern of antisocial behavior for most adolescents.

20. On the path to adolescent delinquency for those with early-onset antisocial behavior, which of the following characteristics defines early childhood rather than middle childhood? (p. 332)
    a. academic failure
    b. commitment to deviant peer group
    c. difficult and fearless temperamental styles
    d. rejection by normal peers

PRACTICE TEST #2

1. According to Erikson, young people who lack a firm sense of self (an identity) to which they can return will find it difficult to risk (p. 315)
    a. intimacy.
    b. security.
    c. shame.
    d. scrutiny.

2. Which of the following parenting styles is linked with positive outcomes in adolescence, including high self-esteem, self-reliance, academic achievement, and work orientation? (pp. 315, 325)
    a. authoritarian
    b. authoritative
    c. permissive
    d. uninvolved

3. When asked about his career plans, Simon says, "Haven't thought about it. Doesn't make too much difference what I do." Simon's identity status is best characterized as (p. 316)
    a. identity achievement.
    b. identity diffusion.
    c. identity moratorium.
    d. identity foreclosure.

4. Adolescents who lack confidence in the prospect of ever knowing anything with certainty and who report low levels of warm, open communication in the home are likely to have which identity status? (p. 316)
    a. identity achievement
    b. identity moratorium
    c. identity foreclosure
    d. identity diffusion

5. _____ typically have close parent–child bonds but lack opportunities for healthy separation. (p. 317)
    a. Identity-achieved adolescents
    b. Adolescents in a state of moratorium
    c. Foreclosed young people
    d. Diffused teenagers

6. Morality is externally controlled at the (p. 320)
   a. preconventional level.
   b. principled level.
   c. conventional level.
   d. postconventional level.

7. When an individual's moral reasoning stems from self-interest, which stage of Kohlberg's theory would best characterize his or her level of moral understanding? (p. 320)
   a. Stage 2: The instrumental purpose orientation
   b. Stage 3: The "good boy–good girl" orientation
   c. Stage 4: The social-order-maintaining orientation
   d. Stage 6: The universal ethical principle orientation

8. In Kohlberg's theory, the _____ individual believes that laws should never be disobeyed because they are vital for ensuring societal order and cooperative relations between individuals. (p. 321)
   a. Stage 1
   b. Stage 2
   c. Stage 4
   d. Stage 6

9. Because situational factors influence moral judgments, Kohlberg's moral stages are shown to be (p. 321)
   a. loosely organized.
   b. tightly organized.
   c. frequently achieved out of order.
   d. inaccurate beyond Stage 3.

10. Which of the following is true with regard to the influences on moral reasoning? (p. 322)
    a. A rigid, closed-minded approach to new information and experiences is linked to gains in moral reasoning.
    b. Peer conflict facilitates moral reasoning by making children aware of others' perspectives.
    c. Strict, authoritarian parenting is associated with more mature moral reasoning.
    d. Movement through Kohlberg's stages is the same in all cultures throughout the world.

11. Research shows that the connection between advanced moral reasoning and moral action is best described as (p. 323)
    a. nonexistent; one does not influence the other.
    b. only modest; moral behavior is influenced by many factors besides cognition.
    c. significant; higher-stage individuals generally report high moral self-relevance.
    d. powerful; mature moral thinkers almost always behave morally.

12. Which adolescent is likely to be psychologically healthiest? (p. 324)
    a. Jasmine, who has a strong feminine gender identity
    b. Luis, who has a strong masculine gender identity
    c. Gabriella, who has an androgynous gender identity
    d. Gordon, who has a feminine gender identity

13. When asked about the meaning of friendship, teenagers stress two characteristics: (p. 326)
    a. intimacy and loyalty.
    b. honesty and loyalty.
    c. intimacy and generosity.
    d. generosity and sincerity.

14. In adolescent friendships, (p. 327)
    a. young people look for common interests and sense of trust, more than any other qualities.
    b. boys engage in more self-disclosure than girls.
    c. cooperation and mutual affirmation increase, while possessiveness of friends decreases.
    d. intimacy has many benefits, and no costs.

15. The first dating relationships of homosexual youths tend to be short-lived and involve little emotional commitment. This is largely because (p. 329)
    a. they are not emotionally ready for more mature, emotionally intense relationships.
    b. they fear peer harassment and rejection.
    c. they are still questioning their sexual identity.
    d. they are looking for relationships that are fun and recreational, with little interest in forming close, long-lasting relational ties.

16. The most common psychological problem of adolescence is (p. 330)
    a. delinquency.
    b. identity diffusion.
    c. gender confusion.
    d. depression.

17. Research examining why girls are more prone to depression than are boys shows that (p. 330)
    a. the biological changes associated with puberty are primarily responsible for the gender gap.
    b. rates of depression for males and females are similar in all developing and industrialized countries around the world.
    c. gender-typed coping styles account for girls' higher rates of depression.
    d. girls with an androgynous or masculine gender identity are as likely as girls with a strong feminine identity to show signs of depression.

18. Which of the following is true of suicide among teenagers? (p. 330)
    a. Boys are four to five times more likely to kill themselves than girls.
    b. African Americans have higher suicide rates than Caucasian Americans.
    c. Rates of teenage suicide are the same among all industrialized nations.
    d. Boys make more unsuccessful suicide attempts than girls.

19. Children or adolescents who engage in illegal acts are considered to be (p. 331)
    a. clinically depressed.
    b. juvenile delinquents.
    c. suicidal.
    d. autonomous.

20. All of the following are associated with successful prevention of juvenile delinquency EXCEPT (p. 332)
    a. authoritative parenting.
    b. high-quality teaching in schools.
    c. positive family relationships.
    d. low monitoring.

CHAPTER 13
PHYSICAL AND COGNITIVE DEVELOPMENT IN EARLY ADULTHOOD

BRIEF CHAPTER SUMMARY

In the modern developed world, the transition to adult roles is prolonged in a new, transitional phase of development, emerging adulthood, which allows for further exploration and identity development before taking on adult roles.

Once body structures reach maximum capacity and efficiency, biological aging begins. The combined result of many causes, it can be modified through behavioral and environmental interventions. In early adulthood, gradual changes occur in physical appearance and body functioning, including declines in athletic skills, in the immune system's protective function, and in reproductive capacity.

SES variations in health over the lifespan reflect differences in both environmental risks and health-related behaviors. Overweight and obesity, strongly associated with serious health problems, have increased dramatically in many Western nations. Young adults are more likely than younger or older people to smoke cigarettes, use marijuana, take stimulants, or engage in binge drinking.

Monogamous, emotionally committed relationships are more typical than casual sex among young adults, and attitudes toward homosexuality have become more accepting as a result of political activism and greater openness on the part of homosexuals. A significant percentage of North American women have endured rape; many more have experienced other forms of sexual aggression, sometimes with lasting psychological effects. Women's menstrual cycle presents unique health concerns, including premenstrual syndrome, an array of symptoms preceding the monthly period. The unique challenges of early adulthood make it a particularly stressful time of life. Social support can provide a buffer against psychological stress, which is related to unfavorable health outcomes, including both unhealthy behaviors and direct physical consequences.

The cognitive-developmental changes of childhood and adolescence extend into adulthood, as seen in the development of epistemic cognition (reflection on one's own thinking process); a movement from dualistic, right-or-wrong thinking toward relativistic thinking; and a shift from hypothetical to pragmatic thought, with greater use of logic to solve real-world problems.

Expertise develops in adulthood as individuals master specific complex domains. College serves as a formative environment in which students can devote their attention to exploring alternative values, roles, and behaviors. Personality, family influences, teachers, and gender stereotypes all influence vocational choice as young adults explore possibilities and eventually settle on an occupation. Non-college-bound young people have a particular need for apprenticeships and other forms of preparation for productive, meaningful lives.

LEARNING OBJECTIVES

After reading this chapter, you should be able to:

13.1 Define emerging adulthood, noting cultural changes that have contributed to the emergence of this period. (pp. 339–340)

13.2 Describe current theories of biological aging, including those at the level of DNA and body cells, and those at the level of tissues and organs. (pp. 340–342)

13.3 Describe the physical changes of aging, paying special attention to the cardiovascular and respiratory systems, motor performance, the immune system, and reproductive capacity. (pp. 342–345)

13.4 Describe the impact of SES, nutrition, and exercise on health, and discuss obesity in adulthood. (pp. 345–348)

13.5 Describe trends in substance abuse in early adulthood, and discuss the health risks of each. (pp. 348–350)

13.6 Summarize young adults' sexual attitudes and behaviors, including sexual orientation, sexual coercion, and premenstrual syndrome. (pp. 350–354)

13.7 Explain how psychological stress affects health. (p. 354)

13.8 Describe characteristics of adult thought, highlighting the theories of Perry and Labouvie-Vief. (pp. 354–357)

13.9 Discuss the development of expertise and creativity in adulthood. (p. 357)

13.10 Describe the impact of a college education on young people's lives, and discuss the problem of dropping out. (p. 358)

13.11 Trace the development of vocational choice, and cite factors that influence it. (pp. 358–361)

13.12 Summarize the problems that North American non-college-bound young people face in preparing for a vocation. (pp. 362)

STUDY QUESTIONS

A Gradual Transition: Emerging Adulthood

1. True or False: Today's young people transition to widely accepted markers of adulthood slowly, often vacillating before making lasting commitments. (p. 339)

2. Describe the developmental period of *emerging adulthood*. (pp. 339–340)

3. How does emerging adulthood prolong identity development? (p. 340)

4. Cite two cultural changes that have contributed to emerging adulthood. (p. 340)
   A. _____
   B. _____

5. True or False: Emerging adulthood is limited or nonexistent for many low-SES young people. Explain your answer. (p. 340)

Physical Development

1. Describe *biological aging,* or *senescence.* (p. 340)
   _____
   _____

2. List four contextual factors that influence biological aging. (p. 340)
   A. _____
   B. _____
   C. _____
   D. _____

Biological Aging Is Under Way in Early Adulthood

1. Briefly explain and evaluate the *"wear-and-tear"* theory of biological aging. (p. 341)
   _____
   _____
   _____
   _____

Aging at the Level of DNA and Body Cells

1. List two current explanations of biological aging at the level of DNA and body cells. (p. 341)
   A. _____
   B. _____

2. Discuss evidence supporting the "genetic programming" theory, which proposes the existence of "aging genes" that control certain biological changes. Note the role of *telomeres* in your response. (p. 341)
   _____
   _____
   _____
   _____

3. Briefly summarize the "random events" theory of biological aging. (p. 341)
   _____
   _____
   _____

4. One probable cause of age-related DNA and cellular abnormalities, implicated in more than 60 disorders of aging, is the release of _____ —naturally occurring, highly reactive chemicals that form in the presence of oxygen. (p. 341)

Aging at the Level of Organs and Tissues

1. According to the _____ *theory of aging,* protein fibers that make up the body's connective tissue form bonds with one another over time. When these normally separate fibers link, tissue becomes less elastic, leading to many negative outcomes. (p. 341)

2. Gradual failure of the _____ system, which produces and regulates hormones, is another route to biological aging. List two examples of decreased hormone production, along with their consequences. (pp. 341–342)

   A. _____

   B. _____

3. Declines in _____ system functioning, which result in increased susceptibility to infectious disease, are related to many conditions of aging. (p. 342)

Physical Changes

Cardiovascular and Respiratory Systems

1. The rate of death from heart disease among (African Americans / Caucasian Americans) is 28 percent higher than among (African Americans / Caucasian Americans). (p. 342)

2. True or False: In healthy individuals, the heart's ability to meet the body's oxygen needs under typical conditions does not change during adulthood. (p. 342)

3. What is *atherosclerosis,* and how does it progress? (p. 342)

   A. _____

   B. _____

4. Explain why rates of heart disease have declined considerably since the mid-twentieth century. (p. 342)
   _____
   _____

5. Cite two ways in which lung functioning changes with age. (pp. 342, 344)

   A. _____

   B. _____

Motor Performance

1. Which athletic skills peak in the early twenties, and which ones usually peak in the late twenties and early thirties? (p. 344)

   Early twenties: _____
   _____

   Late twenties and early thirties: _____
   _____

2. What does research on outstanding athletes reveal about the upper biological limit of motor capacity? (p. 344)
   _____
   _____
   _____

3. True or False: Age-related declines in athletic skill are almost entirely attributable to biological aging. (p. 344)

Immune System

1. Describe two types of white blood cells that are vital in immune system functioning. (p. 344)

    A. _____

    _____

    B. _____

    _____

2. One factor that contributes to age-related declines in the immune response is shrinkage of the _____, which results in decreased production of certain hormones. (p. 344)

3. Explain how stress can weaken the immune response. (pp. 344–345)

    _____

    _____

    _____

Reproductive Capacity

1. Explain why many women experience a decline in fertility across early and middle adulthood. (p. 345)

    _____

    _____

    _____

2. True or False: Male reproductive capacity is unaffected by age. (p. 345)

Health and Fitness

1. Death rates in early adulthood for all causes are (lower / higher) for Canadians than Americans. What factors contribute to this difference? (p. 345)

    _____

    _____

2. Briefly summarize SES variations in health during adulthood, noting factors responsible for these differences. (p. 346)

    Variations: _____

    _____

    Factors responsible: _____

    _____

Nutrition

1. Today, _____ percent of U.S. adults and _____ percent of Canadian adults are obese. (p. 346)

2. True or False: In the United States and Western Europe, 5 to 7 percent more women than men suffer from obesity. In Canada, obesity rates for the two sexes are equal. (p. 346)

3. A (large / small) number of people show large weight gains in adulthood, most often between ages 25 to 40. (p. 346)

4. Define basal metabolic rate (BMR), and describe changes in the BMR during early adulthood that contribute to weight gain. (p. 346)

   Definition: _____

   _____

   Changes: _____

   _____

5. List several health problems associated with being overweight or obese. (p. 346)

   _____

   _____

6. List five elements of effective treatment for obesity. (p. 347)

   A. _____

   B. _____

   C. _____

   D. _____

   E. _____

7. Summarize the detrimental effects of excess dietary fat consumption, noting specific consequences of saturated fat. (pp. 347–348)

   _____

   _____

Exercise

1. Although most North Americans are aware of the health benefits of exercise, about ___ percent in Canada and ___ percent in the United States are inactive. (p. 348)

2. True or False: Exercise helps prevent serious illnesses, such as cancer, adult-onset diabetes, and cardiovascular disease. (p. 348)

3. List five ways that exercise helps prevent serious illnesses. (p. 348)

   A. _____

   B. _____

   C. _____

   D. _____

   E. _____

4. How much exercise is recommended for a healthier and longer life? (p. 348)

   _____

   _____

Substance Abuse

1. True or False: Drug taking peaks among 19- to 22-year-olds and then declines throughout the twenties. (p. 348)

2. What are the two most common substance disorders in early adulthood? (p. 349)

   A. _____

   B. _____

3. Smoking rates have declined very (slowly / rapidly) over the past 40 years. (p. 349)

4. Discuss the consequences of smoking on health. (p. 349)

   _____

   _____

   _____

5. True or False: One out of every three young people who become regular smokers will die from a smoking-related disease. (p. 349)

6. Summarize the benefits of quitting smoking, noting the success rate of those who use cessation aids. (p. 349)

   _____

   _____

7. Describe gender differences in the development and chronicity of alcoholism. (p. 349)

   Men: _____

   Women: _____

8. Twin studies (do / do not) support a genetic contribution to alcoholism. (p. 349)

9. List personal and cultural factors associated with alcoholism. (p. 349)

   Personal: _____

   _____

   Cultural: _____

   _____

10. List some of the health problems associated with chronic alcohol use. (pp. 349–350)

    _____

    _____

11. Cite components of successful treatment programs for alcoholism. (p. 350)

    _____

    _____

Sexuality

1. True or False: Sexual partners tend to be alike in age, education, ethnicity, and religion. (p. 350)

2. True or False: Internet dating services are a successful way for young adults to meet a compatible partner, although conventional strategies for initiating relationships have higher success rates. (p. 350)

3. True or False: Consistent with popular belief, Americans today have more sexual partners than they did a generation ago. Briefly explain your response. (p. 350)

   _____

   _____

4. List three factors that affect frequency of sexual activity. (p. 350)

   A. _____

   B. _____

   C. _____

5. True or False: As the number of sexual partners increases, satisfaction with one's sex life also increases. (p. 350)

6. List the two sexual difficulties most frequently reported by men and by women. (p. 351)

   Men: _____

   Women: _____

7. The majority of Americans (do / do not) support civil liberties and equal employment opportunities for gay men, lesbians, and bisexuals. (p. 351)

8. Heterosexual (women / men) judge homosexuals more harshly. (pp. 351–352)

9. What major factor has limited researchers' access to information about the sex lives of gay men and lesbians? (p. 352)

   _____

10. Explain how the rules for homosexual sex are similar to the rules for heterosexual sex. (p. 352)

    _____

    _____

11. Describe characteristics of gay and lesbian couples, noting living arrangements and level of education. (p. 352)

    _____

    _____

12. An estimated _____ to _____ percent of North American women have experienced rape. (p. 352)

13. Women are most often raped by (strangers / men they know well). (p. 352)

14. Describe the personal characteristics of men who commit sexual assault. (p. 352)

    _____

    _____

    _____

15. Briefly describe three cultural forces that contribute to sexual coercion. (p. 352)

    A. _____

    _____

    B. _____

    _____

    C. _____

    _____

16. True or False: Authorities are just as likely to recognize female-initiated forced sex as illegal as male-initiated forced sex. (pp. 352–353)

17. Summarize the immediate and long-term consequences of rape. (p. 353)

    Immediate: _____

    _____

    Long-term: _____

    _____

18. Cite three critical features in the treatment of rape victims that help foster recovery. (p. 353)

    A. _____

    B. _____

    C. _____

19. List five ways to prevent sexual coercion. (p. 353)

    A. _____

    B. _____

    C. _____

    D. _____

    E. _____

20. List common symptoms of premenstrual syndrome (PMS). (pp. 353–354)

    _____

    _____

    _____

21. Nearly _____ percent of women worldwide experience some form of PMS, but only ____ to ____ percent of women experience symptoms severe enough to interfere with academic, occupational, or social functioning. (p. 354)

22. List common treatments for PMS. (p. 354)

    _____

    _____

Biology and Environment: Sex Differences in Attitudes Toward Sexuality

1. Summarize psychoanalytic, evolutionary, and social-learning perspectives on sex differences in attitudes toward sexuality. (p. 351)

    Psychoanalytic: _____

    _____

    Evolutionary: _____

    _____

    Social-learning: _____

    _____

2. True or False: Women are more opposed to casual sex than men and are only half as likely to engage in it. (p. 351)

3. True or False: Young women's complaints that many men are not interested in long-term commitments are generally unfounded. (p. 351)

Psychological Stress

1. Describe several physical consequences of psychological stress. (p. 354)

2. Explain why early adulthood is a particularly stressful time of life. (p. 354)

Cognitive Development

Changes in the Structure of Thought

1. Cognitive development beyond Piaget's formal operational stage is known as _____ *thought*. (p. 355)

Perry's Theory: Epistemic Cognition

1. What is *epistemic cognition*? (p. 355)

2. Using Perry's research, describe the structure of thought in younger and older college students. Refer to *dualistic* and *relativistic thinking* in your response. (p. 355)

    Younger college students: _____

    Older college students: _____

3. Define *commitment within relativistic thinking,* and provide an example. (p. 355)

    A. _____

    B. _____

4. True or False: Almost all college students reach the stage of *commitment within relativistic thinking*. (p. 355)

5. How do peers contribute to development of epistemic cognition in early adulthood? (pp. 355–356)

6. Explain how peer interaction facilitates individual reflection in early adulthood. (p. 356)

Labouvie-Vief's Theory: Pragmatic Thought and Cognitive-Affective Complexity

1. According to Labouvie-Vief, adulthood marks a shift from hypothetical to _____ *thought*—a structural advance in which logic becomes a tool for solving real-world problems. What motivates this change? (p. 356)

2. Define *cognitive-affective complexity,* noting how it changes in adulthood. Describe its consequences. (p. 356)

   A. _____

   B. _____

   C. _____

Expertise and Creativity

1. Describe *expertise,* noting factors that support it. (p. 357)

   A. _____

   B. _____

2. Summarize differences in problem solving among experts and novices. (p. 357)

   Experts: _____

   Novices: _____

3. True or False: Expertise is necessary for creativity. (p. 357)

4. Describe general trends in the development of creativity across adulthood. (p. 357)

5. In addition to expertise, what other personal qualities foster the development of creativity? (p. 357)

The College Experience

Psychological Impact of Attending College

1. Describe psychological changes that take place during the college years. (p. 358)

   _____
   _____
   _____

2. Cite two factors that jointly contribute to the impact of college. (p. 358)

   A. _____
   B. _____

Dropping Out

1. True or False: Forty-five percent of North American students at two-year institutions and 30 percent of students at four-year institutions drop out, most within the first year and many within the first six weeks. (p. 358)

2. Summarize personal and institutional characteristics that contribute to young people's decision to drop out of college. (p. 358)

   Personal: _____
   _____

   Institutional: _____
   _____

3. True or False: Reaching out to college students, especially during the early weeks and throughout the first year, is critical. Explain your answer. (p. 358)

   _____
   _____
   _____

Vocational Choice

Selecting a Vocation

1. Briefly summarize the three periods of vocational development, noting age range at which each occurs. (p. 359)

   Fantasy period: _____
   _____

   Tentative period: _____
   _____

   Realistic period: _____
   _____

PUZZLE 13.1

Across

2. Cognitive development beyond Piaget's formal operational stage is referred to as _____ thought
4. _____ cognition refers to our reflections on how we arrived at facts, beliefs, and ideas
6. _____ adulthood: a transitional phase of development, extending from the late teens to the mid-twenties
7. _____ thinking: dividing information, values, and authority into right and wrong, good and bad, we and they
8. _____ thinking: viewing all knowledge as imbedded in a framework of thought; favoring multiple truths relative to the context of evaluation
9. During the _____ period of vocational development, children fantasize about career options through make-believe play
11. _____ within relativistic thinking: when one resists choosing between opposing views and instead tries to formulate a more satisfying perspective that synthesizes contradictions
15. _____ aging: genetically influenced, age-related declines in the functioning of organs and systems that are universal in all members of our species
16. _____-_____ theory: the formation of bonds between normally separate protein fibers causes the body's connective tissue to become less elastic
17. During the _____ period of vocational development, adolescents weigh vocational options against their interests, abilities, and values

Down

1. _____-_____ complexity is the awareness and coordination of positive and negative feelings into a complex, organized structure
3. _____ thought: logic becomes a tool for solving real-world problems
5. During the _____ period of vocational development, individuals focus on a general career category and eventually settle on a single occupation
10. The amount of energy the body uses at complete rest (abbr.)
12. Acquisition of extensive knowledge in a field or endeavor
13. Free _____: naturally occurring, highly reactive chemicals that form in the presence of oxygen and destroy cellular material
14. Array of physical and psychological symptoms that usually appear 6 to 10 days prior to menstruation (abbr.)

PRACTICE TEST #1

1. The transition to adult roles includes a phase of development known as emerging adulthood, which (p. 339)
   a. greatly prolongs identity development.
   b. typically extends from about age 18 until the early thirties.
   c. begins after young people have completed their education, regardless of age.
   d. first became common a generation ago.

2. Over the past century in industrialized nations, improved nutrition, medical treatment, sanitation, and safety have resulted in an increase in average life expectancy of about (p. 340)
   a. 10 to 15 years.
   b. 15 to 25 years.
   c. 25 to 30 years.
   d. 50 to 60 years.

3. Biological aging (p. 340)
   a. is the result of "wear and tear" on the body's tissues and organs.
   b. begins in the early twenties.
   c. takes place more rapidly in people who engage in physical work.
   d. is largely the result of heredity, with little influence from environmental factors.

4. According to the "random events" theory of aging, spontaneous or externally caused mutations cause gradual damage to (p. 341)
   a. DNA.
   b. essential vitamins.
   c. the skin.
   d. bone structure.

5. In males, semen volume and sperm concentration and motility gradually decrease after age (p. 345)
   a. 20.
   b. 30.
   c. 40.
   d. 50.

6. Research on health and fitness indicates that (p. 346)
   a. heart disease is the leading cause of death among individuals between ages 25 and 44.
   b. death rates for all causes are essentially equivalent in industrialized nations throughout the world.
   c. income, education, and occupational status show a strong relationship with almost every disease and health indicator.
   d. SES disparities in health and mortality are lesser in the United States than in other industrialized countries.

7. Rising rates of obesity in industrialized nations are the result of (p. 346)
   a. hereditary vulnerability to weight gain.
   b. reduced basal metabolic rate among individuals between ages 25 and 50.
   c. reduced physical labor and increased fat intake.
   d. poor-quality health care and lack of universal health insurance.

8. Adding some weight between ages 25 and 50 is a normal part of aging, resulting from a gradual decline in (p. 346)
   a. basal metabolic rate.
   b. T and B cells.
   c. motor performance.
   d. free radicals.

Factors Influencing Vocational Choice

1. Match each of the following personality types that affect vocational choice with the appropriate description. (p. 359)

   _____ Likes well-structured tasks and values social status; tends to choose business occupations
   _____ Prefers real-world problems and work with objects; tends toward mechanical occupations
   _____ Is adventurous, persuasive, and a strong leader; drawn toward sales and supervisory positions
   _____ Enjoys working with ideas; drawn toward scientific occupations
   _____ Has a high need for emotional and individual expression; drawn to artistic fields
   _____ Likes interacting with people; drawn toward human services

   1. Investigative
   2. Social
   3. Realistic
   4. Artistic
   5. Conventional
   6. Enterprising

2. Research confirms a (weak/moderate/strong) relationship between Holland's personality types and vocational choice. (p. 359)

3. Identify two reasons, other than educational attainment, why young people's vocational aspirations correlate strongly with the jobs of their parents. (p. 360)

   A. _____

   B. _____

4. Teachers (do / do not) play a powerful role in young adults' career decisions. (p. 360)

5. True or False: Over the past three decades, young women's career preferences have remained strongly gender stereotyped. (p. 360)

6. Women's progress in entering and excelling at male-dominated professions has been (slow / rapid). (p. 360)

7. True or False: Sex differences in vocational achievement can be directly attributed to differences in ability. Explain your response. (p. 360)

   _____

8. List three experiences common to young women who show high achievement during college. (p. 361)

   A. _____
   B. _____
   C. _____

Social Issues: Masculinity at Work: Men Who Choose Nontraditional Careers

1. Describe characteristics of men who choose traditionally feminine occupations compared to those who choose traditionally masculine jobs. (p. 361)

   Traditionally Feminine: _____

   Traditionally Masculine: _____

2. True or False: Because of their male minority status in traditionally female occupations, co-workers often assume men are more knowledgeable than they actually are. (p. 361)

3. True or False: Many men in female-dominated occupations express anxiety about being stigmatized for their career choice—by other men, not by women. (p. 361)

Vocational Preparation of Non-College-Bound Young Adults

1. Non-college-bound high school graduates have (more / fewer) work opportunities than they did several decades ago. (p. 362)

2. Summarize the challenges faced by non-college-bound young adults in trying to gain employment, and describe the type of jobs they are likely to find. (p. 362)

   Challenges: _____
   _____

   Type of jobs: _____
   _____

3. Describe the challenges of implementing an apprenticeship program for non-college-bound young adults. (p. 362)

   _____
   _____
   _____

ASK YOURSELF . . .

For *Ask Yourself* questions for this chapter, please log on to the Companion Website at *www.ablongman.com/berk*.

1. Select the Companion Website for *Exploring Lifespan Development*.

2. Use the "Jump to" menu to go directly to this chapter.

3. From the menu on the left side of the screen, select "Ask Yourself."

4. Complete questions and choose "Submit answers for grading" or "Clear answers" to start over.

SUGGESTED STUDENT READINGS

Arnett, J. J. (2006). *Emerging adulthood: The winding road from the late teens through the twenties.* New York: Oxford University Press. Provides a thorough and compelling look at the experiences, challenges, and unique opportunities associated with emerging adulthood.

Massey, D. S., Lundy, G., Charles, C. Z., & Fischer, M. J. (2003). *The source of the river: The social origins of freshmen at America's selective colleges and universities.* New Jersey: Princeton University Press. Using findings from the National Longitudinal Survey of Freshmen, this book examines racial and ethnic differences in academic success, how experiences within the family, peer group, and community contribute to college performance, and how racial stereotypes of intellectual inferiority influence the life chances of many ethnic minority college students.

Smith, M. D. (Ed.). (2002). *Sex without consent: Rape and sexual coercion in America.* New York: New York University Press. A historical look at the experience, prosecution, and meaning of rape in America and how it relates to our understanding of crime and punishment, gender relations, gender roles, and sexual politics.

9. To maintain normal body function and better health, the best rule of thumb is to (p. 348)
   a. eliminate all fat from the diet.
   b. eliminate all unsaturated fats from the diet.
   c. eat less fat of all kinds and substitute unsaturated for saturated fat.
   d. eat less fat of all kinds and substitute saturated for unsaturated fat.

10. Which of the following statements about the value of exercise is accurate? (p. 348)
    a. People who exercise can feel free to eat diets rich in fat, consume alcohol, and smoke, without negative health effects.
    b. Exercise reduces the incidence of obesity.
    c. Regular exercise has not been shown to reduce stress.
    d. Exercise weakens the heart muscle, increasing the risk of cardiovascular disease.

11. The ingredients of cigarette smoke leave their damaging mark (p. 349)
    a. only in the lungs.
    b. only in the mouth and lungs.
    c. only in the lungs and digestive tract.
    d. throughout the body.

12. Which of the following statements about cigarette smoking is true? (p. 349)
    a. Smoking rates have increased among North American adults over the last several decades.
    b. The later people start smoking, the greater their likelihood of continuing.
    c. One out of every three young people who becomes a regular smoker will die from a smoking-related disease.
    d. Despite some improvement in health, those who quit smoking will never return to nonsmoker levels of disease risk.

13. Research on sexual behavior shows that (p. 350)
    a. sexual partners tend to be similar in age, education, ethnicity, and religion.
    b. nearly 50 percent of adults who eventually marry meet at bars, through personal ads, or on vacation.
    c. Americans today have fewer sexual partners than those of a generation ago.
    d. the majority of Americans report having five or more sexual partners in a single year.

14. Men who engage in sexual assault (p. 352)
    a. are less likely to endorse traditional gender roles.
    b. have difficulty accurately interpreting women's social behavior.
    c. usually acknowledge their own responsibility.
    d. are most likely to be from low-SES, ethnic minority groups.

15. According to Perry's work on epistemic cognition, which skill is the first to develop? (p. 355)
    a. Individuals formulate a perspective that synthesizes contradictions.
    b. Individuals give up the possibility of absolute truth.
    c. Individuals choose between many possible, opposing views.
    d. Individuals separate information into right and wrong.

16. Most students who drop out of college (p. 358)
    a. do so during their sophomore or junior year because they are unable to decide on a major.
    b. do not have the ability to succeed at the institution to which they were admitted.
    c. have serious problems with alcohol or drugs.
    d. have problems that are typical rather than catastrophic in nature.

17. Twenty-year-old Dominic explored the possibility of becoming a teacher by tutoring in an after-school program and interviewing several of his previous teachers about their career choice. He then decided to major in education. Dominic is in the _____ period of vocational development. (p. 359)
    a. fantasy
    b. tentative
    c. realistic
    d. acquisition

18. The relationship between personality and vocational choice is (p. 359)
    a. weak, as people rarely choose occupations that complement their personality.
    b. moderate, as most people are a blend of personality types and could do well at more than one kind of occupation.
    c. strong, as career choice, success, and satisfaction are almost entirely attributable to personality factors.
    d. inconclusive, with research findings varying widely on this topic.

19. Young people's vocational aspirations (p. 360)
    a. are generally much higher than their parents'.
    b. are influenced by their fathers' occupations but not by their mothers'.
    c. reflect genetic similarities between parent and child but are unrelated to parenting style.
    d. tend to correlate with their parents' occupations because of similarities in personality, intellectual abilities, and educational attainment.

20. Non-college-bound North American students (p. 362)
    a. are even less likely to find employment than students who drop out of high school.
    b. are typically well prepared for skilled business and industrial occupations.
    c. are better able to find skilled jobs than their counterparts in European nations.
    d. are typically unable to find a job better than the ones they held as students.

PRACTICE TEST #2

1. Which of the following provides support for the programmed effects of "aging genes"? (p. 341)
    a. Human cells that are allowed to divide in the laboratory have a lifespan of 50 divisions, plus or minus 10.
    b. DNA in body cells is gradually damaged through spontaneous or externally caused mutations.
    c. Free radicals released by the body's cells destroy nearby cellular material.
    d. Biological aging does not appear to be affected by environmental factors.

2. Research on the role of key hormones in aging indicates that a gradual drop in growth hormone (GH) is associated with (p. 342)
    a. thickening of the skin.
    b. loss of muscle and bone mass.
    c. reduction in body fat.
    d. increase in cardiovascular functioning.

3. During the twenties and thirties, physical changes of aging (p. 342)
    a. occur only if an individual develops a serious illness.
    b. occur more rapidly than at any other time in the life cycle.
    c. have not yet begun to occur.
    d. occur so gradually that most are hardly noticeable.

4. In healthy individuals, the heart's ability to meet the body's oxygen requirements under normal conditions (as measured by heart rate in relation to volume of blood pumped) (p. 342)
    a. decreases slightly during adulthood.
    b. decreases greatly during adulthood.
    c. does not change during adulthood.
    d. actually increases during adulthood.

5. Studies of outstanding athletes show that (p. 344)
    a. as they begin to age, their attainments fall short of what is biologically possible, even with intensive training.
    b. athletic tasks that depend on endurance peak in the early twenties, while those involving speed, strength, and gross body coordination peak in the late twenties and early thirties.
    c. age-related decline in athletic skill is largely attributable to biological aging.
    d. the upper biological limit of motor capacity is reached in the first part of early adulthood.

6. The immune system declines after age 20 because (p. 344)
   a. production of the thymus hormone increases.
   b. the thymus shrinks, becoming less able to promote full maturity and differentiation of T cells.
   c. the thymus increases in size throughout adulthood.
   d. the stresses of adult life contribute to weakening of the immune system.

7. Treatment for obese adults should (p. 347)
   a. be brief—no more than a few weeks—in order to encourage individuals to take control of their diet and exercise habits on their own.
   b. focus only on changing dietary habits, not on exercise, because it is difficult for obese adults to exercise enough to have any effect.
   c. begin as soon as possible.
   d. focus only on exercise, because regular exercise is more effective than dieting in controlling weight.

8. Which of the following statements about fat consumption is true? (p. 347)
   a. U.S. and Canadian dietary guidelines suggest that dietary fat should make up no more than 30 percent of total caloric intake.
   b. Unsaturated fats are more unhealthy than saturated fats.
   c. To maximize healthy body functioning, dietary fats should be avoided entirely.
   d. Behavioral interventions, such as regular exercise, are largely ineffective in reducing the harmful influence of dietary fats.

9. Among the following groups of North Americans, who is more likely to be inactive compared to their counterparts? (p. 348)
   a. high-SES adults
   b. women
   c. individuals who live in safe neighborhoods
   d. Canadians

10. Which of the following statements about alcoholism is true? (p. 350)
    a. About 50 percent of recovering alcoholics relapse within a few months.
    b. In men, alcoholism usually begins in the late thirties or early forties.
    c. Alcoholism affects more women than men.
    d. The physical effects of alcohol abuse are limited to the liver.

11. The group reporting the highest rates of physical and emotional satisfaction with their sex lives are (pp. 350–351)
    a. individuals in committed relationships who are not yet married.
    b. individuals who have had a large number of sexual partners.
    c. young adults involved in casual dating relationships.
    d. married couples.

12. Victims of sexual coercion (p. 353)
    a. are usually over the age of 30.
    b. rarely know their abusers.
    c. show reactions similar to those of survivors of extreme trauma, including shock, withdrawal, and psychological numbing.
    d. are typically quick to confide in trusted family members and friends about the assault.

13. Premenstrual syndrome (p. 354)
    a. is much more common in women living in industrialized nations than in the developing world.
    b. shows no evidence of having a genetic link.
    c. affects nearly 40 percent of women.
    d. is entirely the result of a genetic predisposition.

14. With regard to epistemic cognition, (p. 355)
    a. students only rarely reach the level of dualistic thinking.
    b. students typically move from relativistic thinking toward dualistic thinking.
    c. as students continue through college, they tend to become less flexible and less tolerant.
    d. the most mature students eventually progress to commitment within relativistic thinking.

15. Compared with novices, experts (p. 357)
    a. reason less effectively.
    b. remember and reason more quickly and effectively.
    c. know fewer domain-specific concepts, because they are focused on underlying principles.
    d. show a more superficial understanding of a larger amount of information.

16. Which of the following statements about expertise and creativity is true? (p. 357)
    a. Experts and novices show remarkably similar reasoning and problem-solving skills.
    b. Creativity takes essentially the same form in childhood and adulthood.
    c. Creativity tends to peak in early adulthood, approximately five years after initial exposure to a field.
    d. Although expertise is necessary for creativity, creativity requires other qualities besides expertise.

17. Those who get an early start in creativity tend to peak and drop off sooner, whereas "late bloomers" reach their full stride at older ages. This suggests that creativity is more a function of _____ than of chronological age. (p. 357)
    a. "actual age"
    b. "career age"
    c. "adult age"
    d. "old age"

18. Cognitive growth during the college years is promoted when (p. 358)
    a. students take online classes rather than enrolling in a postsecondary institution.
    b. students choose a major during their freshman year.
    c. students live in college residence halls and become involved in campus life.
    d. students live at home in order to minimize distractions and promote a higher-quality environment for serious study.

19. Which of the following statements about influences on young people's vocational choices is true? (p. 360)
    a. Because children have considerable knowledge of the drawbacks of their parents' careers, they are likely to choose radically different occupations for themselves.
    b. Teachers are more influential than parents in the career decisions of non-college-bound youths.
    c. Young adults tend to choose occupations that are consistent with their family values, but teachers also play an important role in career decision making.
    d. Neither parents nor teachers have much influence on young adults' career decisions; rather, personality type is the strongest predictor of occupational choice.

20. Teenagers who do not plan to go to college after high school graduation (p. 362)
    a. have a much easier time finding employment than do many college graduates.
    b. are typically limited to temporary, low-paid, unskilled jobs.
    c. often have high-quality vocational preparation, which enables them to enter high-paying, high-skill occupations.
    d. do not have well-developed career aspirations.

CHAPTER 14
EMOTIONAL AND SOCIAL DEVELOPMENT IN EARLY ADULTHOOD

BRIEF CHAPTER SUMMARY

Erikson described the psychological conflict of early adulthood as intimacy versus isolation. In his view, successful resolution of this conflict prepares the individual for the middle adulthood stage, which focuses on generativity, or caring for the next generation and helping to improve society. Levinson suggested that development consists of a series of qualitatively distinct "seasons" in which individuals revise their life structure to meet changing needs. Vaillant refined Erikson's stages, confirming Erikson's stages but filling in the gaps between them.

Although societal expectations have become less rigid, conformity to or departure from the social clock—age-graded expectations for major life events—can be a major source of personality change in adulthood. Following a social clock fosters confidence in young adults, whereas deviating from it can lead to psychological distress.

Although young adults are especially concerned with romantic love and the establishment of an intimate tie with another person, they also satisfy the need for intimacy through relationships with friends, siblings, and co-workers that involve mutual commitment. Romantic partners tend to resemble one another in age, ethnicity, SES, religion, and various personal and physical attributes. Loneliness, as long as it is not overwhelming, can be a motivating factor in healthy personality development.

The family life cycle is a sequence of phases characterizing the development of most families around the world, but wide variation exists in the sequence and timing of these phases. Departure from the parental home is a major step toward assuming adult responsibilities, although nearly half of young adults return home for a brief time after initial leaving. Young adults also delay marriage more today than a half-century ago. Same-sex marriages are recognized in Canada and several other countries, and in the state of Massachusetts; evidence suggests that the factors contributing to happiness for cohabiting same-sex couples are similar to those in other-sex marriages. Women's workplace participation affects both traditional and egalitarian marriages in defining marital roles, with most couplings arriving at a form of marriage somewhere between traditional and egalitarian. Modern couples are having fewer children and postponing parenthood longer than in past generations. Marriages that are gratifying and supportive tend to remain so after childbirth, while troubled marriages usually become more distressed. Parent education programs can help parents clarify their child-rearing values and use more effective strategies.

Today, more adults are single than in the past, and cohabitation without marriage is much more common. The number of couples who choose to remain childless has risen as well. Although childlessness may be distressing when it is involuntary, voluntarily childless adults are just as satisfied with their lives as are parents who have good relationships with their children. Nearly half of all marriages end in divorce, and many people later remarry, often creating blended families that pose their own unique challenges. Never-married parenthood has increased and, for low-SES women, often increases financial hardship. Families headed by homosexuals generally fare well, except for difficulties related to living in an unsupportive society.

Men's career paths are usually continuous, while women's are often discontinuous because of child rearing and other family demands. Although women and ethnic minorities have entered nearly all professions, they still tend to be concentrated in occupations that are less well-paid and that offer little opportunity for advancement. Couples in dual-earner marriages often face complex career decisions and challenges in meeting both work and family responsibilities. When dual-earner couples cooperate to surmount difficulties, they benefit from higher earnings, a better standard of living, and women's self-fulfillment and improved well-being.

LEARNING OBJECTIVES

After reading this chapter, you should be able to:

14.1 Describe Erikson's stage of intimacy versus isolation, noting personality changes that take place during early adulthood. (pp. 366–367)

14.2 Summarize Levinson's and Vaillant's psychosocial theories of adult personality development, including how they apply to both men's and women's lives and their limitations. (pp. 367–369)

14.3 Describe the social clock and how it affects personality in adulthood. (p. 369)

14.4 Discuss factors that affect mate selection, and explain the role of romantic love in young adults' quest for intimacy. (pp. 370–371)

14.5 Explain how culture influences the experience of love. (p. 371)

14.6 Cite characteristics of adult friendships and sibling relationships, including differences between same-sex, other-sex, and sibling friendships. (pp. 371–373)

14.7 Cite factors that influence loneliness, and explain the role of loneliness in adult development. (pp. 373–374)

14.8 Trace phases of the family life cycle that are prominent in early adulthood, noting factors that influence these phases. (pp. 374–381)

14.9 Discuss the diversity of adult lifestyles, focusing on singlehood, cohabitation, and childlessness. (pp. 381–383)

14.10 Discuss today's high rates of divorce and remarriage, and cite factors that contribute to them. (pp. 383–384)

14.11 Summarize challenges associated with variant styles of parenthood, including stepparents, never-married parents, and gay and lesbian parents. (pp. 384–386)

14.12 Describe patterns of career development, and cite difficulties faced by women, ethnic minorities, and couples seeking to combine work and family. (pp. 386–389)

STUDY QUESTIONS

Erikson's Theory: Intimacy versus Isolation

1. According to Erikson, what is the psychological conflict of early adulthood? (p. 366)

2. Explain how a secure identity fosters attainment of intimacy. (pp. 366–367)

3. Describe the characteristics of individuals who have achieved a sense of intimacy versus those affected by isolation. (p. 366)

   Intimacy: _____

   Isolation: _____

Other Theories of Adult Psychosocial Development

Levinson's Seasons of Life

1. True or False: Like Erikson, Levinson regarded development as a sequence of qualitatively distinct eras (stages or seasons). (p. 367)

2. Each era begins with a _____, lasting about five years, which concludes the previous era and prepares the person for the next. (p. 367)

3. Describe the *life structure,* including its central components. (p. 367)

4. Describe differences in the life dreams of men and women. (p. 367)

    Men: _____

    Women: _____

5. How do mentors facilitate realization of young adults' dreams? Who are mentors likely to be? (p. 368)

    A. _____

    B. _____

6. Explain how young people reevaluate their life structure during the age-30 transition. (p. 368)

7. True or False: For men and women without satisfying relational or occupational accomplishments, the age-30 transition can be a relief. (p. 368)

8. Describe women's experiences with "settling down" during their thirties. How do their experiences compare to those of men? (p. 368)

    Women's experiences: _____

    Men's experiences: _____

Vaillant's Adaptation to Life

1. Using Vaillant's theory, explain how men alter themselves and their social world to adapt to life at the following ages: (p. 368)

    Twenties: _____

    Thirties: _____

    Forties: _____

    Fifties and Sixties: _____

    Seventies: _____

2. True or False: When he eventually studied the development of bright, well-educated women, Vaillant found that their development differed sharply from men's. (p. 368)

Limitations of Levinson's and Vaillant's Theories

1. Identify three limitations of Levinson's and Vaillant's theories. (p. 369)

    A. _____

    B. _____

    C. _____

The Social Clock

1. What is the *social clock,* and how does it influence adult development? (p. 369)

    A. _____

    B. _____

2. Describe characteristics of college women born in the 1930s who followed a "feminine" social clock, a "masculine" social clock, or no social clock. (p. 369)

    Feminine: _____

    Masculine: _____

    No social clock: _____

3. How does following a social clock foster confidence during early adulthood? (p. 369)

    _____

Close Relationships

Romantic Love

1. True or False: In selecting a mate, research suggests that "opposites attract." Explain your answer. (p. 370)

    _____

2. In choosing a long-term partner, men and women differ in the importance they place on certain characteristics. How do evolutionary and social-learning perspectives explain this difference? (p. 370)

   Evolutionary: _____
   _____
   _____

   Social learning: _____
   _____

3. True or False: For romance to lead to a lasting partnership, it must happen at the right time for both individuals. (p. 370)

4. List and define the three components of Sternberg's *triangular theory of love.* (p. 370)

   A. _____
   B. _____
   C. _____

5. In the transformation of romantic involvements from passionate to companionate, _____ may be the aspect of love that determines whether a relationship survives. (p. 370)

6. Describe important features of communication that contribute to high-quality intimate relationships. (pp. 370–371)
   _____
   _____
   _____

7. How does the Eastern perspective of love differ from the perspectives of Western cultures? (p. 371)
   _____
   _____
   _____

A Lifespan Vista: Childhood Attachment Patterns and Adult Romantic Relationships

1. Early attachment bonds lead to the construction of a(n) _____, or set of expectations about attachment figures, that serve as a guide for close relationships. (p. 372)

2. Explain how attachment security in childhood influences adult experiences with romantic partners. (pp. 372–373)

   Secure attachment: _____
   _____

   Avoidant attachment: _____
   _____

   Resistant attachment: _____
   _____

3. In addition to child attachment patterns, what other factors contribute to later internal working models and intimate ties? (p. 373)

Friendships

1. Cite three benefits of adult friendship. (p. 371)

    A. _____

    B. _____

    C. _____

2. What features characterize adult friendships? (p. 371)

3. Compare characteristics of women's same-sex friendships with those of men. (p. 371)

    Women: _____

    Men: _____

4. What group of adults has the largest number of other-sex friends? (p. 371)

5. What are some benefits of other-sex friendships? (p. 371)

6. True or False: The majority of other-sex friendships turn into romance. (p. 373)

7. Explain why friend and sibling roles often merge in early adulthood, noting how adult sibling ties resemble friendships. (p. 373)

Loneliness

1. Describe situations in which adults experience *loneliness*. (p. 373)

2. True or False: Loneliness peaks during the teens and early twenties, after which it declines steadily into the seventies. Explain your answer. (p. 373)

3. Under what circumstances are adults likely to experience loneliness? (p. 374)

4. When not involved in a romantic relationship, (men / women) feel lonelier, perhaps because they have fewer alternatives for satisfying intimacy needs. (p. 374)

5. Describe personal characteristics that contribute to loneliness. (p. 374)

6. How can loneliness be motivating? (p. 374)

The Family Life Cycle

1. What is the *family life cycle*? Describe characteristics of individuals in the early adulthood phase. (p. 374)

    A. _____

    B. _____

Leaving Home

1. The average age of leaving the family home has (increased / decreased) in recent years. (p. 374)

2. Nearly _____ percent of young adults return home for a brief time after initial leaving. Those who departed to marry are (most / least) likely to return. Those who left because of family conflict (usually / rarely) return. (p. 375)

3. How do SES and ethnicity contribute to early departure from the family home? (p. 375)

Joining of Families in Marriage

1. Currently, the average age of marriage in the United States is ____ for women and ____ for men. In Canada, the average age of marriage is ____ for women and ____ for men. (p. 375)

2. The number of first and second marriages in the United States and Canada has (increased / declined) over the last few decades. What are some possible reasons for this trend? (p. 375)

3. Nearly _____ percent of North Americans marry at least once. (p. 375)

4. Why is research on same-sex marriages scant? (p. 375)

5. What is the most consistent predictor of marital stability? (p. 376)

   _____

6. Cite differences between *traditional* and *egalitarian* marriages. (p. 376)

   Traditional: _____

   _____

   Egalitarian: _____

   _____

7. In Western nations, men in dual-earner marriages participate much (less / more) in child care than they did in the past. (p. 376)

8. True or False: North American women spend nearly twice as much time as men on housework. (p. 376)

9. List three relationship qualities that contribute to marital satisfaction. (pp. 376–377)

   A. _____

   B. _____

   C. _____

10. True or False: Most couples spend little time reflecting on the decision to marry before their wedding day. (p. 377)

Social Issues: Partner Abuse

1. Partner abuse in which (husbands / wives) are perpetrators and (husbands / wives) are physically injured is the type most likely to be reported to authorities. Why might this not accurately reflect true rates of abuse? (p. 378)

   _____

   _____

   _____

2. True or False: Partner abuse occurs at about the same rate in same-sex relationships as in heterosexual relationships. (p. 378)

3. List three reasons both men and women give for abusing their partner. (p. 378)

   A. _____

   B. _____

   C. _____

4. Describe factors that contribute to partner abuse. (p. 378)

   Psychological: _____

   _____

   _____

   Family: _____

   _____

   _____

   Cultural: _____

   _____

   _____

5. List reasons why many people do not leave destructive relationships before abuse escalates. (p. 378)

6. Describe treatment for victims and perpetrators of partner abuse. (p. 379)

   Victims: _____

   Perpetrators: _____

Parenthood

1. Family size in industrialized nations has (increased / declined). (p. 377)

2. List three factors that affect the decision to have children. (p. 377)

   A. _____
   B. _____
   C. _____

3. True or False: Women with high-status, demanding careers less often choose parenthood and, when they do, more often delay it than women with less time-consuming jobs. (p. 377)

4. Describe reasons for having children that are most important to all groups of people. (pp. 377, 379)

5. Cite two disadvantages of parenthood mentioned most often by young adults. (p. 379)

   A. _____
   B. _____

6. After the arrival of a new baby, the roles of husbands and wives become (more / less) traditional. (p. 379)

7. List factors that contribute to marital satisfaction after childbirth. (p. 379)

8. How does postponing childbearing ease the transition to parenthood? (p. 380)

9. Describe changes in parental roles and responsibilities after the birth of a second child. (p. 380)

10. True or False: Generous, paid employment leave after the birth of a child is widely available in industrialized nations, but not in the United States. (p. 380)

11. In today's complex world, men and women are (more/less) sure about how to rear children than in previous generations. (p. 380)

12. Cite a major struggle for employed parents. Is this more of a problem for men or women? Explain. (p. 380)

    A. _____

    B. _____

13. Identify some benefits of child rearing for adult development. (p. 380)

14. Briefly describe how adolescence brings changes in parental roles. (p. 380)

15. Cite differences in the way mothers and fathers seek information and learn about child rearing. (pp. 380–381)

    Mothers: _____

    Fathers: _____

16. Parent education courses exist to help parents in the following four areas. (p. 381)

    A. _____

    B. _____

    C. _____

    D. _____

The Diversity of Adult Lifestyles

Singlehood

1. Cite two factors that have contributed to the growing numbers of single adults. (p. 381)

    A. _____

    B. _____

2. Because they marry later, more young adult (men / women) are single. But (men / women) are far more likely than (men / women) to remain single for many years or their entire lives. Explain your answer. (p. 381)

3. List the two most often mentioned advantages of singlehood, as well as drawbacks of singlehood. (p. 382)

   Advantages: _____

   _____

   Drawbacks: _____

   _____

   _____

4. Single (men / women) have more physical and mental health problems than single (men / women). Why is this so? (p. 382)

   _____

   _____

Cohabitation

1. Define *cohabitation*, and explain which group of young people has experienced an especially dramatic rise in this type of lifestyle. (p. 382)

   A. _____

   B. _____

2. True or False: Among people in their twenties, cohabitation is now the preferred mode of entry into a committed intimate partnership, with more than 50 percent of North American couples choosing it. (p. 382)

3. How do Western European attitudes toward cohabitation differ from those of North Americans? (p. 382)

   _____

   _____

   _____

4. American and Canadian couples who cohabit before marriage are (more / less) prone to divorce than married couples who did not cohabit. (p. 382)

5. List three types of couples who do not experience the negative outcomes of cohabitation. (p. 383)

   A. _____

   B. _____

   C. _____

Childlessness

1. List reasons couples choose to remain childless. (p. 383)

   _____

   _____

2. (Involuntarily / Voluntarily) childless adults are just as content with their lives as parents who have warm relationships with their children. However, (involuntarily / voluntarily) childless adults are likely to be dissatisfied. (p. 383)

Divorce and Remarriage

1. Explain why divorce rates have stabilized since the mid-1980s. (p. 383)

2. During which periods of adult life are divorces especially likely to occur, and why? (p. 383)

3. Describe maladaptive communication patterns that contribute to divorce. (p. 383)

4. Cite background factors that increase the chances of divorce. (p. 383)

5. Parental divorce (elevates / reduces) risk of divorce in at least two succeeding generations. What explains this trend? (pp. 383–384)

6. True or False: When a woman's workplace status and income exceed her husband's, the risk of divorce decreases. (p. 384)

7. Discuss the consequences of divorce for men and women. (p. 384)

    Men:

    Women:

8. How do men and women differ in their adjustment after divorce? (p. 384)

    Men:

    Women:

9. True or False: On average, people remarry within four years of divorce, women somewhat faster than men. (p. 384)

10. List four reasons that remarriages are especially vulnerable to breakup. (p. 384)

    A. _____

    B. _____

    C. _____

    D. _____

Variant Styles of Parenthood

1. Why are stepmothers especially likely to experience conflict? (p. 385)

   _____

   _____

2. Cite reasons that stepfathers with children of their own have less difficulty adjusting to their role as a stepparent. (p. 385)

   _____

   _____

   _____

3. What are three crucial ingredients of positive stepparent adjustment? (p. 385)

    A. _____

    B. _____

    C. _____

4. In the United States, the largest group of never-married parents is _____. Explain this finding. (p. 385)

   _____

   _____

   _____

5. How do children of never-married parents usually fare? What factors affect their well-being? (p. 385)

    A. _____

    _____

    B. _____

    _____

6. True or False: Gay and lesbian parents are as committed to and effective at child rearing as heterosexual parents. (p. 385)

7. Overall, families headed by homosexuals can be distinguished from other families only by issues related to living in a _____ society. (p. 386)

Career Development

Establishing a Career

1. Men typically have _____ careers—beginning after completion of formal education and ending with retirement. Many women have _____ career paths—ones that were interrupted or deferred by child rearing and other family needs. (p. 386)

297

2. Why can entry into the workforce be discouraging, even for those who enter their chosen field? (pp. 386–387)

3. How do personal characteristics affect career progress? (p. 387)

4. Access to an effective mentor is jointly affected by what two factors? (p. 387)

   A. _____

   B. _____

Women and Ethnic Minorities

1. True or False: Women generally remain concentrated in occupations that offer little opportunity for advancement. (p. 387)

2. Describe reasons why career planning is often short-term and subject to change, especially for women in traditionally feminine occupations. (p. 387)

3. Describe women's career progress in male-dominated fields. (p. 387)

4. Cite examples of racial bias in the labor market. (pp. 387–388)

Combining Work and Family

1. Define *dual-earner marriage*. What are the main sources of strain in these families? (p. 388)

   A. _____

   B. _____

2. Role overload is greater for (men / women). Explain your answer. (p. 388)

3. What strategies can help dual-earner couples combine work and family roles in ways that promote mastery and pleasure in both spheres of life? (p. 388)

___

___

___

ASK YOURSELF...

For *Ask Yourself* questions for this chapter, please log on to the Companion Website at *www.ablongman.com/berk*.

1. Select the Companion Website for *Exploring Lifespan Development*.
2. Use the "Jump to" menu to go directly to this chapter.
3. From the menu on the left side of the screen, select "Ask Yourself."
4. Complete questions and choose "Submit answers for grading" or "Clear answers" to start over.

SUGGESTED STUDENT READINGS

Church, E. (2004). *Understanding stepmothers: Women share their struggles, successes, and insights.* Tornoto: HarperCollins. Presents an extensive overview of research on stepmothers, including the rewards, challenges, and diverse experiences of women who have encountered stepparenthood. An excellent resource for students, teachers, parents, and anyone interested in working with children and families.

Jacobs, J. A., & Gerson, K. (2005). *The time divide: Work, family, and gender inequality.* Cambridge, MA: Harvard University Press. Examines the multitude of benefits and challenges facing dual-earner families. The authors also explore how public policies in the United States and other industrialized nations affect family and work, including gender inequalities in the workplace.

McCarthy, B., & McCarthy, E. J. (2004). *Getting it right the first time.* New York: Brunner-Routledge. Using up-to-date research, detailed case studies, and applied activities, this book examines the most important ingredients for building a successful marriage. The authors also present common marital myths, explain why the early years are so critical, and provide strategies for promoting respect, trust, and intimacy.

PUZZLE 14.1

Across

2. According to Sternberg's _____ theory of love, love has three components—intimacy, passion, and commitment—that shift in emphasis as the romantic relationship develops
4. Feelings of unhappiness that result from a gap between actual and desired social relationships
6. Social _____: age-graded expectations for life events, such as beginning a first job, getting married, birth of a first child, etc.
9. _____ marriage: form of marriage involving clear division of husband's and wife's roles
10. _____ marriage: form of marriage in which husband and wife share power and authority
11. In a _____-_____ marriage, both husband and wife are employed
12. Lifestyle of unmarried individuals who have an intimate, sexual relationship and share a residence

Down

1. Love based on intense sexual attraction
3. Love based on warm, trusting affection and caregiving
5. _____ versus isolation: Erikson's psychological conflict of youth
7. In Levinson's theory, the underlying pattern or design of a person's life at a given time is called the _____ structure
8. _____ life cycle: sequence of phases that characterizes the development of most families around the world

PRACTICE TEST #1

1. When 18- to 25-year-olds are asked what it means to become an adult, most emphasize (p. 366)
   a. career goals.
   b. family goals.
   c. physical qualities.
   d. psychological qualities.

2. The conflict of intimacy versus isolation is successfully resolved when a young adult (p. 366)
   a. establishes a committed, mutually gratifying close relationship.
   b. graduates from a two- or four-year college.
   c. is offered a desirable job in his or her chosen field of work.
   d. leaves the childhood home and begins living independently.

3. In Levinson's concept of the life structure, (p. 367)
   a. men and women typically approach developmental tasks in very similar ways.
   b. ideally, individuals find a desirable life structure in early adulthood and make very few changes after that.
   c. only a few components, related to marriage/family and occupation, are central.
   d. career-oriented women typically construct a dream that is focused entirely on occupational goals, not on relationships.

4. Who among the following is most likely to become a mentor? (p. 368)
   a. a senior colleague to a new coworker
   b. a brother to his older sister
   c. a grandmother to her grandson
   d. a husband to his wife

5. During the age-30 transition, young people reevaluate their (p. 368)
   a. childhood.
   b. sexuality.
   c. life structure.
   d. physical health.

6. According to the social learning perspective, gender roles (p. 370)
   a. profoundly influence criteria for mate selection among individuals of both sexes.
   b. influence men's criteria for mate selection but not women's.
   c. influence women's criteria for mate selection but not men's.
   d. have little influence on criteria for mate selection.

7. At the very beginning of a relationship, the strongest component of love is (p. 370)
   a. passionate love.
   b. compassionate love.
   c. intimacy.
   d. commitment.

8. Couples who report having higher-quality long-term relationships (p. 370)
   a. have sex much more often than the average couple.
   b. somehow manage to keep the mystery in their relationship.
   c. credit their success to being very different, because opposites attract.
   d. consistently communicate their commitment to each other.

9. As people age, intimate, same-sex friendships (p. 371)
   a. increase for both men and women.
   b. increase only for men.
   c. are more numerous for men than they are for women.
   d. are more numerous for women than they are for men.

10. Which of the following have the largest number of other-sex friends? (p. 371)
    a. highly educated, employed women
    b. highly educated, employed men
    c. college-age women
    d. college-age men

11. _____ of young adults return home to live for a brief time after initial leaving. (p. 375)
    a. About one-third
    b. Nearly half
    c. About two-thirds
    d. More than three-fourths

12. Among North Americans, the average age of first marriage is (p. 375)
    a. lower than it was 40 years ago.
    b. the same for men and women.
    c. a little higher in Canada than in the United States.
    d. the same as a generation ago.

13. When asked about the disadvantages of parenthood, young adults most often mention (p. 379)
    a lack of spousal support.
    b. inability to save for their child's college education.
    c. loss of freedom.
    d. unwanted child-rearing advice from in-laws.

14. North American couples who cohabit before becoming engaged are (p. 382)
    a. more committed to each other and display more adaptive patterns of communication than couples who did not cohabit.
    b. more likely to divorce than married couples who did not cohabit.
    c. better prepared for the demands of marriage than couples who did not cohabit.
    d. likely to have conventional values, because cohabitation is widely accepted.

15. When a woman's workplace status and income exceed her husband's, (p. 384)
    a. the couple's likelihood of having children dramatically increases.
    b. the couple's gender-role beliefs are said to be in sync.
    c. the risk of divorce increases.
    d. the risk of divorce decreases.

16. For most divorced adults, negative reactions to divorce subside within (p. 384)
    a. one month.
    b. six months.
    c. two years.
    d. five to seven years.

17. On average, people remarry within (p. 384)
    a. one year of divorce.
    b. two years of divorce.
    c. three years of divorce.
    d. four years of divorce.

18. In the United States, the largest group of never-married parents are young (p. 385)
    a. Asian women.
    b. Mexican-American men.
    c. African-American women.
    d. Caucasian men.

19. Research on gay and lesbian parents indicates that they (p. 385)
    a. have maladjusted children.
    b. are as committed to and effective at child rearing as heterosexual parents.
    c. are less committed to child rearing than heterosexual parents.
    d. are often inconsistent and harsh with their children.

20. Career-oriented, successful ethnic minority women (p. 388)
    a. face racial but not gender discrimination.
    b. rarely receive support from other women.
    c. tend to have mothers who had low expectations for them.
    d. often display unusually high self-efficacy.

PRACTICE TEST #2

1. Like Erikson, Levinson viewed development as (p. 367)
    a. a continuous sequence extending into late adulthood.
    b. especially turbulent for women.
    c. a sequence of qualitatively distinct eras.
    d. biologically determined.

2. Levinson found that during the early adult transition, most individuals construct a(n) (p. 367)
    a. occupational identity.
    b. conceptual identity.
    c. dream.
    d. social clock.

3. Mentors (p. 368)
    a. are usually related to those they guide or educate.
    b. are more readily available to men than to women.
    c. are usually younger than the person they are advising.
    d. usually focus on job training rather than on the values or customs of the occupational setting.

4. In his study of 250 men, Vaillant found that in their fifties and sixties, the men (p. 368)
    a. devoted themselves to intimacy concerns.
    b. became "keepers of meaning."
    c. focused on career consolidation.
    d. pulled back from individual achievement in favor of giving to and guiding others.

5. Ellie's same-age friends all seemed to be getting married and starting families, while Ellie was still single. As a consequence, Ellie felt lonely, had a negative opinion of herself, and questioned her future. The best explanation of Ellie's situation is the (p. 369)
    a. life structure.
    b. social clock.
    c. age-30 transition.
    d. family life cycle.

6. In choosing a long-time partner, men are more apt than women to emphasize (p. 370)
    a. intelligence.
    b. physical attractiveness.
    c. financial status.
    d. moral character.

7. Warm, trusting affection and caregiving in a relationship is (p. 370)
   a. companionate love.
   b. passionate love.
   c. commitment.
   d. intimacy.

8. Compared to Eastern cultural perspectives, Western views of mature love are more likely to focus on (p. 371)
   a. lifelong dependence on one's chosen partner.
   b. obligations to others, particularly parents.
   c. companionship and practical matters, such as similarity of background, career promise, and likelihood of being a good parent.
   d. autonomy, appreciation of the partner's unique qualities, and intense emotion.

9. Highly educated, employed women (p. 371)
   a. have the fewest other-sex friends.
   b. have the greatest number of other-sex friends.
   c. rarely have time for either same-sex or other-sex friends.
   d. often look to other-sex friends for romantic involvement.

10. Loneliness usually peaks in the (p. 373)
    a. mid- to late teens.
    b. late teens and early twenties.
    c. mid- to late twenties.
    d. early thirties.

11. Which of the following adults is likely to experience loneliness? (p. 374)
    a. Meg, a married mother of two who plays cards with a small group of friends twice a month
    b. Joel, a recent college graduate who just started a new job but continues to live with his college roommates
    c. Denzel, a recently divorced father who stays in close contact with his ex-wife and child
    d. Brenda, a college student who still lives at home with her parents

12. Most well-educated, career-oriented women expect a(n) (p. 376)
    a. egalitarian marriage.
    b. traditional marriage.
    c. reverse-role marriage.
    d. same-sex marriage.

13. In partner abuse, women are more often targets of (p. 378)
    a. threats with knives.
    b. slapping.
    c. kicking.
    d. choking.

14. The arrival of a baby results in little marital strain (p. 379)
    a. in supportive marriages.
    b. in troubled marriages.
    c. when women take primary responsibility for caregiving.
    d. in young couples who are just launching their careers.

15. More people seek family therapy during the period when their children are _____ than at any other time in the family life cycle. (p. 380)
    a. young adults
    b. infants
    c. adolescents
    d. starting elementary school

16. Frequently cited advantages of singlehood are (p. 382)
    a. freedom and mobility.
    b. exciting social and sex lives.
    c. greater sense of financial security.
    d. reduced loneliness.

17. Voluntarily childless adults (p. 383)
    a. are just as content with their lives as parents who have warm relationships with their children.
    b. are less content with their lives than parents who have warm relationships with their children.
    c. generally find that their marriages become increasingly unhappy over time.
    d. almost never change their minds about having children later in life.

18. The voluntarily childless usually (p. 383)
    a. are high school dropouts.
    b. are college-educated and have prestigious occupations.
    c. come from large families with many siblings.
    d. are not deeply committed to a career.

19. A factor that increases the chances of divorce is (p. 383)
    a. older age at marriage.
    b. high religious involvement.
    c. high SES.
    d. having parents who divorced.

20. In a study of racial bias in the labor market, researchers found that (p. 387)
    a. résumés with white-sounding names evoked more callbacks than résumés with black-sounding names.
    b. as a result of affirmative action, individuals with black-sounding names received more callbacks than individuals with white-sounding names, regardless of the quality of their résumé.
    c. individuals with high-quality résumés received more callbacks than individuals with low-quality résumés, regardless of whether their names sounded white or black.
    d. individuals with black-sounding names received more callbacks for low-paying jobs, while individuals with white-sounding names received more callbacks for skilled and managerial jobs.

CHAPTER 15
PHYSICAL AND COGNITIVE DEVELOPMENT IN MIDDLE ADULTHOOD

BRIEF CHAPTER SUMMARY

Physical development in midlife continues the gradual changes under way in early adulthood. Age-related deterioration in vision, hearing, and the condition of the skin becomes more apparent. Weight gain coupled with loss of lean body mass is a concern for both men and women, as is a loss of bone mass. Dietary changes and weight-bearing exercise can offset these effects of aging.

The climacteric, or decline in fertility, occurs gradually over a 10-year period for women, concluding with menopause—the end of menstruation and of reproductive capacity. Doctors may prescribe hormone therapy to reduce the discomforts of menopause and to protect women from other impairments due to estrogen loss, but research also shows some potential risks of this therapy. The wide variation in physical symptoms and attitudes indicates that menopause is not merely a hormonal event but is also affected by societal beliefs and practices. Men also experience a climacteric, but the change is less dramatic, limited to a decrease in quantity of semen and sperm after age 40.

Frequency and intensity of sexual activity tends to decline in middle adulthood, although it continues to be an important component of married couples' lives. Cancer and cardiovascular disease are the leading causes of death in middle age. Unintentional injuries continue to be a major health threat, although they occur at a lower rate than in young adulthood, largely because of a decline in motor vehicle collisions. When age-related bone loss is severe, a disabling condition called osteoporosis develops. In both men and women, hostility and anger predict heart disease.

Stress management in middle adulthood can limit the age-related rise in illness and, when disease strikes, reduce its severity. Heredity, diet, exercise, social support, coping strategies, and hardiness contribute to middle-aged adults' ability to cope with stress. Negative stereotypes of aging lead many middle-aged adults to fear physical changes. These unfavorable stereotypes are more likely to be applied to women than to men, yielding a double standard, which may be declining as a result of societal changes.

Although declines in cognitive development occur in some areas, most middle-aged people display cognitive competencies, especially in familiar contexts, and some attain outstanding accomplishment. Consistent with the lifespan perspective, cognitive change in middle adulthood is viewed as multidimensional, multidirectional, and plastic. Crystallized intelligence (which depends on accumulated knowledge and experience) increases steadily through middle adulthood, while fluid intelligence (which depends on basic information-processing skills) begins to decline in the twenties. Research shows that using intellectual skills seems to affect the degree to which they are maintained.

Speed of cognitive processing slows with age, making it harder for middle-aged people to divide their attention, focus on relevant stimuli, and switch from one task to another as the situation demands. With age, the amount of information people can retain in working memory diminishes, but general factual knowledge, procedural knowledge, and knowledge related to one's occupation either remain unchanged or increase into midlife. Middle-aged adults in all walks of life often become good at practical problem solving, largely as a result of development of expertise, and creativity in midlife becomes more deliberately thoughtful.

At all ages and in different cultures, a reciprocal relationship exists between vocational life and cognitive development. Stimulating, complex work and flexible, abstract, autonomous thinking support each other. Often motivated by life transitions, adults are returning to undergraduate and graduate study in record numbers. The majority of adult learners are women, who often experience role overload. Social supports for returning students can make the difference between continuing in school and dropping out.

LEARNING OBJECTIVES

After reading this chapter, you should be able to:

15.1 Describe physical changes of middle adulthood, paying special attention to vision, hearing, the skin, muscle–fat makeup, and the skeleton. (pp. 395–397)

15.2 Summarize reproductive changes in middle adulthood, paying special attention to the symptoms of menopause, the benefits and risks of hormone therapy, and women's psychological reactions to menopause. (pp. 397–400)

15.3 Discuss sexuality in middle adulthood and its association with psychological well-being. (p. 401)

15.4 Discuss cancer, cardiovascular disease, and osteoporosis, noting sex differences, risk factors, and interventions. (pp. 401–403)

15.5 Explain how hostility and anger affect health. (pp. 403–404)

15.6 Discuss the benefits of stress management, exercise, and an optimistic outlook in adapting to the physical challenges of midlife. (pp. 404–406)

15.7 Explain the double standard of aging. (p. 406)

15.8 Describe cohort effects on intelligence revealed by Schaie's Seattle Longitudinal Study. (p. 407)

15.9 Describe changes in crystallized and fluid intelligence during middle adulthood, and discuss individual and group differences in intellectual development. (pp. 407–409)

15.10 Describe changes in information processing in midlife, paying special attention to speed of processing, attention, and memory. (pp. 409–411)

15.11 Discuss the development of practical problem solving, expertise, and creativity in middle adulthood. (pp. 411–412)

15.12 Describe the relationship between vocational life and cognitive development. (p. 412)

15.13 Discuss the challenges of adult learners, ways to support returning students, and benefits of earning a degree in midlife. (pp. 412–413)

STUDY QUESTIONS

Physical Development

Physical Changes

Vision

1. Describe the condition known as *presbyopia,* and explain how changes in the structures of the eye contribute to this condition. (p. 396)

2. Cite declines in visual functioning that are associated with yellowing of the lens, shrinking of the pupil, and increasing density of the vitreous. (p. 396)

3. Describe neural changes in the visual system that occur in midlife. (p. 396)

   _____
   _____
   _____

4. Middle-aged adults are at increased risk for _____ —a disease in which pressure builds up within the eye due to poor fluid drainage, causing damage to the optic nerve. (p. 396)

Hearing

1. Most adult-onset hearing impairments are age-related, declines called _____, meaning "old hearing." (p. 396)

2. Cite two physical changes that lead to age-related hearing loss. (p. 396)

   A. _____
   B. _____

3. (Men's / Women's) hearing tends to decline earlier. Explain your answer. (p. 397)

   _____
   _____

Skin

1. Name and describe the three layers that make up our skin, explaining how each changes with age. (p. 397)

   A. _____
   Changes: _____
   B. _____
   Changes: _____
   C. _____
   Changes: _____

2. Describe changes in the skin at the following ages: (p. 397)

   Thirties: _____
   Forties: _____
   Fifties: _____

Muscle–Fat Makeup

1. Briefly summarize changes in body fat and muscle mass in middle adulthood. (p. 397)

   _____
   _____
   _____

2. Describe sex differences in fat distribution during middle adulthood. (p. 397)

   Men: _____
   Women: _____

3. Explain how weight gain and muscle loss can be prevented. (p. 397)

Skeleton

1. What change leads to substantial reduction in bone density during adulthood? (p. 397)

2. Why are women especially susceptible to loss in bone mass in middle adulthood? (p. 397)

3. Cite one health problem associated with weakened bones. (p. 397)

4. Cite factors that can slow bone loss in postmenopausal women by 30 to 50 percent. (p. 397)

Reproductive System

1. The midlife transition in which fertility declines is called the _____. (p. 397)

2. In women, the climacteric concludes with _____ —the end of menstruation and reproductive capacity. This occurs, on average, in the _____ among North American, European, and East Asian women. (p. 397)

3. Summarize gradual changes that precede menopause, as well as the physical changes that occur after menopause. (pp. 397–398)

    Changes preceding menopause: _____

    Changes after menopause: _____

4. True or False: Research reveals that menopause is not linked to changes in the quantity or quality of sleep. (p. 398)

5. Describe characteristics of women who are likely to experience depressive episodes during climacteric. (p. 398)

6. Describe two types of hormone therapy. (p. 398)

   A. _____

   _____

   B. _____

   _____

7. Briefly summarize the benefits and risks associated with hormone therapy. (p. 398)

   Benefits: _____

   _____

   Risks: _____

   _____

8. Describe factors that affect women's psychological reactions to menopause. (p. 399)

   _____

   _____

   _____

9. Provide an example of ethnic differences in the way women experience and view menopause. (p. 399)

   _____

   _____

   _____

10. True or False: Men lose their reproductive capacity during midlife and can no longer father children. (p. 399)

11. Summarize reproductive changes in middle-aged men. (p. 399)

    _____

    _____

    _____

Cultural Influences: Menopause as a Biocultural Event

1. Summarize the differing views of menopause held by individuals in Western industrialized nations compared to their non-Western counterparts. (p. 400)

   Western: _____

   _____

   Non-Western: _____

   _____

2. True or False: Japanese women and doctors, like their North American counterparts, consider menopause to be a significant marker of female middle age. (p. 400)

3. Compare Mayan and Greek perspectives on menopause, noting similarities and differences. (p. 400)

   Similarities: _____

   _____

   Differences: _____

   _____

Health and Fitness

Sexuality

1. Frequency of sexual activity declines (dramatically / slightly) in middle adulthood. (p. 401)

2. What is the best predictor of sexual frequency in midlife? (p. 401)
   _____

3. How does the intensity of sexual response change during middle adulthood? (p. 401)
   _____
   _____

4. True or False: The majority of people over age 50 say that sex is an important component of their relationship. (p. 401)
   _____
   _____
   _____

Illness and Disability

1. List the two leading causes of death in midlife. (p. 401)
   A. _____
   B. _____

2. Overall, middle-aged (men / women) are more vulnerable to most health problems. (p. 401)

3. In the last 15 years, the incidence of lung cancer dropped in (men / women), but it has increased in (men / women). (p. 402)

4. Describe two types of mutations that contribute to cancer. (p. 402)
   A. _____
   B. _____

5. True or False: Cancer death rates increase sharply as SES decreases and are especially high among low-income ethnic minorities. (p. 402)

6. Provide an example of the complex interaction of heredity, biological aging, and environment on cancer. (p. 402)
   _____
   _____
   _____

7. Name the three most common types of cancer among men and women. (p. 402)
   Men: _____
   Women: _____

8. Describe two ways to reduce cancer illness and cancer death. (p. 402)
   A. _____
   B. _____

9. List three indicators of cardiovascular disease that are known as "silent killers" because they often have no symptoms. (p. 402)

    A. _____

    B. _____

    C. _____

10. List three symptoms of cardiovascular disease. (p. 402)

    A. _____
    _____

    B. _____
    _____

    C. _____
    _____

11. List four ways to reduce the risk of having a heart attack. (p. 402)

    A. _____

    B. _____

    C. _____

    D. _____

12. Accurate diagnosis of cardiovascular disease is of special concern to (women / men), since doctors frequently overlook their symptoms. (pp. 402–403)

13. When age-related bone loss is severe, a condition called _____ develops. (p. 403)

14. True or False: Osteoporosis affects the majority of people of both sexes over age 70. (p. 403)

15. Summarize the symptoms of osteoporosis. (p. 403)

    _____
    _____
    _____

16. List biological and environmental risk factors associated with osteoporosis. (p. 403)

    Biological: _____
    _____

    Environmental: _____
    _____

17. True or False: Men are far less likely than women to be screened and treated for osteoporosis. Explain your answer. (p. 403)

    _____
    _____

18. List several interventions for treating osteoporosis. (p. 403)

    _____
    _____

Hostility and Anger

1. Describe characteristics of the *Type A behavior pattern*. (pp. 403–404)

2. What is the "toxic" ingredient of the Type A behavior pattern? (p. 404)

3. Explain the link between expressed hostility and health problems. (p. 404)

4. True or False: Suppressing anger is a healthier way of dealing with negative feelings than expressing anger. (p. 404)

Adapting to the Challenges of Midlife

Stress Management

1. Identify five strategies for managing stress. (p. 404)

    A.
    B.
    C.
    D.
    E.

2. Distinguish between *problem-centered* and *emotion-centered* coping. (p. 404)

    Problem-centered:

    Emotion-centered:

3. What approach to coping is most effective for reducing stress? (p. 404)

4. Cite several constructive approaches to anger reduction. (p. 405)

5. Summarize changes in coping with stress from early to middle adulthood. (p. 405)

314

Exercise

1. Of those who begin an exercise program in midlife, ____ percent discontinue within the first six months. Among those who stay active, fewer than ____ percent exercise at levels that lead to health benefits. (p. 405)

2. Define *self-efficacy,* and describe the link between self-efficacy and exercise. (p. 405)

    Definition: _____

    Link to exercise: _____

3. Identify characteristics of beginning exercisers that best fit group versus home-based exercise programs. (p. 405)

    Group: _____

    Home-based: _____

4. List barriers to exercise often mentioned by low-SES adults. (p. 405)

An Optimistic Outlook

1. _____ refers to a set of three personal qualities that help people cope with stress adaptively, thereby reducing its impact on illness and mortality. List and describe the three qualities that make up this trait. (p. 406)

    A. _____

    B. _____

    C. _____

2. Summarize the coping strategies of high-hardy and low-hardy individuals. (p. 406)

    High-hardy: _____

    Low-hardy: _____

3. Cite five factors that act as stress-resistant resources. (p. 406)

    A. _____
    B. _____
    C. _____
    D. _____
    E. _____

Gender and Aging: A Double Standard

1. Unfavorable stereotypes about aging are more often applied to (women / men), who are rated as less attractive and as having more negative characteristics. (p. 406)

2. What factor is at the heart of the double standard of aging? (p. 406)
   _____

3. New evidence suggests that the double standard of aging is (increasing / declining). (p. 406)

Cognitive Development

Changes in Mental Abilities

Cohort Effects

1. Schaie examined adult development of intellectual abilities using a _____ design, which combines cross-sectional and longitudinal approaches. Describe differences in Schaie's longitudinal and cross-sectional findings. What accounts for this difference? (p. 407)

   Cross-sectional: _____
   _____

   Longitudinal: _____
   _____

   Difference: _____
   _____

Crystallized and Fluid Intelligence

1. Differentiate between *crystallized* and *fluid intelligence*. (pp. 407–408)

   Crystallized: _____
   _____

   Fluid: _____
   _____

2. (Crystallized / Fluid) intelligence increases steadily throughout middle adulthood, whereas (crystallized / fluid) intelligence begins to decline in the twenties. (p. 408)

3. Using findings from Schaie's Seattle Longitudinal Study, list five crystallized and fluid skills that continue to show gains in midlife and one fluid skill that declines steadily from the twenties to the late eighties. (p. 408)

   Crystallized:

   A. _____
   B. _____
   C. _____
   D. _____
   E. _____

   Fluid:

   F. _____

4. List three reasons why middle-aged adults show stability in crystallized abilities despite a much earlier decline in fluid intelligence. (pp. 408–409)

   A. _____
   B. _____
   C. _____

Information Processing

Speed of Processing

1. True or False: Response time on both simple and complex reaction time tasks remains stable across early and middle adulthood. (p. 409)

2. Provide two explanations for age-related declines in speed of processing. (p. 409)

   A. _____
   _____

   B. _____
   _____

3. How does processing speed affect adults' performance on many complex tasks? (p. 409)

   _____
   _____
   _____

4. True or False: Knowledge and experience help older adults compensate for declines in processing speed. (p. 409)

Attention

1. Studies of attention focus on the following three changes: (p. 409)

   A. _____
   B. _____
   C. _____

2. Explain how declines in attention might be related to a slowdown in information processing during midlife. (p. 410)

   _____
   _____
   _____

3. Describe changes in inhibition in middle adulthood. (p. 410)

   _____
   _____

4. True or False: Practice and experience with attentional skills can help midlifers compensate for age-related declines. (p. 410)

Memory

1. From early to middle adulthood, the amount of information people can retain in working memory (increases / diminishes). What explains this change? (p. 410)

   _____
   _____

2. Memory strategies, such as organization and elaboration, are applied (less / more) often and (less / more) effectively with age. What explains these changes? (p. 410)

   _____
   _____
   _____

3. How can memory tasks be designed to help older people compensate for age-related declines in working memory? (p. 410)

   _____
   _____
   _____

4. Middle-aged people who have trouble recalling something often drawn on decades of accumulated _____ about how to maximize performance. (pp. 410–411)

Practical Problem Solving and Expertise

1. What is *practical problem solving*? (p. 411)

   _____
   _____

2. Expertise (peaks / declines) in midlife. (p. 411)

3. True or False: Advances in expertise are found only among highly educated individuals in administrative occupations. (p. 411)

4. Briefly describe advances in practical problem solving during middle adulthood. (p. 411)

   _____
   _____
   _____

Creativity

1. Summarize three ways that creativity changes with age. (p. 412)

   A. _____
   _____

   B. _____
   _____

   C. _____
   _____

Vocational Life and Cognitive Development

1. Summarize the relationship between vocational life and cognition. (p. 412)

2. Cross-cultural findings (support / refute) the notion that complex work leads to gains in cognitive flexibility. (p. 412)

3. True or False: The impact of challenging work on cognition is greater in early adulthood than in middle adulthood. (p. 412)

Adult Learners: Becoming a Student in Midlife

1. List several reasons why middle-aged adults may decide to enroll in undergraduate and graduate programs. (p. 412)

Characteristics of Returning Students

1. (Men / Women) represent the majority of adult learners. (p. 413)

2. Describe common feelings of women during their first-year reentry as a student. What factors influence these feelings? (p. 413)

   A.

   B.

3. What challenges do middle-aged women who return to college face? (p. 413)

4. What is the most common reason women do not complete their degree in middle adulthood? (p. 413)

Supporting Returning Students

1. List social supports and institutional services that facilitate adult reentry into college. (p. 413)

   Social supports:

   Institutional services:

2. Summarize the benefits of adult reentry to college. (p. 413)

_____

_____

_____

ASK YOURSELF . . .

For *Ask Yourself* questions for this chapter, please log on to the Companion Website at *www.ablongman.com/berk*.

1. Select the Companion Website for *Exploring Lifespan Development*.
2. Use the "Jump to" menu to go directly to this chapter.
3. From the menu on the left side of the screen, select "Ask Yourself."
4. Complete questions and choose "Submit answers for grading" or "Clear answers" to start over.

SUGGESTED STUDENT READINGS

Brim, O. G., Kessler, R. C., & Ryff, C. D. (Eds.). (2005). *How healthy are we? A national study of well-being at midlife.* Chicago, IL: University of Chicago Press. Using results from the Midlife in the United States Study (MIDUS), which included over 7,000 adults between the ages of 25 and 74, this book examines physical health, psychological well-being, and quality of life in middle-aged Americans. Findings represent adults from diverse economic, geographic, and ethnic backgrounds.

Jarvis, P. (2004). *Adult education and lifelong learning: Theory and practice.* New York: Taylor & Francis. Examines current theories of adult learning and education, such as characteristics of adult learners, adult learning needs and opportunities, and distance education.

Levine, S. B. (2005). *Inventing the rest of our lives: Women in the second adulthood.* New York: Penguin. Presents a thorough and optimistic overview of middle adulthood for women, including physical changes, self-discovery, modifications in marital and family roles, and unique career opportunities.

PUZZLE 15.1

Across

3. A disease in which pressure builds up within the eye due to poor fluid drainage, damaging the optic nerve
6. _____ problem solving: requires people to size up real-world situations and analyze how best to achieve goals that have a high degree of uncertainty
7. _____ intelligence: skills that largely depend on basic information-processing skills
10. Treatment in which a woman takes daily doses of estrogen, sometimes combined with progesterone, during the climacteric and after menopause
11. _____ - _____ view: attributes age-related slowing of cognitive processing to greater loss of information as it moves through the system
12. _____ network view: attributes age-related slowing of cognitive processing to breaks in neural networks as neurons die
13. Behavior pattern consisting of competitiveness, ambition, impatience, angry outbursts, and time pressure
14. Set of three personal qualities—commitment, control, and challenge—that help people cope with stress adaptively

Down

1. Condition associated with severe age-related bone
2. Age-related hearing impairments that involve a sharp loss of hearing at high frequencies, gradually extending to all frequencies loss
4. Midlife transition in which fertility declines
5. Condition of aging in which the eye loses its capacity to accommodate entirely to nearby objects
8. _____ intelligence: skills that depend largely on accumulated knowledge and experience, good judgment, and mastery of social conventions
9. The end of menstruation and, therefore, reproductive capacity in women

PRACTICE TEST #1

1. Middle age is loosely defined as taking place between ages (p. 395)
   a. 20 and 35.
   b. 30 and 45.
   c. 40 and 65.
   d. 50 and 75.

2. Throughout adulthood, the size of the pupil shrinks and the lens (p. 396)
   a. yellows.
   b. expands.
   c. thins.
   d. dissolves.

3. Middle-aged adults are at increased risk of _____, a disease in which poor fluid drainage causes a buildup of pressure within the eye, damaging the optic nerve. (p. 396)
   a. glaucoma
   b. presbycusis
   c. presbyopia
   d. climacteric

4. Men's hearing declines (p. 397)
   a. less rapidly than women's.
   b. more rapidly than women's.
   c. at the same rate as women's.
   d. while women's hearing does not decline.

5. Reduction in bone mass during midlife (p. 397)
   a. is caused by increased mineral content.
   b. is more substantial in men than in women.
   c. causes bones to fracture more easily and heal more slowly.
   d. cannot be slowed, even with lifestyle changes such as increased calcium intake.

6. What percentage of individuals affected with cancer are cured? (p. 402)
   a. 10 percent
   b. 20 percent
   c. 40 percent
   d. 60 percent

7. Which indicator of cardiovascular disease is referred to as a "silent killer"? (p. 402)
   a. atherosclerosis—a buildup of plaque in the coronary arteries
   b. a heart attack—blockage of normal blood supply to an area of the heart
   c. arrhythmia—an irregular heartbeat
   d. angina pectoris—indigestion-like or crushing chest pain

8. To treat osteoporosis, doctors recommend a diet enriched with vitamin D and (p. 403)
   a. calcium.
   b. magnesium.
   c. iron.
   d. vitamin C.

9. Expressed hostility (p. 404)
   a. predicts heart disease and other health problems only in men.
   b. is the toxic ingredient in the Type A behavior pattern that predicts heart disease and other health problems.
   c. poses fewer health risks than does suppressed hostility.
   d. elevates heart rate and blood pressure, but reduces levels of stress hormones in the body.

10. Sharon decided that she was unhappy at work. She realized that the primary cause was frustration with an irresponsible co-worker. She met with this individual, came up with strategies to help the young woman meet her responsibilities, and subsequently derived more enjoyment from her job. Sharon used (p. 404)
    a. avoidant coping.
    b. problem-centered coping.
    c. emotion-centered coping.
    d. behavior-focused coping.

11. When a person has a sense of control over life events, a commitment to important activities, and a tendency to view change as a challenge rather than a disappointment, this person is said to display (p. 406)
    a. fluid intelligence.
    b. Type A behavior pattern.
    c. resilience.
    d. hardiness.

12. Hardy individuals (p. 406)
    a. seldom view stressful situations as controllable.
    b. fail to find interest and meaning in daily activities.
    c. more often use emotion-centered coping strategies.
    d. view challenge as a chance for personal growth.

13. The double standard of aging refers to the notion that (p. 406)
    a. middle-aged men become less committed to occupational status and physical fitness, yet they are viewed by the larger culture as powerful and driven.
    b. middle-aged women often feel assertive and confident, yet they are viewed by the larger culture as being less attractive and as having more negative traits than middle-aged men.
    c. middle-aged women gain in positive judgments of appearance, maturity, and power, whereas middle-aged men show a decline in such ratings.
    d. middle-aged adults of both sexes prefer younger sexual partners.

14. Many cross-sectional studies show that _____ increases steadily through middle adulthood, whereas _____ begins to decline in the twenties. (p. 408)
    a. crystallized intelligence, fluid intelligence
    b. fluid intelligence, general intelligence
    c. problem-solving intelligence, crystallized intelligence
    d. fluid intelligence, crystallized intelligence

15. Studies of attention during midlife indicate that (pp. 409–410)
    a. cognitive inhibition—the ability to resist interference from irrelevant information—improves during middle adulthood.
    b. it becomes more difficult to engage in two complex activities at the same time.
    c. decrements in attention are caused by sensory impairments, such as diminished vision and hearing.
    d. practice with attention-related tasks does little to improve these skills.

16. With respect to memory in middle adulthood, (p. 410)
    a. the amount of information people can retain in working memory declines.
    b. adults more often use memory strategies of rehearsal, organization, and elaboration.
    c. recall is better in highly structured than in self-paced conditions.
    d. adults have difficulty compensating for memory limitations.

17. Declines in working memory in midlife largely result from (p. 410)
    a. changes in the structure of the brain.
    b. declines in metacognitive knowledge.
    c. decreased motivation to learn and remember new information.
    d. infrequent and ineffective use of memory strategies.

18. During middle adulthood, creativity (p. 412)
    a. becomes less deliberately thoughtful.
    b. is focused more on generating unusual products and less on combining knowledge and experience.
    c. shifts from an egocentric concern with self-expression to more altruistic goals.
    d. is more spontaneous and intensely emotional.

19. Research on the relationship between vocational life and cognitive development shows that (p. 412)
    a. the impact of challenging work on cognitive growth is greatest for young adults.
    b. people in their fifties and early sixties show as many cognitive gains from complex work as do individuals in their twenties and thirties.
    c. the relationship between challenging work and continued cognitive development is only evident in cultures similar to the United States.
    d. cognition has a unidirectional influence on vocational life—that is, cognitive ability affects vocational choice, but vocational life does not affect cognitive development.

20. Adults who return to college for undergraduate and graduate study are most likely to be (p. 413)
    a. women.
    b. under the age of 35.
    c. divorced, single parents.
    d. free of other career and family obligations.

PRACTICE TEST #2

1. Adult-onset hearing loss (pp. 396–397)
    a. is greater among women than men.
    b. is most often caused by a hereditary condition.
    c. is typically first noticeable by a hearing loss at low frequencies.
    d. is minimal in most middle-aged adults, suggesting that severe hearing problems are caused by factors other than biological aging.

2. As we age, (p. 397)
    a. fibers in the dermis thicken.
    b. the epidermis becomes less firmly attached to the dermis.
    c. fat in the hypodermis increases.
    d. skin becomes much more elastic.

3. Which of the following is true of fat distribution in middle adulthood? (p. 397)
    a. Women accumulate more on the back and upper abdomen.
    b. Men accumulate more around the waist and upper arms.
    c. The rise in fat largely affects the torso as fat levels decline on the limbs.
    d. Men and women both tend to lose fat during middle age.

4. With age, people must gradually reduce caloric intake to adjust for the age-related decline in (p. 397)
    a. presbyopia.
    b. basal metabolic rate.
    c. hormone therapy.
    d. bone mass.

5. The period leading up to and following menopause is often accompanied by (p. 398)
    a. rapid declines in body temperature.
    b. excessive sleep.
    c. a sharp rise in estrogen levels.
    d. mood fluctuations.

6. Hormone therapy (p. 398)
    a. works poorly in counteracting hot flashes and vaginal drying.
    b. is linked to a mild increase in heart attacks, stroke, and blood clots.
    c. is associated with increased depression.
    d. enhances cognitive functioning in 65- to 79-year-old women.

7. The leading causes of death in middle adulthood are (p. 401)
    a. suicide and homicide.
    b. motor vehicle accidents and cancer.
    c. AIDS and heart disease.
    d. heart disease and cancer.

8. Cancer-causing mutations that are due to an inherited predisposition are called (p. 402)
    a. somatic.
    b. BRCA1.
    c. germline.
    d. BRCA2.

9. Mary, a 65-year-old woman, does not exercise regularly, has smoked on and off for thirty years, and is deficient in her vitamin D and calcium intake. As a result, Mary has suffered several minor bone fractures in recent years. Mary most likely has (p. 403)
    a. climacteric.
    b. osteoporosis.
    c. cardiovascular disease.
    d. lung cancer.

10. Which of the following is as vital to adoption and maintenance of an exercise program in midlife as it is to career progress? (p. 405)
    a. intelligence
    b. capacity to cope with stress
    c. self-control
    d. self-efficacy

11. Which group of beginning exercisers is most likely to benefit from a home-based program? (p. 405)
    a. normal-weight individuals
    b. overweight individuals
    c. adults with highly stressful lives
    d. middle-aged women

12. The heart of the double standard of aging may be related to the ideal woman being represented as (p. 406)
    a. passive and submissive.
    b. young and sexually attractive.
    c. indecisive and dependent.
    d. assertive and competent.

13. Which of these tasks most clearly makes use of crystallized intelligence? (p. 407)
    a. in response to a green light, pressing a button as fast as possible
    b. finding hidden figures in a drawing
    c. articulate expression of ideas and information
    d. creating novel pieces of art work

14. According to the neural network view, what causes age-related slowing of cognitive processing? (p. 409)
    a. Neurons continue to increase in size, resulting in crowding and slowing.
    b. Neurons die, resulting in the formation of less efficient connections.
    c. The neural network is adversely affected by changes in the balance of neurotransmitters.
    d. Information loss increases as it moves along the neural network.

15. Researchers who believe that, with age, the entire information processing system slows down to inspect and interpret information espouse the (p. 409)
    a. information-loss view.
    b. theory of successful intelligence.
    c. neural network view.
    d. reaction-time view.

16. As Shamiya gets older, which type of memory task will probably be the most difficult for her? (p. 410)
    a. Recalling meaningful prose
    b. Recalling word lists with a strong category-based structure
    c. Recalling lists of unrelated words or numbers
    d. Recalling information related to her occupation

17. Expertise tends to develop (p. 411)
    a. in those who are highly educated.
    b. in those who reach the top of career ladders.
    c. in those from middle- and high-SES backgrounds, regardless of their own education and occupational status.
    d. among individuals from all fields of endeavor, from food service to upper-level administration.

18. Creative accomplishment tends to peak in the (p. 412)
    a. early thirties.
    b. late thirties or early forties.
    c. late forties or early fifties.
    d. late fifties or early sixties.

19. What percentage of returning student adults are women? (p. 413)
    a. 20 percent
    b. 40 percent
    c. 60 percent
    d. 80 percent

20. The most important factor in the success of returning students is (p. 413)
    a. social support.
    b. high intellectual ability.
    c. full-time attendance.
    d. studying at regular times.

CHAPTER 16
EMOTIONAL AND SOCIAL DEVELOPMENT IN MIDDLE ADULTHOOD

BRIEF CHAPTER SUMMARY

Generativity begins in early adulthood but expands greatly as middle-aged adults face Erikson's psychological conflict of midlife: generativity versus stagnation. Highly generative people find fulfillment as they make contributions to society through parenthood, other family relationships, the workplace, volunteer activities, and many forms of productivity and creativity. From Levinson's perspective, middle-aged adults go through a transition in which they reassess their relation to themselves and the world. At midlife, adults must give up certain youthful qualities, find age-appropriate ways to express other qualities, and accept being older. Rebuilding the life structure depends on supportive social contexts. Vaillant added that middle-aged adults become guardians of their culture, and the most successful and best adjusted enter a calmer, quieter time of life. Few people experience a midlife crisis, although most must adapt to important events, which often lead to new understandings and goals.

Midlife changes in self-concept and personality reflect growing awareness of a finite lifespan, longer life experience, and generative concerns. But certain aspects of personality remain stable, revealing that individual differences established during earlier phases persist. Possible selves become fewer and more realistic. Midlifers also become more introspective, and self-acceptance, autonomy, environmental mastery, and coping strategies improve. Both men and women become more androgynous in middle adulthood—a change that results from a complex combination of social roles and life conditions. Despite changes in the organization of personality, basic, underlying personality traits change little during midlife and beyond.

Because of a declining birthrate and longer life expectancy, the midlife phase of the family life cycle, called "launching children and moving on," has greatly lengthened over the past century. The changes of midlife prompt many adults to focus on improving their marriages, but when divorce occurs, midlifers seem to adapt more easily than do younger people. Gains in practical problem solving and effective coping strategies may reduce the stressful impact of divorce. Most middle-aged parents adjust well to departure of children, especially if the parents have a strong work orientation and if parent–child contact and affection are sustained. When family relationships are positive, grandparenthood is an important means of fulfilling personal and societal needs. A growing number of North American children live apart from their parents in households headed by grandparents, a situation that can create great emotional and financial strain.

A longer life expectancy means that adult children and their parents are increasingly likely to grow old together. The burden of caring for aging parents can be great. Many middle-aged adults become "sandwiched" between the needs of aging parents and financially dependent children. Although middle-aged adults often become more appreciative of their parents' strengths and generosity, caring for chronically ill or disabled parents is highly stressful. Sibling contact and support generally declines from early to middle adulthood, although many siblings feel closer, often in response to major life events, such as parental illness. Friendships become fewer and more selective in midlife and they serve as current sources of pleasure and satisfaction.

Work continues to be a salient aspect of identity and self-esteem in middle adulthood. More so than in earlier or later years, people attempt to increase the personal meaning and self-direction of their vocational lives. Job satisfaction has both psychological and economic significance. Overall job satisfaction improves during midlife, but burnout has become a greater problem in recent years, especially in the helping professions. Vocational development is less available to older workers, and many women and ethnic minorities leave the corporate world to escape the "glass ceiling" limiting their advancement. Still, radical career changes are rare in middle adulthood. Unemployment is especially difficult for middle-aged individuals, and retirement is an important change that is often stressful, making effective planning important for positive adjustment.

LEARNING OBJECTIVES

After reading this chapter, you should be able to:

16.1 Describe Erikson's stage of generativity versus stagnation, noting major personality changes of middle adulthood and related research findings. (pp. 417–418)

16.2 Discuss Levinson's and Vaillant's views of psychosocial development in middle adulthood, noting gender similarities and differences. (pp. 419–421)

16.3 Summarize research on whether or not most middle-aged adults experience a midlife crisis. (p. 421)

16.4 Describe stability and change in self-concept and personality in middle adulthood. (pp. 421–424)

16.5 Describe changes in gender identity in midlife. (p. 424)

16.6 Discuss stability and change in the "big five" personality traits in adulthood. (pp. 424–425)

16.7 Describe the middle adulthood phase of the family life cycle, including relationships with a marriage partner, adult children, grandchildren, and aging parents. (pp. 425–432)

16.8 Describe midlife sibling relationships and friendships. (pp. 432–433)

16.9 Discuss job satisfaction and career development in middle adulthood, paying special attention to gender differences and experiences of ethnic minorities. (pp. 433–435)

16.10 Discuss the importance of planning for retirement, noting various issues that middle-aged adults should address. (pp. 435–436)

STUDY QUESTIONS

Erikson's Theory: Generativity versus Stagnation

1. Define *generativity,* and cite characteristics of generative adults. (p. 417)

    A. _____

    B. _____

2. In addition to parenting, list four ways adults can be generative. (p. 417)

    A. _____   B. _____
    C. _____   D. _____

3. Explain how generativity brings together personal desires and cultural demands. (pp. 417–418)

    Personal desires: _____

    Cultural demands: _____

4. Cite characteristics of adults who develop a sense of stagnation. (p. 418)

    _____

5. Having children seems to foster generative development more in (men / women). (p. 418)

Other Theories of Psychosocial Development in Midlife

Levinson's Seasons of Life

1. According to Levinson, what four developmental tasks do midlifers confront in order to reassess their relation to themselves and to the external world? (p. 419)

    A. _____

    B. _____

    C. _____

    D. _____

2. True or False: Because of the double standard of aging, women are more likely than men to perceive themselves as younger than their chronological age. (p. 419)

3. True or False: Middle-aged men almost never express concern about appearing less attractive as they grow older. (p. 419)

4. How does confronting one's own mortality and the actual or impending death of agemates influence awareness in middle adulthood? (p. 420)

    _____

    _____

5. List four ways the desire for a legacy can be satisfied in midlife. (p. 420)

    A. _____ B. _____

    C. _____ D. _____

6. Explain how men and women reconcile masculine and feminine parts of the self in middle age. (p. 420)

    Men: _____

    _____

    Women: _____

    _____

7. True or False: Midlife requires that men and women with highly active, successful careers reduce their concern with ambition and achievement and focus on themselves. (p. 420)

8. What social contexts support rebuilding the life structure in middle adulthood? (p. 420)

    _____

    _____

    _____

9. How do opportunities for advancement ease the transition to middle adulthood? (p. 420)

    _____

Vaillant's Adaptation to Life

1. According to Vaillant, adults in their late forties and early fifties become _____. (p. 420)

2. What personal changes occur as people approach the end of middle age? (p. 421)

    _____

    _____

Is There a Midlife Crisis?

1. What is a *midlife crisis*? (p. 421)
   _____

2. How do men and women differ in their responses to midlife? (p. 421)

   Men: _____
   _____

   Women: _____
   _____

3. True or False: Sharp disruption and agitation are common in middle adulthood. (p. 421)

4. What are some characteristics of adults who experience a midlife crisis? (p. 421)
   _____
   _____

Stability and Change in Self-Concept and Personality

Possible Selves

1. What are *possible selves,* and how do they change with age? (p. 422)

   A. _____

   B. _____

2. How do possible selves differ from self-concept? (p. 422)
   _____
   _____

3. True or False: Throughout adulthood, people's descriptions of their current selves tend to fluctuate drastically. (p. 422)

Self-Acceptance, Autonomy, and Environmental Mastery

1. Explain why self-acceptance, autonomy, and environmental mastery tend to increase from early to middle adulthood among well-educated adults. (p. 422)

   A. _____

   B. _____

   C. _____

2. Cite two cognitive changes that probably support the confidence, initiative, and decisiveness of middle adulthood. (p. 422)

   A. _____   B. _____

Biology and Environment: What Factors Promote Psychological Well-Being in Midlife?

1. Explain how exercise promotes well-being in midlife. (p. 423)
   _____
   _____

2. What is *flow*, and why does it increase in middle adulthood? (p. 423)

   A. _____
   _____

   B. _____
   _____

3. In a longitudinal study of 90 men, _____ and _____ in early adulthood were among the best predictors of well-being in middle adulthood. (p. 423)

4. True or False: Friendships are more effective than a good marriage in boosting psychological well-being in midlife. (p. 423)

5. True or False: Women are generally happier today than in the past. Explain your answer. (p. 423)
   _____
   _____

Coping Strategies

1. Midlife brings a(n) (increase / decrease) in effective coping strategies. (p. 422)

2. What is *cognitive-affective* complexity, and how might it contribute to effective coping in middle adulthood? (pp. 422, 424)

   A. _____
   _____

   B. _____
   _____

Gender Identity

1. Gender identity becomes (more / less) androgynous in midlife. Explain your answer. (p. 424)
   _____
   _____
   _____

2. How does *parental imperative theory* explain androgyny in later life? (p. 424)
   _____
   _____
   _____

3. Besides reduced parenting responsibilities, what other demands and experiences promote a more androgynous orientation in midlife? (p. 424)

   _____

   _____

Individual Differences in Personality Traits

1. List the *"big five" personality traits.* (pp. 424–425)

   A. _____   B. _____

   C. _____   D. _____

   E. _____

2. Which "big five" personality traits show modest declines in midlife? Which ones increase? (p. 425)

   Declines: _____

   Increases: _____

3. True or False: An individual who scores high or low at one age in the "big five" personality traits is likely to do the same from 3 to 30 years later. (p. 425)

4. How can there be high stability in personality traits, yet significant changes in certain aspects of personality? (p. 425)

   _____

   _____

   _____

Relationships at Midlife

1. Why is the middle adulthood phase of the family life cycle often referred to as "launching children and moving on"? (p. 426)

   _____

   _____

Marriage and Divorce

1. True or False: Middle-aged adults are more likely than younger or older adults to experience financial difficulty. (p. 426)

2. True or False: Midlifers seem to adapt more easily to divorce than younger people. (p. 426)

3. Marital breakup is a strong contributor to the *feminization of poverty*. Explain what this means. (p. 426)

   _____

   _____

   _____

4. List outcomes for middle-aged women who weather divorce successfully. (p. 426)

   _____

   _____

   _____

Changing Parent–Child Relationships

1. True or False: Even when their children are "off-time" in development of independence and accomplishment, middle-aged adults adjust well. (p. 427)

2. Describe how the parental role changes in midlife. (p. 427)

   _____
   _____
   _____

3. When children marry, parents face additional challenges in enlarging the family network to include in-laws. Explain why. (p. 427)

   _____
   _____

4. Once young adults strike out on their own, members of the middle generation, especially mothers, usually take on the role of _____, gathering the family for celebrations and making sure everyone stays in touch. (p. 427)

Grandparenthood

1. On average, American adults become grandparents in their _____, Canadian adults in their _____. (p. 427)

2. List four commonly mentioned gratifications of grandparenthood. (p. 427)

   A. _____
   B. _____
   C. _____
   D. _____

3. How does the grandchild's age affect grandparent–grandchild relationships? (pp. 427–428)

   _____
   _____
   _____
   _____

4. Typically, (same-sex / opposite-sex) grandparents and grandchildren are closer, especially _____ _____ (p. 428)

5. As grandchildren get older, distance has a (greater / lesser) impact on grandparent–grandchild relationships. (p. 428)

6. Explain how SES and ethnicity influence grandparent–grandchild ties. (p. 428)

   SES: _____
   _____

   Ethnicity: _____
   _____

7. True or False: Involvement in care of grandchildren is high among Chinese, Korean, Mexican-American, and Canadian-Aboriginal grandparents. (p. 428)

Social Issues: Grandparents Rearing Grandchildren: The Skipped-Generation Family

1. What are *skipped-generation families*? (p. 429)

2. Cite several reasons that grandparents step in and rear grandchildren. (p. 429)

3. Describe challenges grandparents encounter when they raise grandchildren. (p. 429)

Middle-Aged Children and Their Aging Parents

1. True or False: Mother–daughter relationships tend to be closer than other parent–child ties. (p. 430)

2. True or False: In the non-Western world, older adults often live with their married children. (p. 430)

3. Why are today's middle-aged adults called the *sandwich generation*? (p. 430)

4. Why are women more often caregivers of aging parents? (p. 430)

5. Cite contributions that men make to caring for aging parents. (p. 431)

6. Explain why caring for a chronically ill or disabled parent is highly stressful. (p. 431)

7. What emotional and physical health consequences are associated with parental caregiving? (pp. 431–432)

8. List four ways to relieve the stress of caring for an aging parent. (p. 432)

   A.
   B.
   C.
   D.

Siblings

1. Sibling contact and support (increase / decline) from early to middle adulthood, yet siblings often feel (closer / less close) during this time of life. (p. 432)

2. True or False: As siblings get older, good relationships often strengthen and poor relationships often worsen. (p. 432)

3. Provide an illustration of differences in sibling relationships between village and industrialized societies. (p. 432)
   _____
   _____
   _____

Friendships

1. Briefly describe sex differences in middle-aged friendships. (p. 432)

   Men: _____
   _____

   Women: _____
   _____

2. Number of friends (increases / declines) with age. (p. 433)

3. Explain how family relationships and friendships support different aspects of psychological well-being. (p. 433)

   Family: _____
   _____

   Friendships: _____
   _____

Vocational Life

1. Work (does / does not) continue to be a salient aspect of identity and self-esteem in middle adulthood. (p. 433)

2. What two factors will contribute to the dramatic rise in the number of older workers during the next few decades? (p. 433)

   A. _____
   B. _____

Job Satisfaction

1. Research shows that job satisfaction (increases / decreases) in midlife at all occupational levels. (p. 433)

2. Describe one aspect of job satisfaction that rises with age and one that remains stable. (p. 433)

   Rises: _____

   Remains stable: _____

3. Under what conditions does *burnout* occur, and why is it a serious occupational hazard? (p. 434)

   A. _____

   B. _____

4. How can employers prevent burnout? (p. 434)

   _____

Career Development

1. True or False: Research suggests that training and on-the-job career counseling are more available to older workers. (p. 434)

2. List personal and workplace characteristics that influence employees' willingness to engage in job training and updating. (p. 434)

   A. _____
   _____

   B. _____
   _____

3. How do age-balanced work groups foster on-the-job learning? (p. 434)

   _____

4. Cite workplace factors that contribute to a *glass ceiling* for women and ethnic minorities. (p. 434)

   _____
   _____
   _____
   _____

5. More than _____ of all start-up businesses in the United States are owned and operated by women. How successful are these businesses? (p. 435)

   _____
   _____

Planning for Retirement

1. True or False: Most workers report looking forward to retirement. (p. 435)

2. What are some benefits of retirement planning? (p. 435)

   _____
   _____

3. Less educated people with lower lifetime earnings are (most / least) likely to attend retirement preparation programs. (p. 435)

4. True or False: Financial planning is more important than planning for an active life in promoting happiness after retirement. (p. 435)

ASK YOURSELF...

For *Ask Yourself* questions for this chapter, please log on to the Companion Website at *www.ablongman.com/berk*.

1. Select the Companion Website for *Exploring Lifespan Development*.
2. Use the "Jump to" menu to go directly to this chapter.
3. From the menu on the left side of the screen, select "Ask Yourself."
4. Complete questions and choose "Submit answers for grading" or "Clear answers" to start over.

SUGGESTED STUDENT READINGS

de St. Aubin, E., McAdams, D. P., & Tae-Chang, K. (Eds.). (2003). *The generative society: Caring for future generations.* Washington, DC: American Psychological Association. A multidisciplinary approach to understanding generativity, this book examines the developmental significance of generative behavior in middle adulthood. Other topics include Erikson's theory of generativity, cross-cultural differences in generativity, and the role of volunteerism.

Fingerman, K. L. (2002). *Mothers and their adult daughters: Mixed emotions, enduring bonds.* Amherst, NY: Prometheus Books. A thorough and insightful look at mother–daughter relationships in middle and late adulthood, this book addresses the bond between mothers and daughters, including the challenges they face in maintaining the relationship.

Hayslip, B., & Patrick, J. H. (Eds.). (2005). *Diversity among custodial grandparents.* New York: Springer. Using up-to-date research from leading experts, this book examines the diverse experiences of grandparents raising grandchildren, including role satisfaction in traditional and custodial grandparents, gender and ethnic differences in custodial grandparents, and caregiving interventions and support.

Hedge, J. W., Borman, W. C., & Lammlein, S. E. (2006). *The aging workforce: Realities, myths, and implications for organizations.* Washington, DC: American Psychological Association. Examines the strengths, weaknesses, expertise, and unique needs of workers over the age of 60. The authors also address myths and stereotypes about the aging workforce, age discrimination, and strategies for attracting and retaining older workers.

Kuttner, R. & Trotter, S. (2002). *Family reunion: Reconnecting parents and children in adulthood.* Tampa, FL: Free Press. Emphasizing a lifespan perspective, this book explores the dynamic relationship between adult children and their parents, including how to negotiate changes in a positive way.

PUZZLE 16.1 TERM REVIEW

Across
2. _____ imperative theory claims that traditional gender roles are maintained during the active parenting years to help ensure the survival of children
3. _____ selves: future-oriented representations of what one hopes to become and is afraid of becoming
5. Role assumed by members of the middle generation who take responsibility for gathering the family for celebrations and making sure everyone stays in touch
6. Generativity versus _____ : Erikson's psychological conflict of midlife
8. Middle-aged adults who are squeezed between the needs of aging parents and financially dependent children are known as the _____ generation
9. Glass _____ : invisible barrier to advancement up the corporate ladder faced by women and ethnic minorities
10. The _____ crisis refers to inner turmoil, self-doubt, and major restructuring of personality during the transition to middle adulthood

Down
1. _____ of poverty: trend in which women who support themselves or their families have become the majority of the adult poverty population
4. Condition in which long-term job stress leads to emotional exhaustion, a sense of loss of personal control, and feelings of reduced accomplishment
6. _____-generation family: children live with grandparents but apart from parents
7. _____ _____ personality traits: five basic factors into which hundreds of personality traits have been organized: neuroticism, extroversion, openness to experience, agreeableness, and conscientiousness (2 words)

338

PRACTICE TEST #1

1. In midlife, generativity expands greatly when (p. 417)
   a. individuals become more self-centered and self-indulgent.
   b. midlifers finally place their own comfort above sacrifice.
   c. a focus on what one can get from others replaces a focus on what one can give.
   d. commitment extends beyond oneself to a larger group.

2. According to Erikson, a culture's _____ is a major motivator of generative action. (p. 418)
   a. attitude toward peace
   b. belief in the species
   c. sense of security
   d. set of support systems

3. In middle adulthood, some individuals choose to participate in activities that advance human welfare. Which of Levinson's developmental tasks are these individuals attempting to reconcile? (p. 419)
   a. masculinity–femininity
   b. young–old
   c. engagement–separateness
   d. destruction–creation

4. As people approach the end of middle age, they tend to focus on (p. 421)
   a. shorter-term, career-oriented goals.
   b. personal, physical goals.
   c. longer-term, less personal goals.
   d. specific, household goals.

5. Levinson reported that during the transition to middle adulthood, most men and women in his samples experienced (p. 421)
   a. substantial inner turmoil.
   b. slow, steady changes.
   c. smooth acceptance of aging.
   d. personal and financial gratification.

6. Sharp disruption and agitation during the midlife transition (p. 421)
   a. are common experiences among adults.
   b. are more the exception than the rule.
   c. ultimately result in favorable adjustment.
   d. are more common in men than in women.

7. At lunch, Louisa tells a colleague, "I'm thinking about changing jobs. I feel like I'm doing the same thing day after day. Or maybe I can save some money and start a small business in a few years. I've always wanted to do that, and if I don't do it soon, it will never happen." Louisa is discussing (p. 422)
   a. possible selves.
   b. emotion-centered coping.
   c. environmental mastery.
   d. self-acceptance.

8. Research on well-educated adults ranging in age from the late teens into the seventies, the following three traits increased from early to middle adulthood and then leveled off: (p. 422)
   a. self-acceptance, self-concept, and possible selves
   b. self-acceptance, autonomy, and possible selves
   c. self-concept, patience, and autonomy
   d. self-acceptance, autonomy, and environmental mastery

9. Midlife brings an increase in the use of effective coping strategies. For example, middle-aged people are more likely to (p. 422)
   a. not care very much about problems.
   b. take immediate action to resolve problems.
   c. look for the positive side of a difficult situation.
   d. avoid using humor to express their feelings about problems.

10. Studies of gender identity in midlife reveal (p. 424)
    a. an increase in "masculine" traits in women.
    b. an increase in "feminine" traits in women.
    c. an increase in "masculine" traits in men.
    d. no increase in either "masculine" or "feminine" traits in men.

11. Studies of men and women show that from the teenage years through middle age, (p. 425)
    a. agreeableness and conscientiousness increase.
    b. extroversion and agreeableness increase.
    c. neuroticism and openness to experience increase.
    d. neuroticism and agreeableness do not change.

12. When people in midlife divorce, they usually (p. 426)
    a. have more difficulty adapting than young adults.
    b. adapt in much the same way as young adults.
    c. adapt more easily than young adults.
    d. direct their anger toward their children.

13. In inner cities, welfare recipients, regardless of age and ethnicity, often include a large number of single mothers. This trend is an example of (p. 426)
    a. the parental imperative theory.
    b. the feminization of poverty.
    c. environmental mastery.
    d. feminine midlife crises.

14. Once young adults strike out on their own, members of the middle generation, especially mothers, often take on the kinkeeper role, which involves (p. 427)
    a. supporting their adult children financially.
    b. providing child care for their grandchildren.
    c. moving to a new residence closer to a grown child, usually a daughter.
    d. gathering the family for celebrations and making sure everyone stays in touch.

15. Most people experience grandparenthood as a (p. 427)
    a. burdensome reminder of old age.
    b. significant milestone.
    c. time to reflect on past mistakes.
    d. period of resurgence in youthful energy.

16. Which pair typically has the closest relationship? (p. 428)
    a. maternal grandmother and granddaughter
    b. paternal grandfather and grandson
    c. maternal grandfather and granddaughter
    d. paternal grandmother and grandson

17. In skipped-generation families, grandparents most often step in to raise grandchildren because of (p. 429)
    a. parental physical illness.
    b. parental emotional illness.
    c. child abuse and neglect.
    d. parents' substance-abuse problems.

18. When an aging person's spouse cannot provide care, the relative who is most likely to do so is (p. 430)
    a. an adult son.
    b. a younger sibling.
    c. an adult daughter.
    d. an adult granddaughter.

19. Research shows that in midlife, and at all occupational levels, job satisfaction (p. 433)
    a. increases.
    b. decreases.
    c. remains unchanged.
    d. increases at a higher rate for women than for men.

20. Willingness to engage in job training and updating in midlife is influenced by (p. 434)
    a. co-worker and supervisor encouragement.
    b. participation in work groups that include younger people.
    c. simplified work tasks.
    d. negative stereotypes of aging.

PRACTICE TEST #2

1. Adults with a sense of stagnation (p. 418)
    a. are well-adjusted and report a high level of life satisfaction.
    b. possess leadership qualities and are open to differing viewpoints.
    c. cannot contribute to the welfare of society because they place their own comfort and security above challenge and sacrifice.
    d. view themselves as role models and sources of wisdom for their children.

2. According to Levinson, middle adulthood begins with a transitional period that spans the ages from (p. 419)
    a. 30 to 35.
    b. 35 to 40.
    c. 40 to 45.
    d. 45 to 50.

3. Rebuilding the life structure during middle adulthood depends on (p. 420)
    a. supportive social contexts.
    b. dramatic revision of family and occupational commitments.
    c. success in confronting the double standard of aging.
    d. strengthening of gender-typed characteristics.

4. As a young adult, Christian dreamed of being a great athlete and a very successful businessman. At age 40, as a high-paid administrator for a large corporation, he has largely attained one of those goals. As he enters middle adulthood, Christian will probably (p. 422)
    a. strive harder to make his current self match his early dreams.
    b. become depressed because he has not achieved all of his goals.
    c. focus less on his business success and more on athletic pursuits in an attempt to recapture his youth.
    d. concentrate more on nurturing personal relationships and on performing competently at work.

5. As individuals reach adulthood with less time left to make life changes, their _____ plays a significant role in their well-being. (p. 421)
    a. tendency toward experiencing a midlife crisis
    b. interpretation of life regrets
    c. lack of possible selves
    d. declining sense of autonomy

6. According to parental imperative theory, identification with traditional gender roles is maintained during active parenting years to help ensure (p. 424)
   a. that mothers will remain with children if fathers do not.
   b. that children receive warmth from their mothers and discipline from their fathers.
   c. that children develop androgynous traits.
   d. the survival of children.

7. Neuroticism, extroversion, and openness to experience (p. 425)
   a. show a sharp increase from early to middle adulthood.
   b. are common among well-adjusted adults.
   c. show modest declines or remain unchanged from the teenage years through middle age.
   d. are often transformed into agreeableness and conscientiousness in midlife.

8. Studies show that 9 out of 10 middle-aged North Americans (p. 426)
   a. live with families, usually with a spouse.
   b. live alone after their children are grown.
   c. are or will eventually be divorced.
   d. come from families that have experienced divorce.

9. Although most divorces occur within 5 to 10 years of marriage, ___ percent take place after 20 years or more. (p. 426)
   a. 5
   b. 7
   c. 10
   d. 15

10. In the southern European countries of Greece, Italy, and Spain, middle-aged parents (p. 427)
    a. do not experience the "launching children" phase of the family life cycle.
    b. encourage their children to leave home during the teenage years.
    c. actively delay their children's departure from the home.
    d. have more conflict-ridden relationships with adult children than northern Europeans.

11. When parent–child contact and affection are sustained, (p. 427)
    a. departure of children from the home is a relatively mild event.
    b. mothers and fathers are able to maintain parental authority.
    c. parents' life satisfaction declines.
    d. adult children must struggle to become independent and accomplished.

12. Marcia's ability to keep her family of grown children together by holding bimonthly parties and get-togethers at her home shows that she has (p. 427)
    a. mastered her femininity.
    b. become more androgynous.
    c. adopted the parental imperative theory.
    d. taken on the role of kinkeeper.

13. From 1900 to the present, the percentage of North American middle-aged people with living parents has (p. 428)
    a. risen from 10 percent to 20 percent.
    b. risen from 10 percent to 25 percent.
    c. risen from 10 percent to 50 percent.
    d. fallen from 10 percent to 5 percent.

14. Compared with adult children who assist in the care of aging parents while maintaining a separate residence, those who live with an ill or disabled parent (p. 431)
    a. experience more stress.
    b. are more well-adjusted.
    c. have less role overload.
    d. rarely find rewards in parental caregiving.

15. In the United States and Canada, in-home care of an ill, elder parent by a nonfamily caregiver is (p. 431)
    a. readily available and government supported.
    b. generally not an option because of its high cost.
    c. patterned after the Swedish home helper system.
    d. rarely used because it does not relieve stress on the family caregiver.

16. During middle adulthood, many siblings (p. 432)
    a. spend more time together than they did in early adulthood.
    b. report strained relations.
    c. feel closer than they did in early adulthood.
    d. provide each other with more support than at any other time of life.

17. The aspect of job satisfaction that shows the greatest age-related gain in midlife is (p. 433)
    a. contentment with supervision.
    b. satisfaction with opportunities for promotion.
    c. satisfaction with pay.
    d. happiness with the work itself.

18. Burnout occurs more often in (p. 434)
    a. young workers.
    b. helping professions.
    c. high-income professions.
    d. men.

19. Women face a glass ceiling in their careers because (p. 434)
    a. they are less effective managers than men.
    b. modern businesses realize that the best managers display "masculine" traits.
    c. they have less access to mentors, role models, and informal networks than men.
    d. they are less committed to their careers than men.

20. Even though it is essential for better retirement and adjustment, nearly _____ of middle-aged people engage in no concrete retirement planning (p. 435)
    a. one-fourth
    b. one-third
    c. half
    d. two-thirds

CHAPTER 17
PHYSICAL AND COGNITIVE DEVELOPMENT IN LATE ADULTHOOD

BRIEF CHAPTER SUMMARY

Vastly different rates of aging are apparent in late adulthood. A complex array of genetic and environmental factors combine to determine longevity. Dramatic gains in average life expectancy—the number of years that an individual born in a particular year can expect to live—provide powerful support for the multiplicity of factors that slow biological aging, including improved nutrition, medical treatment, sanitation, and safety. Although most North Americans over age 65 can live independently, some need assistance with activities of daily living or, more commonly, with instrumental activities of daily living, such as shopping and paying bills.

The programmed effects of specific genes as well as the random cellular events believed to underlie biological aging make physical declines more apparent in late adulthood. Although aging of the nervous system affects a range of complex thoughts and activities, research reveals that the brain can respond adaptively to some of these age-related cognitive declines. Changes in sensory functioning become increasingly noticeable in late life: Older adults see and hear less well, and taste, smell, and touch sensitivity may also decline. Hearing impairments are far more common than visual impairments and affect many more men than women.

Aging of the cardiovascular and respiratory systems becomes more apparent in late adulthood. As at earlier ages, not smoking, reducing dietary fat, avoiding environmental pollutants, and exercising can slow the effects of aging on these systems. A less competent immune system can increase the elderly person's risk for a variety of illnesses, including infectious diseases, cardiovascular disease, certain forms of cancer, and a variety of autoimmune disorders.

As people age, they have more difficulty falling asleep, staying asleep, and sleeping deeply. Outward signs of aging, such as white hair, wrinkled and sagging skin, age spots, and decreases in height and weight, become more noticeable in late adulthood. Problem-centered coping strategies yield improved physical functioning in the elderly, and assistive technology is increasingly available to help older people cope with physical declines.

Physical and mental health are intimately related in late life. The physical changes of late life lead to an increased need for certain nutrients, and exercise continues to be a powerful health intervention. Although sexual desire and frequency of sexual activity decline in older people, longitudinal evidence indicates that most healthy older married couples report continued, regular sexual enjoyment. Illness and disability climb as the end of the lifespan approaches. Cardiovascular disease, cancer, and stroke claim many lives, while arthritis and adult-onset diabetes increase substantially. At age 65 and older, the death rate from unintentional injuries is at an all-time high.

When cell death and structural and chemical abnormalities are profound, serious deterioration of mental and motor functions occurs. Alzheimer's disease, the most common form of dementia, can be either familial (which runs in families) or sporadic (where there is no obvious family history). With no cure available, family interventions ensure the best adjustment possible for the Alzheimer's victim, spouse, and other relatives. Careful diagnosis is crucial because other disorders can be misidentified as dementia. Family members provide most long-term care, especially among ethnic minorities. Individual differences in cognitive functioning are greater in late adulthood than at any other time of life. As older adults take in information more slowly and find it harder to apply strategies, inhibit irrelevant information, and retrieve knowledge from long-term memory, the chance of memory failure increases. Research shows that language and memory skills are closely related. Although language comprehension changes very little in late life, retrieving words from long-term memory and planning what to say become more difficult. Finally, traditional problem solving, in the absence of real-life context, declines.

Cultures around the world assume that age and wisdom go together. Older adults with the cognitive, reflective, and emotional qualities that make up wisdom tend to be better educated and physically healthier and to forge more positive relations with others. As in middle adulthood, a mentally active life—above average education, stimulating leisure pursuits, community participation, and a flexible personality—predicts maintenance of mental abilities into advanced old age. And interventions that train the elderly in cognitive strategies can partially reverse age-related declines in mental ability. Elders who participate in continuing education through university courses, community offerings, and programs such as Elderhostel, are enriched by new knowledge, new friends, a broader perspective on the world, and an image of themselves as more competent.

LEARNING OBJECTIVES

After reading this chapter, you should be able to:

17.1 Distinguish between chronological age and functional age, and discuss variations in life expectancy over the past century. (pp. 441–443)

17.2 Describe changes in the nervous system during late adulthood. (pp. 443–445)

17.3 Summarize changes in sensory functioning during late adulthood, including vision, hearing, taste, smell, and touch. (pp. 445–447)

17.4 Describe cardiovascular, respiratory, and immune system changes in late adulthood. (p. 447)

17.5 Discuss sleep difficulties in late adulthood. (p. 447)

17.6 Summarize changes in physical appearance and mobility, including elders' adaptation to the physical changes of late adulthood, and reactions to stereotypes of aging. (pp. 448–450)

17.7 Discuss health and fitness in late life, paying special attention to nutrition, exercise, and sexuality. (pp. 450–452)

17.8 Discuss common physical disabilities in late adulthood, including arthritis, adult-onset diabetes, and unintentional injuries. (pp. 452–455)

17.9 Describe mental disabilities common in late adulthood, including Alzheimer's disease, cerebrovascular dementia, and misdiagnosed and reversible dementia. (pp. 455–459)

17.10 Discuss health care issues that affect senior citizens. (pp. 459–460)

17.11 Summarize memory changes in late life, including implicit, associative, remote, and prospective memories. (pp. 460–463)

17.12 Describe changes in language processing in late adulthood. (p. 463)

17.13 Summarize changes in problem solving during late adulthood. (p. 463–464)

17.14 Discuss the capacities that contribute to wisdom, noting how it is affected by age and life experience. (pp. 464–465)

17.15 Cite factors related to cognitive change in late adulthood. (p. 465)

17.16 Explain how cognitive interventions help older adults sustain their mental abilities. (p. 465–466)

17.17 Describe types of continuing education and benefits of participation in such programs in late life. (pp. 466–467)

STUDY QUESTIONS

Physical Development

1. _____ *age* refers to actual competence and performance of an older adult. (p. 441)

2. True or False: Researchers have identified a single biological measure that predicts rate of aging. (p. 442)

Life Expectancy

1. What is *average life expectancy*? (p. 442)
   _____
   _____

2. In 2004, average life expectancy reached age _____ in the United States and age _____ in Canada. (p. 442)

Variations in Life Expectancy

1. On average, (men / women) can expect to live 4 to 7 years longer than their other-sex counterparts—a difference found in almost all cultures. What accounts for this gender gap in life expectancy? (p. 442)

   _____
   _____
   _____

2. List factors that contribute to SES and ethnic differences in life expectancy. (p. 442)

   _____
   _____
   _____

3. Define *active lifespan,* and indicate how the United States and Canada rank internationally in their measure. (p. 442)

   A. _____
   _____

   B. _____
   _____

Life Expectancy in Late Adulthood

1. The number of people age 65 and older has (risen / declined) dramatically in the industrialized world. (p. 443)

2. Summarize sex differences in life expectancy in late adulthood. (p. 443)

   _____
   _____
   _____

3. True or False: With advancing age, gender and SES differences in life expectancy increase. (p. 443)

4. Describe the *life expectancy crossover.* (p. 443)

   _____
   _____
   _____

5. After age 70, about 10 percent of adults have difficulty carrying out _____, basic self-care tasks required to live on one's own. About 20 percent cannot carry out _____ _____, tasks necessary to conduct the business of daily life and that require some cognitive competence. (p. 443)

6. Summarize evidence that heredity affects longevity. (p. 443)

   _____
   _____
   _____

7. True or False: Twin studies suggest that once people pass age 75 to 80, the contribution of heredity to length of life decreases, while environmental factors play an increasingly large role. (p. 443)

A Lifespan Vista: What Can We Learn About Aging from Centenarians?

1. True or False: Recent increases in the number of centenarians in the industrialized world are expected to accelerate in the years to come. (p. 444)

2. Centenarians are more likely to be (men / women). (p. 444)

3. True or False: Less than 20 percent of centenarians have physical and mental impairments that interfere with independent functioning. (p. 444)

4. True or False: Longevity runs in centenarians' families. p. 444)

5. Describe the health, personality, and activities of robust centenarians. (p. 444)

    Health: _____

    Personality: _____

    Activities: _____

Maximum Lifespan

1. Define *maximum lifespan,* and cite current estimates of it. (p. 443)

    Definition: _____

    Estimates: _____

2. Summarize both sides of the controversy on whether current figures for maximum lifespan represent the upper bound of human longevity or whether lifespan can be extended even further. (p. 443)

    Represents upper bound: _____

    Can be extended further: _____

Physical Changes

Nervous System

1. True or False: Death of neurons and enlargement of ventricles cause brain weight to decrease throughout adulthood. (pp. 443, 445)

2. Describe neuron loss in different regions of the cerebral cortex in late adulthood. (p. 445)

    _____

3. True or False: In healthy older adults, growth of neural fibers takes place at the same rate as in middle-aged adults. (p. 445)

4. Cite two changes in autonomic nervous system functioning in old age. (p. 445)

   A. _____

   B. _____

Sensory Systems

1. What are *cataracts,* and how do they affect vision? (p. 445)

   Definition: _____

   _____

   Impact on vision: _____

   _____

2. Cite two factors that largely account for visual impairments in late adulthood. (p. 445)

   A. _____

   B. _____

3. Depth perception and visual acuity (improve / remain stable / decline) in late life. (p. 445)

4. When light-sensitive cells in the central region of the retina break down, older adults may develop _____ _____, in which central vision blurs and is gradually lost. (pp. 445–446)

5. True or False: Cataracts are the leading cause of blindness in older adults. (p. 446)

6. Describe the consequences of severe vision loss in late adulthood. (p. 446)

   _____

   _____

7. List changes in the ear that cause hearing to decline in late adulthood. (p. 446)

   _____

   _____

   _____

8. Hearing decrements in late life are greatest at (high / low) frequencies. List two additional hearing declines. (p. 446)

   A. _____

   B. _____

9. What hearing difficulty has the greatest impact on life satisfaction? (p. 446)

   _____

10. Most older adults (do / do not) suffer hearing loss that is great enough to disrupt their daily lives. (p. 446)

11. List several ways in which older adults can compensate for hearing loss. (p. 446)

    _____

    _____

12. True or False: Age-related reductions in taste sensitivity are caused by changes in the number and distribution of taste buds. (p. 446)

13. List several factors that contribute to declines in taste sensitivity. (p. 446)

   _____
   _____
   _____

14. Summarize changes in smell during late adulthood. (p. 446)

   _____
   _____
   _____

15. Older adults experience a sharper decline in touch sensitivity on their (arms and lips / hands). (p. 446)

16. What two factors likely account for age-related declines in touch sensitivity? (pp. 446–447)

   A. _____

   B. _____

Cardiovascular and Respiratory Systems

1. List five ways the heart muscle changes with advancing age. (p. 447)

   A. _____
   B. _____
   C. _____
   D. _____
   E. _____

2. What changes in the cardiovascular and respiratory systems lead to reduced oxygen supply to body tissues? (p. 447)

   _____
   _____
   _____

Immune System

1. What is an *autoimmune response*? What are some consequences of a less competent immune system? p. 447)

   Definition: _____
   _____

   Consequences: _____
   _____

2. List an immune indicator that predicts survival in very old people. (p. 447)

   _____

Sleep

1. True or False: Older adults require two to three more hours of total sleep time per night than younger adults. (p. 447)

Nutrition and Exercise

1. Briefly describe the physical and environmental conditions that lead to increased risk of dietary deficiencies in late life. (p. 451)

2. True or False: In several studies, a daily vitamin-mineral tablet resulted in an enhanced immune response and a 50 percent drop in days of infectious illness. (p. 451)

3. True or False: Endurance training and weight-bearing exercise are too strenuous for older adults and present more health risks than benefits. (p. 451)

4. Explain how exercise benefits the brain and cognition in late adulthood. (p. 451)

5. List several barriers to initiation of an exercise program in late life. (p. 451)

Sexuality

1. Virtually all cross-sectional studies report (maintenance / decline) in sexual desire and frequency of sexual activity in old age. Why might this finding be exaggerated? (pp. 451–452)

2. True or False: Most healthy married couples report diminished sexual enjoyment in late adulthood. (p. 452)

3. (Men / Women) are more likely to withdraw from sexual activity in late life. Explain your answer. (p. 452)

Physical Disabilities

1. List the four leading causes of death in late adulthood. (p. 452)

   A.
   B.
   C.
   D.

2. Distinguish between *primary* and *secondary aging*. (p. 452)

   Primary: _____

   Secondary: _____

3. Define *frailty*, and list factors that contribute to it. (p. 453)

   Definition: _____

   _____

   _____

   Contributing factors: _____

   _____

   _____

4. Contrast two forms of arthritis that increase in late life—*osteoarthritis* and *rheumatoid arthritis*. (p. 453)

   Osteoarthritis: _____

   _____

   Rheumatoid arthritis: _____

   _____

5. Describe sex differences in disability due to arthritis. (p. 453)

   Men: _____

   _____

   Women: _____

   _____

6. How can older adults manage arthritis? (pp. 453–454)

   _____

   _____

7. What factors are associated with a risk of developing adult-onset diabetes? (p. 454)

   _____

   _____

8. What treatments are used to control adult-onset diabetes? (p. 454)

   _____

   _____

9. The death rate from unintentional injuries is highest during (adolescence and young adulthood / late adulthood). (p. 454)

10. True or False: Older adults have the lowest rates of traffic violations, accidents, and fatalities of any age group. (p. 454)

11. List three factors that contribute to driving difficulties in older adults. (p. 454)

    A. _____

    B. _____

    C. _____

12. True or False: The elderly account for more than 30 percent of all pedestrian deaths. (p. 454)

13. What is the leading type of unintentional injury among the elderly? (p. 454)

14. List factors that place older adults at increased risk for falling. (p. 455)

15. How does falling indirectly impair health? (p. 455)

Mental Disabilities

1. Define *dementia*. (p. 455)

2. Dementia (declines / rises) sharply with age, striking men and women (disproportionately / equally). (p. 455)

3. The most common form of dementia is _____, in which structural and chemical brain deterioration is associated with gradual loss of many aspects of thought and behavior. (p. 455)

4. What is usually the first symptom of Alzheimer's disease? (p. 455)

5. List personality changes associated with Alzheimer's disease. (p. 455)

6. List three symptoms other than memory loss and personality changes that are associated with the progression of Alzheimer's disease. (p. 455)

    A. _____
    B. _____
    C. _____

7. Explain how Alzheimer's disease is diagnosed. (pp. 455–456)

8. Describe two major structural changes in the cerebral cortex associated with Alzheimer's disease. (p. 456)

    A. _____

    B. _____

9. At one time, researchers thought that plaques contributed to neuronal damage of Alzheimer's. What does new evidence suggest? (p. 456)

10. Explain how declining levels of neurotransmitters contribute to many primary symptoms of Alzheimer's disease. (p. 456)

11. Describe the two types of Alzheimer's disease. (p. 456)

    Familial: _____

    Sporadic: _____

12. Other than genetic abnormalities, cite biological and environmental risk factors for sporadic Alzheimer's disease. (p. 456)

    Biological: _____

    Environmental: _____

13. True or False: Among the Yoruba of Nigeria, the ApoE4 gene is not associated with Alzheimer's. Explain your answer. (pp. 456–457)

14. List four factors that protect against Alzheimer's disease. (p. 457)

    A. _____
    B. _____
    C. _____
    D. _____

15. True or False: Alzheimer's is a curable disease. (p. 457)

16. Describe interventions that help to ensure the best possible adjustment for Alzheimer's victims and their families. (pp. 457)

17. Describe *cerebrovascular dementia*. (p. 457)

18. Summarize genetic and environmental influences on cerebrovascular dementia. (p. 457)

    Genetic: _____

    _____

    Environmental: _____

    _____

19. True or False: Most cases of cerebrovascular dementia are caused by atherosclerosis. (p. 457)

20. Name the disorder that is most often misdiagnosed as dementia, and explain at least one difference between adults with this disorder and those with dementia. (p. 459)

    Disorder: _____

    Difference: _____

21. In addition to the disorder named above, cite three factors that can lead to reversible symptoms of dementia. (p. 459)

    A. _____

    B. _____

    C. _____

Social Issues: Interventions for Caregivers of Elders with Dementia

1. Explain how Alzheimer's disease affects caregivers. (p. 458)

    _____

    _____

    _____

2. List and briefly describe caregiver needs that are addressed by effective interventions. (p. 458)

    A. _____

    B. _____

    C. _____

    D. _____

3. Briefly summarize research on "active" intervention programs, including which caregivers benefit the most. (p. 458)

Health Care

1. True or False: The cost of government-sponsored health insurance for the elderly is expected to double by the year 2025 and triple by the year 2050. (p. 459)

2. True or False: In the United States, Medicare funds 100 percent of older adults' medical expenses. (p. 459)

3. Which disorders of aging most often lead to nursing home placement? (p. 459)

    _____

    _____

4. True or False: Older adults in the Untied States and Canada are less likely to be institutionalized than elders in other industrialized nations. Explain your answer. (p. 459)

5. (Caucasian / African) Americans are more likely to be placed in nursing homes. Why is this so? (p. 460)

6. Describe two recommendations for reducing institutionalized care for the elderly and its associated costs. (p. 460)

   A. _____

   B. _____

7. Briefly summarize ways to improve the quality of nursing home services. (p. 460)

Cognitive Development

1. True or False: Individual differences in cognitive functioning are greater during late adulthood than at any other time of life. (p. 460)

2. Explain how older adults can use *selective optimization with compensation* to sustain high levels of cognitive functioning in late life. (p. 461)

Memory

Deliberate versus Automatic Memory

1. Describe the link between working memory declines and ability to use context cues to aid recall. (p. 461)

2. (Recall / Recognition) memory shows fewer declines in late adulthood. (p. 461)

3. What is *implicit memory*? (p. 461)

4. Age differences are greater for (implicit / deliberate) memory. Explain your answer. (p. 461)

Associative Memory

1. What are *associative memory deficits*? (p. 462)

   _____
   _____

2. True or False: Older adults maintain the ability to recognize single pieces of information but have difficulty with tasks that require them to form associations between multiple pieces of information. (p. 462)

3. List a strategy for improving associative memory in late adulthood. (p. 462)

   _____

Remote Memory

1. True or False: Research shows that memory for recent events is clearer than memory for remote events in late life. (p. 462)

2. Explain why older adults recall their adolescent and early adulthood experiences more easily than their midlife experiences. (p. 462)

   _____
   _____

Prospective Memory

1. What is *prospective memory*? (p. 462)

   _____
   _____

2. Older adults do better on (event-based / time-based) prospective memory tasks. Explain your answer. (p. 462)

   _____
   _____

3. Explain why prospective memory difficulties in the laboratory setting do not always appear in real-life contexts. (p. 463)

   _____
   _____

Language Processing

1. What factors help older adults maintain their language comprehension skills? (p. 463)

   _____
   _____

2. Describe two aspects of language production that show age-related declines, and note factors that contribute to these changes. (p. 463)

   A. _____

   B. _____

   Factors that contribute to changes: _____

   _____

3. List two ways that older adults often compensate for difficulties with language production. (p. 463)

   A. _____

   B. _____

Problem Solving

1. (Traditional / Real-life) problem solving declines in old age. Explain why. (p. 463)

   _____

2. What types of everyday problems are of concern to most older adults? (p. 463)

   _____

   _____

3. Summarize adaptive problem-solving strategies used by older adults to solve problems of daily living. (pp. 463–464)

   _____

   _____

   _____

4. Older adults are (quicker / slower) than younger adults to make decisions about seeking health care. (p. 463)

5. True or False: Older couples are less likely than younger couples to collaborate in everyday problem solving. (p. 464)

Wisdom

1. Define *wisdom,* noting characteristics often used to describe this quality. (p. 464)

   A. _____

   _____

   B. _____

   _____

2. True or False: Cultures around the world assume that age and wisdom go together. Explain your answer. (p. 464)

   _____

   _____

3. True or False: Research shows that age is more important than life experience in the development of wisdom. (pp. 464–465)

4. In addition to age and life experience, what other factor contributes to late-life wisdom? (p. 465)

   _____

5. True or False: Wisdom is a strong predictor of psychological well-being, and wise elders seem to flourish, even when faced with physical and cognitive challenges. (p. 465)

Factors Related to Cognitive Change

1. List four factors that predict maintenance of mental abilities in late life. (p. 465)

   A. _____

   B. _____

   C. _____

   D. _____

2. Explain how retirement can affect cognitive change both positively and negatively. (p. 465)

   Positively: _____
   _____

   Negatively: _____
   _____

3. Define *terminal decline*, and note its average length. (p. 465)

   Definition: _____

   Average length: _____

Cognitive Interventions

1. For most of late adulthood, cognitive declines are (rapid / gradual). (p. 466)

2. Summarize findings from the Adult Development and Enrichment Project (ADEPT) and from the Advanced Cognitive Training for Independent and Vital Elderly (ACTIVE). (pp. 466–467)

   ADEPT: _____
   _____

   ACTIVE: _____
   _____

Lifelong Learning

1. Elders' participation in continuing education has (increased / declined) over the past few decades. (p. 467)

2. Describe characteristics of Elderhostel programs, noting opportunities that they offer. (pp. 467–468)
   _____
   _____

3. Describe the University of the Third Age and similar programs offered in Europe and Australia. (p. 468)
   _____
   _____

4. Summarize three ways to increase the effectiveness of instruction for older adults. (p. 468)

   A. _____

   B. _____

   C. _____

5. List five benefits of elders' participation in continuing education programs for the elderly. (p. 468)

   A. _____
   B. _____
   C. _____
   D. _____
   E. _____

ASK YOURSELF...

For *Ask Yourself* questions for this chapter, please log on to the Companion Website at *www.ablongman.com/berk*.

1. Select the Companion Website for *Exploring Lifespan Development*.
2. Use the "Jump to" menu to go directly to this chapter.
3. From the menu on the left side of the screen, select "Ask Yourself."
4. Complete questions and choose "Submit answers for grading" or "Clear answers" to start over.

SUGGESTED STUDENT READINGS

Achenbaum, W. A. (2005). *Older Americans, vital communities: A bold vision for societal aging.* Baltimore, MD: Johns Hopkins University Press. In an ecological approach to understanding the health, vitality, and productivity of today's elders, the author describes how increases in life expectancy have transformed America's aging society.

Ballenger, J. F. (2006). *Self, senility, and Alzheimer's disease in modern America: A history.* Baltimore, MD: Johns Hopkins University Press. Based on current research in psychiatry and gerontology, this book provides an extensive overview of Alzheimer's disease, including health concerns, neurological changes, cultural perceptions about cognitive decline, and treatment options.

Cabeza, R., Nyberg, L., & Park, D. (Eds.). (2005). *Cognitive neuroscience of aging: Linking cognitive and cerebral aging.* New York: Oxford University Press. A collection of chapters examining the effects of aging on cognition. Topics include age-related changes in neural activity, the effects of aging on memory and perception, recent advances in the field of neurology, and the benefits of cognitive training.

Ellis, N. (2004). *If I live to be 100: Lessons from the Centenarians.* New York: Three Rivers Press. Based on extensive research and a year of interviews, this book highlights the extraordinary lives of centenarians, including their unique life experiences and secrets to living a long, healthy life.

PUZZLE 17.1

Across

2. _____ lifespan: the number of years of vigorous, healthy life that an individual born in a particular year can expect
3. _____ lifespan: genetic limit to length of life for a person free of external risk factors
9. Bundles of twisted threads that are the product of collapsed neural structures are called _____ tangles.
10. Life expectancy _____: age-related reversal in life expectancy of sectors of the population
11. Cloudy areas in the lens of the eye that result in foggy vision and (without surgery) eventually blindness
12. _____ life expectancy: the number of years that a person born in a particular year can expect to live
13. _____ degeneration is a blurring and eventual loss of central vision due to a break-down of light sensitive cells in the center of the retina

Down

1. Form of arthritis characterized by deteriorating cartilage on the ends of bones of frequently used joints
4. Set of disorders occurring almost entirely in old age; many aspects of thought and behavior are so impaired that everyday activities are disrupted
5. _____ dementia: a series of strokes leaves areas of dead brain cells, producing degeneration of mental abilities
6. _____ disease is the most common form of dementia in which structural and chemical deterioration in the brain is associated with gradual loss of many aspects of thought and behavior.
7. _____ response: abnormal response of the immune system in which it turns against normal body tissues
8. _____ plaques: dense deposits of a deteriorated protein surrounded by clumps of dead neurons

363

PUZZLE 17.2

Across

3. Type of memory deficit that involves difficulty creating or retrieving links between pieces of information
5. Memory without conscious awareness is called _____ memory
7. _____ activities of daily living: tasks necessary to conduct the business of daily life and that require some cognitive competence, such as telephoning, shopping, housekeeping, and paying bills
9. _____ of daily living: basic self-care tasks required to live on one's own, such as dressing, bathing, or eating
10. _____ age: actual competence and performance of an older adult
11. _____ memory involves remembering to engage in planned actions at an appropriate time in the future
12. _____ aging: declines due to hereditary defects and environmental influences
14. _____: form of cognition that combines breadth and depth of practical knowledge, ability to reflect on that knowledge in ways that make life more bearable and worthwhile, emotional maturity, and creative integration of experience and knowledge into new ways of thinking and acting

Down

2. Compression of _____: public health goal of reducing the average period of diminished vigor before death as life expectancy extends
4. Selective _____ with compensation: strategies that permit older adults to sustain high levels of functioning
6. _____ involves weakened functioning of diverse organs and body systems, which profoundly interfere with everyday competence, leaving the older adult highly vulnerable to infection, temperature changes, or injury
8. _____ decline is a steady, marked decrease in cognitive functioning prior to death
11. _____ aging: genetically influenced age-related declines in functioning of organs and systems that affect all members of our species and take place in the context of overall good health
13. _____ memory: recall of events that happened long ago

PRACTICE TEST #1

1. Today, average life expectancy in North America is approximately (p. 442)
   a. 40 to 45 years.
   b. 55 to 60 years.
   c. 75 to 80 years.
   d. 95 to 100 years.

2. When researchers estimate the active lifespan, the country that ranks first is (p. 442)
   a. the United States.
   b. Canada.
   c. Japan.
   d. Sweden.

3. Which of the following statements is true of the brain in late adulthood? (pp. 443, 445)
   a. Brain weight can decline by as much as 5 to 10 percent by age 80.
   b. Neuron loss occurs only in the temporal lobe of the cerebral cortex.
   c. The brain is incapable of overcoming late adulthood declines.
   d. Glial cells increase in size and number throughout late adulthood.

4. Which of the following statements is true of eyesight in late adulthood? (pp. 445–446)
   a. Macular degeneration is the leading cause of blindness among older adults.
   b. Cataracts are cloudy areas in the lens of the eye that cannot be repaired and usually lead to blindness.
   c. Dark adaptation usually becomes easier in late adulthood.
   d. More than three-fourths of people age 85 and older experience visual impairment severe enough to interfere with daily living.

5. Ellen is worried about developing cataracts or macular degeneration. To reduce her risk of developing these conditions, she can (p. 446)
   a. spend fewer hours working at the computer.
   b. wear glasses for reading.
   c. take a daily multivitamin pill.
   d. eat a diet rich in green, leafy vegetables.

6. Age-related declines in hearing (p. 446)
   a. are greatest at low frequencies.
   b. have the greatest impact on life satisfaction when speech perception declines.
   c. are severe enough to disrupt the daily lives of nearly all elders.
   d. have a greater impact on self-care than does vision loss.

7. Aging of the cardiovascular system causes the (p. 447)
   a. heart muscle to become less rigid, so it pumps less efficiently.
   b. cells within the heart to shrink and multiply.
   c. artery walls to stiffen and accumulate some plaque.
   d. heart muscle to become more responsive to signals from pacemaker cells.

8. Older adults need about 7 hours of sleep per night, which is about _____ younger adults require. (p. 447)
   a. the same amount as
   b. twice as much as younger adults
   c. an hour more than younger adults
   d. an hour less than

9. Declines in mobility in late adulthood are the result of (p. 448)
   a. diminished muscle strength.
   b. visual declines associated with depth perception and acuity.
   c. changes in body structure, particularly height and weight.
   d. age-related changes in the structure of the middle ear, which affect balance.

10. Research demonstrates that over the past two decades, compression of morbidity has occurred in developed countries due largely to (p. 450)
    a. a decrease in rates of obesity and sedentary lifestyles.
    b. a reduction in the number of major surgical procedures performed.
    c. medical advances and improved socioeconomic conditions.
    d. an increase in the age at which the average person retires.

11. The leading cause of death among individuals age 65 and older is (p. 453)
    a. respiratory disease, such as pneumonia.
    b. cardiovascular disease.
    c. cancer.
    d. unintentional injury.

12. The most common type of arthritis afflicting older adults is (p. 453)
    a. osteoarthritis.
    b. rheumatoid arthritis.
    c. diabetic arthritis.
    d. Alzheimer's arthritis.

13. Diabetes (p. 454)
    a. is not hereditary but results only from environmental factors such as obesity and lack of exercise.
    b. is a disease of the bones that usually develops after age 60.
    c. affects people of all ages.
    d. always requires daily medication; it cannot be treated with diet.

14. Older adults are particularly susceptible to motor vehicle injury because they (p. 454)
    a. tend to drive at much higher speeds than younger adults.
    b. are likely to have visual impairments and slower reaction time than younger people.
    c. are less cautious than younger drivers.
    d. are more decisive than younger drivers, but often in a reckless way.

15. Among the earliest symptoms of Alzheimer's disease is (p. 455)
    a. the disintegration of skilled, purposeful movements.
    b. severe loss of memory for such items as names, dates, appointments, familiar routes of travel, and everyday safety precautions.
    c. disruption of sleep by delusions and imaginary fears.
    d. loss of the ability to comprehend and produce speech.

16. Which of the following statements about Alzheimer's disease is true? (p. 455)
    a. It can result in coma and, eventually, death.
    b. It affects only the mind and emotions, not the physical aspects of life.
    c. Memory problems usually present themselves at the end stages of the disease.
    d. The disease follows the same course in nearly all individuals.

17. The disorder most often misdiagnosed as dementia is (p. 459)
    a. depression.
    b. Alzheimer's disease.
    c. diabetes.
    d. arthritis.

18. Which of the following statements about memory in late adulthood is true? (p. 463)
    a. Recognition suffers more than recall.
    b. Associative memory deficit is usually not a problem.
    c. Problems with prospective memory are more evident in the laboratory than in real life.
    d. Remote memory is usually much clearer than memory for recent events.

15. Sporadic Alzheimer's disease (p. 456)
    a. tends to run in families.
    b. is linked to genes on chromosomes 1, 14, and 21.
    c. is associated with an abnormal gene on chromosome 19, resulting in excess levels of ApoE4.
    d. has an earlier onset and a more rapid progression than does familial Alzheimer's disease.

16. Of the following individuals, the most likely to be placed in a nursing home is (p. 460)
    a. a Caucasian American with Alzheimer's disease.
    b. an African American with cardiovascular disease.
    c. a Native American with cancer.
    d. an Asian elder with a hip fracture.

17. Research on memory capacity in late adulthood shows that (p. 461)
    a. age-related memory declines are greatest for automatic activities, whereas memory for tasks requiring deliberate processing does not change much in old age.
    b. recognition memory suffers less in late adulthood than does recall memory.
    c. older adults recall remote personal experiences more easily than recent ones.
    d. older adults perform better on time-based than event-based prospective memory tasks.

18. Which of the following statements about problem solving in old age is true? (p. 463)
    a. Older adults solve everyday problems more effectively than complex hypothetical problems.
    b. Problems encountered in late adulthood are nearly identical to those encountered earlier in life.
    c. Because older adults view most problems as beyond their control, they seldom use adaptive coping strategies.
    d. Compared to younger married couples, older married couples are less likely to collaborate in everyday problem solving.

19. Wisdom (p. 465)
    a. is directly related to age and is seen at high levels in virtually all older adults.
    b. is more common in early and middle adulthood than in late adulthood.
    c. is closely linked to life experiences, particularly exposure to and success in overcoming adversity.
    d. shows no relationship to life satisfaction.

20. Elderhostel, Routes to Learning, and similar programs (p. 466)
    a. combine educational programs and recreational activities.
    b. provide direct instruction in compensatory strategies to help elders address cognitive processing declines.
    c. are only beneficial for active, wealthy, well-educated older adults.
    d. are specially designed to meet the needs of elders with little education and few economic resources.

19. The Adult Development and Enrichment Project (ADEPT) was an intervention program that (pp. 465–466)
    a. contributed to improved memory and problem-solving abilities among elderly participants.
    b. hastened the rate of terminal decline among elderly participants.
    c. provided better strategies for overcoming the physical declines of aging.
    d. was designed to assist caregivers of older adults with Alzheimer's disease.

20. Which of the following language processing skills changes very little in late life? (p. 463)
    a. retrieving words from long-term memory
    b. understanding the meaning of spoken words
    c. planning what to say
    d. planning how to say something

PRACTICE TEST #2

1. A North American baby born in 1900 had an average life expectancy of just under 50 years. In 2004, this figure reached _____ in the United States and _____ in Canada (p. 442)
    a. 57.9; 59.9
    b. 67.9; 65.9
    c. 77.9; 80.1
    d. 87.9; 92.2

2. The likely reason that women live 4 to 7 years longer than men, on average, is that women have (p. 442)
    a. less stressful lives.
    b. better access to health care.
    c. more supportive social relationships.
    d. the protective value of their extra X chromosome.

3. Declines in brain weight throughout adulthood largely result from (pp. 443, 445)
    a. shrinkage of the ventricles within the brain.
    b. death of neurons.
    c. myelination of neural fibers.
    d. increased incidence of stroke.

4. The leading cause of blindness among older adults is (p. 446)
    a. glaucoma.
    b. cataracts.
    c. macular degeneration.
    d. neural death in the visual cortex of the brain.

5. Aging of the immune system (p. 447)
    a. leads to increased production and responsiveness of T-cells.
    b. results in profound loss of function for most older adults.
    c. shows little variation from one person to the next.
    d. is related to increased malfunction, so that the immune system is more likely to turn against normal body tissues.

6. Among the best ways to foster restful sleep is (p. 447)
    a. to use long-term medication.
    b. to try to stay in bed for longer periods of time.
    c. to establish a consistent bedtime and waking time.
    d. to take naps during the daytime.

7. Creasing and sagging of the skin and the appearance of age spots all extend into old age. The face is especially likely to show these effects because it is (p. 448)
    a. frequently exposed to the sun.
    b. the area that is most elevated in relation to the heart.
    c. in constant motion.
    d. damaged by lotions, shaving cream, and other products.

8. Older adults who use _____ coping strategies adapt more favorably to the everyday challenges of aging and show improved physical functioning. (p. 448)
    a. problem-centered
    b. cognition-centered
    c. emotion-centered
    d. avoidant

9. Older adults are generally _____ about their own health. (p. 450)
    a. optimistic
    b. pessimistic
    c. indifferent
    d. uninformed

10. By very old age (85 and beyond), women are more impaired than men because (p. 450)
    a. women are more prone to fatal diseases.
    b. men are more prone to non-life-threatening disabling conditions.
    c. only the sturdiest men have survived.
    d. men have longer life expectancies.

11. Your elderly grandparent is wondering whether to take a daily vitamin–mineral nutritional supplement. What useful information should you offer? (p. 451)
    a. There is no evidence that vitamin–mineral supplements offer health benefits.
    b. Vitamin–mineral supplements are only advantageous to older adults who are sedentary.
    c. Daily vitamin–mineral supplements are probably unnecessary as older adults require fewer nutrients and have fewer dietary deficiencies.
    d. Daily vitamin–mineral supplements have been linked to an enhanced immune response and a 50 percent drop in days of infectious illness.

12. Which of these is the best example of primary aging? (p. 452)
    a. Farsightedness resulting from stiffening of the lens of the eye
    b. Lung cancer caused by smoking cigarettes
    c. Weight gain resulting from a sedentary lifestyle
    d. High blood pressure resulting from prolonged stress in the workplace

13. Although _____ contributes to frailty, researchers agree that _____ plays a larger role, through genetic disorders, unhealthy lifestyle, and chronic disease. (p. 453)
    a. secondary aging; primary aging
    b. primary aging; secondary aging
    c. functional aging; biological aging
    d. biological aging; functional aging

14. Dementia (p. 455)
    a. is usually, though not always, irreversible and incurable, depending on the type.
    b. never affects the subcortical regions of the brain.
    c. causes deterioration in quality of life, but is not, in itself, a cause of death.
    d. can occur at any age, not just in the elderly.

2. Describe sleep difficulties common in older adults, and cite two factors that are largely responsible for these problems. (p. 447)

   Sleep difficulties: _____

   _____

   Factors responsible: _____

   _____

3. Describe ways to foster restful sleep in late adulthood. (p. 447)

   _____

   _____

   _____

Physical Appearance and Mobility

1. Describe changes in the skin in late adulthood. (p. 448)

   _____

   _____

2. True or False: The face is especially likely to show signs of aging because it is frequently exposed to the sun. (p. 448)

3. Describe facial changes that occur in late adulthood. (p. 448)

   _____

   _____

4. True or False: Both height and weight tend to decline in late adulthood. (p. 448)

5. List three age-related changes that affect mobility. (p. 448)

   A. _____

   B. _____

   C. _____

Adapting to the Physical Changes of Late Adulthood

1. True or False: Outward signs of aging, such as graying hair, facial wrinkles, and baldness, are closely related to sensory, cognitive, and motor functioning, as well as longevity. (p. 448)

2. Explain how problem-centered coping strategies help older adults adjust to the physical changes of late life. (p. 448)

   _____

   _____

   _____

3. Define *assistive technology,* and provide several examples of devices that help older adults cope with physical declines. (pp. 448–449)

   Definition: _____

   _____

   Examples: _____

   _____

4. Like gender stereotypes, aging stereotypes often operate _____. Explain what this means. (p. 449)

5. How do stereotypes of aging affect older adults' functioning and self-esteem? (pp. 449–450)

6. Summarize cross-cultural evidence from Inuit and Japanese populations suggesting that positive cultural views of aging contribute to better mental and physical health in the elderly. (p. 450)

Health, Fitness, and Disability

1. The majority of older adults rate their health (favorably / unfavorably). (p. 450)

2. Explain how physical and mental health are intimately related in late life. (p. 450)

3. Summarize SES and ethnic variations in physical functioning during late life, noting reasons for these differences. (p. 450)

    SES: _____

    Ethnic variations: _____

4. True or False: Beyond age 85, women are more impaired than men and are less able to remain independent. (p. 450)

5. Define *compression of morbidity,* noting recent trends. (p. 450)

6. Describe evidence indicating that compression of morbidity can be greatly extended. (pp. 450–451)

CHAPTER 18
EMOTIONAL AND SOCIAL DEVELOPMENT IN LATE ADULTHOOD

BRIEF CHAPTER SUMMARY

The final psychological conflict of Erikson's theory, ego integrity versus despair, involves coming to terms with one's life. Adults who arrive at a sense of integrity feel whole, complete, and satisfied with their achievements, whereas despair occurs when elders feel they have made many wrong decisions. In Peck's theory, ego integrity requires that older adults move beyond their life's work, their bodies, and their separate identities. Joan Erikson, widow of Erik Erikson, believes that older people can arrive at a psychosocial stage she calls gerotranscendence—a cosmic, transcendent perspective directed beyond the self. Labouvie-Vief addresses the development of adults' reasoning about emotion, pointing out that older adults develop affect optimization, the ability to maximize positive emotion and dampen negative emotion. Although researchers do not yet have a full understanding of why older people reminisce more than younger people do, current theory and research indicate that reflecting on the past can be positive and adaptive.

Older adults have accumulated a lifetime of self-knowledge, leading to more secure and complex conceptions of themselves than at earlier ages. During late adulthood, shifts in three personality traits take place. Agreeableness and acceptance of change tend to rise, while sociability dips slightly. Although declining health and transportation difficulties reduce organized religious participation in advanced old age, informal religious activities remain prominent in the lives of today's elders.

In patterns of behavior called the dependency–support script and independence–ignore script, older adults' dependency behaviors are attended to immediately, while their independent behaviors are ignored, encouraging elders to become more dependent than they need or want to be. Physical declines and chronic disease can be highly stressful, leading to a sense of loss of personal control—a major factor in adult mental health. In late adulthood, social support continues to play a powerful role in reducing stress, thereby promoting physical health and psychological well-being.

In late adulthood, extroverts continue to interact with a wider range of people than introverts and people with poor social skills. Disengagement theory, activity theory, continuity theory, and socioemotional selectivity theory offer varying explanations for the decline in amount of social interaction in late adulthood. The physical and social contexts in which elders live affect their social experiences and, consequently, their development and adjustment. Seniors tend to prefer to live independently as long as possible, but different communities, neighborhoods, and housing arrangements (including congregate housing and life care communities) vary in the extent to which they enable aging residents to satisfy their social needs.

The social convoy is an influential model of changes in our social networks as we move through life. Marital satisfaction rises from middle to late adulthood as perceptions of fairness in the relationship increase, couples engage in joint leisure activities, and communication becomes more positive. Most gay and lesbian elders also report happy, highly fulfilling relationships. Couples who divorce in late adulthood constitute a very small proportion of all divorces in any given year. Compared to divorced younger adults, divorced elders find it harder to separate their identity from that of their former spouse, and they suffer more from a sense of personal failure. Wide variation in adaptation to widowhood exists, with age, social support, and personality making a difference. Today, more older adults who enter a new relationship choose to cohabit rather than remarrying.

Siblings, friends, and adult children provide important sources of emotional support and companionship to elders. Although the majority of older adults enjoy positive relationships with family members, friends, and professional caregivers, some suffer maltreatment at the hands of these individuals.

Financial and health status, opportunities to pursue meaningful activities, and societal factors (such as early retirement benefits) affect the decision to retire. Retirement also varies with gender and ethnicity. Most elders adjust well to retirement. Involvement in satisfying leisure activities is related to better physical and mental health and reduced mortality. Successful aging, which involves maximizing gains and minimizing losses, is best viewed as a process rather than a list of specific accomplishments. Social contexts that permit elders to manage life changes effectively foster successful aging.

LEARNING OBJECTIVES

After reading this chapter, you should be able to:

18.1 Describe Erikson's stage of ego integrity versus despair. (p. 471)

18.2 Discuss Peck's tasks of ego integrity, Joan Erikson's gerotranscendence, and Labouvie-Vief's emotional expertise. (pp. 471–473)

18.3 Describe the functions of reminiscence and life review in older adults' lives. (p. 473)

18.4 Summarize stable and changing aspects of self-concept and personality in late adulthood. (pp. 473–474)

18.5 Discuss spirituality and religiosity in late adulthood, and trace the development of faith. (pp. 474–475)

18.6 Discuss individual differences in psychological well-being as older adults respond to increased dependency, declining health, and negative life changes. (pp. 475–476, 477))

18.7 Summarize the role of social support and social interaction in promoting physical health and psychological well-being in late adulthood. (pp. 476, 478)

18.8 Describe social theories of aging, including disengagement theory, activity theory, socioemotional selectivity theory, and continuity theory. (pp. 478–480, 481)

18.9 Explain how communities, neighborhoods, and housing arrangements affect elders' social lives and adjustment. (pp. 480, 482–483)

18.10 Describe changes in social relationships in late adulthood, including marriage, gay and lesbian partnerships, divorce, remarriage, and widowhood, and discuss never-married, childless older adults. (pp. 483–486)

18.11 Explain how sibling relationships, friendships, and relationships with adult children change in late life. (pp. 486–488)

18.12 Discuss elder maltreatment, including risk factors and strategies for prevention. (pp. 488–490)

18.13 Discuss the decision to retire, adjustment to retirement, and involvement in leisure activities. (pp. 490–492)

18.14 Discuss the meaning of successful aging. (pp. 492–493)

STUDY QUESTIONS

Erikson's Theory: Ego Integrity versus Despair

1. Cite characteristics of elders who arrive at a sense of integrity and those who experience despair. (p. 471)

   Integrity: _____

   _____

   Despair: _____

   _____

Other Theories of Psychosocial Development in Late Adulthood

Peck's Tasks of Ego Integrity and Joan Erikson's Gerotranscendence

1. Cite three tasks that Peck maintained must be resolved for integrity to develop. (p. 472)

   _____

   _____

   _____

2. Recent evidence suggests that body transcendence and ego transcendence (decrease / increase) in very old age. (p. 472)

3. Describe and evaluate Joan Erikson's psychosocial stage of *gerotranscendence*. (p. 472)

   Description: _____

   _____

   Evaluation: _____

   _____

Labouvie-Vief's Emotional Expertise

1. Describe *affect optimization*. (p. 472)

   _____

2. How do gains in affect optimization contribute to resilience in late adulthood? (pp. 472–473)

   _____

   _____

3. Explain how older adults' emotional perceptiveness influences their coping strategies. (p. 473)

   _____

   _____

4. True or False: A significant late-life psychosocial attainment is becoming expert at processing emotional information and regulating negative affect. (p. 473)

Reminiscence and Life Review

1. True or False: Older people *reminisce* to escape the realities of a shortened future and nearness of death. (p. 473)

2. Define *life review*, and explain why it is an important form of reminiscence. (p. 473)

   Definition: _____

   _____

   Explanation: _____

   _____

3. Besides life review, cite three other purposes of reminiscence. (p. 473)

Stability and Change in Self-Concept and Personality

Secure and Multifaceted Self-Concept

1. True or False: Older adults have accumulated a lifetime of self-knowledge, leading to more secure and complex conceptions of themselves than at earlier ages. (p. 473)

2. Explain how a firm, secure, and multifaceted self-concept relates to psychological well-being. (p. 474)

   _____

   _____

   _____

3. In what areas do elders continue to mention hoped-for selves? (p. 474)

4. How do elders reorganize their possible selves? (p. 474)

Resilience: Agreeableness, Sociability, and Acceptance of Change

1. Cite three shifts in personality characteristics that take place during late adulthood. (p. 474)

    A. _____

    B. _____

    C. _____

2. When elders take personality tests, agreeableness rises—especially among (men / women). (p. 474)

Spirituality and Religiosity

1. Older adults attach (great / moderate / little) value to religious beliefs and behaviors. (p. 474)

2. North American elders generally become (less / more) religious or spiritual as they age—a trend that (is / is not) universal. Explain your answer. (p. 474)

3. Involvement in both organized and informal religious activities is especially high among _____ _____ elders. (p. 475)

4. (Men / Women) are more likely to be involved in religion. What might explain this trend? (p. 475)

5. Briefly summarize the benefits of religious involvement. (p. 475)

Individual Differences in Psychological Well-Being

Control versus Dependency

1. Describe two complementary behavior patterns people often use when interacting with older adults. (p. 475)

    A. _____

    B. _____

2. What factors determine whether elders will react positively or negatively to social contact and caregiving? (p. 476)

3. In (Western / non-Western) societies, many elders fear becoming dependent on others. (p. 476)

4. Why do family members or other caregivers often respond to elders in ways that promote excess dependency in old age? (p. 476)

Health

1. What late-life situation is among the strongest risk factors for depression? (p. 476)

2. Summarize the impact of physical health on psychological well-being in late adulthood. (p. 476)

3. True or False: People age 65 and older have the lowest suicide rate of any age group. (p. 476)

4. Cite factors that help elders surmount physical impairment. (p. 476)

Social Issues: Elder Suicide

1. Cite sex and age differences in elder suicide. What explains these trends? (p. 477)

    A.
    B.
    C.

2. What factors help prevent suicide among ethnic minority elders? (p. 477)

3. Failed suicides are much more (common / rare) in old age than in adolescence. (p. 477)

4. List two reasons why elder suicides tend to be underreported. (p. 477)

    A.
    B.

5. What two types of events often prompt suicide in late life? (p. 477)

   A. _____

   B. _____

6. List several warning signs of elder suicide. (p. 477)

   _____

   _____

7. Describe the most effective treatment for depressed, suicidal elders. (p. 477)

   _____

   _____

   _____

Negative Life Changes

1. True or False: Negative life changes are less stressful for elders than for younger people. (p. 476)

2. Briefly describe sex differences in elders' coping skills. (p. 476)

   _____

   _____

Social Support and Social Interaction

1. Summarize the benefits of social support in late adulthood. (p. 476)

   _____

   _____

   _____

2. Many older adults place a high value on (dependency / independence) and (do / do not) want a great deal of unreciprocated support from people close to them. (p. 476)

3. List two factors that make ethnic minority elders more likely to accept formal support. (pp. 476, 478)

   A. _____

   B. _____

4. True or False: Perceived social support is associated with a positive outlook in older adults with disabilities, whereas the amount of help from family and friends has little impact. Provide research to support your answer. (p. 478)

   _____

   _____

A Changing Social World

Social Theories of Aging

1. According to _____ theory, mutual withdrawal between elders and society takes place in anticipation of death. Why does this theory not adequately explain the reduced social activity of older people? (p. 478)

2. _____ theory states that social barriers to engagement, not the desires of elders, cause declining rates of interaction. (p. 478)

3. True or False: Consistent with *activity theory*, studies show that simply offering older adults opportunities for social contact leads to greater social activity. (p. 479)

4. _____ theory posits that most aging adults strive to maintain a personal system that ensures consistency between their past and anticipated future, which promotes life satisfaction. (p. 479)

5. Describe ways that reliance on continuity benefits older adults. (p. 479)

6. According to *socioemotional selectivity theory*, how do the functions of social interaction change from middle to late adulthood? (p. 479)

7. According to socioemotional selectivity theory, what explains changes in the function of social interaction in late adulthood? (p. 479)

8. How do older adults apply their emotional expertise to promote harmony in social interactions? (pp. 479–480)

Biology and Environment: Aging, Time Perception, and Social Goals

1. True or False: Socioemotional selectivity theory underscores that our time perspective plays a crucial role in the social goals we select and pursue. (p. 481)

2. How do the social perspectives of men with AIDS support socioemotional selectivity theory? (p. 481)

3. Mainland Chinese elders express a (stronger / weaker) desire for familiar social partners because they perceive their future as (more / less) limited. (p. 481)

4. True or False: The preference for close partners when time is short stems from a need for social support, not meaningful interactions. (p. 481)

Social Contexts of Aging: Communities, Neighborhoods, and Housing

1. True or False: About half of American and three-fourths of Canadian ethnic minority elders live in cities, compared to only one-third of Caucasians. (p. 480)

2. The majority of senior citizens reside in _____, where they moved earlier in their lives and usually remain after retirement. (p. 480)

3. How do suburban elders differ from inner-city elders? (p. 480)

   A. _____

   B. _____

4. What aspects of smaller communities foster gratifying relationships for older adults? (p. 480)

   _____
   _____

5. Presence of family members (is / is not) as crucial to older adults' well-being if they have neighbors and nearby friends who can provide support. (p. 480)

6. Older adults in Western industrialized nations want to (leave / stay in) the neighborhoods where they spent their adults lives. (p. 481)

7. List three factors that prompt elder relocations. (p. 481)

   A. _____

   B. _____

   C. _____

8. Which setting affords the greatest possible personal control for the majority of elders? Under what conditions does this setting pose risks? (p. 481)

   A. _____

   B. _____

9. Although increasing numbers of ethnic minority elders want to live on their own, _____ often prevents them from doing so. (p. 482)

10. During the past half-century, the number of unmarried, divorced, and widowed elders living alone has (declined / risen) rapidly. This trend (is / is not) evident in all segments of the elderly population. (p. 482)

11. Cite factors that contribute to rising poverty rates among elderly women. (p. 482)

    _____
    _____

12. Identify and define two types of residential communities available to North American seniors. (p. 482)

    A. _____
    _____

    B. _____
    _____

13. Discuss the positive effects of residential communities on physical and mental health. (p. 483)

14. What factors enhance older adults' life satisfaction in residential communities? (p. 483)

15. Which residential setting represents the most extreme restriction of autonomy? (p. 483)

16. How do North American nursing homes differ from European facilities? (p. 483)

Relationships in Late Adulthood

1. How does the *social convoy* support adaptation to old age? (p. 483)

Marriage

1. Provide four reasons why marital satisfaction increases from middle to late adulthood. (pp. 483–484)

    A. _____
    B. _____
    C. _____
    D. _____

2. When marital dissatisfaction is present, it takes a greater toll on (men / women), who tend to confront marital problems and try to solve them. (p. 484)

Gay and Lesbian Partnerships

1. True or False: Most elderly gays and lesbians in long-term partnerships report happy, highly fulfilling relationships. (p. 484)

2. What unique challenges do aging gays and lesbians face? (p. 484)

Divorce, Remarriage, and Cohabitation

1. What reasons do men and women give for initiating divorce in late life? (p. 484)

    Men: _____

    Women: _____

2. Following divorce, older adults find it (easier / harder) to separate their identity from that of their former spouse, and they suffer (more / less) from a sense of personal failure. (p. 484)

3. Why do women suffer more than men from late-life divorce? (p. 484)

    _____

    _____

4. List three reasons why late adulthood remarriages are more frequent after divorce than widowhood. (p. 485)

    A. _____

    B. _____

    C. _____

5. True or False: Rather than remarrying, today many older adults who enter a new relationship choose cohabitation. What explains this trend? (p. 485)

    _____

    _____

    _____

Widowhood

1. True or False: Widows make up one-third of the elderly population in the United States and Canada. (p. 485)

2. True or False: Ethnic minorities with high rates of poverty and chronic disease are more likely to be widowed. (p. 485)

3. The greatest problem for recently widowed elders is _____. (p. 485)

4. (Men / Women) find it more difficult to adjust to widowhood. Cite three reasons for this gender difference. (p. 485)

    A. _____

    B. _____

    C. _____

5. True or False: Older widowers report the most depression and the slowest rate of improvement in the two years following the death of a spouse. Explain your answer. (p. 485)

    _____

    _____

    _____

6. True or False: Providing older widows and widowers with information and support in acquiring daily living skills promotes favorable adjustment. (p. 486)

Never-Married, Childless Older Adults

1. Cite examples of alternative, meaningful relationships formed by adults who remain single and childless throughout life. (p. 486)

   _____
   _____

2. In a large, nationally representative sample of Americans over age 70, childless (men / women) without marital partners were far more likely to feel lonely. (p. 486)

Siblings

1. Both men and women perceive bonds with (sisters / brothers) to be closer. (p. 487)

2. Under what circumstances are elders likely to turn to siblings for assistance? (p. 487)

   _____

3. Cite the benefits of joint reminiscing between siblings in late adulthood. (p. 487)

   _____
   _____
   _____

Friendships

1. List four functions of elder friendships. (p. 487)

   A. _____
   B. _____
   C. _____
   D. _____

2. True or False: Friendship formation continues throughout life. (p. 487)

3. Describe characteristics of older adult friendships. (p. 488)

   _____
   _____
   _____

4. What are *secondary friends,* and why are women more likely than men to have them? (p. 488)

   A. _____
   B. _____

Relationships with Adult Children

1. As with other ties, the (quality / quantity) of interactions between elders and their adult children affects older adults' life satisfaction. (p. 488)

2. Explain how warm bonds between elders and their adult children foster psychological well-being. (p. 488)

   _____
   _____

3. (Moderate / Extensive) support from adult children is psychologically beneficial to elders. (p. 488)

4. As social networks shrink in size, _____ become more important sources of family involvement. (p. 488)

Elder Maltreatment

1. List and briefly describe five forms of elder maltreatment. (p. 489)

    A. _____

    _____

    B. _____

    _____

    C. _____

    _____

    D. _____

    _____

    E. _____

    _____

2. What forms of elder maltreatment occur most frequently? (p. 489)

    _____

    _____

3. Perpetrators of elder abuse usually (are / are not) family members. (p. 489)

4. Describe a type of neglect, which the media refers to as "granny dumping." (p. 489)

    _____

    _____

5. List five risk factors that increase the likelihood of elder abuse. (p. 489)

    A. _____
    B. _____
    C. _____
    D. _____
    E. _____

6. Why is preventing elder maltreatment by family members especially challenging? (p. 490)

    _____

    _____

7. Identify several components of elder maltreatment prevention programs. (p. 490)

    _____

    _____

    _____

8. True or False: Combating elder maltreatment requires efforts at the level of the larger society. Explain your answer. (p. 490)

_____
_____

Retirement and Leisure

1. What social changes have led to a blurring of the distinction between work and retirement? (p. 490)

_____
_____

The Decision to Retire

1. What is usually the first consideration in the decision to retire? List additional considerations. (p. 490)

   First: _____

   Additional: _____
   _____
   _____

2. Provide an illustration of how societal factors affect older adults' retirement decisions? (pp. 490–491)

   _____
   _____

3. How do retirement programs in many Western countries compare to programs in the United States? (p. 491)

   A. _____
   _____

   B. _____
   _____

Adjustment to Retirement

1. True or False: For most people, mental health is fairly stable from the pre- to postretirement years. (p. 491)

2. Cite workforce and psychological factors that predict retirement satisfaction. (p. 491)

   Workforce: _____
   _____

   Psychological: _____
   _____

3. How can retirement enhance marital satisfaction? How does marital satisfaction, in turn, influence adjustment to retirement? (p. 492)

   A. _____

   B. _____

Leisure Activities

1. What is the best preparation for leisure in late life? (p. 492)
   _____

2. List several benefits of involvement in leisure activities. (p. 492)
   _____
   _____

3. List four characteristics of elders who become involved in volunteer work. (p. 492)

   A. _____
   B. _____
   C. _____
   D. _____

4. Older adults report (less / more) awareness of public affairs and vote at a (lower / higher) rate than other adults. (p. 492)

Successful Aging

1. Define *successful aging,* and cite characteristics of successful agers. (p. 492)

   A. _____
   B. _____
   _____

2. Explain how views of successful aging have changed in recent years. (p. 493)
   _____
   _____

3. List eight ways that older adults realize their goals. (p. 493)

   A. _____
   B. _____
   C. _____
   D. _____
   E. _____
   F. _____
   G. _____
   H. _____

4. Cite societal contexts that permit elders to manage life changes effectively. (p. 493)
   _____
   _____
   _____

ASK YOURSELF...

For *Ask Yourself* questions for this chapter, please log on to the Companion Website at *www.ablongman.com/berk*.

1. Select the Companion Website for *Exploring Lifespan Development*.
2. Use the "Jump to" menu to go directly to this chapter.
3. From the menu on the left side of the screen, select "Ask Yourself."
4. Complete questions and choose "Submit answers for grading" or "Clear answers" to start over.

SUGGESTED STUDENT READINGS

Eyetsemitan, F. E. & Gire, J. T. (2003). *Aging and adult development in the developing world: Applying western theories and concepts*. West Point, CT: Greenwood Publishing. A collection of chapters highlighting the influence of environmental contexts on the aging process. According to the authors, Western theories of aging may be inappropriate for understanding the experiences of elders in developing societies.

Podnieks, E., Lowenstein, A., & Kosberg, J. (2005). *Elder abuse*. New York: Haworth Press. A multidisciplinary approach to understanding elder abuse, this book presents up-to-date research on domestic violence in late adulthood, including risk factors, characteristics of abusers, cultural perceptions of elder abuse, and practical strategies for dealing with elder abuse.

Roose, S. P., & Sackeim, H. A. (2004). *Late-life depression*. New York: Oxford University Press. Presents a thorough overview of late-life depression. Topics include symptoms of late-life depression, diagnosis and treatment options, the relationship between depression and mortality, elder suicide, and bereavement.

Vaillant, G. E. (2002). *Aging well: Surprising guideposts to a happier life from the landmark Harvard Study of Adult Development*. Boston: Little Brown. Based on a longitudinal study of 824 participants followed from adolescence through old age, this book explores the multitude of factors contributing to resilience across the lifespan. Vaillant concludes that individual lifestyle choices play a greater role in successful aging than genetics, wealth, race, and gender.

PUZZLE 18.1

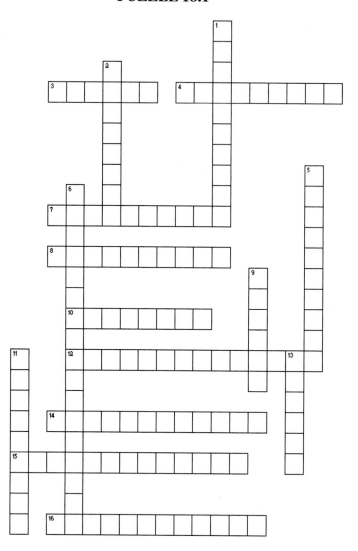

Across

3. Life _____: process of calling up, reflecting on, and reconsidering past experiences and contemplating the meaning with the goal of achieving greater self-understanding
4. Ego _____ versus despair: Erikson's psychological conflict of late adulthood
7. _____-support script: pattern of interaction in which elders' dependency behaviors are attended to immediately, thereby reinforcing those behaviors
8. _____ housing: housing for elderly that adds a variety of support services
10. According to _____ theory, declines in social interaction during late life are due to failure of the social environment to offer opportunities for social contact, not the desires of elders
12. _____ selectivity theory: declines in social interaction in late adulthood are due to physical and psychological changes, which lead elders to emphasize the emotion-regulating function of interaction
14. _____-ignore script: pattern of interaction in which elders' independent behaviors are largely ignored, leading them to occur less often
15. According to _____ theory, declines in social interaction during late adulthood are due to a mutual withdrawal between elders and society in anticipation of death
16. The process of telling stories about people and events from the past and reporting associated thoughts and feelings

Down

1. _____ theory states that social barriers to engagement, not the desires of elders, cause declining rates of interaction.
2. _____ _____ communities: housing for elderly that offers a range of options, from independent or congregate housing to full nursing home care (2 words)
5. _____ aging: gains are maximized and losses are minimized
6. A psychosocial stage proposed by Joan Erikson that represents development beyond ego integrity; when attained, there is a heightened inner calm, contentment, and additional time spent in reflection.
9. Social _____: views the individual within a cluster of relationships moving throughout life
11. _____ friends: people who are not intimates but with whom the individual spends time
13. _____ optimization: the ability to maximize positive emotion and dampen negative

PRACTICE TEST #1

1. According to Erikson, adults who arrive at a sense of integrity (p. 471)
    a. feel they have made many wrong decisions throughout their lives.
    b. feel whole, complete, and satisfied with their achievements.
    c. feel contempt toward themselves and others.
    d. dealt with significant psychological problems early in life.

2. According to Labouvie-Vief, elders display a compensating emotional strength in their ability to maximize positive emotion and dampen negative emotion, or (p. 472)
    a. gerotranscendence.
    b. ego integrity.
    c. disengagement.
    d. affect optimization.

3. As 75-year-old Margaret tells her grandchildren of times long ago, when she was just a small child, she is engaging in (p. 473)
    a. reminiscence.
    b. disengagement.
    c. affect optimization.
    d. geotranscendence.

4. In old age, the majority of older adults (p. 474)
    a. fail to replace possible selves with new ones.
    b. characterize hoped-for selves as "declining" and "missing out on."
    c. continue to mention, but fail to pursue, hoped-for selves in areas of good health and social responsibility.
    d. continue to actively pursue hoped-for selves.

5. Longitudinal research suggests that religious involvement (p. 474)
    a. declines sharply in late adulthood.
    b. remains fairly stable throughout adulthood.
    c. is especially low among low-SES ethnic minority elders.
    d. has little impact on physical and psychological well-being.

6. As a result of negative changes, 82-year-old Jada is more likely to report _____ than her 85-year-old brother. (p. 476)
    a. a higher sense of psychological well-being
    b. a similar sense of psychological well-being
    c. a lower sense of psychological well-being
    d. higher self-esteem

7. According to _____, social barriers to engagement, not the desires of elders, cause declining rates of social interactions as people age. (p. 478)
    a. activity theory
    b. socioemotional selectivity theory
    c. continuity theory
    d. disengagement theory

8. Compared to younger adults, older adults place greater emphasis on (p. 479)
    a. seeking affirmation from social partners.
    b. information seeking and future contact as a basis for selecting social partners.
    c. the emotional-regulating function of their social interactions.
    d. increasing the size of their social networks.

9. Both urban and rural older adults report greater life satisfaction when _____ reside in their neighborhood (p. 480)
   a. many senior citizens
   b. many children
   c. few people
   d. many young adults

10. Although increasing numbers of ethnic minority elders want to live on their own, _____ often prevents them from doing so. (p. 482)
    a. pride
    b. cultural values
    c. their children
    d. poverty

11. From middle to late adulthood, marital satisfaction (p. 483)
    a. rises.
    b. remains stable.
    c. declines.
    d. has little impact on psychological well-being.

12. Elderly gay and lesbian couples in long-term partnerships typically (p. 484)
    a. have great difficulty achieving a sense of integrity.
    b. experience less hostility and discrimination than younger gay and lesbian couples.
    c. report happy, highly fulfilling relationships.
    d. turn to family members and friends instead of their partners for social support.

13. Couples who divorce in late adulthood constitute only about _____ of all divorces in a given year. (p. 484)
    a. 20 percent
    b. 10 percent
    c. 5 percent
    d. 1 percent

14. Compared with widowed women, divorced older women may be more motivated to remarry because of (p. 484)
    a. greater fear of living alone.
    b. more extreme economic circumstances.
    c. greater desire for companionship.
    d. greater interest in a male role model for their children.

15. Compared with younger adults, elders who must cope with the death of a spouse typically show (p. 485)
    a. the same type and intensity of reactions.
    b. a less intense but longer-lasting reaction.
    c. less resiliency in the face of loneliness.
    d. fewer lasting problems adjusting to the death.

16. The kind of assistance that elders most often receive from their adult children is (p. 488)
    a. emotional support.
    b. help with day-to-day living tasks.
    c. financial assistance.
    d. assistance with medical emergencies.

17. Which of the following is among the most frequently reported type of elder maltreatment? (p. 489)
    a. physical abuse
    b. financial abuse
    c. sexual abuse
    d. racial discrimination

18. Elder maltreatment is more likely to occur in nursing homes (p. 489)
    a. with many visitors.
    b. that have plentiful staff.
    c. that are overcrowded.
    d. with low staff turnover.

19. The first consideration in the decision to retire is usually (p. 490)
    a. relocation possibilities.
    b. affordability of retirement.
    c. accessibility to assisted living.
    d. physical health of the retiree.

20. Recent views of successful aging focus on the (p. 493)
    a. achievements of individuals with outstanding life accomplishments.
    b. processes people use to reach personally valued goals.
    c. social lives of successful and unsuccessful agers.
    d. identification of a single set of standards for aging well.

PRACTICE TEST #2

1. At age 80, Barbara can't face the idea that she will die and the world will go on. She has children and grandchildren but has little interest in their lives. According to Peck, Barbara needs to work on (p. 472)
    a. body transcendence.
    b. ego transcendence.
    c. ego differentiation.
    d. future differentiation.

2. Bruce, age 74, has lately been recalling events of his past, reflecting on and reconsidering experiences, and contemplating their meanings with the goal of achieving greater self-understanding. Bruce has been engaging in (p. 473)
    a. life review.
    b. affect optimization.
    c. ego transcendence.
    d. geotranscendence.

3. During late adulthood, self-concept becomes (pp. 473–474)
    a. more insecure.
    b. more complex and multifaceted.
    c. less self-accepting.
    d. simpler and more streamlined.

4. Compared with people of other age groups, elders have the (p. 476)
    a. lowest suicide rate.
    b. highest suicide rate.
    c. lowest rate of depression.
    d. lowest rate of suicide but highest rate of depression.

5. Women over age 75 are far more likely than men of the same age to (p. 476)
    a. have others depend on them for emotional support.
    b. be married.
    c. be healthy.
    d. have higher incomes.

6. Ethnic minority elders are more likely to accept agency-provided support services when they are (p. 476)
   a. connected to a familiar neighborhood organization, such as the church.
   b. arranged and paid for by their adult children.
   c. delivered by people they do not know.
   d. motivated by obligation rather than care and concern.

7. According to disengagement theory, declining rates of interaction in late adulthood are caused by (p. 478)
   a. social barriers to engagement.
   b. life-long selection processes.
   c. the desire of elders to reduce social interaction.
   d. mutual withdrawal between elders and society in anticipation of death.

8. Among ethnic minority older adults, about _____ percent of Americans and _____ percent of Canadians live in cities. (p. 480)
   a. 10; 40
   b. 25; 50
   c. 50; 75
   d. 75; 50

9. The majority of older adults in Western nations want to live (p. 481)
   a. in their own homes and neighborhoods, and 90 percent of them do.
   b. in their own homes and neighborhoods, but only 50 percent do.
   c. in a warmer climate like that found in Florida and Arizona.
   d. with their children or other family members.

10. Older Americans experience the most extreme restriction of autonomy if they live (p. 483)
    a. in a nursing home.
    b. at their own home.
    c. in congregate housing.
    d. in a life care community.

11. The influential model of changes in our social networks as we move through life is known as the (p. 483)
    a. socioemotional group.
    b. continuity group.
    c. social convoy.
    d. affect optimization convoy.

12. When marital dissatisfaction is present in late adulthood, it (p. 484)
    a. takes a greater toll on men than on women.
    b. takes a greater toll on women than on men.
    c. affects men and women similarly.
    d. often results in domestic violence.

13. When asked about the reasons for divorce, (p. 484)
    a. elderly men typically mention difficulty adjusting to spending more time with their spouse following retirement.
    b. elderly women typically mention boredom with the relationship and a desire to form new, more rewarding relationships.
    c. both elderly men and women mention interest in a younger partner.
    d. elderly men typically mention lack of shared interests and activities, while elderly women typically mention their partner's refusal to communicate and emotional distance.

14. The greatest problem for recently widowed elders is (p. 485)
    a. profound loneliness.
    b. poverty.
    c. declining physical health.
    d. housing.

15. In late adulthood, sibling relationships (p. 487)
    a. are closer with brothers.
    b. become more emotionally distant.
    c. more often involve direct assistance than socializing.
    d. involve increased levels of support when siblings live close to each other.

16. Older women, more often than older men, have friends who are not intimates but with whom they spend time occasionally, such as a group that meets for lunch. These friends are termed (p. 488)
    a. occasional friends.
    b. social friends.
    c. loose friends.
    d. secondary friends.

17. In relationships between elders and their adult children, which of the following is linked to positive psychological well-being? (p. 488)
    a. mild support, with expected reciprocation
    b. moderate support, with no opportunities to reciprocate
    c. moderate support, with opportunities to reciprocate
    d. extensive support, with no opportunities to reciprocate

18. Elder maltreatment is more common when caregivers (p. 489)
    a. are emotionally and financially independent.
    b. have a history of family violence.
    c. are not related to the victim.
    d. work in nursing homes, even those with good working conditions.

19. Involvement in leisure activities (p. 492)
    a. is related to better physical and mental health and reduced mortality.
    b. is related to better physical health, but has relatively little impact on mental health.
    c. does not change much over the course of late adulthood.
    d. most often develops suddenly, as new retirees gain free time.

20. Which of the following is true of volunteerism among older adults? (p. 492)
    a. Less-educated elders are more likely to volunteer.
    b. Older elders are more likely to volunteer than younger elders.
    c. Elder women are more likely to volunteer than elder men.
    d. Volunteer work usually begins in late adulthood.

CHAPTER 19
DEATH, DYING, AND BEREAVEMENT

BRIEF CHAPTER SUMMARY

When asked how they would like to die, most people say they want death with dignity—either a quick, agony-free end during sleep or a clear-minded final few moments in which they can say farewell and review their lives. In reality, death is long and drawn out for three-fourths of people—many more than in times past, as a result of medical advances that have prolonged life.

In general, dying takes place in three phases: the agonal phase, clinical death, and mortality. In most industrialized nations, brain death is accepted as the definition of death, but thousands of patients who remain in a persistent vegetative state reveal that the brain-death standard does not always solve the dilemma of when to halt treatment for the incurably ill. Because most people will not experience an easy death, we can best ensure death with dignity by supporting dying patients through their physical and psychological distress, being candid about death's certainty, and helping them learn enough about their condition to make reasoned choices about treatment.

In early adulthood, many people brush aside thoughts of death, perhaps prompted by death anxiety or relative disinterest in death-related issues. Overall, fear of death declines with age, reaching its lowest level in late adulthood and in adults with deep faith in some form of higher being.

According to Kübler-Ross, dying people typically express five responses, which she initially proposed as "stages": denial, anger, bargaining, depression, and acceptance. Rather than stages, these five reactions are best viewed as coping strategies that anyone may call on in the face of threat. A host of contextual variables—nature of the disease; personality and coping style; family members' and health professionals' truthfulness and sensitivity; and spirituality, religion, and cultural background—affect the way people respond to their own dying and, therefore, the extent to which they attain an appropriate death.

Although the overwhelming majority of people want to die at home, caring for a dying patient is highly stressful. Hospital dying takes many forms, each affected by the physical state of the dying person, the hospital unit in which it takes place, and the goal and quality of care. Whether a person dies at home or in a hospital, the hospice approach strives to meet the dying person's physical, emotional, social, and spiritual needs by emphasizing quality of life over life-prolonging measures.

The same medical procedures that preserve life can prolong inevitable death, diminishing the quality of life and personal dignity. In the absence of national consensus on passive euthanasia, people can best ensure that their wishes will be followed by preparing an advance medical directive—a written statement of desired medical treatment should they become incurably ill. Although the practice has sparked heated controversy, public support for voluntary euthanasia is growing; slightly less public consensus exists for assisted suicide.

Although many theorists regard grieving as taking place in orderly phases of avoidance, confrontation, and restoration, in reality, people vary greatly in behavior and timing and often alternate between these reactions. Like dying, grieving is affected by many factors, including personality, coping style, and religious and cultural background. Circumstances surrounding the death—whether it is sudden and unanticipated or follows a prolonged illness—also shape mourners' responses. When a parent loses a child or a child loses a parent or sibling, grieving is generally very intense and prolonged. People who experience several deaths at once or in close succession are at risk for bereavement overload that may leave them emotionally overwhelmed and unable to resolve their grief.

Preparatory steps can be taken to help people of all ages cope with death more effectively. Today, instruction in death, dying, and bereavement can be found in colleges and universities; training programs for doctors, nurses, and helping professionals; adult education programs; and even a few elementary and secondary schools.

LEARNING OBJECTIVES

After reading this chapter, you should be able to:

19.1 Describe the physical changes of dying, along with their implications for defining death and the meaning of death with dignity. (pp. 499–501)

19.2 Discuss factors that influence attitudes toward death, including death anxiety. (pp. 501–502)

19.3 Describe and evaluate Kübler-Ross's theory, citing factors that influence dying patients' responses. (pp. 503–504)

19.4 List goals associated with an appropriate death, and summarize contextual factors that influence a person's adaptation to death. (pp. 504–506)

19.5 Evaluate the extent to which homes, hospitals, and the hospice approach meet the needs of dying people and their families. (pp. 506–508)

19.6 Discuss controversies surrounding euthanasia and assisted suicide. (pp. 509–512)

19.7 Describe bereavement and the phases of grieving, indicating factors that underlie individual variations in grief responses. (pp. 512–515)

19.8 Explain the concept of bereavement overload, and describe bereavement interventions. (pp. 515–517)

19.9 Explain how death education can help people cope with death more effectively. (pp. 517–518)

STUDY QUESTIONS

How We Die

Physical Changes

1. True or False: Most people experience a quick, agony-free death. Explain your answer. (p. 499)

2. Describe physical and behavioral changes in the days or hours before death. (p. 500)

3. Describe the three phases of dying. (p. 500)

   Agonal phase: _____

   Clinical death: _____

   Mortality: _____

Defining Death

1. What definition of death is currently used in most industrialized nations? (p. 500)

   _____
   _____

2. Describe the definition of death used by doctors in Japan, citing cultural beliefs that have led Japan to use this definition. (p. 500)

   _____
   _____

3. Explain why the brain death standard does not solve the dilemma of when to halt treatment. (p. 500)

   _____
   _____
   _____

Death with Dignity

1. Summarize three ways that we can foster dignity in death. (pp. 500–501)

   A. _____
   _____

   B. _____
   _____

   C. _____
   _____

Attitudes Toward Death

1. Compared with earlier generations, today more young people reach adulthood (with / without) having experienced the death of someone they know well. (p. 501)

2. What is *death anxiety*? (p. 501)

   _____
   _____

3. Research reveals (few / large) individual and cultural differences in the anxiety-provoking aspects of death. (p. 501)

4. Identify two personal factors that minimize death anxiety. (p. 502)

   A. _____
   _____

   B. _____
   _____

5. Death anxiety (declines / increases) with age, reaching its (highest / lowest) level in late adulthood. What accounts for this trend? (p. 502)

   _____
   _____

6. Explain how death anxiety can motivate people in positive ways. (p. 502)

7. Regardless of age, cross-cultural studies show that (men / women) are more anxious about death. (p. 502)

8. Explain the link between death anxiety and mental health. (p. 502)

9. Children (frequently / rarely) display death anxiety. Cite exceptions. (p. 502)

Thinking and Emotions of Dying People

Do Stages of Dying Exist?

1. List and describe Kübler-Ross's five typical responses to dying, and explain how family members and health professionals can best react to the first four. (p. 503)

   A. _____
   Reactions: _____

   B. _____
   Reactions: _____

   C. _____
   Reactions: _____

   D. _____
   Reactions: _____

   E. _____

2. True or False: Kübler-Ross viewed the responses listed above as a fixed sequence that is universally experienced by all individuals. (p. 503)

3. Summarize criticisms of Kübler-Ross's theory. (pp. 503–504)

Contextual Influences on Adaptations to Dying

1. Describe an *appropriate death*. (p. 504)

2. Cite five goals that patients mention when asked about a "good death." (p. 504)

    A. _____
    B. _____
    C. _____
    D. _____
    E. _____

3. True or False: Dying people display similar reactions, regardless of the nature of their disease. (p. 504)

4. True or False: The way an individual views stressful life events and has coped with them in the past is likely to be closely related to the way the person manages the dying process. (p. 504)

5. A candid approach, in which those close to and caring for the dying person acknowledge the terminal illness, is (ill-advised / recommended). (p. 505)

6. True or False: In Asia and the Middle East, it is common for doctors to withhold information about a dying patient's prognosis. (p. 505)

7. Describe features of effective communication with dying people. (p. 505)

8. Explain how Buddhist practices and beliefs foster acceptance of death. (p. 505)

9. Describe beliefs and customs, guided by religious ideas, that shape dying experiences in the following cultures. (p. 506)

    Native-American: _____

    African-American: _____

    Maori of New Zealand: _____

A Place to Die

Home

1. True or False: Eighty to 90 percent of North Americans would prefer to die at home; however, only about one-fourth of Canadians and one-fifth of Americans experience home death. (p. 506)

2. Summarize the advantages and disadvantages of dying at home. (p. 506)

    Advantages: _____

    _____

    Disadvantages: _____

    _____

3. True or False: Family members report more prolonged psychological stress following a home death than a death that occurred elsewhere. (p. 506)

Hospital

1. How can emergency room staff help family members cope with the sudden loss of a loved one? (p. 507)

    _____

    _____

2. Patients with (cancer / cardiovascular disease) account for most cases of prolonged dying. (p. 507)

3. Explain the conflict of values between dying patients and health professionals in hospital settings, especially in intensive care units. (p. 507)

    _____

    _____

4. True or False: The majority of U.S. hospitals have comprehensive treatment programs to ease physical, emotional, and spiritual pain at the end of life. (p. 507)

The Hospice Approach

1. Describe the hospice approach, noting its seven main features. (p. 507)

    Description: _____

    _____

    A. _____
    B. _____
    C. _____
    D. _____
    E. _____
    F. _____
    G. _____

2. What is *palliative care*? (p. 507)

    _____

    _____

3. Hospice programs offer a continuum of care. Explain what this means. (p. 507)

4. Explain how hospice care contributes to improvements in family functioning. (p. 508)

5. The majority of North Americans (are / are not) familiar with the philosophy of the hospice approach. (p. 508)

Biology and Environment: Music as Palliative Care for Dying Patients

1. Define *music thanatology*. (p. 508)

2. How is music applied in palliative care? (p. 508)

3. True or False: Since hearing typically functions longer than other senses, an individual may be responsive to music until his or her final moments. (p. 508)

The Right to Die

1. The United States and Canada (do / do not) have uniform right-to-die policies. (p. 509)

2. Define *euthanasia,* and list its four forms. (p. 509)

    Definition: _____

    A. _____
    B. _____
    C. _____
    D. _____

Passive Euthanasia

1. Define *passive euthanasia*. (p. 509)

2. True or False: When there is no hope of recovery, the majority of North Americans support the patient's or family members' right to end treatment. (p. 509)

3. Passive euthanasia (is / is not) widely practiced as part of ordinary medical procedure. (p. 509)

4. (Religion / Ethnicity) strongly contributes to people's views of passive euthanasia. (pp. 509–510)

5. Without a national consensus on passive euthanasia, how can people best ensure that their wishes will be followed if they become terminally ill or fall into a persistent vegetative state? (p. 510)

6. Name and describe two types of *advance directives* recognized in U.S. states and Canadian provinces. (p. 510)

   A. _____

   B. _____

7. Cite two reasons why living wills do not guarantee personal control over treatment. (p. 510)

   A. _____

   B. _____

8. The durable power of attorney for health care is (more / less) flexible than the living will. Explain your answer. (p. 510)

9. True or False: Over 70 percent of North Americans have executed a living will or durable power of attorney. (p. 510)

Voluntary Active Euthanasia

1. True or False: *Voluntary active euthanasia* is a criminal offense in most countries, including almost all U.S. states and Canada. (p. 510)

2. True or False: About 70 to 90 percent of people in Western nations approve of voluntary active euthanasia. (pp. 510–511)

3. Summarize the controversy over the legalization of voluntary active euthanasia. (p. 511)

Assisted Suicide

1. True or False: Assisted suicide is tacitly accepted in many Western European countries. (p. 512)

2. Describe Oregon's Death with Dignity Act. (p. 512)

3. True or False: 75 percent of North Americans approve of assisted suicide. (p. 512)

4. Briefly describe dilemmas associated with assisted suicide. (p. 512)
_____
_____

5. Public opinion consistently favors (active euthanasia/assisted suicide) over (active euthanasia/assisted suicide). (p. 512)

Bereavement: Coping with the Death of a Loved One

1. Distinguish among *bereavement, grief*, and *mourning*. (p. 512)

   Bereavement: _____
   _____

   Grief: _____
   _____

   Mourning: _____
   _____

Grief Process

1. List four tasks of the grieving process that help people recover and return to a fulfilling life. (p. 513)

   A. _____
   B. _____
   C. _____
   D. _____

2. Match each of the following grief reactions with the appropriate description. (p. 513)

   _____ The bereaved individual must balance emotional consequences of his/her loss with attending to life changes associated with the loved one's death.
   _____ A numbed feeling serves as "emotional anesthesia."
   _____ The mourner confronts the reality of the loss and experiences a cascade of emotional reactions.
   _____ The bereaved individual yearns for the deceased and obsessively reviews the circumstances of the death.
   _____ The mourner may show a variety of behavioral changes, including absent-mindedness, poor concentration, self-destructive behavior, and/or depression.
   _____ Emotional energy shifts toward life-restoring pursuits.
   _____ The bereaved person experiences shock followed by disbelief and is unable to comprehend the death.

   1. Avoidance loss
   2. Confrontation
   3. Restoration

3. True or False: Grieving can accurately be described as a fixed series of three phases. (p. 513)

4. Describe the *dual-process model of coping with loss*. (p. 513)
   _____
   _____
   _____

Personal and Situational Variations

1. True or False: Compared with men, bereaved women typically express distress and depression less directly and seek less social support. (p. 513)

2. Explain differences in grieving when death is sudden and unexpected versus prolonged and expected. (pp. 513–514)

    Sudden and unexpected: _____

    _____

    Prolonged and expected: _____

    _____

3. What is *anticipatory grieving*? (p. 514)

    _____

    _____

4. Compared with survivors of other sudden deaths, people grieving a suicidal loss are (more / less) likely to blame themselves for what happened. (p. 514)

5. List three reasons why the death of a child is the most difficult loss an adult can face. (p. 514)

    A. _____

    B. _____

    C. _____

6. Why is the loss of a family member likely to have long-standing consequences for children? (p. 514)

    _____

    _____

    _____

7. Briefly describe the physical symptoms often displayed by children who are grieving the loss of a family member. (p. 514)

    _____

    _____

    _____

8. True or False: When children maintain mental contact with a deceased parent or sibling by dreaming about or speaking to the loved one, this hinders the child's ability to cope with the loss. (p. 514)

9. Describe the link between cognitive development and children's ability to grieve, noting how adults can help young children better understand the person's death. (p. 514)

    _____

    _____

    _____

10. Grief-stricken (school-age children / adolescents) tend to keep their grieving from both adults and peers, often leading to depression and attempts to escape the grief through acting out behavior. (p. 515)

11. Younger adults display (more / fewer) negative outcomes than older adults following the death of a spouse. Explain your answer. (p. 515)

12. Describe the unique challenges that gay and lesbian partners face when they experience the death of an intimate partner, including disenfranchised grief. (p. 515)

13. Describe *bereavement overload*, and note how it influences one's ability to cope with grief. (p. 515)

    Description: _____

    Impact: _____

14. Identify three groups of individuals who are at risk for bereavement overload. (p. 515)

    A. _____
    B. _____
    C. _____

Cultural Influences: Cultural Variations in Mourning Behavior

1. Describe mourning behaviors and beliefs about death in the following religious and cultural groups. (p. 516)

    Jews: _____

    Quakers: _____

    African Americans: _____

    Balinese of Indonesia: _____

2. Summarize the benefits of Internet, or Web, memorials. (p. 516)

Bereavement Interventions

1. List five suggestions for resolving grief following the death of a loved one. (p. 517)

   A. _____

   B. _____

   C. _____

   D. _____

   E. _____

2. Self-help groups that bring together mourners who have experienced the same type of loss (are / are not) highly effective for reducing stress. (p. 517)

3. Describe characteristics of bereavement interventions for children and adolescents. (p. 517)

   _____

   _____

   _____

4. Cite four instances in which grief therapy may be necessary to help the mourner overcome his/her loss. (p. 517)

   A. _____

   B. _____

   C. _____

   D. _____

Death Education

1. List four goals of death education. (p. 517)

   A. _____

   B. _____

   C. _____

   D. _____

2. Compared to lecture-style programs, experiential programs that help people confront their own mortality are (less / more) likely to heighten death anxiety. (p. 518)

ASK YOURSELF...

For *Ask Yourself* questions for this chapter, please log on to the Companion Website at *www.ablongman.com/berk*.

1. Select the Companion Website for *Exploring Lifespan Development*.
2. Use the "Jump to" menu to go directly to this chapter.
3. From the menu on the left side of the screen, select "Ask Yourself."
4. Complete questions and choose "Submit answers for grading" or "Clear answers" to start over.

SUGGESTED STUDENT READINGS

Byard, R. W., & Cohle, S. D. (2004). *Sudden death in infancy, childhood, and adolescence.* New York: Cambridge University Press. Presents an extensive overview of infant, child, and adolescent death, including current research on SIDS, intentional and unintentional deaths, and suicide.

Corless, I. B., Germino, B. B., & Pittman, M. (Eds.). (2006). *Dying, death, and bereavement: A challenge for living.* New York: Springer. A multidisciplinary approach to understanding death and bereavement, this book highlights a diverse range of end-of-life issues, including communicating about the dying process, death education, a place to die, the bereavement process, and the importance of social support.

Walsh, F., & McGoldrick, M. (Eds.). (2004). *Living beyond loss: Death in the family* (2nd ed.). New York: Norton. A collection of chapters examining the effects of death on the family system. Topics include death in the family life cycle, reactions to death, cultural variations in mourning behavior, religion and spirituality, and personal reflections on death and loss.

PUZZLE 19.1

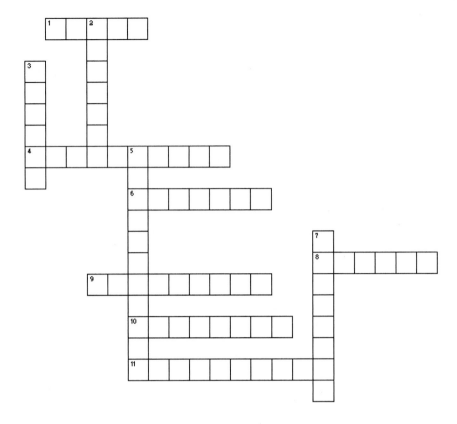

Across

1. _____ death: irreversible cessation of all activity in the brain and brain stem
4. Persistent _____ state: cerebral cortex no longer registers electrical activity, but the brain stem remains active
6. _____ euthanasia: withholding or withdrawing life-sustaining treatment, permitting the patient to die naturally
8. _____ will: written statement specifying the treatments a person does or does not want in case of terminal illness, coma, or other near-death situation
9. Phase of dying in which an individual passes into permanent death
10. Durable power of _____ for health care: written statement that authorizes another person to make health care decisions on one's behalf in case of incompetence
11. Practice of ending the life of a person suffering from an incurable condition

Down

2. _____ medical directive: written statement of desired medical treatment should a person become incurably ill
3. Voluntary _____ euthanasia: practice of ending a patient's suffering, at the patient's request, before a natural end to life
5. _____ death: a death that makes sense in terms of the person's pattern of living and values, and at the same time, preserves or restores significant relationships and is as free of suffering as possible
7. _____ death: phase of dying in which heartbeat, circulation, breathing, and brain functioning stop, but resuscitation is still possible

PUZZLE 19.2

Across

2. Culturally specified expression of a bereaved person's thoughts and feelings
3. Comprehensive program of support services that focuses on meeting terminally ill patients' physical, emotional, social, and spiritual needs and that offers follow-up bereavement services to families
5. _____ care: aimed at relieving pain and other symptoms in terminally ill patients in order to protect the person's quality of life rather than prolonging life
6. Death _____: fear and apprehension of death
7. The experience of losing a loved one by death
8. _____-_____ model of coping: oscillation between dealing with emotional consequences of loss and attending to life changes

Down

1. _____ grieving: acknowledging that the loss is inevitable and preparing emotionally for it
4. Intense physical and psychological distress following a loss
9. Phase of dying in which gasps and muscle spasms occur during the first moments in which the body cannot sustain life anymore

PRACTICE TEST #1

1. Death is long and drawn out for what percentage of people? (p. 499)
   a. 50%
   b. 66%
   c. 75%
   d. 90%

2. The definition of death that is currently used in most industrialized nations is (p. 500)
   a. loss of heartbeat and respiration.
   b. lack of activity in the cerebral cortex, even if the brain stem remains active.
   c. irreversible cessation of all activity in the brain and the brain stem.
   d. muscle spasms indicating that the body can no longer sustain life.

3. "Death with dignity" refers to (pp. 500–501)
   a. dying in one's sleep.
   b. receiving sufficient medication to ease pain during a prolonged death.
   c. dying at home, where one is likely to be most comfortable.
   d. being well informed about one's condition and receiving assurance of support and compassionate care.

4. Who among the following Westerns is LEAST likely to experience death anxiety? (p. 502)
   a. a religiously committed woman
   b. an adult with deep faith in a higher being
   c. an adult with contradictory religious beliefs and behaviors
   d. an adolescent with no personal philosophy on death

5. Death anxiety is largely limited to (p. 502)
   a. adolescence and adulthood.
   b. childhood.
   c. extreme old age.
   d. men of any age.

6. Elisabeth Kübler-Ross's stages of dying (p. 504)
   a. should be viewed as a fixed sequence displayed by all individuals.
   b. provide an exhaustive list of people's responses to death.
   c. are best viewed as coping strategies that individuals can call on in the face of threat.
   d. do not accurately represent people's reactions to their own impending death.

7. Which of the following statements accurately describes how those who are terminally ill cope with impending death? (pp. 504–505)
   a. They almost never come to accept their fate.
   b. They use diverse coping strategies, influenced by personality and by others' responses.
   c. At first, they are usually depressed.
   d. They rarely show anger about impending death.

8. When asked to describe a "good death," dying patients typically say that they hope to (p. 504)
   a. maintain a sense of identity, or inner continuity with their past.
   b. achieve financial autonomy before they die.
   c. avoid death as long as they possibly can.
   d. find spiritual guidance in their remaining days.

9. In communicating with a dying person, it is best to (p. 505)
   a. give only vague information about the diagnosis and the course of the disease.
   b. avoid any discussion of death-related issues.
   c. discourage the person from maintaining hope, because a favorable outcome is unlikely.
   d. foster a trusting relationship by listening attentively and accepting the person's feelings.

10. Which of the following statements about dying at home is true? (p. 506)
    a. Home is the least stressful place to care for a dying person.
    b. Although most older adults would prefer to die at home, they express concern about the burden placed on family members.
    c. A home death often leads to deterioration in relationships between the dying person and caregivers.
    d. Most homes are better suited than hospitals to handling the comfort-care needs of the dying.

11. One disadvantage of dying in a hospital is that (p. 507)
    a. a hospital death places high physical, psychological, and financial demands on caregivers.
    b. family members experience more prolonged psychological distress when a loved one dies in the hospital rather than at home.
    c. privacy and communication with family members are secondary to monitoring the patient's condition.
    d. hospitals tend to overemphasize palliative care.

12. Central to the hospice approach is that the dying person and his or her family be offered (p. 507)
    a. choices that guarantee an appropriate death.
    b. choices that guarantee an end to life free of death anxiety.
    c. an array of life-saving treatments regardless of cost.
    d. care at home, rather than in inpatient settings like hospitals and nursing homes.

13. The right of a dying patient or family members to choose passive euthanasia (p. 509)
    a. receives almost no support from Catholics because it is seen as a first step toward government-approved mercy killing.
    b. has similar levels of support across all North American ethnic groups.
    c. has very little support in North America because of controversial cases like that of Terri Schiavo.
    d. is supported by more than three-fourths of North Americans in cases where there is no hope of recovery.

14. The best way for people to ensure that they will have access to passive euthanasia should they desire it is by (p. 510)
    a. asking their doctors to record their wishes in their medical file.
    b. informing a close friend or relative.
    c. preparing and signing a living will.
    d. preparing and signing a durable power of attorney.

15. Assisting a suicide is (p. 512)
    a. legal in Canada.
    b. legal in all U.S. states.
    c. illegal in many, but not all, U.S. states.
    d. illegal in Germany.

16. Among the various forms of euthanasia, North Americans are LEAST supportive of (p. 512)
    a. voluntary passive euthanasia.
    b. voluntary active euthanasia.
    c. assisted suicide.
    d. all forms.

17. Theorists formerly believed that bereaved individuals moved through three phases of grieving. A more accurate account, however, compares grief to a (p. 513)
    a. roller-coaster ride, with many ups and downs.
    b. pinwheel, with many points of spinning emotions.
    c. washing machine, with anger, fear, and frustration all mixing together.
    d. rocket launch, with a huge surge of emotion followed by a settling-down period.

18. The major difference between a sudden, unexpected death and a prolonged death is that when dying is prolonged, the bereaved person has had time to engage in (pp. 513–514)
    a. restoration.
    b. dual-process coping.
    c. anticipatory grieving.
    d. confrontation.

19. Bereavement interventions typically (pp. 515, 517)
    a. advise people to reflect on their loss internally and privately.
    b. discourage people from involving themselves in self-help groups.
    c. encourage people to draw on their existing social network.
    d. are ineffective in relieving stress or anxiety about a loss.

20. Compared to lecture-format death education programs, experiential programs are (pp. 517–518)
    a. less likely to heighten death anxiety and may sometimes reduce it.
    b. more likely to result in gains in knowledge about the death process.
    c. less likely to help people confront their own mortality.
    d. more likely to heighten death anxiety by exposing people to the reality of death.

PRACTICE TEST #2

1. Technological advances have changed our thinking about death by (p. 499)
    a. providing reliable ways to restore functioning when an individual is in a persistent vegetative state.
    b. providing so many means of keeping death at bay that death has become a forbidden topic for many people.
    c. providing a clear, universally accepted definition of the end of life.
    d. easing the acceptance of death by providing increased scientific understanding of the death process.

2. About ___ percent of people experience a quick, agony-free death. (p. 499)
    a. 80
    b. 45
    c. 20
    d. 5

3. Resuscitation is NOT possible in (p. 500)
    a. brain death.
    b. clinical death.
    c. the agonal phase of death.
    d. a persistent vegetative state.

4. Compared with earlier generations, today's children and adolescents in industrialized nations are (p. 501)
    a. more comfortable dealing with death because they play a greater role in caring for dying family members.
    b. more accepting of death because they see frequent images of death in TV shows, movies and videos, and news reports.
    c. less likely to experience death anxiety because of their heightened religious awareness.
    d. more insulated from death because they are more likely to reach adulthood without experiencing the death of someone they know well.

5. Death anxiety (p. 502)
    a. increases with age, as individuals experience more deaths of family and friends.
    b. declines with age, reaching its lowest level in late adulthood.
    c. is greater in men than in women.
    d. is an individual trait that remains stable from childhood into late adulthood.

6. _____ predicts low death anxiety (p. 502)
   a. Terminal illness in children
   b. Physical health in adulthood
   c. Symbolic immortality
   d. Religiousness

7. A patient who _____ is most likely to cope well with dying and attain the goals of an appropriate death. (p. 505)
   a. feels she has much unfinished business to attend to
   b. has family members who participate in the patient's denial
   c. views dying as part of life's journey
   d. experiences an extended disease, accompanied by depression

8. Effective communication with the dying should include (p. 505)
   a. withholding information about the terminal nature of the illness, to reduce anxiety.
   b. gradually withdrawing social support, to help the dying person separate permanently from family members.
   c. avoiding family "unfinished business," to ease the stress of dying.
   d. building a trusting relationship that maintains hope as long as possible.

9. When a dying person feels a strong sense of spirituality, it tends to produce (p. 505)
   a. less fear of death.
   b. more anger at God for not preventing one's death.
   c. confusion and distress about what dying really means.
   d. anger and resentment toward those who go on living.

10. Today, about _____ percent of deaths in the United States and _____ percent in Canada take place in hospitals. (p. 506)
    a. 50; 40
    b. 60; 60
    c. 70; 80
    d. 80; 70

11. Eighty to 90 percent of North Americans say that they would prefer to die (p. 506)
    a. at home.
    b. in a hospital.
    c. in a hospice.
    d. in a doctor's office.

12. The central belief of the hospice approach is that (p. 507)
    a. medical choices should be made by an objective third party in order to ease the psychological strain on the dying person and his or her family.
    b. quality of life is the most important issue surrounding a person's journey toward death.
    c. terminally ill patients should always be able to die in their own homes.
    d. contact with family members should be secondary to monitoring the condition of the dying patient.

13. In North America, use of passive euthanasia for terminally ill patients and those in a persistent vegetative state is considered (p. 509)
    a. immoral and unethical.
    b. an extreme procedure that must be approved by the courts.
    c. permissible only for the most elderly patients.
    d. an ordinary part of normal medical practice.

14. In case of a terminal illness, coma, or other near-death situation, people specify the treatments they do or don't want in a(n) (p. 510)
    a. durable power of attorney for health care.
    b. living will.
    c. health care proxy.
    d. advance medical directive.

15. The U.S. state of _____ has passed a law, the Death with Dignity Act, that allows physicians to prescribe drugs so that terminally ill patients can end their own lives. (p. 512)
    a. California
    b. New York
    c. Oregon
    d. Massachusetts

16. Grief refers to (p. 512)
    a. acknowledging that loss is inevitable.
    b. the experience of losing a loved one by death.
    c. culturally specified expressions of the bereaved person's thoughts and feelings.
    d. intense physical and psychological distress.

17. Adjusting to death is easier when (p. 514)
    a. the survivor understands the reasons for the death.
    b. the death is sudden and unanticipated.
    c. the death is the result of a suicide.
    d. a person experiences several deaths in close succession.

18. Compared to those grieving other types of loss, people who have lost a loved one to suicide are (p. 514)
    a. less likely to feel profound guilt and shame.
    b. more likely to conclude that they contributed to or could have prevented the death.
    c. likely to self-blame only if their religion condemns suicides as immoral.
    d. more likely to get over the bereavement period quickly.

19. Children who experience the loss of a parent or sibling (p. 514)
    a. adjust quickly because they cannot yet comprehend the permanence of the loss.
    b. respond best when adults tell them that the missing family member has merely gone to sleep.
    c. should be discouraged from maintaining mental contact with the deceased, such as by dreaming about or speaking to the person regularly.
    d. often display persistent mild depression, anxiety, and angry outbursts.

20. One of the best ways to help a grieving person is by (p. 515)
    a. giving advice aimed at hastening recovery.
    b. discussing one's own experiences with death.
    c. listening sympathetically and "just being there."
    d. encouraging the person to spend some time alone.

CROSSWORD PUZZLE SOLUTIONS

PUZZLE 1.1

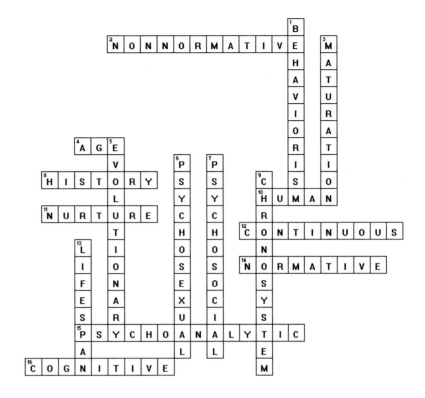

PUZZLE 1.2

PUZZLE 1.3

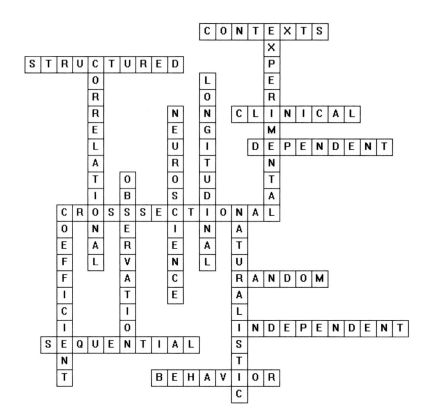

PUZZLE 2.1

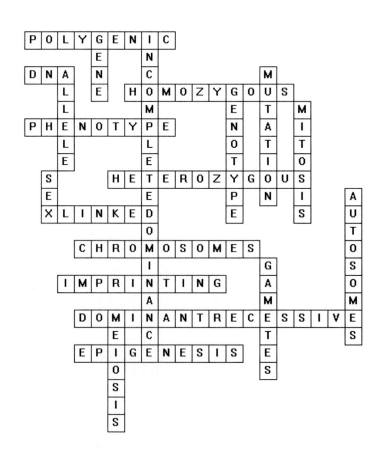

414

PUZZLE 2.2

PUZZLE 3.1

PUZZLE 3.2

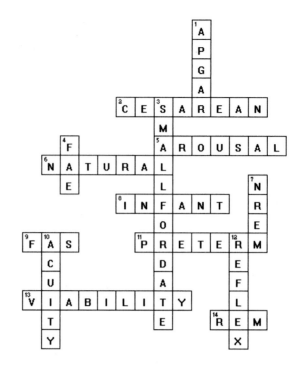

PUZZLE 4.1

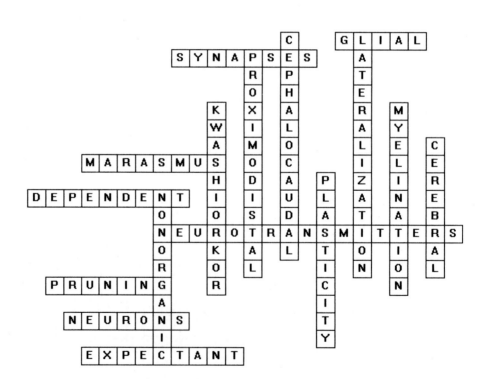

PUZZLE 4.2

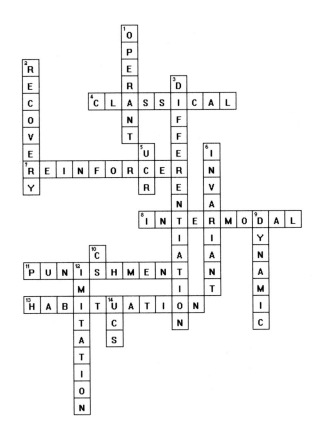

PUZZLE 5.1

417

PUZZLE 5.2

PUZZLE 6.1

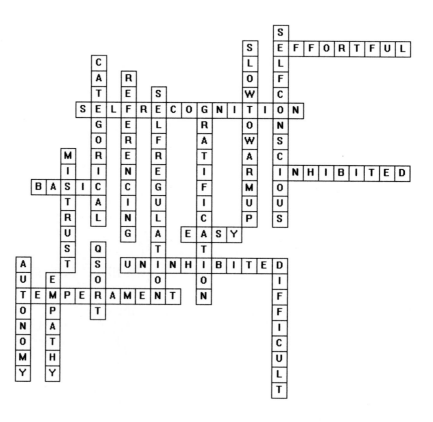

PUZZLE 6.2

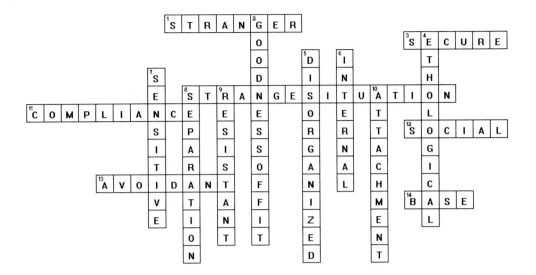

PUZZLE 7.1

PUZZLE 7.2

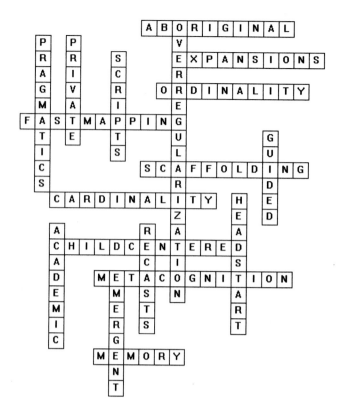

PUZZLE 8.1

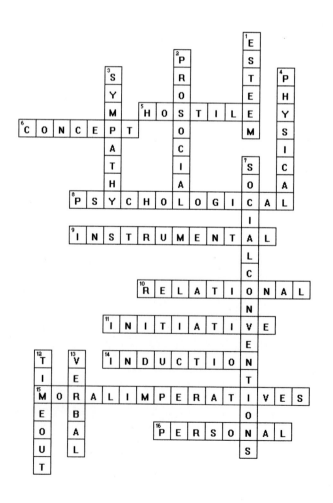

PUZZLE 8.2

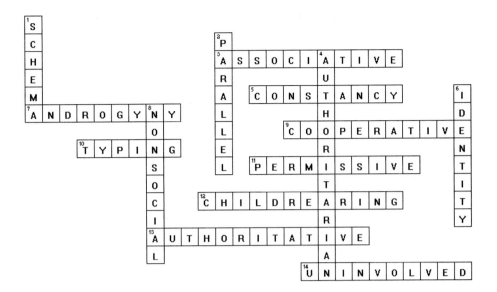

PUZZLE 9.1

PUZZLE 9.2

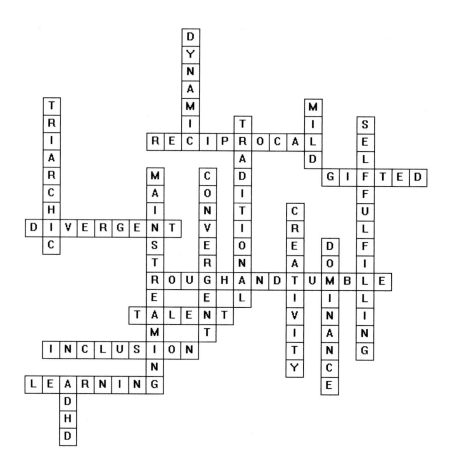

PUZZLE 10.1

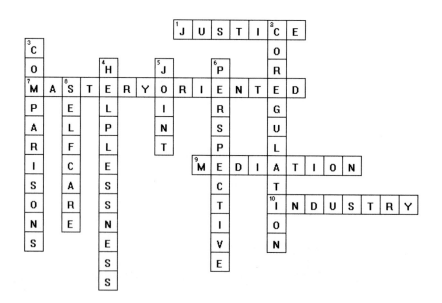

PUZZLE 10.2

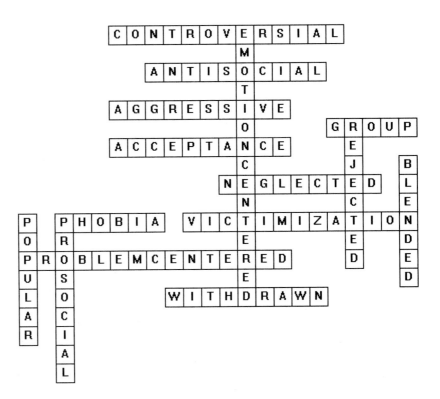

PUZZLE 11.1

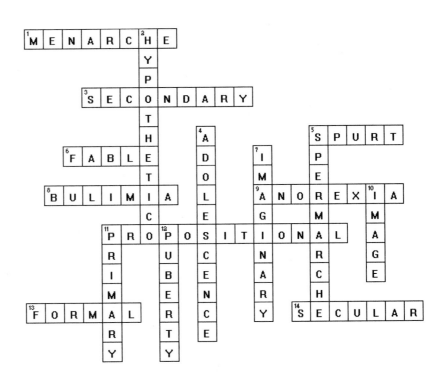

PUZZLE 12.1

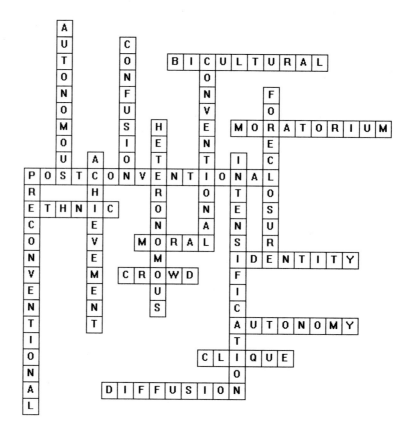

PUZZLE 13.1

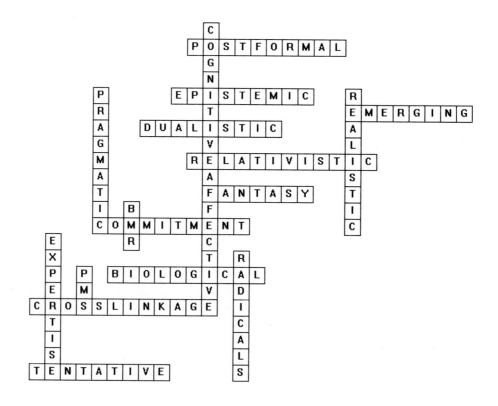

PUZZLE 14.1

PUZZLE 15.1

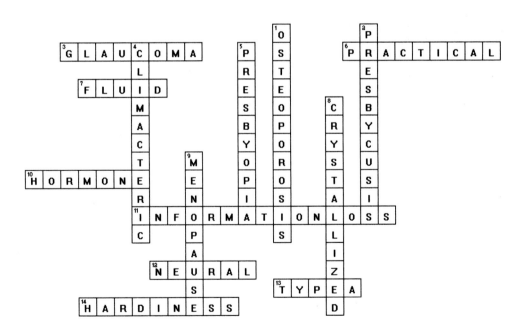

PUZZLE 16.1

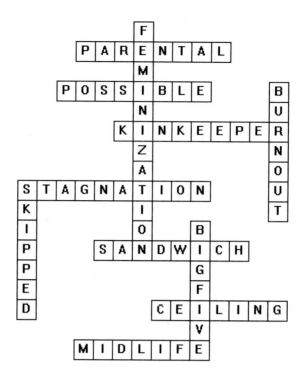

PUZZLE 17.1

PUZZLE 17.2

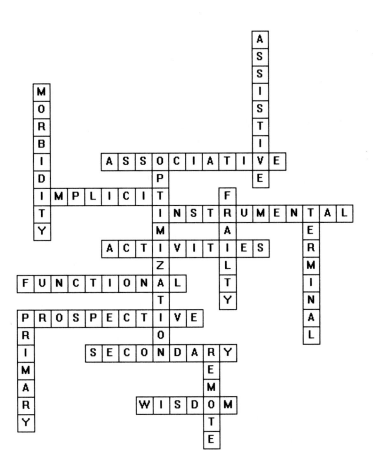

PUZZLE 18.1

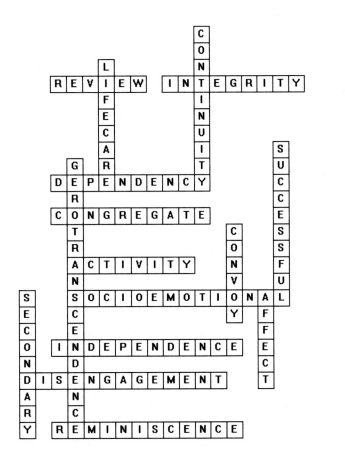

PUZZLE 19.1

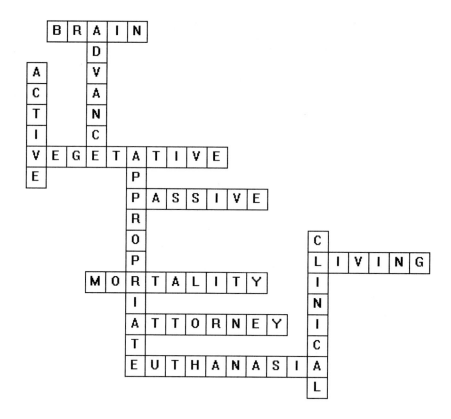

PUZZLE 19.2

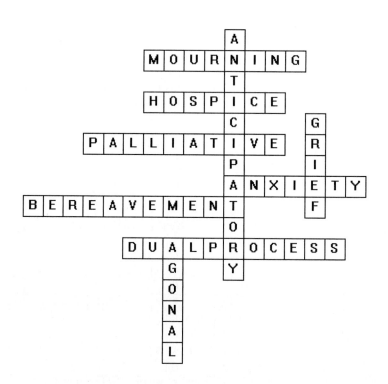

ANSWERS TO PRACTICE TESTS

CHAPTER 1

Practice Test #1

1. b	2. d	3. a	4. d	5. b
6. c	7. b	8. c	9. a	10. a
11. d	12. d	13. b	14. b	15. c
16. d	17. d	18. a	19. b	20. a

Practice Test #2

1. c	2. a	3. d	4. d	5. b
6. b	7. b	8. c	9. c	10. a
11. a	12. b	13. d	14. a	15. d
16. a	17. c	18. b	19. c	20. c

CHAPTER 2

Practice Test #1

1. a	2. b	3. b	4. d	5. d
6. a	7. c	8. a	9. b	10. c
11. b	12. b	13. c	14. c	15. b
16. a	17. a	18. c	19. c	20. c

Practice Test #2

1. c	2. c	3. d	4. a	5. a
6. a	7. a	8. c	9. b	10. c
11. d	12. c	13. b	14. a	15. a
16. d	17. a	18. a	19. a	20. c

CHAPTER 3

Practice Test #1

1. b	2. b	3. c	4. c	5. d
6. a	7. c	8. a	9. c	10. c
11. b	12. c	13. b	14. b	15. b
16. a	17. b	18. d	19. c	20. c

Practice Test #2

1. b	2. b	3. d	4. b	5. c
6. b	7. c	8. d	9. d	10. a
11. c	12. a	13. d	14. d	15. c
16. b	17. d	18. a	19. a	20. b

CHAPTER 4

Practice Test #1

1. c	2. b	3. a	4. a	5. d
6. d	7. d	8. d	9. d	10. b
11. c	12. c	13. c	14. d	15. b
16. a	17. b	18. b	19. a	20. a

Practice Test #2

1. d	2. b	3. c	4. d	5. d
6. c	7. a	8. b	9. c	10. c
11. b	12. c	13. a	14. b	15. b
16. c	17. a	18. a	19. b	20. a

CHAPTER 5

Practice Test #1

1. a	2. d	3. b	4. c	5. a
6. a	7. b	8. a	9. c	10. d
11. b	12. b	13. a	14. c	15. b
16. b	17. c	18. d	19. a	20. b

Practice Test #2

1. b	2. c	3. a	4. a	5. d
6. a	7. d	8. d	9. c	10. a
11. c	12. d	13. b	14. b	15. c
16. c	17. b	18. d	19. a	20. a

CHAPTER 6

Practice Test #1

1. c	2. c	3. a	4. b	5. b
6. d	7. b	8. b	9. b	10. c
11. b	12. d	13. c	14. a	15. d
16. d	17. c	18. c	19. b	20. b

Practice Test #2

1. b	2. d	3. b	4. c	5. a
6. b	7. d	8. a	9. d	10. b
11. b	12. d	13. b	14. c	15. d
16. a	17. d	18. b	19. a	20. d

CHAPTER 7

Practice Test #1

1. c	2. c	3. a	4. b	5. d
6. c	7. a	8. c	9. d	10. d
11. b	12. a	13. c	14. d	15. b
16. a	17. c	18. b	19. b	20. d

Practice Test #2

1. a	2. d	3. a	4. c	5. a
6. d	7. c	8. a	9. b	10. c
11. b	12. b	13. a	14. b	15. c
16. b	17. a	18. c	19. c	20. d

CHAPTER 8

Practice Test #1

1. a	2. d	3. b	4. a	5. b
6. c	7. a	8. c	9. b	10. b
11. c	12. a	13. a	14. d	15. c
16. c	17. d	18. a	19. a	20. d

Practice Test #2

1. a	2. a	3. b	4. b	5. a
6. d	7. c	8. d	9. b	10. a
11. b	12. a	13. b	14. b	15. a
16. a	17. c	18. a	19. a	20. b

CHAPTER 9

Practice Test #1

1. c	2. a	3. b	4. b	5. d
6. d	7. c	8. b	9. d	10. a
11. b	12. c	13. a	14. b	15. c
16. d	17. d	18. a	19. b	20. d

Practice Test #2

1. b	2. c	3. c	4. a	5. c
6. a	7. c	8. d	9. c	10. c
11. c	12. a	13. d	14. d	15. d
16. c	17. b	18. a	19. c	20. b

CHAPTER 10

Practice Test #1

1. b	2. a	3. b	4. c	5. d
6. a	7. b	8. c	9. b	10. a
11. d	12. c	13. b	14. d	15. b
16. c	17. a	18. a	19. b	20. c

Practice Test #2

1. c	2. d	3. a	4. b	5. c
6. a	7. b	8. d	9. c	10. b
11. b	12. a	13. d	14. d	15. c
16. a	17. c	18. b	19. c	20. d

CHAPTER 11

Practice Test #1

1. c	2. d	3. a	4. c	5. b
6. b	7. d	8. a	9. b	10. c
11. a	12. c	13. b	14. b	15. c
16. a	17. d	18. d	19. d	20. b

Practice Test #2

1. b	2. d	3. c	4. a	5. b
6. a	7. b	8. b	9. a	10. b
11. a	12. d	13. b	14. a	15. b
16. c	17. c	18. c	19. d	20. a

CHAPTER 12

Practice Test #1

1. b	2. a	3. c	4. d	5. a
6. c	7. b	8. b	9. c	10. b
11. b	12. c	13. a	14. c	15. a
16. b	17. a	18. d	19. a	20. c

Practice Test #2

1. a	2. b	3. b	4. d	5. c
6. a	7. a	8. c	9. a	10. b
11. b	12. c	13. a	14. c	15. b
16. d	17. c	18. a	19. b	20. d

CHAPTER 13

Practice Test #1

1. a	2. c	3. b	4. a	5. c
6. c	7. c	8. a	9. c	10. b
11. d	12. c	13. a	14. b	15. d
16. d	17. c	18. b	19. d	20. d

Practice Test #2

1. a	2. b	3. d	4. c	5. d
6. b	7. c	8. a	9. b	10. a
11. d	12. c	13. c	14. d	15. b
16. d	17. b	18. c	19. c	20. b

CHAPTER 14

Practice Test #1

1. d	2. a	3. c	4. a	5. c
6. a	7. a	8. d	9. d	10. a
11. b	12. c	13. c	14. b	15. c
16. c	17. d	18. c	19. b	20. d

Practice Test #2

1. c	2. c	3. b	4. b	5. b
6. b	7. a	8. d	9. b	10. b
11. c	12. a	13. d	14. a	15. c
16. a	17. a	18. b	19. d	20. a

CHAPTER 15

Practice Test #1

1. c	2. a	3. a	4. b	5. c
6. c	7. a	8. a	9. b	10. b
11. d	12. d	13. b	14. a	15. b
16. a	17. d	18. c	19. b	20. a

Practice Test #2

1. d	2. b	3. c	4. b	5. d
6. b	7. d	8. c	9. b	10. d
11. b	12. b	13. c	14. b	15. a
16. c	17. d	18. b	19. c	20. a

CHAPTER 16

Practice Test #1

1. d	2. b	3. d	4. c	5. a
6. b	7. a	8. d	9. c	10. a
11. a	12. c	13. b	14. d	15. b
16. a	17. d	18. c	19. a	20. a

Practice Test #2

1. c	2. c	3. a	4. d	5. b
6. d	7. c	8. a	9. c	10. c
11. a	12. d	13. c	14. a	15. b
16. c	17. d	18. b	19. c	20. c

CHAPTER 17

Practice Test #1

1. c	2. c	3. a	4. a	5. d
6. b	7. c	8. a	9. a	10. c
11. b	12. a	13. c	14. b	15. b
16. a	17. a	18. c	19. a	20. b

Practice Test #2

1. c	2. d	3. b	4. c	5. d
6. c	7. a	8. a	9. a	10. c
11. d	12. a	13. b	14. a	15. c
16. a	17. b	18. a	19. c	20. a

CHAPTER 18

Practice Test #1

1. b	2. d	3. a	4. d	5. b
6. c	7. a	8. c	9. a	10. d
11. a	12. c	13. d	14. b	15. d
16. a	17. b	18. c	19. b	20. b

Practice Test #2

1. b	2. a	3. b	4. b	5. a
6. a	7. d	8. c	9. a	10. a
11. c	12. b	13. d	14. a	15. d
16. d	17. c	18. b	19. a	20. c

CHAPTER 19

Practice Test #1

1. c	2. c	3. d	4. b	5. a
6. c	7. b	8. a	9. d	10. b
11. c	12. a	13. d	14. d	15. c
16. c	17. a	18. c	19. c	20. a

Practice Test #2

1. b	2. c	3. a	4. d	5. b
6. c	7. c	8. d	9. a	10. d
11. a	12. b	13. d	14. b	15. c
16. d	17. a	18. b	19. d	20. c

NOTES

NOTES

NOTES